AFRICA'S BEST & WORST PRESIDENTS:
How Neocolonialism & Imperialism Maintained Venal Rules in Africa

Nkwazi Nkuzi Mhango

Langaa Research & Publishing CIG
Mankon, Bamenda

Publisher:
Langaa RPCIG
Langaa Research & Publishing Common Initiative Group
P.O. Box 902 Mankon
Bamenda
North West Region
Cameroon
Langaagrp@gmail.com
www.langaa-rpcig.net

Distributed in and outside N. America by African Books Collective
orders@africanbookscollective.com
www.africanbookscollective.com

ISBN: 978-9956-764-72-3

© Nkwazi Nkuzi Mhango 2016

Table of Contents

List of Figures

List of Abbreviations

AIDS–Acquired Immune Deficiency Syndrome
ANC–African National Congress
AU–African Unity
BDP–Botswana Democratic Party
BoT–Bank of Tanzania
CAR–Central African Republic
CBC–Canadian Broadcasting Corporation
CCM –*Chama Cha Mapinduzi*
CEO–Chief Executive Officer
CIA–Central Intelligence Agency
CNN–Cable News Network
CNU–Cameroonian National Union
COD–Coordination of Democratic Opposition
CONAKAT–*Confédération des Associations Tribales du Katanga*
DP–Democratic Party
DRC–Democratic Republic of Congo
DSP–Division *Speciale Presidentielle*
FLS–Frontline States
FRELIMO–*Frente de Libertação de Moçambique or Mozambique Liberation Front*
GM–General Manager
GNP–Gross National Product
GOB–Government of Botswana
GOU–Government of Uganda
HIV–Human Immunodeficiency Virus
IDP–Internally Displaced Person
IFI–International Financial Institutions
IMF–International Monetary Fund
IPS–Inter Press Service
KADU–Kenya Democratic Union
KANU–Kenya African National Union
KAR–King's African Rifles
KCA–Kikuyu Central Association
LSE–London School of Economics
MCP–Malawi Congress Party

MK–*Umkhoto we Sizwe*
MNC–Multinational Corporation
MPLA–*Movimento Popular de Libertação de Angola*
MPR–*Mouvement Populaire de la Révolution or Popular Movement of the Revolution*
NAM–Non-Aligned Movement
NASB–New American Standard Bible
NGO–Non-Governmental Organisation
NP–National Party
OAU–Organization of African Union
PEV–Post-Election Violence
RDPC–*Rassemblement Démocratique du Peuple Camerounais*
RENAMO–*Resistência Nacional Moçambican*
SAS–Special Air Service
SSA–Sub-Sahara Africa
SWAPO–South West Africa People's Organization
TNC–Transnational Corporation
TPDF–Tanzania People's Defence Force
TRC–Truth and Reconciliation Commission
UDSM–University of Dar es Salaam
UK–United Kingdom
UNIP–United National Independence Party
UN–United Nations
UPC–Uganda People's Congress
URT–United Republic of Tanzania
USA–United States of America
VP–Vice President
VRP–Volta River Project
WB–World Bank (WB)
WHO–World Health Organisation
ZAPU–Zimbabwe African People's Union

Preface

When it comes to the terms of understanding any propounded philosophy or theme, before delving into the corpus of the discourse, we need to define them in order to have a single–or a likely–definition of the matter for the purpose of perceiving things in the same footing. Therefore, before delving into the analysis of this volume, it is better for us to define the term management. The definition of management differs from one discipline of social science to another. *Ipso facto*, there cannot be a watertight definition of the term. However, for the purpose of this volume, management denotes the power, legality or otherwise of managing the business of the state as opposed to the management of a private or public firm or company. I must emphasise from the outset that the type of management discussed in this volume is strictly and distinctly different from business as a profession. It is the management of public affairs without hoping to get profit or using purely business tactics to reach the goal. The business in question needs trust and readiness to serve others as opposed to normal business where shrewdness is *sine qua non* in making sure that one gets the profit. This is the business of delivering social services to the citizens whose country leaders manage. It is the business of promoting and protecting their rights. It sometimes is the business of protecting the interests of the citizenry against the interests of other business firms such as investments and neoliberal policies especially in Africa where such interests are always in a collision course with the citizenry. I am making this distinction to avoid creating the impression of instrumetalizing profit making as opposed to serving providing. This volume, therefore, is about a bigger entity, a country, a state or public entity but not about a company or anything like it in size and scope. So, arguably, when we say the best or worst management, impliedly, however, we might sound as the managers everybody knows. The difference, however, is that here the general manager (GM) or the Chief Executive Officer (CEO) of our unity of analysis–which is a country–is the president or the Prime Minister all depending on the system one country uses to govern its citizens. You can call this *presidentialism* or the system under which the president heads the government but not the Prime Minister, or Monarch. While other entities such as companies and corporations are ontologically formed to exclusively deal with business aimed at making profits, the entity in this discourse does many things such as providing, *inter alia*, security, services, leadership and vision all aimed at providing social service as the primary duty of any government.

Besides, when it comes to managing firms or businesses, the one operating them is obligated to have some related academic qualifications. However, in running the business of the state, sometimes, the situation is different in that academic requirements are immaterial. However, it is better to have some qualifications, due to a life-long tradition emanating from colonial times that allows politicians—whether they are qualified or otherwise—to seek public offices based on the consent of the constituency. This is done by politicians instead of economists or whoever that academically qualifies for or fits in to take up the task of running the organisation.

Furthermore, every doctrine must have some philosophical underpinnings to back it in order to make a clear sense and meaning to whoever comes across it. We, therefore, cannot complain that there is no watertight definition of management of the business of the state and thereby leave the dialogue just there without trying to give the readers a hunch of perceiving the matter. At least, in this volume, we will borrow from other fields in defining management as we keep the meaning as handy as possible to the issues we are discussing. Otley (1999) defines management as 'control systems' that provide information that is intended to be useful to managers in carrying out their responsibilities aiming at assisting the organisations in 'developing and maintaining viable patterns of behaviour,' (p.364). We prefer this definition to be functional in this volume due to a few reasons. Firstly, when we talk of the best and the worst managers Africa has ever had, we mean political leadership qualities in which, as argued above, presidents are the managers or CEOs of this entity known as government. Secondly, leadership is, essentially, the power or means which one uses in addressing the underlying problems or gains a particular country faced or gained. Furthermore, C. Barnard cited in Gray and Macpherson (2001) defines leadership noting that it "refers to the quality of the behavior of the individuals whereby they guide people or their activities in organized effort," (p.708). If anything, management of whatever firm–of whatever size and nature–is a behavioural attribute that aims at affecting others either positively or negatively; all depending on the evaluation of the performance (s) of the manager (s) in question. So, management is about leadership that provides the direction of the entity so managed for that matter.

Thirdly, our definition deals with the management of the entity without specifying or limiting itself to the typology of the organisation. So, this definition is an open-ended one; and it is not a full-loaded one. Fourthly, the definition refers to *control* which–in essence–is the aim of the manager of whatever organisation. Arguably, control is all about power that enables somebody to do something which is the major domain of our managers in this tome. Again, this power can be power over or power with all depending on the structure of the organisation and the way it is managed or mismanaged. Sixth, the definition, further, refers to *performance* which is what those managed or manned expect of the manager and vice versa all depending on reciprocity as agreed in the rules and regulations of the organisation. Again, for any manager to succeed there must be *reciprocity* between the manager and those he or she leads or controls. Seventh, the definition touches on *behaviour*. Yes, in this volume the unit of analysis is the state ran by the government which all is managed by the President or the Prime Minister. Given that our unity is a state or country, it therefore means having a certain set of behaviour that differentiates the citizens of one country from those of the others. We, therefore, can confidently and comfortably argue that our definition fits in the discourse of this volume. Importantly, as argued above, it must be noted that the manager or managers or call them directors in this discourse are the presidents or premiers depending on who is the head of the state. We are going to present those who had what it takes or those who fit the bill and those who ended up being but let-downs to their countries.

Oftentimes, whatever happens under the sun must have a reason be it real or farfetched. Africa is relatively poor by all standards; however, if we go deeper and fairly interrogate the real situation, Africa is not that poor as it is wrongly and biasedly perceived. When it comes to conceivable poverty that Africa faces, there are some explanations and reasons of such effects and situations based on history, politics and the *realpolitik* of the world. In other words, there is no way one can well evaluate Africa's performance without consulting its history as it was written by either Africans themselves or non-Africans depending on the angle anybody took in so doing. Generally, in Africa, and particularly in every country in the discourse, some of the reasons that caused poverty and miseries are internal while others are external by nature and essence. So, our discourse will deal with both as it explores the big players in the management of Africa as a unit of analysis based on exploring chosen countries severally. Thereafter, it will be easier to show how Africa notwithstanding, the matter is to gauge how Africa was ruined, doing so cannot be done by solely using Africa as a unity of analysis without exploring individual countries. However, the results will show it as one entity so explored.

This book aims at bringing back and tagging some reasons *inter alia* that saw Africa becoming poor and underdeveloped. Given that whatever happens under the sun has a human hand on it including running the business of the state, we are trying to show the world how some personalities contributed immensely in the mess Africa is in currently. Either by intention, ignorance, greed or otherwise, human contribution (s)–for better or for worse as far as Africa is concerned–is inevitable given that organizations are the creatures of humans aimed at serving them and regulating their relationship as a society or a people. On the other hand, we will present those who managed Africa well so as to balance the impact of two groups explored in this discourse. We, therefore, would like to present heroes and villains *vis-à-vis* Africa's predicaments and tribulations so that the coming generations can have somewhere to commence as far as revamping Africa from the miseries is concerned. This volume provides analytical tools based on historical realities in an academic manner aimed at helping anybody who wants to evaluate our leaders and rulers to do so scientifically and easily. Most importantly, this book is but a barometer with which one can evaluate our past leaders so as learn from both their strength and weaknesses. So, let us state it from the outset that we are not witch hunting or trying to shame anybody but presenting the facts as raw as they are. We will start with the heroes and end up with villains whose lessons are great for us, especially, currently when the quest for reclaiming and rejuvenating

Africa's place among the countries of the world is higher than at any time of Africa's history. The twenty-first century saw a close contact among the countries of the world, especially, through globalization which—up till now—works to the advantage of Western countries as opposed to those of Africa.

The information contained in the book is *a posteriori* based on media, historical, experiential and academic sources. We decided to make this volume academic due to the fact that it is the only way by or through which one can make a valid and acceptable claim as a contribution to exhuming Africa's problems based on its history, thus, contribute to finding solutions by expanding and contributing to the dialogue about tackling Africa's problems. Also, it is very important to mention our bias or interests in this discourse. The author is an African who would like to see Africa becoming self-sufficient and self-reliant so as to contribute to the development of its own and that of the world just like others. However, we know that information about Africa's history can be obtained from various non-academic sources which lack authenticity and high academic acceptance due to the nature of compiling them which makes the reliability of such information to become questionable and unbelievable altogether. When it comes to media source, being primary sources, are authentic especially when we consider that the rules demand that they collaborate their sources. Again, this does not exempt some media, especially, Western ones from biases and vexations particularly against those they perceive to be their enemies. So, too, not all people like to go through different academic sources to elicit information knowing that it is unauthentic. We, thus, intend to put such information in one piece so that it can be much easier for those interested in knowing the root causes of Africa's predicaments to reach it easily and quickly. By adding pictorial information, we are sure that readers will get close to home by imagining and evaluating the protagonists be they good or notorious. A picture is worth a thousand words. Additionally, the truth and experiences discussed make this analysis more of tragicomic as far as African history and politics are concerned; in that it analyses and presents the story of the same entity (Africa) from both sides of the coin. More importantly, this volume is not going to dissect or analyse all players in African affairs due to the magnitude of the contributions some individuals had in shaping the history of Africa compared to others. So, some will miss out; while others will have a few pages compared to others who will appear and have more information about them. All depends on an individual's contribution positively or negatively. We are dissecting a club of exceptionally a few select individuals who rightly or accidentally happen to be at the pinnacle of their countries as far as managing their affairs is concerned.

Arguably, many African youths born after independence or born of those who were born after independence, do not know Africa's movers and shakers *vis-à-vis* its management and mismanagement altogether. This is historically true due to the fact that most of them exited political scenes many years ago. We are presenting the personalities that shaped the politics of our continent either positively or negatively. By presenting these personalities once again, we are trying to draw a picture of the trajectory of the path the continent has gone through up to this point and time. Such presentation will help readers to judge by themselves why Africa is like it is today. Another nugget is that some academics or historians will come forth either to support or critique if not to oppose this discourse; thereby we will get rich resource based on comparative study of the history of Africa.

We understand that many syllabi in many African countries have always undergone some changes based on the needs and challenges of the time. Some are manipulated to suit political needs of those in power while others do so to suit academic needs of the time and the country altogether. There are those who were phased out after either being overthrown or falling out with those who took the reins of power after them. Therefore, some personalities that shaped the history of Africa are no longer taught in schools as it was after independence when the quest for decolonisation was high, not to mention introducing new players in the affairs of Africa. This is logical. After independence, every African country wanted its people to know how independence was fought for and gained so as to protect it at all costs. This is the time Africa evidenced great drive for its reunification. Slowly however, the theme changed from post-colonial awareness to political configuration and synchronisation, development, globalization and technology among other concepts that took over from colonial epoch. Again, how can one know who he or she actually is the make of African history without knowing her or his history? We need to make history tell their history so as to form the part of today's efforts by African academics aimed at securing the future of Africa. It is unfortunate that the history of Africa was erroneously written by the victors who are colonial monsters in this case. In this book, we want history to be written by victims or losers namely Africans themselves. Ours is the beginning of a new paradigm shift. Experts in this area will help us a great deal more. For, those of us who went to school in the seventies and eighties were taught this fake history about the discovery of Africa. It is time now we tell the history of conspiracy in which some of our brothers and partly sisters conspired with our tormentors in creating our miseries. By teaching this true history written by African, we slowly, will be embarking on its decolonisation, thus, its emancipation for the better future of the victims. By decolonising history, we will be creating an emancipatory history that aims at emancipating our people.

Popkewitz (1997) argues that "History, in its modern senses, involves procedures that construct objects through conceptual lenses," (p.133). In other words, the aim of this book is to deconstruct archaic history by exposing its fallacy and richness as far as the management of African states is concerned. The book wants to show what colonial lenses concealed and distorted. Therefore–in this case–the lenses used are that of an Africa who questions the *status quo* that our tormentors wanted, and still want us, to take as the normal nature of things while it is not at all. Moore (2007) argues that "'History will have its say one day,' we hear. 'It won't be a history written in Brussels, Paris or Washington. It will be ours, the history of a new Africa,'" (p.3) written by Africans of course. One may add. Whatever history that is not written by Africans themselves, such a history cannot be new but a prolongation that can lead and lean on the same meme colonial monstered authored. Arguably, although this book is not the only one about the issue, it subscribes to the *wake-up call* that a true history of Africa must, and will be written by the Africans themselves the same way the Westerners wrote theirs before crossing over to write ours with all bigotries and lies they heinously made part of our history. Arguably, when it comes to Africa, there are so many histories about it. Africa needs to have one true history authored by Africans themselves after deconstructing all fake histories and stories about Africa.

Just like any human beings, Africans know how history plays an important role in the lives of all human beings. This is why–despite being the science of past things–history will always be taught, researched, written and preserved at all costs. For example, when someone wants to start a family, he or she collects information about the partner with whom he or she wants to start the said family. Both parties do the same thing namely gathering information on and about each other in order to see if they are going to get what they want and desire. They try to see if the intended partner has dangerous diseases such as epilepsy, leprosy, or any desirable or undesirable qualities and others. This is the role of history. It tells us who we are and why we are how we are. It also helps us in preparing the coming generations we create through marriage. As well, history can predict who we are going to be; if we examine our past. The drunkard of today is able to know who he or she will become in the future. All depends on the direction one is going to take for better or for worse. Due to its importance, history will always be studied and taught; and definitely, it will remain an academic discourse just like other social sciences. So, letting someone else to write your history is as good as committing suicide. For, such a person can describe you the way he or she likes: even misrepresenting you to suit her or his interests as it happened in writing and presenting African history. Everybody has a history to write or narrate; and story to tell. It is only the dead that do not tell stories or narrate their histories. Africa is alive, as it has been. Therefore, it has the wherewithal of authoring its own history based on reality; but not lies and bigotry as it has always been in the case of representing African history. Consequently, one of the ways of truly and accurately rewriting African history is through examining those who managed or mismanaged, especially soon after African countries gained their independence.

Wayne and Kimenyi (1986) note that, "Examples of inefficient managers are common in Africa. Nigeria, Kenya, Zaire, Uganda, Burundi, and Zambia are only a few countries where inefficient managers hired by the dictator have caused major reductions in the national product," (p.38). This episode fits in our discourse in that presidents–being the CEOs of the countries they are managing–are responsible for whatever their appointees do due to the fact their appointees act vicariously on behalf of their makers who in this case are the presidents. We will delve into and shed light on vicarious liability shortly hereunder. Importantly, the managers who happen to be dictators manage the empire as a project that defines and dictates almost everything in the state. This is a norm of any government that runs the empire especially where the citizenry are hijacked or sidelined from running the business of the state. The difference, however, is that, in Africa; many governments run the empire discretionary based on the whims of the rulers as opposed to the needs and interests of the citizenry. As argued above, the citizenry in such countries are sidelined and hijacked. Therefore, they cannot be blame for anything that happens wrongly or negatively. Their managers are the ones to should the blames. Essentially, this is why Africa has always lagged behind as far as real and meaningful development, human rights and self-reliance that do not depend on cooked statistics are concerned. Thompson (2005) observes that, "the central project of Empire follows a relatively conventional Marxist mode of discovery: define the enemy and locate the conditions of its reproduction, then identify its gravedigger/s and the material foundations of that power," (p.74). Therefore, whatever happens in the business of the state, the managers of the said state have solely big role to play. As a result, we must treat those failures resulting from the agents of the presidents as theirs but not of the appointees. Under vicarious responsibility–which historically entails the choice for a master to give orders to his servant (Laski, 1916, p.105) to carry them out–whatever the servant does, one sending or appointing her or him automatically gets the rewards or blames or faces the consequences resulting from the work of the appointee which, essentially, is the work of who sent or him to act as her or his messenger to others. In simple African conceptualization of the concept based on Swahili (the biggest African language spoken in eastern, central, and partly southern Africa) philosophy, whatever the messenger does, it is not hers or his but the master's. Swahili sage has it that, "*Mbwa akining'ata siongei na mbwa bali mwenye mbwa* literally: When a dog bites me, I do not talk to the dog but to the owner. Therefore, the dog acts vicariously whereby the owner takes liability. Or put it this way using Swahili sage that has it that "*Usiue mjumbe*" namely, "why killing a messenger?" When the messenger abuses an elder in the society, the liability falls on your shoulders however the master who sent her or him did not sent that messenger to do what is done. Nyamnjoh (2012) sums it up that real life is bigger than logic.

All over again, when you examine how our states and their systems work—under the discretionary powers some of our rulers especially in dictatorships—you end up wondering; if they ever think about the future. They do things as if there is no future or as if they are the first and the last in this world. It is sad to note that nobody has ever examined mental health of many African thieves and dictators to see which types of mental diseases they were suffering from or which backgrounds they came from based on the mental history of their families. Apart from greedy, manipulation, there must be something else that fooled such people to behave as if a human life does not have an end which is death. It is sad that even those who were overthrown; their netherworld-cum-underworlds were not explored well to see how they operated so as to be able to gander into their psyches in particular. Knowing such hidden things about venal dictators that ruined Africa is an important thing that will avert Africa from getting more of the same in the future. One may ask: Why many venal dictators Africa has ever had did what they did. Arguably, one of the reasons of their *faux pas* may be the fact that they came to power, first of all, without the consent of the people. And secondly, they did not have any wherewithal or plans to serve and develop the countries but only to rob them. Thirdly, the people they ruled did not know their true selves as far as their weaknesses, sicknesses and whatnot are concerned. As Foucault (1984) puts it, "There is no external position of certainty, no universal understanding that is beyond history and society," (p.4) especially of a person or thing one deals with. Based on its history, the society needs to know and select its leaders grounded in its needs and desires instead of letting external players do so. If this goes on, Africa will always remain an experimental object for others to benefit while the Africans suffer more and more pointlessly thanks to having bad management of their affairs in many countries. The society needs to know behavioural conditions of its leaders before entrusting them the noble duty of leading it; failure to which it can end up in a calamity as it happened in many countries whose worst managers we will discuss later hereunder.

All those who got in power–either by carrying out *coup d'états* or through the barrel of the gun–are no different from mere coldblooded thugs who break into the house, terrorize its occupants and make away with everything or anything they are able to put a hand on. However, there is an exception to every general rule. Freedom fighters in Angola, Mozambique and Zimbabwe, among others, who were forced to take up arms and bring down illegal and colonial regimes, cannot fall under this category all depending on how they managed the affair of the citizenry thereafter. So, too, coups–such as the one in Burkina Faso in 1984, under the legendary Thomas Sankara that brought about humongous change–do not also fall under this category.

Also, regimes that were propelled to power by mass actions such as the one in Tunisia are acceptable but all depends on if they conditionally met the expectations of the mass of the citizens who sacrificed everything to see to it that they pulled corrupt and inept regimes down. The Democratic Republic of Congo (DRC), Egypt, Libya, and Uganda provide ideal examples whereby the mass overthrew long time dictatorial regimes to end up ushering more of the same. Such regime cannot be legalised in any way or sense. For, they are the typical replica of what they replaced. They are but the betrayals of the mass. Foucault (Ibid) answers the question of how should one actively self-form and position by observing "twin terms of power and knowledge" (p.12) as the driving forces behind whatever goes on in the society. Foucault (op.cit) argues, "That the real political task in a society such as ours is to criticise the working institutions...," (p.6) but not to be hijacked or cowered by them. Shall this happen, the mass shall pull down such managers who use power as the means of humiliating and exploiting the citizenry they are supposedly duty bound to serve. Power and knowledge play a very crucial role in the management of any society. And this is very obvious in that our rulers had, and still have power while academics have knowledge. If we put these twin variables at a collision course, chances of reconciling them is very high especially at this time when democratic ideas are taking roots in Africa despite being borrowed from the West. Again, this begs and challenges us to formulate our modes and models of democracy suitable to our needs and environment. We need to transit from depending on conditional-Western democracy by creating our own brand of democracy. Western-funded and-borrowed democracy will obviously serve those who fund it but not those they fund. Recipients always face conditions on whatever they receive. *Blessed is the hand that giveth than the one that taketh*. Therefore, Africa needs to reinvent itself so as to come up with its own version of democracy based on its needs, aspirations, dreams, expectations and environment. Importantly, when, and if academics decide to take on those in power abusing and misusing it, they must be braced to face many challenges such as being regarded as witch hunters, dreamers; *provocateurs,* and above all, they will be branded agents of imperialists by those opposing them even the known agents of imperialists they will decide to take on. Ironically, those who are in bed with the so-called imperialists are, sometimes, good at accusing others of the same sin they have been committing for decades. Ugandan long-time president Yoweri Museveni provides a very ideal example of failing to reflect on his own actions. The *News 24* (19 March, 2014) quoted Museveni saying that African government need to be strong enough to prevent Western countries from meddling in their national and continental affairs. Museveni blatantly accuses the West of greedy as a driving force behind snooping into Africa's affairs. How can African countries become strong and oppose Western meddling into their affairs while they willingly and blindly go there begging to get money to run their governments? He who pays the piper calls the tune. It is as logically simple as that. If one does not want to receive orders, must stop beggarliness and misuse of public office. It is good that Museveni castigates *greedy West.* However, he forgets about greedy Museveni who has been in power over three decades geared and enhanced by the same vice he is purportedly accusing others of. Greed is greed regardless whoever is behind it. At least, Western countries have something to say in that they run many African governments. What does a person like Museveni say about his long-time rule over Ugandans apart from the same vice-cum-meme of which he accuses the West? If we face it, Museveni does not have any *locus standi* whatsoever to accuse the West of what he has been doing for the entire period time he has been in power manipulating people and tampering with the constitution so as to remain in office illegally. According to International Monetary Fund (IMF) country *Report no.05/307*, 2005, Uganda government's dependency on donor aid has increased the vulnerability of the budget to sudden cut-back in donor aid. In 1997/98 domestic revenues were sufficient to fund 79% of the Government Of Uganda (GOU) expenditure plus external debt payments but this has fallen only to 60% in 2001/02, (p.41). Can such a government exonerate itself from entertaining West's meddling without becoming self-reliant really?

As Chomsky (2013) puts it, academics need to be ready to take on what he called *thought control*, which the governments all over the world like to do. This is done in two ways, by force or by manipulation, especially, through buying out or getting rid of thorny academics. Knowing this danger helps academics to devise methods by which to avert it and stay course with what they desire to do and achieve, which in this discourse, is freeing Africa from the fangs of its tormentors. Some governments used their agents to hunt and, either silence detractors or offer them some bribes so as to force them to stop pursuing what is regarded as dangerous undertakings to the state or the government. It is always a carrot-and-stick technique that is oft-used in dealing with academics that seem not to toe the line as far as the management of the business of the state is concerned.

For that reason therefore, when it comes to assessing African managers, be they the best or the worst, we will not address ourselves to those who were under their watch. Instead, by and large, we will judge everybody as a CEO under whose watch things went well or awry. It is very important to clarify this in order to avoid letting the CEOs jump the smoking gun while they actually had the power to turn things around where things went wrong; or influence things where things went well. The role of leadership is very crucial in managing or mismanaging the business of the state as we will see later in this lucubration.

Lastly, but not least, when we evaluate the works of past African managers, although there is one serving manager, we will build the stamina of taking on current managers who openly seem to mismanage our countries. We will ask how they got in power, what they achieved or failed to achieve, how accountable/unaccountable, credible/uncredible, trustworthy/untrustworthy and competent or incompetent they are and what have you as far as their scores are concerned. Good news is; after gaining the stamina and resolve, we will ask all such inevitably important and thorny questions openly and fearlessly as we seek logical and right answers to our problems as they authored them. For those who performed deservedly, we will seek to build or expand, if not to scoop from, their noble works in managing the business of the state for the time being and the future. All in all, there are some vital lessons from these subjects for us as a society that intentionally aspires to forge ahead.

Acknowledgments

As our tradition, I would like to candidly and profoundly acknowledge the contribution that my wife, Nesaa, has made. She has always stood by me in my writing escapades doing alone all things we are supposed to share. Her support has always been immense especially encouraging me not to give in or up whenever the goings get tough. Our children too, have contributed a lot in this undertaking. The older one never stopped to ask when a new book would come out. For them, I am a book factory that never goes bankrupt as far as writing is concerned.

Langaa Publishers have always been kind to me whenever my works come to their attention. They have never sat on them. I sincerely and humbly acknowledge the encouragements I got from my brothers Professors Sean Byrne and Munyaradzi Mawere; and Dr. Artwell Nhemachena (who meticulously and expediently reviewed this volume).

I would like to also acknowledge my friend and brother Professor Hans Werner not to forget Professor Eliakim Sibanda (all of the University of Winnipeg) for encouraging me to take on critical issues that many hate to love.

Lastly, though not least, I would like to thank all readers who will read this tome and work on its nuggets.

Chapter 1

Lumumba the Martyr Who Defined Africa

"We will show the world what the black man can do when he works in freedom and we shall make the Congo an example to the whole of Africa," Lumumba in Gerard-Libois, (1966, p. 267).

Figure 2: P. E. Lumumba DRC's 1st PM (image courtesy of Kalangu Voice of Africa)

We will kick-start this discourse–about the best and the worst African managers–with the late Patrice Lumumba, the founding father of Congo, now the Democratic Republic of Congo (DRC), as means of showing our respect and empathy to him and his country due to what transpired resulting into the loss of his life at his prime. Lumumba opens the curtain not just because he was better than others in this discourse. This volume decided to start with Lumumba thanks to his selfless and true contribution, particularly to the course of his country and Africa in general. More importantly, starting with Lumumba is one way of acknowledging and paying tributes to his contribution for our wellbeing as Africans and victims of what he ferociously and tirelessly fought against. Essentially, we start with him because his life was cut short before even putting a hand on what he wanted to do for his country and Africa. What makes Lumumba unique compared to other is the fact that he knew the dangers his stance posed. Again, he did not cower or waver when the hour of truly offering himself as a *sacrificial lamb* arrived. We are doing this the same way Christians literally do in remembering and acknowledging the role Jesus played in their *salvation*. Our experience shows that humans are always afraid of death. This is why many security and protective gadgets are invented and supplied every day. This is why Jesus is treated exceptionally. Shedding somebody's blood for others is not an easy thing that everybody can do, mainly at one's prime time or age. This is why Lumumba is referred to as a martyr in this volume. If we examine his history without any bias, it verily shows that his few and short acts even before being assassinated had already showed that he was a shooting star that would have pulled his country out of colonial grip; and contributed immensely to his continent had he lived to fulfil his plans and dreams. Lumumba was not only just a shooting star but huge and magnificent star. Nonetheless, Lumumba's tragic death dashed Congolese's hopes as we will later show. True, his fiery and unwavering words quoted above can show the readers the type of person and leader Lumumba actually was. Lumumba was born on July 2nd, 1925 in the Wembonya village in the Katoko-Kombe district of Sankuru, Central Kasai province of what was then known as the Belgian colony of the Congo, (Lumumba, 2003, p. 113). Lumumba was the first prime minister of Congo who was overthrown, captured, tortured and, later, tragically assassinated by Joseph Desire Mobutu, former DRC's dictator and thief under the order of the Central Intelligence Agency (CIA) and Belgium authorities on 17th January, 1961 after refusing to become a straight partner of the West in exchange with his life. He is the only founder of his nation who spent the shortest time in office in Africa. One would want to know why Lumumba was overthrown under the orders of the West, especially Belgium and the United States (US); and what went wrong at such very nativity of the nation where things were supposed to be hilarious thanks to the euphoria of gaining independence. Further, one would, likewise, want to know the position the international community took and the role it played at this *hour of need* for Lumumba and his new country. So, too, one would want to know and explore what transpired after the assassination of Lumumba. We will answer all these questions, *inter alia*, in this volume. However, it is not easy for one chapter to exhaustively cover everything that this giant, Lumumba, did even in the short time he lived. This chapter explores Lumumba the person not the legendary figure of the politics of Africa that his death created subsequently.

When he discovered that the situation was out of control, according to Klein and Licata (2003) Lumumba sought assistance from the UN peacekeeping force but was denied under the pretext of neutrality "which in effect, legitimized the secession of Katanga," (p. 577) which, in a sense, was the straw that broke the camel's back *vis-à-vis* the toppling, and later, the assassination of Lumumba. It is obvious blamable that UN's *neutrality* was nothing but a perfidy to Lumumba who had immense trust in this international body to which his new country was a member. Sadly, the same organisation that Lumumba trusted ended up stabbing him in the back. Ontologically, the so-called international organisations and the international community have always machinated with the West in sticking up and sullying Africa. And this was not the first or the last time for such bodies to practically sabotage Africa. Refer to how the International Monetary Fund (IMF) and the World Bank (WB) have always misguided African economies by introducing detrimental and exploitative measures that have kept Africa in abject poverty wantonly.

Ironically, the sacrilegious sin that Lumumba committed so as to be shunned and assassinated by those he trusted most was nothing but to say "no" to the machinations of the West that wanted to laughably offer him ceremonial independence while it wanted to keep on robbing the country using the same fake independence. De Vos (1961); Klein (2000); and Willame (1994) cited in Klein and Licata (Ibid) claim that Lumumba did not want to become Belgium's colonial project (p. 577); instead he tried to ally himself with communist Russia the move that the West misconstrued as being a threat-cum-danger to their hidden interests in the Congo which at the time was the sole African producer of uranium. Lumumba did not want to hear anything short of total and true independence let alone subscribing to blackmail and neocolonialism that wanted to turn him into a stooge the West could use to rob his country and his people. For Lumumba, myopic and humdrum personal glories—just like the ones that lulled his betrayers—had no place even when it meant to die for refusing them. In other words, Lumumba refused to be a good *black blue-eyed boy* to the West and their allies wanted him to be like Ivorian Felix Houphouët-Boigny, Kenyan Jomo Kenyatta, Malawian Hastings Kamuzu Banda and many more who decided to vend their people in order to look good in the eyes of the West. They decided to become the enemies of the people whom, in some cases, the West used to kill the men of the people like Lumumba, Kwame Nkrumah (Ghana), Salvador Allende (Chile), Jacobo Albenz (Guatemala) and Thomas Sankara (Burkina Faso) among others that became the victims of imperialism as the continuance of colonialism.

Despite knowing the danger of his choice and undertaking, in fact, Lumumba willingly, heroically and unequivocally opted to become the *black sheep* rather than betraying his conscience and his people. Death, for him, was better than slavery. To Lumumba, his life was nothing bigger or more important than the wellbeing of his people. For him, even if it begged to gulp *hemlock*, it would not have been an issue subject to guessing or second thought. He believed in truth so as to die for it. What a selfless person who practically proved to die for the truth he knew and believed in! To the contrary, after Lumumba was assassinated, his infamous antithesis (Joseph Desire Mobutu later Mobutu Sese Seko) took over so as to sell the whole country, including himself, to his cloners. There is no way one can write an accurate history of corruption, power abuses and duplicity in Africa without touching on Mobutu whom we will explore in an independent chapter henceforward. From the look of things soon after independence, it was obvious that Lumumba would not succeed in his stance against the West. One thing Lumumba did not know is that those around him were not sailing in the same boat with him. He wrongly thought that all of *comrades* and *compatriots* were on the same page as people of vision, probity, conscience and belief in freedom and justice of the whole country. He did not know that he was sharing a bed with hyenas and foxes that would devour him and his people when the right time to do so arrived. For, they were hell-bent to rock the boat or throw Lumumba overboard if the boat were to survive. Those he thought were his friends turned out to be his nemeses who, like the UN, the international community and the West, stabbed him in the back.

Metaphorically, Lumumba concentrated on the *elephant* without looking at the *monkeys* that the *hunters* used to finish him up; and thereby ruin what he lived and died for. Swahili have a saying that when you laugh with monkeys, you will harvest chaff. The West had already studied Lumumba so as to know his weaknesses and strengths. There were three *mauvais mousquetaires or* three bad musketeers in this betrayal namely Mobutu who later took over after betraying his co-conspirators, Moise Tshombe, the founder of *Confédération des Associations Tribales du Katanga* (CONAKAT) and Joseph Kasa-vubu, president of Congo's new national assembly, who waged the war of destroying Lumumba to end up being thrown out of the bandwagon-cum-gravy train thereafter. Live by sword, die by sword. The sage has it. You may call them three monkeys who greedily and blindly authored the destruction of the DRC (themselves included). This being the real situation, Lumumba, thus, was to be eliminated at all costs as soon as possible before entrenching himself in power; and thereby spoil things. And this plot of eliminating Lumumba would be fulfilled by local murderers who were promised the pomp and yum-yum of the high echelons of power. Lumumba (2003) notes that "only a few days after independence, Belgian army officers provoked a mutiny amongst the 24,000 African soldiers in the *Force Publique* and the Belgian government sent troop reinforcements to the Congo," (p. 115). Lumumba goes on arguing that amidst the mutiny; Colonel Mobutu, "formerly one of the commanders of the *Force Publique* appointed by Lumumba, announced that this force, renamed the *Armée Nationale Congolaise*," and staged a coup that saw Congo being plundered and ruined for over thirty years thereafter as you will see. This macabre act became, if anything, a myth, especially as to who actually was behind the assassination of Lumumba up until the US declassified some of CIA's confidential documents. For many years, Lumumba's death was subject to many conspiracy theories; however all tied on one nexus that the West and local players hatched a plot that culminated into the assassination of Lumumba and his two confidants, Maurice Mpolo and Joseph Okito. See Langer, 2014.

Be that as it may be, what is obvious is the fact that when Congo was preparing itself for its independence, one opportunistic and controversial figure, Joseph Desire Mobutu burst onto the scene after conspiring with the West to either derail or hijack the whole process. There are some literatures which claim that Mobutu, on the one hand, was a double agent in that he was one of Lumumba's consigliore; and a CIA agent, on the other hand. The convolution of this situation led to many conclusions about the motive; and who actually was behind the assassination of Lumumba. By implications and circumstantially, Mobutu is the only visible assassin due to the fact that he was the only beneficiary from Lumumba's assassination. Again, after Mobutu being used and misused like any tool in the hands of anybody, the actual killer became the West. However, by pinning down Mobutu, many were left guessing; even exonerating the West by just blaming Mobutu alone without looking at who was actually in bed with him in raping the DRC. Luckily, as indicated above, after the US declassified its confidential documents, at least, this action started to shed light on the macabre truth *vis-à-vis* the ghoulish capture; and later, the assassination of Lumumba. Indeed, this is when the world–that used to guess about who actually killed Lumumba–woke up to such an ugly and gut-wrenching new reality that squarely implicated the US. First of all, many were shocked to learn that the country that presented itself as the *champion* of democracy and human rights could commit such a heinous crime (see Mhango (2015). Yet again, knowing what the US has been doing not only in the DRC but all over the world, for some, especially in the ranks, this was but an open secret. Essentially, the fact that the US ordered the assassination of Lumumba was known based on assumptions–but not facts–due to how it overtly and covertly dealt with Mobutu. So, putting CIA's dirty linens on the agora acted as one way of getting strong evidence against the US; however there was no pending case on the issue. How did the US order the assassination of Lumumba? De Witte (2000) notes:

Richard Bissell, the CIA's Deputy Director for Plans and its head of clandestine operation said later, The agency has put a top priority, probably on range of different methods of getting rid of

Lumumba in the sense of either destroying him physically, or incapacitating, or eliminating his political influence, (p. 17).

Such revelations are unswervingly self-inculpatory for the CIA and the US in general. If there were an international mechanism to be used to force such culprits to be brought to book or being forced to redress the victims, maybe, just maybe, the situation in the DRC would not have always been as tense and volatile as it has been since the assassination of Lumumba over five decades ago that evidenced big violence and pillaging of the country *inter alia*.

If anything, the CIA did not succeeded in destroying Lumumba physically, politically and forever. Spiritually Lumumba is still alive. He is the part of glorious history of Africa. If the US succeeded in destroying Lumumba, it successfully did it partially and momentarily. However, the US failed to destroy one important fact-cum-facet that shaped Lumumba as a leader. It did not destroy what he fought and died for, justice and freedom of Africa. Up until now, Congolese are still crying for justice, chiefly being able to truly benefit from abundant resources their country is endowed with. Although Lumumba died many years ago, he is still living with his people in the sense that whenever they come across problems such as violation of human rights, neocolonialism, national vandalism, violence and exploitation, they fondly remember him. Lumumba will always be a reminder that Africa is not totally and truly free; thus, there is a need to fight for freedom to see to it that Africans are treated equally and justly just like any others. So, the precedent that Lumumba set will never be easily erased from the hearts and history of Africa.

Although Lumumba did not live to lead his country as he hoped, he truthfully proved to be a visionary, charismatic but noncompliant leader who was ahead of his time. Academics need to keep on reminding the world of evil and diabolic forces and the reasons behind killing Lumumba for refusing to become a Western stooge. More outstandingly, Lumumba had the window to negotiate. Yet, he did not want to betray his people and their cause. He, thus, faced death heroically hoping that–maybe–things would change for the better. Sadly though, the death of Lumumba pulled the DRC back after being savagely exploited and maltreated by king Leopold of Belgium for decades before it was handed over to Mobutu to rape even more for over three decades thereafter. As the DRC neared to attaining its independence early in the 60s, the CIA and Belgium hatched a plan to eliminate Lumumba after finding that he was incorruptible and unintimidatable. They, consequently, earmarked some stooges led by Mobutu–who, as noted above was Lumumba's Chief of Staff and one of the people that Lumumba wrongly trusted the most–and Kasa-vubu and Moise Tshombe whom Mobutu fixed after getting what he wanted. Daniel P. Moynihan (1989 cited in Johnson III, 1992) notes that:

> Regarding the assassination of Lumumba, the Committee discovered that in the summer of 1960, the C.I.A. Deputy Director of Plans, Richard Bissell, asked the Chief of the African Division, Bronson Tweedy, to explore the feasibility of assassinating Lumumba, Congo's prime minister. Bissell also asked a C.I.A. scientist, Joseph Scheider, to prepare to assassinate or incapacitate an unidentified "African leader." Scheider testified that Bissell said that the assignment had the "highest authority," (p. 406).

Such information was circulating in academic circles even before the White House declassified CIA's files on foreign leaders that it was contracted to kill under the instructions or orders of the presidency and the senate. Since the allegations that the CIA assassinated Lumumba came to light, neither the government of the US nor the CIA itself has ever refuted the allegations. Now the whole world knows who killed Lumumba; and why he was killed. Gerald and Kuklik (2015) maintain that "after Lumumba's death, the United States had propped up Mobutu who ruled Congo for thirty years," (p. 3). Here we are talking about the role the US played in killing Lumumba. There are yet other culprits that you cannot expect. If we face it without beating around the bush, the UN is also to blame. Looking at its incompetence, conspiracy and powerless, one would argue that it ceased to have any meaning for the DRC and Africa ever since. Ironically, Africa has always trusted the same let-downs as we saw it in 1994 during the 100-day genocide in Rwanda when, once again, the same UN proved to be but a letdown even more not to mention being an international-lame duck. However, people tend to treat what happened in Rwanda in 1994 as an accident-cum-common mistake. It was not at all. It started long time ago as Gerald and Kuklik (Ibid) note that the Africans seem to have little knowledge of the UN and did not understand its American origins not to mention its weakness, particularly before powerful nations, (p. 30). And, indeed, Africans still lack the said *knowledge* about the whole international system and the way it works against them based on overt and covert international racism. They are always fooled by making them a part of it even by offering some high offices to manage in the UN. Once again, the UN and the US are tied together in the conspiracy to assassinate Lumumba. Neither the UN nor the US has ever repudiated such damning allegations. Why should they do so while they know Africa–as it has always been–cannot do anything thanks to being scuttled since 1884? I still wonder how Africa could keep good ties with these entities despite their criminality against it. Does this need a PhD in political science or philosophy to understand; and thus decide? Who will take on these two entities if at all brave personalities such as Lumumba, Nkrumah and others were felled while others had to cower or fight it alone as Nyerere did and finally fail after many African stooges either abandoned or betrayed him? Lumumba is long gone; Nyerere is no more. Mandela, too, is gone. Nonetheless, what these heroes and others fought for is still around. Africa is still ours. It still needs our contribution which essentially is for ourselves and the generations to come. Although I hate colonialism, it had something that Africa lacks. It was able to envision the future. This is why colonial monsters dubiously divided Africa in order to weaken it so as to keep on exploiting it, (Mhango 2015). For how long shall Africa go on this self-inflicted suttee while it actually knows its consequences? I think; the new African generation needs to know what and who their enemies are. And once they know, they can arguably avoid repeating the same mistakes that the post-colonial generation committed. By revisiting the assassination of Lumumba, among others, the new African generation will be able to choose to keep in on with the *status quo* or do otherwise for its future betterment. Admittedly, the post-colonial generation has failed in some ways however still there are some good things to learn from it. For instance, the present and the coming generations will be able to see the detriment of dependence on Western countries in lieu of interdependence among themselves. Lumumba epitomises this in that he tried to encourage other post-colonial-African leaders to embark on the reunification of Africa in order to chart their own way towards advancement and development of their own continent and people. The critique one can make is: For how long will we go on failing while we know the root causes of our quandaries? This becomes obvious due to the fact that Africa—under corrupt and inept regimes that betrayed and sold their people in exchange with stupid and nonsensical glories—has been repeating the same mistakes that it has been committed for over fifty years of its controversial and wanting independence.

On betrayal, one wonders about how the US—that pretends to champion human rights in the world—has always failed or kept quiet, or negated to even issue an apology to the people of the DRC and Africa in general for the role it played in ruining many African countries and the lives of the people in those countries. Is it wrong to demand that the US, apart from officially issuing an apology, must pay compensation to Congolese and other victims of its criminal policies all over the world? There are a couple of reasons why the US, and all those who conspired with it, plotted, and later, assassinated Lumumba to pay compensation to his country and his people for wronging and robbing them for many years. First, the US and Western countries that conspired against the DRC must do so for killing Lumumba and DRC's economy. Secondly, the conspirators must be forced to pay compensation for installing a corrupt and venal ruler who terrorised Congolese for over thirty years, *inter alia*. And thirdly, the US and its connivers must redress the DRC for robbing the country of its resources for the whole period the country was miserably misruled by Mobutu and his cabal of thieves the whole period he was in power in the DRC and thereafter under Kabila. Fourthly, the US and the West must redress the DRC for causing many violent conflicts resulting from the struggle for controlling resources the DRC is endowed with. When you look at the numbers of raped women, displaced people and those who lost their beloved ones, you do not understand if the US and the West have any morality as the pretend or portray themselves to be. Sixthly, all those who profited and profiteered from the DRC must cancel all loans they extended to Mobutu knowingly; he would steal and squander them wantonly as they stayed side and looked. Seventhly, all conspirators behind the robbing of the DRC must rebuild the country that Mobutu and his kit and caboodle of criminals destroyed as means of reconciliation between them and the Congolese who—for a long time—bore the consequences of the criminality that they caused it.

Essentially, Lumumba's assassination is said to have involved the entire colonial West led by Belgium and the US as Eyskens the son of Gaston Eyskens who was Belgium premier during the killing of Lumumba, cited in Bustin (2002) discloses that "in his times, Lumumba was considered a Communist, with so many deaths on his conscience that a consensus to eliminate him developed in the West," (p. 539). There is a lot of evidence all over the place that show that the West assassinated Lumumba; simply because he was not ready and willing to betray his people in order to protect personal, evil and stinking interests of the West just like Mobutu and others did. Lumumba gets a very special place in the history of the DRC and Africa in general as the best manager however he did not live to manage the affairs of his country. His staunch stand against imperialists has many lessons for Africa today. Swahili sage has it that *Nyota njema huonekana asubuhi* literary; the lucky star is seen at dawn. As well, Lumumba, just like the late Steve Biko (South African freedom fighter), and Thomas Sankara (former Burkina Faso president), was like a lucky star for Africa; however he did not get enough time to shine. If Lumumba decidedly and willingly chose to betray his people like Mobutu and others did for a mere survival, he would easily have had done so. Yet again, he chose to die a dignified person rather than living like a dog even if he was the Whiteman's dog. In his thirties, just like Biko and Sankara, Lumumba still had a lot to desire to live for, and do. But he heroically offered his life for the sake of his country. As argued above, Lumumba saw that his life was not more important than the cause he lived and died for. Such a spirit is important for Africa that has—for a long time, and for no more logical reasons than greed and myopia—suffered from betrayal and greed. So, when the coming generations judge us—at least—they will have a point of reference on personalities such as Lumumba who stood firm for their wellbeing even at the time when he had to sacrifice his own life. Moore (2007) maintains that "history will have its say one day. It won't be a history written in Brussels, Paris or

Washington. It will be ours, the history of a new Africa," (p. 3). This is the history we are writing in order to fulfil Lumumba's prophecy. Re-narrating Lumumba's noble cause; and life are our responsibility. All this aims at trying to address collective account of what pushed Africa to cascade into a morass it is currently in economically and politically despite a lie behind aid Africa receives from those who destroyed it (the volume of dependency and aid will be out soon). However, donors—who happen to be the same colonial monsters and imperialists—always pretend to help when the going gets tough. Notably, aid and handouts have never alleviated the problem rather than exacerbating dependence and indebtedness Africa has faced since independence. Lumumba did not want to live in such Africa that any quack can easily abuse and misuse as it currently is.

By and large, Africans and those who despise them need to know why some Africans have always been in bad hands of corrupt, inept and banditry regimes. The DRC is the leading country in Africa to have suffered more injustices and being mismanaged, plundered, vandalised and abused since gaining its independence. Mobutu—as promised above, that we will discuss later under the category of the worst managers—presided over a very kleptocratic regime that culminated in mega theft, gross violations of human rights, and miseries of all kinds. No country in Africa can be at par with the DRC as far as political banditry and vagabondage are concerned. Even if we go down the history lane, the DRC tops the list of African countries that colonial monsters brutalised before handing them over in the hands of some black colonialists who did exactly the same even at a very big enormousness and viciousness. For that reason, we can argue that long-time and long-lasting injustices hardened Lumumba. This is why it was more important for him to die on his feet fighting than living as a betrayal on his knees. Basically, Lumumba was hardened by the injustices and the violence; his country, and his people went through. The DRC has always suffered all sorts of injustices; and still suffers because of nothing but its resources as Boschini, *et al.*, (2007) argue that "natural resource abundance is negative for economic development only if the country lacks the proper institutions to deal with rent-seeking behaviour that resources otherwise may result in," (p. 9). This is exactly what happened in the DRC after the assassination of Lumumba. The country was pointlessly mismanaged due to the death of the best manager who would have wrestled it from the fangs of hyenas. When it comes to rent-seeking behaviours, Mobutu's venal rule; was unparalleled. The West installed a corrupt Mobutu whose role was to vend everything that his makers-cum-masters wanted or ordered him to offer. Moore (2007) underscores and pins down what geared the West to conspire with greedy Congolese thugs and betrayers such as Mobutu, Moise Tshombe and Joseph Kasa-vubu to assassinate Lumumba saying that:

> His assertion that the resources of his country would be used for the benefit of the Congolese sounded suspiciously like socialism, too. The American–the neo-colonialists hoping to gain strategic minerals from countries like the Congo (remember, the uranium that bombed Hiroshima was from the DRC!)," [Sic] (p. 4).

Lumumba's visibly proclivity towards the then Union of Soviet Socialist Republics (USSR) irked the US to the extent of creating fear that its arch nemesis would get hands on uranium so as to add more threat; and thus, tilt power balance in which the US would end up losing its grip on the world. So, something had to be done urgently to stop such a shift in world power and *realpolitik* of the time. The US had already developed what was known as *Manhattan project* in Kinshasa (Daly, *et al.*, 2005, p. 56). It did not like to see the DRC slinking into the hands of its arch nemesis, the USSR. Thus, apart from being forced by economic drive, there was a cold war phobia of each of the drive of the then sharply divided and highly antagonistic superpowers which were centred on the belief that whoever controls nukes and uranium control the world. Thus, Lumumba was the victim of nuke politics of the time between the then superpowers whose ideologies and strategies were always at loggerheads with each other. So, whoever that was caught in between was not spared. Africans have a saying that "when two elephants fight, it is the grass that suffers." Mhango (2015) calls this dichotomous situation ideological divide and rule of Africa which led to the current scramble for and partition of Africa for the aim of selling weapons in order to get cheap resources.

Even after the death of Lumumba, it is unfortunate that *multinational robbery* has been going on unremittingly ever since the DRC gained its independence. The US–a self-appointed *champion and guardian* of democracy–has always been in the big picture as far as the plundering of the DRC is concerned not to mention the death of the country's first Prime Minister, Lumumba. So, too, the US and Belgium have never distanced themselves from such damning allegations of the assassination of Lumumba. What else do we need to implicate the US in the assassination of Lumumba which is crime against sovereignty? Ironically, Lumumba was not the first or the last to die under the instructions of the US as the UN stood aside and watched. Others died under the same orders from the same criminality. Johnson III (1992) names leaders such as "Rafael Trujillo of the Dominican Republic, Ngo Dinh Diem of South Vietnam, and General Rene Schneider of Chile," (p. 404) as victims of this criminality committed by the country that aggrandises itself of being the *guardian* of democracy in the world. Others like Salvador Allende (Chile), Kwame Nkrumah (Ghana), Jacob Albenz (Guatemala) and unknown others were either assassinated or overthrown due to being obstacles to surreptitious interests of the US. Has the US stopped these machinations towards less powerful countries it seeks to exploit, especially in Africa? The death of Lumumba speaks volume. That is Patrice Emile Lumumba, the true son and undisputable hero of Africa who was assassinated simply because he did not offer to be in bed with hyenas and eagles of this world.

His last words adapted from the letter he wrote to his wife before being murdered tell it all. Lumumba says:

> Do not weep for Me. History will one day have its say; it will not be the history taught in the United Nations, Washington, Paris, or Brussels, but the history taught in the countries that have rid themselves of colonialism and its puppets. Africa will write its own history and both north and south of the Sahara it will be a history full of glory and dignity, (Cole, 2006, p. 26).

For Lumumba, Africa was bigger and more precious than his life, family and everything. His words are not the words of a coward who is afraid of death. They are the words of the person who knows what is waiting for him; however painful and nerve-wracking it may seem for others as it was the case of Lumumba. Despite that, Lumumba stood firm to see to it that he did not betray his ideas, dreams and people. This is why Lumumba, like Mandela, has always been idolised and eulogised not only in the DRC but all over Africa and the world in general. He willingly paid the price dearly more than even Jesus, who according to Christian dogma, complained when the moment of truth arrived saying *"Eli, Eli, lama sabachthani,"* literary "My God, My God, why you have forsaken me?" (Matthew 27:45-46, NASB). Jesus had God's assurance that he would be resurrected. Lumumba faced his death courageously; and he knew there was no assurance except the emancipation of Africa.

In sum, the assassination of Lumumba, tragically, dealt a death blow to the DRC that ever since has never gotten any respite as far as good governance, human rights, democracy and economic recovery are concerned. It is as if Lumumba died with his country. For, soon after his assassination, there came one barbarous and disastrous Mobutu who abused and mismanaged the country for over three decades. As mentioned above, we will delve into Mobutu's venal and terrorist rule later in the section of the worst African managers of state affairs.

What's more, despite such macabre act that imperialists and criminals committed, neither the US nor Belgium has ever thought about redressing the DRC for the loss they caused it. Since then, Lumumba assassins have treated his loss just like anything normal to happen to a person and worse enough to the whole country. The international community, too, conspired with Lumumba's assassins by indifferently maintaining silence as if his rights—just like any human being—did not count. If they failed to view him as a leader, at least, they would have viewed him as a human being whose human rights were created even before he was killed. For, ever since, nobody has ever condemned this barbaric act that left the DRC bleeding to death. Ironically, when wild animals such as elephants and rhinoceroses are killed today, the same people holler at the top of their lungs while they have kept mum about Lumumba's death.

Let us sum up Lumumba's chapter with his last words to his wife that turned up to be the last also to the world in the letter he wrote that reads:

My dear wife,

I am writing these words not knowing whether they will reach you, when they will reach you, and whether I shall still be alive when you read them. All through my struggle for the independence of my country, I have never doubted for a single instant the final triumph of the sacred cause to which my companions and I have devoted all our lives. But what we wished for our country, its right to an honourable life, to unstained dignity, to independence without restrictions, was never desired by the Belgian imperialists and the Western allies, who found direct and indirect support, both deliberate and unintentional, amongst certain high officials of the United Nations, that organization in which we placed all our trust when we called on its assistance.

They have corrupted some of our compatriots and bribed others. They have helped to distort the truth and bring our independence into dishonour. How could I speak otherwise?

Dead or alive, free or in prison by order of the imperialists, it is not myself who counts. It is the Congo; it is our poor people for whom independence has been transformed into a cage from whose confines the outside world looks on us, sometimes with kindly sympathy, but at other times with joy and pleasure. But my faith will remain unshakeable. I know and I feel in my heart that sooner or later my people will rid themselves of all their enemies, both internal and external, and that they will rise as one man to say No to the degradation and shame of colonialism, and regain their dignity in the clear light of the sun.

We are not alone. Africa, Asia and the free liberated people from all corners of the world will always be found at the side of the millions of Congolese who will not abandon the struggle until the day when there are no longer any colonialists and their mercenaries in our country. As to my children whom I leave and whom I may never see again, I should like them to be told that it is for them, as it is for every Congolese, to accomplish the sacred task of reconstructing our independence and our sovereignty: for without dignity there is no liberty, without justice there is no dignity, and without independence there are no free men.

Neither brutality, nor cruelty nor torture will ever bring me to ask for mercy, for I prefer to die with my head unbowed, my faith unshakable and with profound trust in the destiny of my country, rather than live under subjection and disregarding sacred principles. History will one day have its say, but it will not be the history that is taught in Brussels, Paris, Washington or in the United Nations, but the history which will be taught in the countries freed from imperialism and its puppets. Africa will write its own history, and to the north and south of the Sahara, it will be a glorious and dignified history.

Do not weep for me, my dear wife. I know that my country, which is suffering so much, will know how to defend its independence and its liberty.

Long live the Congo! Long live Africa!

Patrice Lumumba

Source:

http://ziomania.com/lumumba/The%20Last%20Letter%20of%20Patrice%20Lumumba.htm Accessed on January 3, 2016.

Lumumba's legacy

Lumumba will always be remembered for his unwavering resolve that was aimed at emancipating his country from the clutches of colonialism and injustices. His selflessness is another nugget, among many, that Lumumba left behind as a legacy for true and patriotic African leaders, and Africans in general, to ape and to venerate. He knew the danger his stand posed; but he was consequentially and willingly ready to pay the price even if it meant to lose his life if such a sacrifice destined to achieving what he stood for, the total and true liberation of Congo. For Lumumba, the country was bigger than a leader; thus dying for it was a worthy thing to do for whoever that described himself as its leader. His openness and uprightness, despite being detrimental for his success, are something that Africa will always miss. His faithfulness and commitment to what he believed in are his nuggets that Africa misses and lacks today in its attempts to make headways almost in all spheres of life for its bright future. Lumumba sets an example as a fearless, selfless and trustworthy leader who did not amass any wealth by robbing his country just like his successor-cum-betrayer, Mobutu. Lumumba died an innocent politician who is rare, especially in Africa of today where leadership has been turned into an enterprise that enhances quick and big bucks to those in power, to get. Lumumba, arguably, was a needle in a very huge haystack, that is Africa. Above all, Lumumba, just like Mandela, sacrificed his blood for the wellbeing of his country. His words in the last letter to his wife, Pauline Lumumba, suffice to say it all:

Dead or alive, free or in prison by order of the imperialists, it is not myself who counts. It is the Congo; it is our poor people for whom independence has been transformed into a cage from whose confines the outside

17

world looks on us, sometimes with kindly sympathy, but at other times with joy and pleasure.

As a selfless, brave, committed and focused manager of public affairs, Lumumba left a very shinning legacy as a good manager of public affairs even if he paid dearly for the love of his country, his people, and above all Africa.

Like Samora Machel, Lumumba was a staunch believer in radical changes. He lacked one thing that the West has always used to dupe others. He was not a hypocrite. Generally, he left a shining legacy in that he refused to compromise the rights and freedom of his people even when it meant to be assassinated. Despite spending a short time in power, Lumumba seemed to be honest and a down-to-earth person who would have propelled his country and Africa forward.

Again, when it comes to weakness, Like Thomas Sankara, Lumumba was too open that he gave ammunitions to his enemies. Sometimes, in politics, especially during the cold war, it was like willingly signing your own death warrant whenever you divulged your plans against two superpowers. Lumumba divulged a lot, and too much, so as to be cut short easily after he proved to be a threat to the interests of the colonial monsters.

Chapter 2

The Juggernaut of African Union

"For, we have dedicated ourselves to the attainment of total African freedom. Here is one bond of unity that allies free Africa with unfree Africa, as well as all those independent states dedicated to this cause," Nkrumah (1963, xi).

Figure 1: Kwame Nkrumah Ghana's 1st President (image courtesy of Anti-Imperialism.Com)

After Lumumba who was heartbreakingly assassinated by those he wrongly trusted for his staunch stand against colonialism, comes Dr. Kwame Nkrumah who was, *inter alia*, the political juggernauts that Africa has ever had. Apart from being the founding father of Ghana, Nkrumah was the first African leader to bring independence; thereby opening the doors for other African countries to gain their

19

independence, especially in 1960s which was known as Africa's era. He was born on 21st September 1909 in Nkroful, Ghana (Lawson 2010, p. 15) and died on 27th April, 1972 in Bucharest, Romania where he was flown for treatments. Under Nkrumah, Ghana was the first African country to gain independence on March 6th, 1957. Nkrumah is renowned for championing the fast-track unification of Africa based on the vision of a strong, abler and economically-self-sufficient-continental country of Africa (Mhango, 2015). Well educated and travelled, Nkrumah is credited to have popularised the concept of the unification of Africa which he died fighting for. Apart from Nyerere, since Nkrumah died, nobody has ever championed this idea with the same vigour and magnitude as he did. Essentially, Nkrumah wanted Africa fast united—although other leaders such as Julius Nyerere (Tanganyika)—wanted the unification of Africa to be done slowly after acquiring independence. Others such as Hasting Kamuzu Banda, Felix Houphouët-Boigny did not like the idea for the fear of losing their power. Basically, whereas Nkrumah believed in a fast-track union, Nyerere preferred piecemeal unification commencing with regional blocks which would later lead to the total unification of Africa. Nkrumah and Nyerere are among few thinkers who became politicians that Africa has ever produced. Therefore, their philosophical scrimmage was seen as the *rumbling battle* of the giants. Like Nyerere, Nkrumah was one of the founders of the Organisation of African Unity (OAU) in 1963 in Addis Ababa that ever since became the headquarters of the OAU; and thereafter the African Union (AU). Before the formation of the OAU, Nkrumah convoked the First Conference: Accra, 5th–13th December, 1958 which laid foundations for the unification of Africa; and hence paved the way for the birth of the OAU. True, Nkrumah was the force—among the forces to reckon with—as far as combating neocolonialism in Africa and the world in general is concerned. Along with Nyerere, Nkrumah challenged independent African countries to unite as means of doing away with colonialism. Nkrumah (1966) argues:

> In the neo-colonialist territories, since the former colonial power has in theory relinquished political control, if the social conditions occasioned by neo-colonialism cause a revolt the local neo-colonialist government can be sacrificed and another equally

20

subservient one substituted in its place. On the other hand, in any continent where neo-colonialism exists on a wide scale the same social pressures which can produce revolts in neo-colonial territories will also affect those States which have refused to accept the system and therefore neo-colonialist nations have a ready-made weapon with which they can threaten their opponents if they appear successfully to be challenging the system, [Sic] (p. 3).

For Nkrumah, the independence that African countries gained was imperfect; and incomplete due to the fact that economic dependency; and underdevelopment were still in existence. He used to say that no African country can take any pride in itself for being independent if there was still an inch of African soil that was under colonialism or tyranny. Just like Nyerere, Nkrumah wanted Africa to control its economy; and thus, destiny by dictating the price of its products in order to benefit Africans. To achieve this, Nkrumah, firstly, espoused the unification of Africa based on having a powerful, strong and united front that would enable Africa to decisively participate in international affairs so that it could tip the balance of power at the time Africa was discredited and looked down upon negatively. Also, Nkrumah wanted a self-sufficient, and self-regulating united Africa that would have a big and vocal say in international affairs; as opposed to taking a back seat as it has always been after his dream failed to materialise. Nkrumah started by proposing that Africa had to form its own cartels which would enable it to market, and henceforth manage its products without depending on dubious and exploitative Western markets. He wanted to start with Ghana as a launching pad by using the then chief product, cocoa. In a sense, such an idea did not augur well with imperialists and Western countries in general that used to exploit Africa under their own cartels and policies that were totally and visibly hostile and exploitative to Africa. For, having its own cartels, Africa would not only negatively affect Western economies, but would, also, deny or foil them from getting cheap products as they were used; and thus, lead to their economic downturn unexpectedly. On their side, Western countries would not wait to lose given that–just like Lumumba–Nkrumah had openly indicated his desire—to side with

21

their arch rival, the Union of Soviet Socialist Republics (USSR). Thus–to foil such manoeuvres–something had to be done straightaway to circumvent this obviously looming endangerment Lumumba and Nkrumah posed, especially to the interests of the West. Henceforth, Western countries understood that Nkrumah was agitating Africa to cut their tap offs; something that, among other reasons and forces, eventually led to his toppling in 1972. After being toppled, Africa lost a true-cum-great-champion of true independence based on its unification as a tactical move to counter imperialistic exploitation; thereafter, the dream of unifying Africa slowly stonewashed away. It can be argued that Nkrumah was a big fish in a small pond; and–to his detriment nevertheless–his vision was not clearly understood by his colleagues in Ghana and Africa in general. Like his brother, friend and compatriot, Lumumba, this is why the forces that destroyed them came from within and without his fold. Nkrumah was among the first African presidents, himself and Maurice Yameogo of the then Upper Volta later Burkina Faso, to spearhead the reunification of Africa in 1961. Hagberg and Tegan (2000) observe that:

> In the following days the two delegations elaborated an agreement to be signed 17 June 1961. Ten days later the boundary separating Upper Volta and Ghana was symbolically destroyed at the ceremony in Paga, (pp. 9-10).

However, unfortunately for Nkrumah's vision, a few weeks after this symbolic and foundational reunion, the president of Ivory Coast, Felix Houphouët-Boigny, under the machinations spearheaded by the West, lulled president Yameogo out of this novel union; and this started sending shockwaves all over Africa and the world at large. Sadly, that became the end of such a short-lived first union in Africa.

Nkrumah's vision and aim were matter-of-factly clear. He wanted to offer stable and reliable social services to his people. Nkrumah (1963) argues when he sat with his party colleagues after independence to examine their priorities, they framed a short list among which was to "abolish poverty, ignorance, illiteracy and improve our health services," (p. 118).

22

Abolishing—not eradicating poverty disease and ignorance, among other things that preoccupied Nkrumah—was his number one priority not only for his country Ghana but also for the entire continent. Selfless as he was, he devoted much of his time and energy to the wellbeing of Africa which he regarded as one big country that would perform miraculously had—what he envisaged—been fulfilled. Arguably, Nkrumah's priorities were in conflict with the interests of Western countries whose colonial and exploitative policies enabled them to hold Africa at ransom which they desired to continue even after giving freedoms to their former colonies. To the Western countries, even as of today, exploiting Africa—for the benefits and betterment of their people—is the right thing to do next to God-given one. Due to their double standard, Western countries—that sing democracy and human rights—have failed to incorporate economic rights in their *diktat* and aid to Africa. Why? It is simple; they do not want Africa to care for/about its people something that would enable them to become self-confident so as to challenge even topple Western-backed regimes. This is why corrupt and inept rulers such as Mobutu easily survived the wrath of their citizens.

You can see this almost in everything otherwise known as international policies from human rights to global warming whereby Africa is taken for a ride simply because it must act as their backdrop *ad infinitum* as it has been since colonial era. Therefore, whoever wanted or implied, rightly and wrongly to turn tables on this lie—by debunking it—he or she had to, subsequently, be eliminated as soon as possible. And indeed, after the demise of the dream of unifying Africa, the West went on to keep on exploiting Africa up to this date as it deceptively thinks it will do continually shall the situation remain as it is currently. A divided-and-disunited Africa became a soft target for Western countries, and later, China, and India, to exploit; and get cheap-raw materials for many of their industries and markets. This is why world markets of almost everything are based in the capitals cities of Western countries which do not produce any of the products auctioned in these markets, (Mhango 2015). Take—for example—coffee and tea. No country in Europe produces coffee or tea. Yet, their corporations make more *big bucks*—from advertising and selling coffee and tea based on having the headquarters of the world markets for the same—than producers in Africa and elsewhere; simply because

23

Africa is divided and weak when it comes to dealing with and in, marketing and managing its products. When he consequently, announced his priorities for Africa, Nkrumah meant to stop exploitation that would badly and negatively affect the economies in the West. From this time forth, Nkrumah became an enemy number one that had to be stopped by all means; even if it meant to assassinate, or overthrow him as it later happened. Such a move was undesirable and contra-; and counterproductive against the interests of Western countries. So, Nkrumah, just like Lumumba, had to be stopped by either eliminating or toppling him. The later was preferred as indicated above. The West knew too well how influential and instrumental Nkrumah was as far as the liberation of Africa was concerned. Biney (2008 cited in Chimuka 2012) concurs by quoting former Zambia President Kenneth Kaunda as saying that "Nkrumah inspired many people of Africa towards independence and was a great supporter of the liberation of southern Africa from apartheid and racism." Former Namibian president, Sam Nujoma cited in Biney (Ibid), maintains that:

> Ghana's fight for freedom inspired and influenced us all, and the greatest contribution to our political awareness at that time came from the achievements of Ghana after its independence. It was from Ghana that we got the idea that we must do more than just petition the UN to bring about our own independence, (p. 66).

To make matters worse, Nkrumah did not only want changes for Ghana alone but also for the whole continent that he wanted to see quickly and truly united. Nkrumah (1963) notes that when returned back home in 1947, he had the intention of using Ghana (then the Gold Coast) as a *launching pad* for African independence and unity, (p. 136). His vision was across-the-board and ambitious something that shook former colonial monsters greatly. As aforementioned, this is why we see him as a big fish in a small pond that is easy–for his enemies–to spot and take on or fix; and possibly get rid. Nkrumah did not see Africa as fragmented continent the same way colonial monsters divided and saw it; but instead, he viewed Africa as a country, one big continental country with immense potentials that was naturally united before being partitioned and divided at the

24

Berlin Conference in 1884 during the scramble, partition and division of Africa as a way of avoiding the confrontations among colonial monsters. For Nkrumah, Africa was a naturally-united entity that was not supposed to be divided as it happened thanks to colonial machinations. Mhango (2015) addresses this issue extensively going further arguing that Africa does not need unification; but instead, it needs to be reunification given that it was naturally united. His main argument is that you cannot unify the entity that is naturally united. Instead, you can reunify the same by returning it to its natural form and order. Arguably, at the time, Nkrumah propounded the unification of Africa; such a view was radical, robust and ahead of time. If he were a selfish and myopic person, Nkrumah would have concentrated on thinking about how to manage Ghana by leaving others out. Essentially, Nkrumah's vision would have been "everybody for his survival" just like other first presidents who acted as thus when their countries were under colonial hazard or rule and thereafter.

By and large, by championing the unification of Africa that was able to depend on itself, Nkrumah was attempting to emancipate Africa economically while suffocating Western economies that ever since have depended on Africa for supply of cheap raw materials. This move was unacceptable before the eyes of Western countries which stood to lose big. Therefore, the scheme was to be hatched quickly to finish Nkrumah the same way they did with Lumumba. Essentially, what tragically brought Nkrumah down is nothing but his vision of a united and economically powerful Africa as a continental country he envisaged to rival the US. You can see this in the European Union (EU) or the US today. Those countries are becoming more powerful not just because they have something different from what others do not have. They are stronger because of their unity that is missing in Africa. This is why the call for the unification of Africa is still relevant shall Africa aspire to do away with the current backwardness and dependency. If the US were to be divided into over fifty countries, obviously, many countries created thereafter would become poor and US's economic and military clouts would go under due to the fact that countries formed out of the US would spend much money on weapons for fear of their neighbours just like African countries have done ever since they gained their political and incomplete independence, (Mhango 2015). Try to imagine. How many jobs, policies and strategies would be affected by Nkrumah's move of truly unifying Africa aimed at economic autonomy? How much money would the West lose that Africa has always lost to this inequitable and exploitative business whose causes are disunity and divisions?

Practically, Nkrumah went further planning to form some cartels that would be used in selling African products to the world market in order to control the prices. This also did not augur well with the West. Nkrumah (1963) notes:

> In November 1959, representatives of trade unions all over Africa met in Accra to organize an All-African Trade Union Federation. The African labour movement has always been closely associated with the struggle for political freedom, as well as with economic and social development, (p. 137).

To know how this was viewed, one can look at the Organisation of Petroleum Exporting Countries (OPEC) that has always caused a headache to Western economies through controlling and regulating oil prices, supply and demand globally. Suppose Nkrumah executed his plans under the united Africa. Obviously, the Western economies would have been negatively affected even more. Essentially, this is why the unification of Africa has never been favoured within and without Africa. To mislead them, African countries are now encouraged to embark on regional cooperation and groupings instead of a total unification of Africa. Regional groupings are but the repetition of the mistake that was committed after some African leaders opposed Nkrumah's fast-track unification. The East African Community (EACI) provides an ideal example of such a failure.

To avoid economic and financial apocalypse that would result from the unification and cartelisation of Africa, the West had to urgently eliminate Nkrumah through a *coup d'état* that worked successfully as it was in the case of the Democratic Republic of Congo in which–as indicated above–Lumumba was tragically assassinated by the West in order to foil the danger he posed to its interests. Just like it was for Lumumba whom the West tried to poison to no avail, Nkrumah is likely to have faced the same before being toppled so as to end up dying in exile. For, Nkrumah was overthrown in February 1966 by lieutenant General Emmanuel Kwasi Kotoka when he was on a state visit to North Vietnam and China. The difference however is that Lumumba was captured and later assassinated while Nkrumah was just toppled and left to go to exile to end up dying there. The toppling of Nkrumah's government, apart from being a bad precedent, dealt a big blow to Africa as far as unification was concerned. For, Nkrumah was very instrumental in seeing to it that Africa was united as it was before being divided and partitioned by the colonial monsters. Live by sword, die by sword. Fortunately, even Kotoka did not stay in power longer. What you sow is what you reap. Kotoka was deposed and killed just after a year since taking over from Nkrumah. The toppling of Nkrumah was the second big blow that Africa received after the toppling and killing the first Nigerian Prime Minister, Sir Abubakar Tafawa Balewa just a month before Nkrumah was toppled. For, in the following year, Ghana had a new military regime. Before then, Africa evidenced the first coup that was successfully carried out in Togo where Emmanuel Bodjollé, Etienne Eyadema and Kleber Dadjo toppled Togolese founding father, President Sylvanus Olympio in a bloody *coup d'état*. For the first time, West Africa was leering with the fear of coups. For, thereafter, Ghana and Nigeria experienced many more *coup d'états* that left these countries paralysed after being robbed and mismanaged for many years they were under corrupt dictators whose missions were nothing but brutalising and robbing the countries.

Arguably, Nkrumah envisioned a very united, powerful, self-reliant Africa that would be like China is today had his ideas been put into actions. Again, Nkrumah did not live to execute his missions. When it comes to the unification of Africa, Nkrumah will always be remembered for his vision. Mhango (2015, p. 431) argues that Nkrumah wanted Africa to be united in the fast-track move in order to circumnavigate and avoid Western machinations. Despite this vision, Nkrumah faced fierce opposition from within and without Africa, among others. Tanzania's first president, Julius Nyerere, was the one who wanted Africa to be unified in a step-by-step manner which Nkrumah viewed as dangerous for the cause. For the enemies of the idea would sabotage the process. Nkrumah was right. Nyerere was wrong. The two would rumble at the meetings of the then OAU so as to polarise the continent. Despite these philosophical differences between the two, they were good friends still; and their passion for the unification of Africa was unquestionably firm despite choosing different approaches. For them, Africa came first before anything. They all wanted to delay the independence of their countries in order to wait for other African countries to become independent so that they could be united to form one united Africa. What they did not know is the fact that not all African post-colonial leaders shared the same vision. When it comes to the unification of Africa, for Nkrumah, it was not an option but an obligation. His book *Africa Must Unite* speaks volumes. Nkrumah (1963) maintains that they had dedicated themselves to the attainment of total African freedom which would form "a bond of unity that allies free Africa with unfree Africa, as well as all those independent states dedicated to this cause," (xi). To gauge how Nkrumah loved a united Africa, he wrote in his book as thus: "dedicated To George Padmore (1900-1959) and to the African Nation that must be." This can clearly show how Nkrumah viewed Africa as a country but not a divided continent as she currently is.

Furthermore, Nkrumah had a very broad and grand vision for the economy of the united Africa something that African countries currently lack; and still need nonetheless. However, due to his socialist inclination, there are those who argue that some pro-capitalistic African countries were afraid that they would be swayed or forced to his direction. Additionally, this fear seemed real due to the fact that Nkrumah was a no-nonsensical and ebullient person whose arguments were strongly backed by scientific evidence which cowed his opponents. After teaming up with Nyerere, Nkrumah became even more a threat to colonial monsters and their stooges than ever before. To see how farsighted and committed Nkrumah was, his own words speak volumes. Nkrumah says:

My purpose now is to trace briefly the African background and the effects of centuries of colonialism on the political, economic and social life of Africa as a whole; to place developments in Ghana in the broader context of the African revolution; and to explain my political philosophy based on my conviction of the need for the freedom and unification of Africa and its islands, (ix).

Such a vision, apart from being expressly logical and workable, was a threat to the stooges the West had already planted in some countries like Kenya, Malawi, the DRC, Ivory Coast and others that hated the idea of unifying Africa either for the fear of losing their power or for the purpose of carrying the orders of their masters who cloned them. Therefore, Nkrumah's vision did not only disturb imperialists and colonial monsters but it also irked their stooges whose vision for being in power was a self-help project.

Things became even complicated due to the fact that the chief proponents of the unification of Africa namely Nkrumah and Nyerere were all inclined to East. Metz (1992) argues that "Nkrumah and Nyerere were cognisant of the impact of capitalism in their societies. Thus, for them, socialism was an objective to be sought as a primary goal but not an extra condition," (p. 379). Such a claim holds water in that pro-capitalist countries–of which most were ruled by the stooges of the West–viewed Nkrumah's and Nyerere's visions differently and unfavourably as opposed to pro-socialist countries which looked at the impact of capitalism negatively; and thus, supported and teamed up with whoever opposed capitalism as it is in case and point. Countries such as Uganda under Milton Obote, and Zambia under Kenneth Kaunda threw their weights behind Nkrumah's and Nyerere's visions. Arguably, such an undertaking was dangerous for pro-capitalist countries such as Kenya, Malawi, Ivory Coast and others that were openly in bed with the West. Such agents of colonialism saw Nkrumah as their nemesis whose destruction they would fully like and support. The West used this schism among African leaders in meddling with African affairs by using Africans themselves. Once again, soon after becoming free Africa was facing a catch-22 sort of situation that threatened the fabrics that were supposed to bring it together. So, Nkrumah had two types of enemies, namely the West and his own African brothers in power. The credulous leaders of such countries–apart from being restricted by their capitalist masters–would not easily support the whole move of the total unification of Africa. They would not do so because of the fear of losing their fake and ephemeral powers they waged in vending their own people pointlessly for personal glories. Such a trend perpetrated by such a rotten crop of post-colonial rulers, unfortunately, still goes on in Africa even to date whereby some African rulers care a lot about their personal glories as opposed to the glory of Africa. To some extent, Nkrumah's and Nyerere's vision and policies were not only seen as threats and impediments to other African countries under gullible rulers but also a danger to the interests of the West in Africa. Thus, many Western-tamed-and-cloned rulers had to avoid the unification of Africa at all cost; for fear of either losing power or favours from those who cloned, abused, used, and nourished them. Conversely, I do not think that rulers like Mobutu, Kenyatta and Banda–to mention but a few–would risk supporting such a radical change that Nkrumah and Nyerere propounded. Evidentially, this can be seen in the demise of the then EACI that was made of Kenya, Tanzania and Uganda. Hazlewood (1979) notes that ideological division between 'capitalist' Kenya and 'socialist' Tanzania (p. 52) was among the causes of the demise of the EACI. Sadly, such schisms still go on even after learning a lesson the hard way. Many myopic and selfish African rulers are still at home with the idea of a divided Africa provided that they remain in power; and their power remains unchallenged, intact and untouched. This informs us that some of our leaders who took over after the founders have maintained such a suicidal and tunnel vision by concentrating on their political survival without underscoring that in both ideologies there were good and bad things Africa would have learned and benefitted from. Again, after the demise of the East, what is preventing African countries to go on with the project of unifying Africa as envisaged by the founders led by Nkrumah? Another question is: Where are committed and visionary leaders of Nkrumah and Nyerere brand currently when neocolonialism has claimed a lot of Africa's freedom due to the reign of selfish and myopic rulers?

At the time of independence and soon after, however, fear of socialism could be seen as valid or otherwise reason; we need to underscore one important thing in that ideological divisions were not a bigger danger than keeping Africa fragmented as it currently is. This argument makes more sense, especially when we look at African economic preconditions and economic systems that were in place before the coming of colonialism. However the concept of socialism can be regarded as a new thing to Africa, looking back at African traditions, it is evident that communalism–however distinct from the socialism the East propounded–existed almost in the whole continent. Etekpe and Okolo (2010) note that Nyerere's socialism:

Reflects African communal pattern of life fondly styled, "African Socialism". This form of socialism was fairly different from that of Karl Marx and Lenin's version in the sense that African socialism "is recapturing the values of Africans to build African Society," (p. 6).

Being naturally collectivistic, African society had a degree or degrees of socialism based on African traditional communalism which should not be mistaken for communism. Arguably, Africa was naturally socialistic; that is why when colonial economy was introduced in Africa, it became hard, and sometimes, impossible to understand and cope with it. I think the spirit of African socialism was behind Nkrumah's and Nyerere's drive for the unification of Africa. Quite contrary however, Nkrumah did not live to exercise and implement his policies aimed at fulfilling his dreams of seeing a strong and a united Africa. Notably however, Nkrumah's contribution to Ghana and Africa will always be historically notable. For instance, after being overthrown, Ghana's economic health did not improve. Instead, the 70s evidenced the country that was grappling with *coup d'états* and economic holdups after many projects that Nkrumah inaugurated became obsoletely crippled due to the lack of visionary and abler leadership. The toppling, and later, the death of Nkrumah marked the beginning of the end of the Africa unity as he envisaged it. Only one mover, Nyerere was left struggling to maintain the Union of Tanganyika and Zanzibar and the EACI which came to an end in 1977 after fissures surfaced resulting from ideological differences and oft-squabbling among member states. However, the union of Tanganyika and Zanzibar that gave birth to the United Republic of Tanzania (URT) still goes from strength to strength and it stands as the testimony by being the only practical unity in Africa. In this way, we can say that Nyerere succeeded where Nkrumah failed. Again, nobody can blame Nkrumah for not succeeding; because he did not get enough time in power to fulfil his dreams of the unification of Africa.

Furthermore, even if you look at African countries after the demise of socialism, you find that economically and socially they are still identical so to speak. Poor farmers in Kenya and Tanzania, for instance, are still facing the same enemies; and becoming poorer and poorer by days even though they experience some degrees of difference in the magnitude of their poverty. Again, poverty is poverty even if there are some disparities; all depends on the policies a particular country puts in place. You will see hereunder how poverty levels in Kenya and Tanzania differ due to the foundations which the founders of these two nations laid down.

In sum, it can be argued that the toppling, and later, the demise of Nkrumah sent Africa many years back as far as its unification is concerned. Now Nkrumah is no more but Africa still remains. His economic hallmark on Ghana, Akasombo Dam, still exists as it bemoans at us and wonders why we did not understand and keep this pace and vision alive for our own good. Many factories, despite the truncation, he built, however ghostlier they look, are still there. Nkrumah's vision of wanting Africa to create cartels to protect its produces still makes more sense, mainly today even if it has never been worked on. All technical schools he envisioned are still there calling and crying for him. Africans, too, still remain not to mention their problems and needs for their solutions. Africa's problems are doubling day by day. So, Africans, as a people, need to find solutions for their problems. Essentially, times have changed dramatically; however the problems remained the same. This makes sense in that we still can retrieve some strategies from gurus such as Nkrumah in trying to solve the problems Africa has been facing ever since. Again, we can still draw from Nkrumah's experience and insights for Africa to forge ahead but conditionally that Africa should be united. Notably, Nkrumah was one of the great managers as far as running the business of the state, and the continent in general, is concerned. However, his nemeses and detractors say he was irascible and aloft. They say that power climbed to his head so as to create many more enemies at home and abroad something that led to his fall from grace. Moreover, they say that after coming to power, he became a much know-all that would not listen to anybody. Others say that he had good intentions that he wanted to fulfil with bad means by not educating his people to know his vision. Anybody can say anything as far as Nkrumah is concerned. However, it is evident that–as a big fish in a small pond–Nkrumah tried as much as he could, particularly if we underscore the fact that freedom meant different things in Africa at his time. His zeal of seeing Africa excelling like the US–maybe, if it were not cut short–was not well articulated so as to sink in the hearts and minds of his people and Africans in general. Again, Africa will miss him forever.

There are some observations we can make about Nkrumah in that:

Firstly, despite performing poorly economically–for he spent much money helping other African countries–Nkrumah provided exemplary and pragmatic leadership, specifically about the dream of unifying Africa. No literature can be completed about the unification of Africa without mentioning Nkrumah's name. Arguably, one of the reasons why some of Nkrumah policies failed is the fact that he had a gargantuan dream about Africa. Therefore, his plans were so extensive and ambitious and needed a long time to materialise. Sadly however, even his colleagues did not understand the scope of his vision and how to deliver it, Nkrumah's spirit of one united Africa–in spite of not materialising–is still felt all over Africa.

Secondly, Nkrumah left a mode of infrastructure, mainly power generation aimed at industrialising the country. As aforementioned, Akosombo dam is nothing but Nkrumah's vision of Ghana and Africa in generally *vis-a-vis* industrialisation. The Government of Ghana (1961 cited in für Entwicklungsforschung, 2000) notes that "Ghana's leaders saw industrialization as essential to the development of the country and electric power from the Volta River Project (VRP) as central to that industrialization," (p. 2). Nkrumah had a vision of self-sufficient country that aimed at countering capitalist exploitation and domination altogether. He aimed at using Ghana as a laboratory of his ambitions that aimed at covering the whole continent. As indicated above, this is one of the reasons that led to his toppling. Like Thomas Sankara, the lack of hypocrisy and secrecy in his dreams and plans made Nkrumah vulnerable and easy to defeat.

Thirdly, just like any honest manager of public affairs, Nkrumah did not leave behind a very affluent family whose wealth was ill-gotten by embezzling public funds. Hayward and Dumbuya (1983) note that 'the last year of Nkrumah were marked with intolerance of opposition, repression, corruption, economic disruption and political decay,'" (p. 647) after those surrounding Nkrumah let him down. As an individual and a leader, Nkrumah was not at home with such vices. This is why those surrounding him hated and disliked him for denying them the opportunities to fleece the country. This is Nkrumah, the man who wanted to see Africa united so as to move forward as a continental country. Nkrumah's legacy will always remain an irony for the current crop of African rulers who do not want to reunify Africa for fear of losing presidency and powers. Arguably, just like Lumumba and Nyerere, Nkrumah was ahead of his time; and, indeed, he was a big fish in a small pond which made it easier for capitalists and colonialists to see and deal with. He was open to everybody not to forget trusting all African leaders wrongly thinking they shared his dreams and ambitions. Africa will always miss him dearly as a person who championed its wellbeing and prosperity to end up being betrayed by his colleagues and their masters.

"*Their history of colonialist subjection differs from ours only in detail and degree, not in kind. Some there are who make fine distinctions between one brand of colonialism and another, who declare that the British are 'better' masters than the French, or the French 'better' than the Belgian, or the Portuguese or the white settlers of South Africa, as though there is virtue in the degree to which slavery is enforced. Such specious differentiations come from those who have never experienced the miseries and degradation of colonialist suppression and exploitation,*" Kwame Nkrumah, in Nkrumah, Arigoni and Napolitano (1963, xii).

Nkrumah's legacy

As legendary as Kwame Nkrumah was–of course, larger than life–left a very shinning legacy, exclusively on collective and strenuous efforts of liberating and unifying Africa. Like any good manager of public affairs, Nkrumah did not amass any wealth by means of robbing his country. Like an intellectual, Nkrumah wrote books to express his views and vision of Ghana and Africa in general. He died a hero that Africa venerated, principally for being instrumentally a stumbling block against colonialism, divisionism, imperialism and *politique de l'autruche* many African stooges embarked on. His vision for Africa was bigger than any single country could accommodate. His economic vision was superb, particularly trying to unify Africa into a cartel to market and manage its produces. Industrialisation was his major theme based on electrification of Africa. Hate or love him. Nkrumah did not make do with corruption, red type, rent seeking or any malpractices in the public offices. His zeal and commitment however created many enemies who later toppled him as a means of stopping Africa from its total liberation based on self-reliance and self-sufficiency.

Like Lumumba above, apart from being a radical believer of whatever he envisaged, Nkrumah was too open so much that his own words became the impetuses-cum-missiles his nemeses used to get rid of him. Also, Nkrumah had a blanket belief that all of his African compatriots were like him while some of them were hyenas in sheep's clothing. Nkrumah was not as cunning as Nyerere was. Again, this should not be misconstrued as being inept and careless.

One of the ways of emulating Nkrumah is to bring him back to the current dialogue, especially to launch him to the new generation that did not live at his time however he fought for it. The new generation needs to know him. For, our understanding is that our history is one of the tools we can use to fight for our emancipation as people and as a continent that has always been exploited. Nkrumah is one of the makers of this history that we need in making the case for our emancipation. This is the major theme and aim of this volume. What a big fish in a small pond that Nkrumah was! We have adopted a style of starting the dialogue about the subjects of this volume by using the words of those we deliberate about. The same way, we wind up their treatises with their own words. We sign off from Nkrumah chapter with his words in order to give the readership more insights about the person. Here we finish with his legacy thereafter.

It is clear that we must find an African solution to our problems, and that this can only be found in African unity. Divided we are weak; united,

Africa could become one of the greatest forces for good in the world,
Nkrumah (1961, p. 1).

Chapter 3

Nyerere the Philosopher King Who Shook the West

"I believe that, left to ourselves, we can achieve unity on the African Continent. But I don't believe that we are going to be left to ourselves! I believe that the phase from which we are now emerging successfully in the phase of the First Scramble for Africa, and Africa's reaction to it. We are now entering a new phase—the phase of the Second Scramble for Africa. and just as, in the First Scramble for Africa, one tribe was divided against another tribe to make the division of Africa easier, in the Second Scramble for Africa one nation is going to be divided against another nation to make it easier to control Africa by making her weak and divided against herself,"
Julius K. Nyerere, 1961 cited in Nyerere (1962).

Figure 2: Julius K. Nyerere Tanzania 1st President (image courtesy of Ippmedia.com)

Mwalimu Julius Kambarage Nyerere was born on 13th April, 1922 in Mwitongo, Northern Tanzania on the shores of Lake Nyanza to a chief of Zanaki community. Like Sir Seretse Khama (Botswana) that we will discuss later, if Nyerere wanted to become a chief of his people he would. But Nyerere did not like to become a chief. Nyerere did not believe in leadership resulting from pedigree; but, instead, he believed in leading ability based on deliverance, competence and the consent of the ruled. Nyerere died naturally on 14th October, 1999 in London where he was admitted suffering from leukemia that later killed him. He was the first president of Tanganyika; and later, Tanzania after Tanganyika united with Zanzibar to form the United Republic of Tanzania (URT) in 1964. Nyerere was a charismatic leader who, apart from leading, wrote many books. While his counterpart, Nkrumah, can be termed as a juggernaut of African politics, Nyerere was something else, a genius, selfless and giant as far as good management of the business of the country is concerned. As a decent and trustworthy man, Nyerere did not allow even his family to use his power as a ladder to opulence simply because it was related to him. When it came to his party, he was even sterner than anybody would think. Cooksey and Kellsal (2011) note that:

> Nyerere worried that local party cadres were using the party as a vehicle for personal accumulation, and in 1962 he resigned as Prime Minister and toured the party grassroots in an attempt to instil a socialist spirit, (p. 15).

And indeed, Nyerere reached at the point of threatening to walk out of his party and join the opposition after noting that his party the *Chama Cha Mapinduzi* (CCM) (Revolutionary Party) was hijacked by dubious businesspeople whose goals were to use it to exploit poor Tanzanians. So, Nyerere wanted to see his party changed by going back to its ethics and foundations. And indeed, it did, at least, during his life. That is when Nyerere remained in his party up until his death conditionally that his party was to remain as the party of the poor but not the rich. Nyerere wanted justice for all but not for a select few as it was in many African corrupt countries. Burrowess (1996) argues that:

> Security for the people of the South requires the restoration of political processes that allow decisions about the production and distribution of resources to be made by the people themselves (rather than local or foreign elites) in accordance with their needs for participation, distributive justice and control, (p. 144).

Despite ruling under one-party system which was an in-thing at his time, Nyerere allowed his people to participate fully in many areas such as politics whereby voters had the power and responsibilities to tell what their representatives should go and say before the parliament. Comparably, under Nyerere, the parliament was more vibrant and closer to the people than soon after he willingly relinquished power. Also, Tanzanians enjoyed equal and equitable opportunities in economic activities that were engrained in the philosophy of *Ujamaa* and *Kujitegemea* or familyhood (Fouéré 2014, p. 3) and Self-reliance by producing and sharing equally and equitably as a community. Nyerere used to collect taxes and pay for social services such as education, and health something that enabled many Tanzanians to acquire primary, secondary, and tertiary education equally and free. Under Nyerere, even corruption was minimal due to his disciplinarian nature of seeing to it that ethics were followed. Nobody would become rich without showing how one made her or his wealth. Again, after Nyerere relinquished power, neoliberal policies kicked in so as to cultivate rent-seeking behaviour. The equal and equitable Tanzania the world used to evidence under Nyerere is long gone now.

When it comes to land, it became a right for every Tanzanian while in many countries it was taken by elites and rich people depriving poor people the opportunity to own this vital means of production. Nyerere strove to build an egalitarian country. And indeed, he tried and partly succeeded. Arguably, if we look at the population of Tanzania in general, poor Tanzanians are better than their Kenyan counterparts due to the fact that the spirit of socialism, brotherhood and sharing is higher in the former than in the latter. For example, all Tanzanians are entitled to owning land; and the land is owned by the government on behalf of the citizens. To the contrary, in Kenya, the right for every citizen to own land does not exist; and the land is privately owned. Miguel (2004) notes that:

Tanzania-nation building approach has allowed ethnically diverse communities in rural Tanzania to achieve considerable success in fund-raising for local public goods, while the diverse communities in the nearby Kenyan region typically fail," (pp. 327-328).

This finding speaks volumes. I was in Kenya from 2002 to 2006. I found Miguel assertion above to be true due to the fact that many Kenyans still feel secured in their tribal cocoons while Tanzanians feel secured in the national unity. I would argue. Tanzania's land policies of making sure that every Tanzanian has the right to owning a piece of land while in Kenya it is not a right, has a lot to do with the peaceability of the country and the wellbeing of rural and poor Tanzanians. After over five decades of independence, Kenya still has high rates of landlessness.

Apart from sound and sustainable land policies, Nyerere adds another feather in his cap. He was a very honest and trustworthy man who did not fear to express his weakness among much strength he had. Nyerere proved his honesty when he willingly decided to relinquish power in 1985 after noticing that neoliberal economic policies had crippled his government after sabotaging his policies. Although he was regarded as a benevolent dictator, admitting that his policies had failed after the IFIs sabotaged them is a democratic virtue and the conceptualisation of the term. At the time he bowed out so as to openly admit there is nothing new he would do, he was just 63 years old while in the neighbouring Malawi, the president had already declared himself president for life. Nyerere, therefore, openly told Tanzanians that he was not ready to turn back (embrace capitalistic policies and implement them as president) and become a proverbial *salt pillar*. How many African rulers, we have even today, that have willingly turned themselves into *salt pillars* that are littering our continent today? Nyerere decided to quit at the time many Tanzanians wanted him to soldier on. He flatly refused and told Tanzanians that what he had had done was enough.

Who actually was Nyerere? To get to know the true Nyerere, one must get out of his inner sanctum and the media. Academics may be a good source that can unearth who actually Nyerere was. Academics like Ali Mazrui, one of those renowned for criticising African leaders, may provide the answer as to who Nyerere actually was. Mazrui (2003) notes that Nyerere was one of the most intellectual of East Africa's Heads of State at the time whom he says was a true philosopher, president and original thinker, (p. 136). Mazrui's observation truly reflects on who actually Nyerere was. I decided to use Mazrui due to the fact that—as indicated above—was renowned for fearlessly and honestly faulting rulers among whom were Amin and Kenyatta who sent him packing after uttering things that nobody at the time would have guts to. Nyerere was at home with those who faulted his policies. Instead of sending them packing or detaining even killing them like Banda, Kenyatta and Houphouët-Boigny did, Nyerere wanted whoever made a claim to substantiate or defend it. Again, not all that saw Nyerere with the same lenses, the *Newsweek* (25 October, 1999 cited Ibhahow and Dibua 2003) queries asking as to "how does a leader wreck a country's economy yet die a national hero? Julius Nyerere's inefficient leadership dried Tanzania of funds, but his personality was irresistible," (p. 59). It depends on the source one uses in analysing and evaluating Nyerere and his deeds. Western media did not like him at all due to being an open socialist.

Arguably, his academic acumen applied almost in everything he did. He, also, faulted others as well as Nyerere (1966, p. 3 cited in Gade, 2011) notes:

> Years of Arab slave raiding, and later years of European domination, had caused our people to have grave doubt about their own abilities. This was no accident; any dominating group seeks to destroy the confidence of those they dominate because this helps them to maintain their position, and the oppressors in Tanganyika were no exception, (p. 305).

If there is anything Nyerere did successfully, as a good and competent manager of state affairs, is nothing but decolonising the minds of his people; thereby stamping out tribalism and nepotism that have become very big stumbling blocks for many African countries. It is only Tanzania, among many African countries, whose people do not talk about tribalism. Up until his death, Nyerere enjoyed the legacy of making Tanzanians more a nation than a group of warring tribes that calls itself a nation. So, one of Nyerere's tactics of taking on and defeating the enemies, mainly colonialism be it religious or political, was to build a nontribal nation. Many African leaders used tribal differences and divisions as the tools for dividing and hence ruling them while Nyerere did exactly the opposite. For example, while many African leaders of his time groomed their children by taking them to study abroad or enrolling them in private and expensive schools, Nyerere's children went to normal public schools where they lived and mingled with other children from poor backgrounds. While some of his successors manoeuvred to see their children being appointed ministers or given high positions in the government, as it happened for the son of his successor, Ali Hassan Mwinyi, whose son was appointed a minister in two successive governments that followed after Mwinyi completed his two terms in office, Nyerere did neither allow his wife nor his children to participate in the running of either his party or government. Nor did Nyerere secure any lucrative jobs for his children in public firms that were under his government like many of his successors and their friends who littered the Bank of Tanzania (BoT) with their children did. Nyerere was a normal human being just like others save that he comparably had better and more qualities than many African leaders of his time and thereafter. Honest, straightforward and judicious as Nyerere was, left a very glossy legacy where other left gross ones. Nyerere is still respected in Tanzania and all over the world posthumously. In Tanzania, in particular, Nyerere's posthumous instrumentality and vitality can be seen during election campaigns in Tanzania. For, it has become a cardinal rule that every politician who wants to win or influence voters always pays homage to Nyerere's grave in his village, Butiama. Nyerere's *necropolis* has become another shrine for politicians in Tanzania to go for their political pilgrimages. This trend has been going on ever since Nyerere relinquished power; and it has doubled posthumously. The Catholic Church was sometimes in the process of beatifying Nyerere due to his selfless, trust and true love for people not only in his country but all over the world. If he were alive, Nyerere would not have accepted such an offer due to the fact that he once said that he was the son of his father's fifth wife which by all neo-religions, he was a bastard. Nyerere is renowned to have spent much of time and resources to see to it that all African countries acquired independence. Nyerere was the happiest person the day South African Apartheid regime was pulled down in 1997. This is why the first indigenous African president of South Africa Nelson Mandela made his first trip abroad by visiting Tanzania. Mandela did so in order to show his appreciation for the role Nyerere and Tanzania played in the liberation of South Africa not to mention other countries in Southern region such as Angola, Mozambique, Namibia and Zimbabwe to whose independence Tanzania was very instrumental under Nyerere's stewardship. Due to his love of, and commitment to freedom, humanity and equality, Nyerere turned Dar es Salaam into the Magnet for freedom fighters in the region to congregate and live as they waged wars for freedom of their countries. Nyerere's desire for seeing Africans becoming independent and dignified did not end with the countries in the Southern Africa region. In 1978, he took on autocratic regime in neighbouring Uganda that was under Dictator Idi Amin who was renowned for being a ruthless-mass murderer. Nyerere, a peaceful man, knew the consequences of such a war, mainly for a poor country like Tanzania; the West had shunned as a punishment. But due to his love of freedom and human rights, Nyerere risked everything to see to it that Ugandans were freed from the fangs of Amin who ruthlessly used to kill them. Nyerere fully fulfilled his mission in Uganda by booting Amin out despite heavy cost Tanzania paid. Thereafter, Tanzania paid dearly economically. For, its economy took a hit that has taken a very long time to recover. Despite that, Nyerere was unapologetic up until he willingly retired from office. For him, stopping Amin from killing his people was a duty but not a favour.

Despite all consequences, Nyerere did not waiver his resolve to liberate Uganda from Idi Amin. For, the Tanzania People's Defence Force (TPDF) entered Uganda and flushed Amin out after a very gruelling battle which consequentially cost Tanzania a lot economically thereafter. Nyerere's prominent slogan was: Africa will never be truly free if an inch of its land is still under colonial grip. He fulfilled this vow-cum-vision of seeing to it that all Africans became independent. He spent much resources and money on this dream, in particular when he championed and chaired the Frontline States (FLS), an alliance of the independent countries of Southern Africa that was established in 1975 under the auspices of the three Pan-Africanist leaders of Zambia, Tanzania and Botswana to play a pivotal role in dismantling white colonial rule and Apartheid in the sub-region, *Daily News* (17 May, 2015). Being a good manager, Nyerere made sure that post-colonial Tanzania should not succumb before division, tribalism and exploitation of one person by another. In 1967, Nyerere shocked many when he nationalised all means of production as the move of empowering his people economically. Shocked were not only foreigners but also some of his consigliore such as his then foreign minister Oscar Kambona who fled the country thereafter due to not being ready to live under a socialist country. As mentioned above, Nyerere made sure that every Tanzanian had the right and access to land which is an important part of African identity. This is why Tanzania has never suffered from systemic land grabbing. However, after introducing neoliberal policies in Tanzania, slowly; Nyerere's foundations are being felled. Arguably, it will take many generations to erode Nyerere's land policies which are enshrined in the constitution.

Under Nyerere, Tanzanians enjoyed free social services such as education, health and others that the government provided free of charge. It is just recently, the new president under Nyerere's party, CCM, Dr. John Pombe Magufuli–whom we will explore later–seriously started to revisit the provision of free education to all Tanzanians starting with primary and secondary education. Nyerere built many schools, clinics and hospitals aiming at having a healthy and educated nation. Oketch and Rolleston (2007) maintain that, being a teacher, Nyerere put more emphasis on education for national development, (p. 132). Ironically, despite such a good vision, neoliberal economic policies faulted; and thereafter felled this emancipatory system that Nyerere laid down. Today one wonders to find countries such as Canada and Germany doing the same thing Nyerere envisage in the late 60s. Nyerere's vision on education was clear. Nyerere (1967) opines that:

> The education provided by colonial government in the two countries now forming Tanzania had a different purpose. It was not designed to prepare young people for the service of their country; instead it was motivated by a desire to inculcate the values of colonial society and to train individual for the service of the colonial state, (p. 2).

Further, Nyerere wanted to stop the trend of providing education for the production of cheap labours and colonial puppets that would serve, entrench and enhance swift function of the colonial rule in their country. He wanted to cultivate a crop of academics, and literate people that would take the baton up and fulfil his dreams for the good of others. Nyerere wanted to create the society of thinkers that would challenge the *status quo* so as to liberate Tanzania and Africa once and for all. During Nyerere's presidency, the only University in Tanzania, the University of Dar es Salaam (UDSM) was renowned for convening academic symposia and debates in which Nyerere actively participated without missing or sending those who opposed his policy packing as it was in Malawi, Kenya and other African countries at the time. Rajani (2003) notes that Nyerere raised the kinds of questions that encouraged the public to participate and debate due to the fact that Nyerere believed that technocrats and bureaucrats have a key role to play in this discourse, (p. 8). Due to his honesty, even those who participated in the symposia and debates at the UDSM were not intimidated or manipulated or being forced to follow his *diktat* or biddings. The debates were as open and straightforward as possible so as to assure participants that whatever they said was subject to discussion. Nyerere did not like praise singers and bootlickers who would sing his praises just like other dictators wanted their people to become. Some of the students and participants in these symposia and debates such as the later Dr. John Garang de Mabior (the first president of South Sudan) and Yoweri Museveni went on to becoming leaders of their countries. It must be noted that Nyerere personally sponsored Dr. Garang so as to get his secondary and tertiary education free in Tanzania. Nyerere did that knowing that Dr. Garang would become an asset to his country and Africa in general which he later became. Garang is the founding father of the youngest nation in the world, South Sudan that he wrestled from the fangs and twinges of North Sudan that brutally and racially colonised it for many generations. Sadly, though, Dr. Garang died shortly after his country seceded from North Sudan; after waging gruelling war of liberation for over twenty years. Ironically, he ruled his country for only 21 days. During his life Nyerere mentored three presidents namely Garang, Museveni and Samora Machel. Those are the ones we know publicly. There might be others that we do not know who also Nyerere mentored. So, it can be argued that the type of education Nyerere envisaged and espoused aimed at pragmatic decolonisation of his people so that they could build their country based on their ways of life, in lieu of aping everything from outside just like many other African countries, did to end up in crises hopelessly. For Nyerere, education was for self-awareness, self-actualisation, self-reliance and development. He wanted to offer an education that would make a human more human than a materialist or a consuming machine as espoused by capitalism. Indeed, Nyerere wanted to build a country of equal and dignified people who could eat what they produce and produce what they eat. Raikes (1975) notes that Nyerere wanted to transform his country from the states of underdevelopment and dependency which can be defined as "convergence of resources use the needs of the mass of the people," (p. 33).Where would have Africa been had all founders envisaged the future of their countries the same way Nyerere did?

For Nyerere, Raikes (Ibid.), "...colonial education induced attitudes of human inequality, and in practices underpinned the domination of the weak by the strong, especially in economic field." If anything, economic domination and the domination of the weak by the strong is what the world has experienced before and after colonialism. This was made possible by the fact that after many countries were given their flag or political independence, neocolonialism and neo-imperialism maintained the *status quo* under which Africa was left behind acting as a source for raw material and a market for processed goods from rich countries. To crown it all, imperialists cloned African stooges to do their dirty laundries by running the show in their countries presumed to be free although they actually were not. To the contrary, Nyerere did not like this at all; and he was ready for whatever consequences rather than becoming a stooge that would vend his own people for the promises of power and protection. Knowing how African economies were servicing and sustaining Western economies, Nyerere embarked on African traditional socialism or *Ujamaa* to use as a vehicle to serve and develop his country so that it could become self-reliant, *kujitegemea* in Swahili; thus *Ujamaa na Kujitegemea* policies. For over twenty years he was in power, Nyerere soldiered on without necessarily subscribing to Western policies despite being shunned and sabotaged along the way. Such a staunch stand had its consequences on Nyerere's policies. Thanks to globalised neoliberal policies, Nyerere decided to throw a game after noticing that he could not go on ruling a country that was cascading economically not because of having bad management; but because of refusing to subscribe to neoliberal policies. Nyerere found that clinging to power would hugely affect his country even more. Therefore, he had to willingly relinquish power so as to allow others to try turning the situation around. This is when he openly admitted that sabotage by the West–as a way of punishing him for his noncompliance–had taken a toll on the economy of his country. Although his policies were people-geared, people-oriented, and people-centred, they were more of an antithesis to neoliberal policies based on exploitation and unfair relationship between poor and rich countries. When he found that he could not run the country after International Financial Institutions (IFIs) shunned him not to mention suffocating his government, he decided to willingly relinquish power in 1985. Interestingly, many Tanzanians urged him to soldier on, but Nyerere refused squarely saying that what did not work for all twenty-four years he was in power would not work even if he were given a hundred years more to rule the country. Nyerere used to say that he would not look back and become a Biblical *pillar of salt* politically. And indeed, to the fulfilment of his vows, Nyerere died still believing in socialism and self-reliance as opposed to the capitalism, he fiercely opposed up until he breathed the last. Despite being no more, Nyerere still has very big influence in Tanzania's political landscape as mentioned above that, in Tanzania today, nobody can come to power without going to Nyerere's grave to show his respect as means of convincing Tanzanians that he or she is Nyerere's good student. It reached the point when some thinkers argued that the dead Nyerere is more powerful than many living politicians. One Swahili weekly *Dira ya Mtanzania* (July 13th, 2015) wrote, "*Inashangaza kuona Nyerere anakuwa na nguvu kuliko hata walio hai. Je hawa hawajafa kiroho na kubakia kimwili kiasi cha kuishiwa na kutegemea kuwatumia marehemu kufikia malengo yao machafu?* ("It baffles to find that Nyerere is more powerful than living people. Aren't these dead spiritually by just being alive physically; but are politically bankrupt so as to depend on using the dead to reach their dirty goals?") Such a claim shows us how strong Nyerere has remained posthumously. It is because of his policies and his managerial skills that have enhanced this as one of his legacies.

Apart from fighting for the wellbeing of his people, like his friend and compatriot, Nkrumah, Nyerere wanted the whole Africa to be reunited however step by step the move that Nkrumah vehemently opposed so as to stall the process of reunifying Africa. Nyerere preached what he lived and lived what he preached. He was a doer more than a preacher. The URT he engineered and crafted has stood the test of time as the only successful and long-time union Africa boast of having today thanks to Nyerere ingenuity. Essentially, this is the only union that exists today in Africa. Looking at its exiguity and vitality, one can say that Nyerere succeeded in what failed many, especially if we look at some of the unions such as the East African Community (EAC) and Senegambia, to mention a few. Furthermore, Nyerere's economic policies aimed at benefiting many but not a few as it became a norm in many African countries after acquiring their independence. Whereas many African countries saw their leaders and rulers becoming tycoons overnight, Nyerere died a poor person whose house was built by the government as its appreciation for his patriotism and truthfulness to his people and his county. His children and his widow Mama Maria (as Tanzanians refer to her); still live normal live just like any ordinary Tanzanians which it is in itself an exception to the general rule *vis-a-vis* the current crop of rulers who took office after Nyerere. To make sure that all Tanzanians are equal and one, Nyerere abolished tribalism and nepotism; thereby creating an equal society in which there was no tribalism. Tanzanians identify themselves with their nationality but not tribes which is unique in Africa. Even intertribal marriages are more common among Tanzanians minus the minority Indians who clung to their racist caste system that they exported to Tanzania and other African countries the colonial monsters brought them to. Importantly, Nyerere invested wisely and heavily almost in all types of industries and factories in order to create jobs and offer services to his people. When he asserted that his *Ujamaa* and *Kujitegemea* aimed at self-reliance, he meant exactly it. Nyerere (1985) argues that Tanzania's educational policy is based on three philosophical assumptions namely equality, membership to the society and acquisition of basic literacy and numeracy which contribute to the person and the nation at large, (p. 45).

What a powerful statement that intertwines Nyerere's educational and economic policies under one parasol! As argued above, under Nyerere, Tanzanians enjoyed free education from primary school to PhD among others. This was incredibly like a miracle compared to other African countries of the time. Again, how much Nyerere succeeded or failed in his quest and experimentation of the unification of Africa, it all depends on exegeses one applies on the matter. Nyerere will always be remembered as the father of the Union of Tanganyika and Zanzibar and the liberation of Southern African countries to which he unquestionably contributed massively.

Nyerere had another feather in his cap. More than any African leader of the time and thereafter, Nyerere was instrumental in bringing down the Apartheid regime in South Africa. The words of the first president of Mozambique, the late Samora Machel (1985 cited *mutatis mutandis* in Ishemo 2000) suffice to sum up who Nyerere actually was as far as the total liberation of Africa was concerned. He says that:

> When in Mozambique we speak of Nyerere, we remember the names that are the landmarks of our history. When we invoke the name Julius Nyerere, we remember Kongwa, the military camp where we trained the guerrillas that purified liberation struggle; we remember Tunduru, where our children learned a new life that we are building,; we remember Bagamoyo, our education centre that prepared the cadres for the victory that we knew was certain, we remember Mtwara, our rearguard hospital, where we treated our war wounded, and where we formed new cadres for our health services. With the name of Nyerere, we remember, with profound emotion, Nachingwea, the laboratory of our struggle, the camp where we trained our best soldiers, and where, in our day to day work, a New Man was constructed. With president Nyerere, we live the moment that can never been extinguished from our memory, (p. 87).

Such eulogy based on figures and facts shows how selfless Nyerere was. All mentioned are the parts of Tanzania which Nyerere offered to the *Frente de Libertação de Moçambique* (FRELIMO) to launch and operate from in its struggle to liberate Mozambique which culminated in 1975 when Mozambique became independent after Portuguese ruled it for many years. Nyerere did not only offer bases to the FRELIMO but he also offered the same to Zimbabwean freedom fighters under the Zimbabwe African Nation Union (ZANU) led by Reverend Ndabaningi Sitole before Robert Mugabe. So too, Nyerere supported Joshua Nkomo (with his Zimbabwe African People's Union (ZAPU), Namibians under South Western African People Organization (SWAPO) led by Sam Nujoma, the African National Congress (ANC) under Nelson Mandela and many more. As noted above, Nyerere's slogan, just like Kwame Nkrumah's, was that the liberation of Africa would never be completed if there was an inch of the soil of any African country that was still under colonial rule or tyranny.

Nyerere did not only offer land to freedom fighters for establishing bases, but also he offered financial, military, political, moral and social supports as well. For instance, refugees from all Southern African countries that were under colonial rule were equally and unquestionably entitled to social services such as health and education along with Tanzanians. Due to the maturity of Tanzanians then, there was no conflict between them and the freedom fighters that Tanzania hosted. As the members of African communal society, Tanzanians and the freedom fighters shared whatever was available at the time despite the economy of the country performing poorly due to the reasons mentioned above. Under Nyerere's policies of *Ujamaa* and *Kujitegemea* based on African brotherhood, every African had the right to enjoy whatever was available in Tanzania. Theoretically, for Nyerere, Africa was one country waiting to be reunited to the tune it was before the coming of colonial monsters. This is why refugees enjoyed the same rights Tanzanians enjoyed. Ironically however, when South Africa acquired its independence after pulling Apartheid regime down in 1997, a few years thereafter, its citizens were involved in xenophobic attacks against their sisters and brothers from neighbouring countries among whom were Tanzanians. Thank heavens that this sacrilege occurred almost 16 years after Nyerere's death. It would have affected him negatively to find that the people he supported became new black Boers as he used to call whoever wanted to divide Tanzanians along colour, region, religion or tribe. No words may describe who actually Nyerere was as far as accountability and good quality of management are concerned. He, indeed, was what one can call one of the *Incredibles* Africa has ever had.

Hate him or love him; this is Mwalimu Julius Kambarage Nyerere, the philosopher king whose indelible marks, legacy and ingenuity as far as economic, social and political management are concerned that will remain for many generations to come. Nonetheless, his *Ujamaa* and *Kujitegemea* policies are no longer applied in Tanzania, their spirit and successes will always speak volumes *vis-a-vis* the wellbeing of Tanzanians. Nyerere was able to bridge the gap between the poor and the rich in Tanzania during his leadership. The salt of the earth and down to earth person, Nyerere has always been a point of reference in leadership. Nyerere left behind a very shining legacy, especially, the URT as mentioned above that he engineered and crafted as a symbol and desire for African colonial-demarcated and created countries to reunite to the tune they were before the partition and division of Africa in 1884. At the national level, Nyerere left behind a very cohesive, united and levelled country compared to many sharply divided African countries.

Furthermore, Nyerere greatly reduced tribalism. Tanzanians are impressively an exception to the general rule in Africa *vis-à-vis* tribalism. The problem of tribalism in Tanzania is very negligible compared to its neighbours that have always suffered from the vice since independence. However, tribalism has recently crawled back as Tillmar (2006) notes that "common to both areas was also 'tribalism', in the sense that 'immigrant' business owners from other parts of the country were distrusted with regard to their goodness and 'locals' were distrusted with regard to their competence," (p. 103). If Tanzania goes on divorcing Nyerere's foundations, chances of witnessing tribalism resurging are very high however successive governments have tried to put a lid on it. Again, due to the surge of corruption, tribalism, just like any vices such as drug peddling, embezzlement of public funds and others, is as well cropping up as the days go by. Despite all, the strong sense of nationalism still exists among Tanzanians compared to the neighbours. And this is why the country has always been stable since independence as opposed to other countries in the region.

Secondly, Nyerere left a very narrow gap between who-have and who-have-not; however since he departed things have changed negatively. However, income inequality is on the increase in Tanzania as Deininger (1996) argues that the Gini coefficient for the country as a whole rising from 0.34 to 0.37 between 1991–92 and 2000–01, and for Dar es Salaam from 0.30 to 0.36, (p. 1669). Under Nyerere, income inequality was very negligible due to the fact that he enforced the code of ethics that was observed by all Tanzanians equally and sternly. After the neoliberal policies–that the International Monetary Fund (IMF) and the World Bank (WB) spearheaded–kicked in, everything changed. All of a sudden, Tanzanians, for the first time, started to see evolving millionaires who robbed public parastatals under privatisation which turned out to be disastrous to the county. Before his death, Nyerere castigated this trend saying that it would divide the country between the rich and poor so as to compromise its security and stability.

Thirdly, Nyerere left a very vast infrastructure of roads, schools, hospitals, factories and whatnot in the country. Nyerere had a very ambitious plan to industrialise the country. Van der Straeten (2015) claims that:

> After independence Julius Nyerere adopted the colonialist view that successful economic development requires a strong state. Consequently, Tanzania's natural, industrial, and communications resources were nationalized in the Arusha Declaration in 1967, (p. 275).

Comparably, when it comes to social infrastructure, Tanzania is better-off than its neighbours. So, too, the signs and remnants of an egalitarian country Nyerere build are still evident in Tanzania. However, as time goes by, chances of being eroded are higher and visible after the country embraced neoliberal policies as propagated and executed by the IFIs steered by the WB and the IMF. Nyerere died believing in social justice and his *Ujamaa* and *Kujitegemea* which gave him guts and conviction to stand against the new world order that systematically exploits poor countries for the benefit of the West. Leys (1996 cited in MacGuinty and William 2009) argues that "modernising elites were really... lumpen-bourgeoisies serving their own and foreign interests," (p. 10). Basically, Leys underscores the current world order in which the West designs development strategies for poor countries to work on as it aimed at benefiting the West. This is colonial superimposition by the West. Even if we consider the way the process is conducted, we find that the West has always dealt with local elites; thereby excluding the majority of citizens. Nyerere did not want to be among local elites who acted as good boys for the West so as to sink their countries in utter exploitation that has been going on up till now. Being a visionary-cum-thinker, Nyerere saw it coming; and thus, avoided it even at the expense of relinquishing power willingly at the age of 63 years which, at the time, was regarded as a good age for being a leader. This can be seen on the fact that his successor, Mwinyi took over from him when he was 61years old. Nyerere was a principled and strict man to his beliefs and vision. He preached water and drank water which is totally different from many of his colleagues at the time. Land was one of Nyerere's favourite topic and policy matter. His words suffice to show how he felt about land distribution.

"The foreigner introduced a completely different concept —the concept of land as a marketable commodity. According to this system, a person could claim a piece of land as his own property whether he intended to use it or not. I could take a few square miles of land and call them 'mine' and then go off to the moon. All I have to do to gain living from 'my' land was to charge to a rent to the people who wanted to use it," Julius Nyerere in Nyerere (1968, p. 4).

Nyerere's legacy
Mwalimu (teacher) Julius Kambarage Nyerere will always be remembered for his love and commitment to Africa. Accountable, selfless and trustworthy, Nyerere left a very shinning legacy many African leaders do not have. He united Tanganyika and Zanzibar to form the United Republic of Tanzania (URT) set the pace for other African countries to follow. He is credited for being instrumental in the formation of the East Africa Community (EACI) not to mention being a linchpin in the business of the Non-Aligned Movement and the South Commission which he once chaired.

Just as any intellectual, Nyerere wrote profusely. His works are still the point of reference in many social sciences. Apart from unifying Tanganyika and Zanzibar, Nyerere abolished tribalism in Tanzania. Up until now, Tanzania is the only country in the East and Central Africa region that does not suffer from tribalism. As a trustworthy manager, apart from managing the business of his country well, he did not rob his country. His family, up until now many years after his death, is still living a normal life as mentioned above. So, too, Nyerere has another accolade. He willingly relinquished power in 1985 after diligently and trustworthily serving his country for 24 years. Notably, Nyerere championed and chaired the Frontline States, countries that spearheaded the liberation of South Africa on top of providing heaven for freedom fighters in Angola, Mozambique, Namibia, South Africa and Zimbabwe. Also, Nyerere overthrew Idi Amin after finding that the international community maintained silence while Amin was mercilessly butchering innocent Ugandans in 1979. It is not easy to contort Nyerere's legacy in one chapter. Again, Nyerere will be always remembered as a good manager of his country whose bigger dream was to see the entire continent of Africa united to form one powerful country of AFRICA.

Nonetheless, despite having a very shinning legacy, Nyerere had his weakness. For example, when he willingly relinquished power, he admitted that things were not going according to what he expected. So, for him, this was a failure in spite of the fact the IFIs sabotaged his policies as indicated above. Again, he boldly used to say that if someone would wake up in the middle of the night asking him where he put the money the country used to get, he would show her or him what he called the *graveyard* of the said money. He meant that he would show empty schools, hospitals, clinics, roads that were starting to dilapidate, and above all, Tanzanians who got social services free and equally. At the time his enemies and detractors were scorning Nyerere, most of his neighbours were ruling the majority or people who barely had anything congenial comparably *vis-à-vis* free provisions of social services. Nyerere was different from squanderers such as Bokassa and Houphouët-Boigny who burnt much public monies on obsolete *black elephants* while their people were starving and dying. Nyerere is one of a few presidents who admitted to have failed so as to bow out uprightly and willingly in order to give room for others to try and manage the affairs of the country. Arguably, Nyerere did not seek to build a paradise. Instead, he wanted to equally and equitably uplift Tanzanians from poverty, ignorance and diseases that the colonial government left behind. Notably, whether Nyerere's policies were a failure or not depends on the lenses one uses. In the eyes of capitalist, Nyerere left a bankrupt country. Again, in the eyes of socialists or humanists, Nyerere's policies were a success story, especially if we consider the number of Tanzanians he uplifted from ignorance and diseases. While many of his colleagues were collecting taxes and spending them on living large, Nyerere heavily invested in his people. Samoff (1990 cited in Ibhawoh and Dibua 2003) concurs noting that "by the early 1980s, even in the face of economic difficulties, Tanzania had one of the highest literacy rates in Africa with every village boasting of at least a primary school," (p. 71). Ibhawoh and Dibua go on citing the *Africa Now* (December, 1981, p. 58) which reported that 90 percent of these villages had, at least, one village cooperative store while over 60 per cent had relatively easy access to safe water supply, a health centre or dispensary. Can we call this a failure if we underscore the reasons that led to the impracticability of Nyerere's policies? It is upon the reader to judge.

Despite some policy shortfalls and flaws in his management, Nyerere's legacy can be summarised in the words of Deininger (1996) noting that "Nyerere will be remembered internationally as an African leader of moral integrity who contributed greatly to the campaign against apartheid in South Africa" (p. 1369). Like Mandela, Nyerere was no saint. However, he was a great manager of public affairs who tried harder so as to leave a very shinning legacy as a diligent and honest manager of public affairs. Nyerere died in 1999 after willingly relinquishing power in 1985. Many Tanzanians, especially the poor miss him dearly. Africa too will always miss him. This is Mwl Julius Kambarage Nyerere whose words hereunder wrap up his chapter.

"And in rejecting the capitalist attitude of mind which colonialism brought into Africa, we must reject also the capitalist methods which go with it. One of these is the individual ownership of land. To us in Africa land was always recognized as belonging to the community. Each individual within

our society had a right to the use of land, because otherwise he could not earn his living and one cannot have the right to life without also having the right to some means of maintaining life. But the African's right to land was simply the right to use it; he had no other right to it, nor did it occur to him to try and claim one," Nyerere (1987, p. 7).

Figure 3: Nyerere punishing Kikwete after Mkapa (image courtesy of Daily Nation)

Chapter 4

Samora the Hero Who Died Mysteriously

"Our state apparatus is corrupted. It is sick, full of parasites, come clinging to the skin and others internal...We are going to define tasks for everyone to carry out. We will be ruthless with the undisciplined, the incompetent, the lazy, the negligent, the careless, the corrupt, those who go in for red tape, for inertia, those who cultivate a spirit of routine, those who despise the people," Machel cited in Meyns (1981, p. 60).

Figure 6: Samora M. Machel Mozambique's 1st President (image courtesy of free encyclopaedia)

Africa has had all crops and kinds of leaders and rulers from good to bad, sane and ridiculously insane and what have you. True, comrade

Samora Moises Machel was among the most articulated, committed and selfless leaders just like his mentor Mwalimu Nyerere was. Machel was born in Chilembene, Gaza Province, Mozambique on September 29th, 1933; and died October 18th, 1986 of the plane crash at Mbuzini; Eastern Transvaal, South Africa; at the time the country was still under the Apartheid regime. Like Lumumba above, Machel died in very murky and mysterious environment that left many speculations and many conspiracy theories behind. Machel's death left many more questions than answers. Machel died in a plane crash on his way back home from attending a Summit with the heads of states of Angola, the DRC (then Zaire) Mozambique and Zambia in Mbala, Zambia. Machel was the leader of the *Frente de Libertação de Moçambique* (FRELIMO) or the Mozambican Liberation Front which was founded in Dar es Salaam in 1962 to spearhead the struggle against Portuguese colonial government in Mozambique; which it later defeated; and thereby liberated Mozambique on 25th June, 1975.

When the media broke the news that Machel was no more, many people in Mozambique, Africa and the world in general were shocked and dismayed. However, his enemies were happy that, at last, they got themselves rid of a thorn in their side. When it comes to the majority Africans, particularly in the countries in the then known as the Frontline States for the liberation of South Africa, Machel's death was a big loss and a big blow altogether. I remember how I received such bad news of the untimely demise of Machel. I remember a friend of mine saying as he held his head in his hands with disbelief noting that "it can't be? God, why should it be Samora but not the *Kaburu* (Boer) in the first place?" This can show you how Machel was loved and revered in some countries. Arguably, Machel was not only the president of Mozambique—for other countries likes Tanzania and Zambia—he was one of theirs, a true son of Africa. Again, this shows the ephemerality of human life and predicaments. I remember, as a young boy then, how in the morning of 20th October, 1986, I was in my small café. We surrounded my transistor radio to hear the late Julius Nyerere announce the tragic death of the true son of Africa. We were all touched due to the fact that, at school, we were used to Machel's famous slogan of *A Luta Continua* namely struggle continues. Also, we use to sing the then famous liberation song from

Mozambique *FRELIMO ya winna* or *FRELIMO has won*. We use to sing in our corrupted childish language:

Ife ana Frelimo zowona tina pata ku Mozambique
Ife ana Nyerere zowona tina pata ku Tanzania
If ana Samora zowona tina pata ku Mozambique
Frelimooo yaawina, frelimooo yaawina
Zowona, tina pata ku Mozambique

Ironically, we did not understand the whole meaning of the song. However, we knew it was about victorious struggle that culminated in the freedom of Mozambique in 1975. When we heard Mwalimu Nyerere heartbreakingly announce the death of the true son of Africa who happened to be his friend and mentee, we were all touched as if the deceased was either our neighbour or the person we knew however, some, and most of us, of course, had never met with Machel. The shock of the loss started to sink in and the death became a reality after this time. No way would Mwalimu Nyerere joke about the death of his friend and mentee whom we knew through the media. The radio was the most trusted tool and the most powerful source of information, especially at that time when there were no Television services in Tanzania. So, whatever the radio reported was taken to be serious and true including government propagandas. Machel's slogan of *A Luta Continua* was known everywhere in the country. We used to hear his voice on the radio, mainly at the time the FRELIMO was fighting against Portuguese colonial regime in Mozambique. We, sometimes, interacted with some Mozambicans who were given sanctuary in Tanzania. So, too, we used to see Machel's picture on newspapers and in books. At that time, as noted above, Tanzania did not have Television services all over the country. So, most of us saw Machel after the coming of internet which– through YouTube–enabled us to see and listen to our hero posthumously. Despite seeing him posthumously, some of us liked him even before seeing him. So, seeing him added more closeness so as to feel writing something about this icon of independence struggle in Mozambique. On the material day Nyerere announced the demise of Machel, I vivid remember how my business boomed. Many people would come and speculate about Machel and the way they knew him. Personally, it was one of the most sombre days in my life so to speak.

There are those who allegedly claimed that the crash of Machel's presidential jet was caused by Apartheid regime in South Africa after tampering with communication, and thus, misdirected the plane to the hill where it tragically crashed. The *New African* (December, 1986, No: 23) quoted one of the survivals, Fernando Manuel Joao, president Machel's bodyguard as saying that soon after 9:00pm that Sunday night, the stewardess told the passengers on the presidential jet to prepare for landing in Maputo. However, five minutes passed without receiving any more instructions. Joao went on saying that he heard "a sound like a shot. Suddenly we heard plane screech," (p. 9). Machel and his mentor Julius Nyerere were known to be thorny to the Apartheid regime which they wanted to dismantle and get Africa rid of as the last bastion of colonialism. Some made allegations that the plane did not crash but the missile brought it down. Munslow (1998) notes that the government of Mozambique said that the "crash" to have occurred under "circumstances not clarified," (p. 23) to mean that there was a foul play behind this tragedy for Mozambique and Africa in general. The paper went on writing that some African leaders "believe the aircraft was shot down." Whether the plane was shot down or not, what was obvious was the loss of a true son of Africa, Samora Moise Machel. However, Machel had a premonition of his death as he used to say, *Independência ou morte* (Darch and Hedges 2013, p. 59) literary "independence or death" especially if there was a single inch of African soil that was still in colonial grip. He consequently died with his belief in freedom, not only for Mozambique but the entire continent. As aforementioned, at the time of the death of Machel, neighbouring South Africa was still under Apartheid. Despite being an occupied country, South Africa posed a great danger to many, if not all, of its neighbours with the exception of Malawi that intimately cooperated with it after betraying its African counterparts. Dying in South African soil–which was among Machel's arch nemeses that was in bed with Portuguese colonial rule–created many conspiracy theories on whether what brought down Machel's aircraft was a bomb, a missile or a mere accident. Machel was not a fainthearted person. He was not afraid of death, instead he was prepared for it if need be. You can see how death was not Machel's threat in the words he wrote soon after the death of his first wife Josina Machel.

Machel cited in Chirere (2005) writes:

Josina, you are not dead
Because we have assumed
Your responsibilities…
Out of your memory
I will fashion a hoe to turn the sad
Enriched by your sacrifice
And new fruits will grow (p. 4).

Machel interprets death as a duty, specifically when one has
achieved her or his goals. So, too, he believes in the continuity and
the hard work all collectively shared and borne. Like her husband,
Josina, too, was ready to die for the course she believed in. Cited in
Chirere (Ibid) she writes:

The blood shed by our heroes
Make us sad but resolute.
It is the price of our freedom
We keep them close in our hearts…
Revolutionary generations
are already being born, (p. 4).

Nature has its way of shaping and equipping humans with the
tools they need for survival. As if it were a divine, Josina speaks the
same language with the one her husband speaks. Her poem speaks
volumes as far as her preparedness to face death is concerned. For
the couple, death did not kill. But instead it motivated and hardened
those left behind to carry on with the journey as they also prepare
themselves to meet their deaths, if needs be, provided the struggle
continues. For, Machel, as a committed revolutionary, blood was
there to nourish the struggle to see to it that the sacrifice for the
nation is made. To the contrary, to the fainthearted and fake
revolutionists like Muamar Gaddafi, death was something to avoid at all
costs even if it meant to kill innocent people wrongly perceived to be
enemies.

Due to being a good manager of the affairs of his state, the
sudden death of Machel did not destabilise his country subsequently.

The transition in Mozambique took place smoothly even before his body was buried. There were no squabbles over power or any divisions in his country and party which was different from countries that were under dictators whose toppling marked another era of divisions and the failure of the states. Libya, Egypt and the DRC epitomise how leadership plays a very important role on the integrity or failure of the country after a long-time leader or ruler dies or being pulled down as it happened in these countries after being under long-time dictatorships. Smooth transition in Mozambique gives Machel a credit of running the business of the state by establishing the system that did not depend on a single person as it was in Somalia, Libya, Rwanda and Egypt after rulers either were kicked out, or died; thereby their countries cascaded into chaos, anarchy and the status of failed states. This means that Machel had already established a very reliable and sustainable system that would operate even in his absence as it later happened.

True, Machel was among Africa's shining stars whose life was cut short at the time his country and Africa needed him the most. Vocal as he was, Machel was very instrumental in bringing down Apartheid regime in South Africa. He always showed his dislike of Apartheid despite the danger such a stance posed given that Mozambique is next door to South Africa. Being a brave leader, he did not cower or hide his uneasiness while other carbuncular rulers such as Malawian, Hastings Kamuzu Banda who shared the bed with a racist regime in South Africa, either for fear of being attacked, toppled; or because of being Western straight men who were ready to do whatever their masters ordered them to do even if it meant to betray or vend their people. Even before the release of South African first indigenous president, Nelson Mandela, Machel had already declared war against this notorious regime. While other African rulers such as Banda, Joseph Mobutu (DRC), Jomo Kenyatta (Kenya) and others dragged their feet as far as getting Africa rid of Apartheid is concerned, Machel, like Nyerere and Kaunda, openly and boldly declared war against Apartheid regime in the neighbouring South Africa. Being a powerful neighbour, South Africa posed a great danger to Mozambique. Militarily, financially and technically, South Africa was ahead of Mozambique. Intimidating as the Apartheid regime was, needed a courageous man to declare war against it, especially when such a person was neighbour that could be attacked easily. Machel's philosophy and stance against South African Apartheid regime were clear and open. Machel (1987) notes in his then blockbuster book, *Apartheid Must be Eradicated* that:

> The South Africa armed forces are waging a colonial war in Namibia, invaded and partly occupied Angolan territory, and carry our operations and aggression against Swaziland, Lesotho, Botswana, Zambia, Zimbabwe and Mozambique," (p. 26).

Machel tries to show the size and magnitude of the problem so that those responsible for dealing with it prepare themselves well to match with its nature, size and magnitude. Machel and Nyerere were instrumental in convincing other Frontline states to impose sanctions against Apartheid South Africa. He campaigned tirelessly internationally; and the results were tremendous; when the international community responded by supporting Liberation Movements; and thereby imposing sanctions against Apartheid which authored the beginning of the end of the regime that officially crumbled in 1994 twelve years after Machel's death. Interestingly, despite Machel's absence on the day South Africa became independent, his widow, Grace was there as she stood hand in hand with her second husband, Nelson Mandela. When it comes to defining Apartheid, Machel (Ibid) goes on saying:

> There is no such a thing as democratic apartheid. There is no humane apartheid. There is no peaceful apartheid. Apartheid is the denial of justice, equality and social norms. It is an institutional violation of human rights. Apartheid, like colonialism, cannot be reformed. Apartheid, like colonialism, must be eradicated, (p. 29).

So, for Machel, there was no compromise, no negotiation; no what except to bring down Apartheid regime. He minced no words on this as his words show. His resolve to pull down Apartheid regime was unquestionable by all standards. Maybe, this is why the Apartheid regime hated and feared him so as to be allegedly behind his death. However, he died before Apartheid was pulled down; Machel's

contribution to the eradication of Apartheid was key and humongous. His slogan, *"A Luta Continua"* is a hallmark that Machel left behind. He used to say *"A Luta Continua"* and then asked, *"Conta Que?* Or against what? Then, he would answer "Against tribalism, nepotism, ignorance, exploitation of person by a person, superstition, hunger, miseries, lack of clothing,"
https://www.youtube.com/watch?v=bvj0Feq5vpI
Accessed September 22, 2015.

Indeed, tribalism, nepotism and superstition among other vices, constituted a big problem to post-colonial African countries. As we will see later, some leaders used tribalism and nepotism to hang onto power as opposed to the will of the people.

Machel's vision and commitment were unshakably clear that the struggle continues; and someday all people will be equal and free. He used to say. In the above clip, Machel is quoted saying that there are some who feel a certain pride because they were colonised by English because English are civilised because they build a great empire. He went on talking about those who took pride in their colonial masters such as English, French and Portuguese. He refers to Portuguese as a most backward country in Europe. He argues that colonialism is a crime against humanity. There is no humane colonialism or democratic. Colonialism is naturally inhumane and savagery.

Like his mentor and comrade, Nyerere, Machel took back the land that was held for about 500 years by Portuguese settlers and redistributed to the people of Mozambique without illegally or preferentially apportioning any to himself or his friends as it was in many countries. He believed that every human being is rooted on the land which has a very special relationship in many African cultures. He, therefore, saw no bright future for his people without owning land they belonged to and some fought and died for. Such a move was not liked by Western countries, especially Portuguese. Apartheid South Africa did not like land acquisition and land redistribution given that it was sitting on the same land a few whites stole from Africans whom they rendered landless. When he was fighting for the liberation of Mozambique, many African and Western countries used to deny him support and aid. Yet, Machel did not give in. He went on with his Marxist policies up until his death. For Machel, economic and socio-economic justice was the apogee of any ideal and free society. He had to fight colonialism because it was exploitative. As a good manager, Machel knew how painful it was for someone to be exploited by another. Machel cited in Leao (2005) maintains:

> We were obliged to sell our products to the traders at prices fixed by the administration... We would produce and sell one kilo of beans at three and a half escudos while European farmers produced and sold at five escudos the kilo.... If on occasion, by special agreement, we managed to sell direct to a caterer or trader... we were compelled to receive payment half in cash and half in goods.... We couldn't become traders. 'Natives' couldn't enter into any form of commerce. They can only be producers for European traders. African cows are not registered and cannot bear their owners' brand. This enabled the European farmers to steal African cattle, (p. 33).

Exploitation becomes even more notorious when a person is rendered landless. Knowing the significance of land as a natural right and means of production to humans, Machel nationalised land when Mozambique became independent. Like his mentor, Nyerere, Machel wanted every Mozambican to have means of production under her or his disposal. As mentioned above, differently from Mugabe and Kenyatta who used land as source of power they used to reward their cronies and courtiers to gain more leverage, and make them party to their criminality, Machel did not take any land for his private use and ownership. Many African leaders and rulers succumbed to the lures of land acquisition and land grabbing when they had the responsibility of redistributing wealth such as land. There are some who did not apportion any parcels of land or a cent to themselves like Machel and Nyerere while Kenyatta, for example, acquired millions of hectares. I am not trying to be a devil's advocate. When it comes to land grabbing, and amassing wealth, former Ugandan dictators, Amin, shocked many. He scores higher than many in the region. Despite being accused of mass murder, brutality and cannibalism, there is nowhere Amin was accused of apportioning to himself even an inch of land or shops he took from Asians. Nor were there any allegations that Amin stashed even a cent in the foreign banks like Abacha, Mobutu and many more that are not yet unearthed. However, Amin failed the test after offering Asian shops to his soldiers and friends. Machel and Nyerere are still an exception to the general rule when it comes to managing public affairs at a state level. When it comes to being selfless, Machel and Nyerere are second to none in Africa.

Henderson (1976) notes that:

Samora Machel stated that economic priority must be given to agricultural development. Mozambique's economy is, and is likely to remain for the near future, an agriculturally-based one. In order to assess Mozambique's future economic development, it is important to consider land settlement policies within the country in the past, (p. 142).

Apart from taking land from Portuguese settlers, Machel nationalised schools and hospitals that were used by only the privileged, mostly Portuguese and their African collaborators. Machel cited in (Darch and Hedges 2011) nationalised land so to do and bring justice to the country after finding that, in Mozambique, "everything for the benefit of Portuguese colonialism; to benefit imperialism," (p. 69). Land is very precious to those who underscore its value and significance. Land is everything, chiefly for traditional farmers whose lives depend on it. Machel, as a son of a farmer, understood this very well. Further, Machel wanted every Mozambican to have good health so that he or she could produce for her/himself and for the country. Machel envisaged a very egalitarian country just like his mentor, Nyerere, who nationalised all means of production including land in 1967 just six years after gaining independence. To Machel, a country with landless citizens was like a time-ticking bomb that we recently saw exploding in Zimbabwe as it waits to explode in South Africa, Kenya, Namibia and other countries that did not sort out land issues after acquiring their independence. Indeed, Machel and Nyerere shared the same vision on land; and their visions obviated land-conflicts in their countries. What puts Machel and Nyerere ahead of others *vis-a-vis* socio-economic justice and moral grounds is the fact that they refused to use the power to allocate themselves or their friends, family, relatives anything just like other African rulers we will see who used their power to grab land

and rob their countries. There are so many examples, mainly in Kenya and Zimbabwe where lands reacquisition and land redistribution ended up being used as a token to reward loyalty, friendships and whatnot. When it comes to healthy relationship, Machel regarded Nyerere as a comrade, father, friend and mentor. Their relationship was so unique that it needs volumes to explain. Even when he was killed, Nyerere was badly affected with this death. To know well who Machel was, Meseses (2013) answers the question referring to Machel as "…the man Mandela labelled 'a true African revolutionary'," (p. 514). Despite the weight and truthfulness of Mandela, no doubt Machel was a true son and an African revolutionary whose marks will always remain indelible on the struggle and wellbeing of African continent. Machel was a true revolutionary who lived; and ultimately died a revolutionary. His ideas speak to this; and his actions practically imply this too. It is very interesting to note that despite his modesty level of education, Machel wrote books something most of our current rulers cannot do. This shows how consistent, able and bright Machel was as far as the cause he fought for is concerned.

Furthermore, Machel used to say that his philosophy was based on concrete things such as land, life, and all amenities every human being deserves to have and enjoy. So, to Machel, *abstractisation* of some items was a misnomer. Interestingly, Machel did not mince words when he propounded this kind of philosophical interpretation of things. In other words, he added more value to the things that many would take for granted or underestimate such as life and all of its amenities. This is a new and radical approach many of his colleagues lacked. This approach, apart from being philosophical, is totally distinct from most of intellectual African leaders who basically employed more theories than actions. One of them is the late Leopold Sedar Senghor, Senegalese founding father with his *negritude* philosophy. Ironically, Senghor was more at home in Paris than Dakar despite championing *negritudes* which he did without neglecting Western culture. Comparably, Machel, along with Kaunda and Nyerere, was a creature of another planet as far as talking and walking the talk is concerned. Machel's complexification of human amenities helped him to implement his policies. He was able to on all those who grabbed land and sat on it while the majority of the rightful owners, namely Mozambicans, were suffering from landlessness which rendered them poor unnecessarily in the country they bled and died for. You can see this colonial mentality of holding on important and natural resources such as land in Kenya, Jamaica, and South Africa where the majority of citizens wallow in manmade abject poverty wantonly whereas the minority sits on big chunks of land without developing them. Looking at what transpired in Zimbabwe recently whereby the government took land and farms from white settlers and how it distributed them speaks volumes about Machel vision and integrity. Instead of using land and farms to reward his cronies and courtiers, Machel understood that owning land was but a human right that everybody, regardless who needed it or not, must have. For the person who abhorred and abolished tribalism and superstition, doing differently would have tarnished his image not to mention defeating his goal and cause. This is one of the reasons why Machel appears in the list of the best managers of their countries. However, he did not live long enough to see what he fought for. Instead, he died for the course of the people of Mozambique and Africa in general.

"It was in the course of political-military training that we forged national unity, and developed a common outlook, a patriotic consciousness and a class consciousness. We came (to the camp at Nachingwea in Tanzania) as Makondes, Makuas . . . Rongas or Senas, and we left as Mozambicans. We came in as black, white, coloured and Indian persons, and we went out as Mozambicans. We came with a limited vision, because the only zone we knew was our zone. It was there that we took on the full dimension of our country and the values of the revolution," Machel (cited by Nwafor, 2003, p. 39 cited in Reis 2012, p. 4).

Machel's legacy

Machel left a very united and cohesive government under his party, the FRELIMO despite the fact that there were still some pockets of those who opposed him under the Mozambican National Resistance (RENAMO) or *Resistência Nacional Moçambican* led by his arch nemesis, Alphonso Dhlakama. Despite RENAMO's aggression through a gruesome and long-time civil war, Mozambique has remained intact even after the death of Machel. Like any trustful managers of public affairs, there are no any corruption allegations involving Machel that his estate faces. His stanch and staunch belief in equality and justice enhanced him to rule diligently and trustworthily so as to die without robbing his country. More importantly, Machel's stand against imperialism and colonialism has always been a reference point as far as decolonisation of Africa is concerned. Machel died too early; and he will always be remembered as a true son of Africa who practically and theoretically showed the way of how to decolonise Africa. Machel was a leader who knew what he wanted; and what his people wanted and needed and how to get it. The *eNCA* (13 June, 2013) observes that:

> Most African leaders can learn from Machel; here is a leader who had time for his people, who defended his people, would chat to people on the side of the road and console ... could confront his leaders for being corrupt, I think that's the type of governance and the type of leadership we need in Africa.

When it comes to weakness, Machel was too radical and forceful sometimes. As well, Machel believed in Marxism as the only way of life that would deliver his country. This may make him not only a radical but also a conservative as far as his ideology was concerned. Also, his move to sign the Nkomati accord (Mzumara 2011, p. 360) between Mozambique and South Africa shocked and angered many. This created some elements of controversy even narrow interests in which Machel considered Mozambique's interests instead of the interests of the whole region. However, Erasmus (1984) notes that:

> The Accord of Nkomati is undoubtedly the most sought after breakthrough in Pretoria's relations with Southern Africa. Among the Black States of the region Mozambique enjoys a unique position. It is a self-declared Marxist People's Republic and ideologically completely opposed to South Africa. President Machel is a highly-respected figure in African politics and no other African country was prepared to lend support to the ANC to the degree that Maputo had done, a factor of considerable annoyance to the South African government, (p. 2).

Many were shocked and irked by Machel's move due to the fact that on the one hand, he was heavily supporting the ANC while on the other hand, he was signing an agreement of nonaggression with Apartheid regime that the ANC was seeking to topple. Balancing such a situation needed a skilful manager whose decisions were to be genuine and understandable by both sides. However, Machel's move to sign a peace agreement with a violent regime was seen as trying to save two masters at one time.

Special tributes

Along with Samora Machel was the late Dr. Eduardo Modlane (20 June, 1920–3 February, 1969) who essentially was the leading founder of the FRELIMO. Modlane was assassinated in Dar es Salaam Tanzania when a bomb was planted in the book destined to the FRELIMO. After Modlane's death, Machel took the baton and liberated Mozambique. Modlane contributed immensely in founding and running the FRELIMO. Just like Amical Cabral (12 September, 1924–20 January, 1973) of Guinea Bissau who was also assassinated just about eight months to independence of his country, Modlane will be remembered as the architect of the liberation of Mozambique. Forlornly tough, he did not live to see the independence of his country. Again, as noted above in Machel's and his wife's poems, Machel notes that "the blood shed by our heroes makes us sad but resolute. And of course, as Machel would put it, "we have assumed Your responsibilities…" Machel took the responsibility of liberating Mozambique. It makes no sense whatsoever to discuss the history of Mozambique without mentioning the name Eduardo Modlane. He, too, was one of the best managers of African affairs who will always be missed dearly for the contribution and sacrifice he made to the liberation of Mozambique.

So, important too, was Josina Muthemba Machel (August 10, 1945–April 7, 1971) Machel's first wife who died a natural death at the age of 25 years. She was, along her husband, a freedom fighter *per se* whom death did not intimidate.

"Não, nós não somos inferiores. Não devem pensar assim. Não devem pensar assim [No, we are not inferior. You must not think like that. You must

not think like that]," Machel (cited in Darch and Hedges 2011, p.63).

Figure 4: Botha and Machel's caricature (image courtesy of mozambiquehistory.net)

72

Chapter 5

Kaunda the Humanist Per se

"The planned economy for some of us was an extremely important area in human life. How do you meet these challenges that God has given us in our lives if you don't help plan the economy? If you don't plan your economy, you are leaving everything in the hands of some other people, not yourself. You are leaving the door wide open for others to misbehave, to complicate your own life," Kaunda in the *Mail and Guardian* (27 October, 2014).

Figure 5: Kenneth D. Kaunda Zambia's 1st President (image courtesy of BBC)

Dr. Kenneth David Kaunda, the founder of Zambia, is a record breaker in some sense. Apart from holding a record of being one of the last two living first African presidents along Sir Dawda Jawara, Gambia's first president, Kaunda has another record breaking. He was the first sitting president in Africa to convene elections and make them free and fair so as to lose in the same elections. This was new and a misnomer to his colleagues at the time Kaunda bowed out of the office of the president which also saw him exiting political scene in general. So, too, he is the first founding president to willingly and quickly concede defeat. Kaunda went on breaking records even after exiting power as we will see later as far as transparency and fight against HIV/ADS are concerned.

Who is Kaunda? Kaunda was born at Lubwa in Chinsali District on 28th April, 1924 to a Church of Scotland missionary father David Kaunda from Malawi. Kaunda became Zambia's first president on 24th October, 1964 till November 2nd, 1991 after his ruling party the United National Independent Party (UNIP) was badly defeated by the opposition in general elections. Kaunda shocked many, friends and enemies alike even those you would not expect after conceding defeat; and thereby vacating the state house right away on the same day he was defeated. Another shocker that proved Kaunda's diligence and trustworthiness is being able to convene transparent, free and fair elections in which he lost without even attempting to rig or change the results as what transpired in Kenya in 2007 tells. Such a shock was valid given that at the time Kaunda was defeated multiparty politics was relatively new in Africa. Again, Kaunda proved to be a very astute student who learned things quickly. He did not ignore the writing on the wall or pretend that he did not see the signs of time. For, instead of attempting to cling unto power, Kaunda willingly relinquished it after conceding defeat something that was rare at the time in Africa. He had what it takes to preplan and preordain the results but he did not do so. Once again, Kaunda turned his defeat into victory *vis-a-vis* democracy and honesty. Arguably, Kaunda transformed himself from a one-party dictator to the father of democracy in Zambia just over night by being honest and transparent. Kaunda had what it takes to manipulate and rig elections. But he chose not to. For, he knew the haunting and costly jeopardies of doing so. Many will concur with us that Kaunda was ahead of his time as far as power is concerned. It is over twenty years since Kaunda willingly relinquished power through a ballot box. Ironically, some presidents such as Robert Mugabe, Yoweri Museveni, Paulo Kagame, Joseph Kabila, Denis Sassou-Nguesso and Pierre Nkurunzinza are amending the constitutions of their countries to remain in power. This, for the matter-of-factly, can show us the type of visionary Kaunda is. For, what he qualified to do—even at the time nobody would force him to abide by the constitution and tenets of democracy—has failed many at this precariously tricky time.

Although Kaunda was not as vocal as Nkrumah and Nyerere were, he managed Zambia responsibly and diligently despite presiding over a one-party rule for a long time. Venter and Olivier

(1993) note that "Kaunda became renowned as a passionate proponent of human rights in Africa and sometimes depicted as conscience of Africa," (p. 25). However, Venter and Olivier on arguing that Kaunda calls his philosophy humanism; and others call it *Kaundaism*. If we interpret humanism in African sense of the word we end up having Ubuntu which was historically the guiding principle in all societies in Central, East and South Africa region. However, Ubuntu is misconstrued to have originated from South Africa, (See Gade 2013; Mbigi and Maree 1995) while it actually was practised by all Bantu people. Under his humanism philosophy, Kaunda coined a very powerfully effective slogan of *One Zambia, One Nation* which has since became one of the things that differentiate Zambians from non-Zambians. Under, and, after Kaunda's watch, Zambia has remained one nation. Power never climbed into Kaunda's head. Vengeance never became his weapon of silencing dissenting voices. As argued in this volume that management is about controlling and inculcating a certain set of behaviour, Kaunda positively and diligently did exactly this. Under his rule, he tried as much as he could to be as transparent and as humane as he could which he did successfully. There perhaps can be systemic failures that occurred under his rule. Again, Kaunda was not an angel or a know-all person. He knew; power was like a coat on somebody's back. He knew power belongs to his citizens; and his being in power was but just people's trust in him. This is why when time for him to exit the political scene, he did not cling to power or try to rig or manoeuvre elections. He conceded defeat with a big and clean heart. He proved this by vacating the state house–as indicated above–on the same day Fredrick Chiluba–who later humiliated and imprisoned him in 1997 accusing him of coup attempt against his government which was totally politically motivated–defeated him. Ironically, Chiluba ended up badly mismanaging the business of running the state. Another thing that has shocked many up until now is Kaunda's resilience on living up to his words. Before going to elections in which he was defeated, he told Zambians that he felt that he still had something to offer to Zambia. Again, he did not hide his future plans by telling Zambians that if they voted him out, he would not turn back as he did thereafter even after being asked to make a comeback which was very possible thanks to how Chiluba had mismanaged the country so as to force Zambians to regret their action of voting Kaunda out. If he were a power monger or a monster, Kaunda would have seized this opportunity to make a comeback like his friend Obote, whom Kaunda gave refuge before returning to power to end up messing even more.

Furthermore, Kaunda was the man of his own words. At the time he willingly conceded defeat (de Gaay-Fortman 2000, p, 4; Mutonga 2003, p. 95; Mapuva 2013, p. 107; and Larcom, Sarr and Willems 2014, p. 5), if he wanted to try to tamper with the constitution to remain in power or rig the elections, he would. But he chose not to. So, too, Kaunda did not groom either his son or any protégé to take over after relinquishing power. And this move helped Zambia to create a precedent and change leadership harmoniously then and thereafter. The *New York Times* (November 2nd, 1991) wrote that:

> The conciliatory tone of the televised coverage and a newspaper editorial praising the "exemplary" conduct of the elections that had "done Africa proud" indicated that Mr. Kaunda, who remained silent during the day, would retire from the scene gracefully, many Zambians said.

Once again, this verily shows how Kaunda embraced democratic transition without any ill will or reservations. For, the *Los Angeles Times* (November 3rd, 1991 quoting the Africa South of Sahara *World Tables* 1991, p. 7) wrote on the day Kaunda was defeated quoting him as saying "you win some, and you lose some elections." What else would we want such an honest man to say? Kaunda went on saying that elections were not the end in themselves. This statement can be construed to mean that there is life out of the state house. Essentially, Kaunda's openness and courage enabled him to concede defeat acted as a motivation for other African leaders who were afraid of taking such a less-travelled road. For, three years after Kaunda exited power honourably, in the neighbouring Malawi, a long-time dictator, Hastings Kamuzu Banda found himself facing the same predicament. As well, Banda was defeated in the elections; and unexpectedly though, conceded defeat. Arguably, after evidencing peaceful transition in Zambia, Malawi was encouraged and motivated to believe that the fear for reprisal was immaterial at this time of democratic changes in Africa. Coincidentally, Malawi is Kaunda's ancestral land whose politics after Banda seems to be identical to Zambia's. The same was replicated in Kenya in 2002 when a long-time dictator, former president Daniel arap Moi, agreed to step down; and let his party field another person other than himself. In the same elections, Moi's protégé, Uhuru Kenyatta, was defeated by the opposition; and Moi had to concede the defeat of his person who was known as Moi's project or project Uhuru. Since then, Africa has witnessed many replications of conducting transparent, free and fair elections in some countries such as Nigeria in 2015 where the incumbent president Goodluck Ebele Jonathan was defeated by opposition candidate Muhamad Buhari. So, by underscoring such replications in various Africa countries, one can say that Kaunda did not only transform himself from a one-party dictator to the father of democracy of Zambia but also created a precedent in the whole continent. Kaunda's faith in democracy enabled other leaders to follow suit at the very time nobody expected they thought about that let alone doing it.

Arguably, Kaunda's sense of humanity–like Nyerere's–made him a benevolent dictator who did not kill his opponent or rob Zambia. As a down-to-earth or a salt-of-the-earth person, Kaunda was open and straightforward in his policies. He may have some failures just like any manager; Kaunda still performed his duties as a president humbly and compassionately. Despite ruling under one party as it was a norm then. I must emphasise this. Kaunda has never been accused of killing or sending his opponents to exile just like his counterpart in neighbouring Malawi did. This is phenomenal so to speak. So, too Kaunda has never faced any corruption allegations. No rumours have ever made any round in Zambia alleging that Kaunda amassed wealth.

Before the tumble of copper price, Zambia's chief export, Kaunda and his wife, the late Betty, used to bike and appear in public without any security details. At the time, Zambians used to enjoy copper money. Verily, Kaunda understood that the *love* Zambians showed him had the strings attached. This love was basically revolving around positive economic performance. He knew that it would not exist or be there forever. He knew this *copper love* would quickly evaporate when things took a slump. And indeed, after the economy tanked, the very love evaporated. English proverb has it that when poverty comes in at the door, love flies out of the window. Therefore, after the price of copper plummeted; and Zambia's economy took a hit, Kaunda openly told Zambians that they would not see him anymore in the streets freely biking with his wife as he used to do. Again, the plunge of copper price could not be blamed on Kaunda. The *New York Times* (Ibid), wrote that "Mr. Kaunda imposed economic sanctions against the secessionist white Rhodesian Government of Ian D. Smith at great cost to the Zambian economy and its prime product, copper." Like his great friend Nyerere, Kaunda contributed immensely to the liberation of Southern African countries that were still under the grip of colonialism in Angola, Mozambique, Namibia, South Africa and Zimbabwe. As the head of the state, Kaunda had to sacrifice a lot to see to it that these countries gained their independence. There was nothing eminently dangerous for Zambia's security like Kaunda's decision to allow the *Umkhoto we Sizwe* (MK) or the spear of the nation, the African National Congress' (ANC) military wing to establish its headquarters in Lusaka from where it carried its attacks on South Africa. Due to the proximity, this action put Zambia in more danger than Tanzania which does not share border with South Africa. The editorial of Tumfweko Zambia *News and Entertainment* (December 27th, 2013) noted that "the ANC was headquartered in Roma while members of the military wing of ANC, MK, were based in Lilanda area." Looking at the proximity, Kaunda's decision was the result of a daring and fearless leader who is not afraid of taking risks. The Newspaper went on complaining that Kaunda's contribution in championing the freedom of Mandela was underestimated by international media. Essentially, the falling of copper price became another straw that broke the camel's back. Zambia had much on its table than it could chew. Again, based on humanism, Kaunda would not stop taking such a risk. He cherished and accentuated the centrality of freedom to human life which—to him—was nonnegotiable and deserved any sacrifice as long as his actions would add up as they did. Knowing how hard the situation would become, Kaunda, *sans doute*, had to face Zambians and tell them what they did not like to hear. Such a situation was tricky and tremendously tantalising. For, telling Zambians the real situation would discourage them. Again, Kaunda did not hesitate to do so. If he did not tell them the truth, Zambians would not have prepare themselves to take the challenge up as they heroically did for the whole period their country supported the struggle in South Africa. Therefore, Kaunda told the Zambians the bitter truth that he knew many people would hate him due to the predicaments they were facing; and the hard times that would follow thereafter. Such a move did not need only the courage but the courage of the mad and big heart altogether. What straightforwardness! How many African managers were able to say such things knowingly their consequences?

The other time Kaunda shocked Zambians is the time they asked him to retire from presidency. He openly said that his heart still needed to be in office. Therefore, Kaunda would retire when voters vote him out as they did in 1991. To live up to his words, when his successor started to mess and monkey with everything, the same Zambians who voted Kaunda out wanted him to come back. As noted above, he refused telling them that he knew they would remember and want him back. But it was too late. He did not run or influence the politics of Zambia to his advantage or like or interest. Furthermore, as honest, trustworthy and straightforward person, Kaunda left Zambians and the world at large wondering when he publicly said that one of his sons, Masuzgo Gwebe Kaunda, died of HIV/AIDS (Dec. 21st, 1986). The *New York Times* (October 5th, 1987) quoted Kaunda as saying "how my son got AIDS I don't know." Kaunda admitted of the death of his son at the time HIV/AIDS deaths were treated as a secret for fear of embarrassment and stigmatisation for the family of the deceased. As a powerful person, Kaunda would have coerced or coxed doctors to write a favourable report on the death of his son. But he did not. He wanted his people and the world to know that HIV/AIDS was the menace that would kill everybody regardless her or his station in the society. Thereafter, another prominent son of Africa, Nelson Mandela, did exactly the same by openly saying that his elder son, Makgatho Lewanika Mandela, died of HIV/AIDS. The *Washington Post* (January 5th, 2005) quoted Mandela as saying, "My son has died of AIDS," (p. 10). Such admission needs honesty and big heart, especially, for the person who was president. Again, Kaunda, and Mandela did it *manifestment*.

Kaunda's leadership skills kept Zambia united and harmonious for the whole time he was in power. The foundations Kaunda laid down have kept Zambia peaceable and one even after vacating the office of president. For, Zambia is among a few African countries that have never been under military junta. All this tranquillity, and of course, stability are credited to Kaunda's charisma and skills as a manager of state affairs. The foundations he laid are firm. Kaunda was not afraid of openly showing his true self, hobbies and aversions. Many Zambians remember his love of soccer and music that gave Zambia National Football Team a moniker of KK or Kenneth Kaunda. His song *Tiende pamodzi ndi mtima umwe* or *Let's Walk Together in One Spirit* has never escaped the hearts and minds of Zambians. Kaunda had a very unique rapprochement with his people. However, he was accused of being undemocratic. Easterly (2001) maintains that Kaunda discriminated against Bemba, one of the biggest tribe in Zambia for sympathising with opposition, by favouring his Nyanja speaking tribe, (p. 688). Whether this is true or not depends on how one looks at Kaunda. Arguably, despite such accusations, there is no recorded time at which Zambia tangibly suffered from any tribalism under Kaunda's watch. I remember; sometimes, in Tanzania, his friend, Mwl Julius Nyerere was accused of favouring Roman Catholics simply because he was one of them. When research was conducted, it came to light that he was the only practising catholic in his government; and the second was his minister who had already acquired a second wife as opposed to catholic *diktat*. To gauge the truth and just accusations, Sklar (1983) differs with Easterly (Ibid) observing that:

> In Zambia, the concept of participatory democracy was introduced as a national goal by President Kenneth D. Kaunda (1968, p. 20) in 1968. Subsequently, Kaunda (1971, p. 37) construed the concept to connote democratic participation in all spheres of life, so that "no single individual or group of individuals shall have a monopoly of political, economic, social or military power," (p. 16).

As argued above, whether Kaunda was a tribal leader or not, depends on how you look at him. Looking at Sklar compared to

Easterly, one can notice a schism in analysing Kaunda. This is normal in social sciences given that whenever one makes a claim, has to substantiate it. To avoid confusion and misleading allegations, there is a simple barometer one can use to gauge whether a former leader was fair or unfair. Normally, especially in Africa, gauging how former leaders performed becomes easy. You just look at how they are treated by the successors after relinquishing power. Even though, Kaunda was maltreated by Chiluba, this move did not succeed. And in some African countries former leaders are protected by the successor for the fear of facing the same after retiring or just because they are their protégés or such leaders are spotless. When Chiluba humiliated Kaunda, many Zambians condemned it. Kaunda's personal integrity saw him out of this manmade debacle by which his successor wanted to humiliate him in vain. Ironically, Chiluba ended up in a bigger quandary than the one he had created to shame and humiliate Kaunda. Many Zambians would testify that Kaunda would not harm anybody let alone attempting to overthrow the government which is a political crime of high order in many African countries which is punishable by death. When it comes to other criminal cases, two things oft-haunt Africa former presidents, either they live by being protected by their successors, or their dirty linens are put on the agora; and thereby become a laughingstock if not ending up behind bars. Kaunda did not face any of the two. First of all, he had no protégé to protect him due to the fact that he did not handpick or support or groom anybody to take over after him. Secondly, Kaunda did not need or want protection. Instead, his personal integrity and clean records enabled him to live comfortably after exiting power which is rare in Africa. A noticeable few former presidents lived honourably and without any disturbance thanks to their integrity. These are Kaunda, Mandela, Nyerere and Leopold Sedar Senghor. However, there were other honest and diligent leaders who were maltreated by their successors despite having committed no crimes whatever. Such are former and first president of Cameroon Ahmadou Ahidjo who died in exile in Senegal and his remains have never been returned home and be reburied honourably by the person he ceded power to, Paul Biya, Cameroonian long-time dictator. Another victim of political uprightness was Somali's first president, Aden Abdullah Osman Daar, after being defeated in election by his

81

former Prime Minister; Abdirashid Ali Shermarke in 1967. Daar lived a normal life up until he was imprisoned in 1990 for expressing his views against the former tyrant Mohamed Siad Barre. Daar was released after the fall of Barre a year after and lived a normal life until he died in Somalia at the age of 99 years old. Those were the lucky ones. Most of the founders of African countries were toppled and other killed.

What's more, dignified life after presidency shows how trustworthy and incorrupt Kaunda was. Different from many who abused their offices, Kaunda, just like Nyerere (who died honourably in Tanzania) still lives in Zambia where he is revered as the founder of the nation. His life is different from the lives of former presidents such as Milton Obote (Uganda) whom Kaunda accommodated for long time; and Kwame Nkrumah (Ghana) who were overthrown so as to die in exile.

> *"We have no choice, as a young Nation landlocked and surrounded by hostile forces, but to work very hard for national survival and national fulfilment. Drunkenness, road accidents, indiscipline, laziness, selfishness, exaggerated feelings of self-importance; ignorance and disease are among the worst enemies of our society. They frustrate the efforts of selfless, dedicated workers. We must fight with a will to win. We cannot afford to lose. Our first victory against the enemy lies in the unity of purpose and action to build a free, strong and prosperous Zambia,"* Kenneth Kaunda, in Nkosi (2011, pp. 65-66).

Kaunda's legacy

Kenneth Kaunda (KK) will be remembered as the manager of public affairs who did not rob his country. Even after relinquishing power, he is still living comfortably and honourably in his country as a founding father and a statesman. No corruption allegations have ever heaved on him. As noted above, Kaunda united Zambia under his slogan of *One Zambia, One Nation* which made the country peaceable despite being surrounded by countries that were still under colonialism. Like Nyerere, Kaunda turned Zambia into a hub for freedom fighters in Southern African region by providing headquarters to many liberation movements. Kaunda's leadership was guided by the philosophy of collectively running of the business of the state. His famous song *Tiende Pamodzi* or *Let us Walk Together* referred to above speaks volume not to mention his love of football which resulted to calling Zambia's national football team KK the initials of his name. Also, Kaunda left another indelible mark on fashion. His Kaunda suit will always be called so and worn by many in Africa not to forget his white handkerchief that has always been in his hands as a symbol of peace for the man and his mission not to forget the nation. One Zambian once said that Kaunda was more than a president. He was a marque, especially if we consider what came to be Kaunda Suit, a simple suit unique and that started to surface after Kaunda invented it. Indeed, even this is his legacy for future generations.

Kaunda will also be remembered as the leader who wanted to see Africa united. His vision for Zambia was huge, mainly thwarting tribalism without using force. He will always be a point of reference *vis-à-vis* conceding defeat as he did in 1991 when he lost in the general elections that saw his exit from power. So, too, Kaunda will be remembered and honoured for not interfering in the government of his successor something he would have done if he wanted.

Just like anybody else, Kaunda was no angel. One of the weaknesses is that he left power unwillingly, as noted above, after being defeated in the general election in 1991. Furthermore, Kaunda will be remembered for his inability to conceal his emotions. When anything that would trigger his tears happened, contrary to African beliefs that a man should not cry, Kaunda would not subdue or conceal his emotion even where he is supposedly expected to "tough it out" as an African man who should not show his weakness like a woman. Such a trait depends on how you look at it. Sometimes, it can be seen as a sign of sincerity and openness or weakness.

"No price is too high to pay for freedom," Kaunda (January 1, 1998).

PHILIPS

PHILIPS

45

Prod. by
**Philips
Electrical Ltd.
Zambia**

PZ 1B

PZ 1

TIYENDE PAMODZI
Zambia Cabinet and Central
Committee led by President
KENNETH KAUNDA
Recorded at State House, Lusaka by
Zambia Broadcasting Services

Chapter 6

Balewa the Symbol of National Unity

Figure 9: Sir Abubakar T. Balewa Nigeria's 1st PM (image courtesy of BBC)

Sir Abubakar Tafawa Balewa (December, 1912–15 January, 1966) inherited a sharply divided country (Kirk-Green, 1975; Nwozor 2014; and Tsaior 2015). The country was dividing along north-south and Christian-Muslim divide that the British colonial rule created under its famous divide-and-rule strategy which was firstly introduced in Nigeria by Fredrick Lugard. It was aimed at weakening Nigeria in order to perpetually exploit it even after the British colonial monsters had left. Delicate as the situation was, it needed a person like Balewa whom Brown-Peterside (1966) defines as an "incarnation of faith and love, and a symbol of national unity and peace," (p. 15). Sir Balewa was not only a symbol of unity for Nigeria but also a trustworthy manager of the business of the state. Nyerere cited in Brown-Peterside (Ibid) defines him as "a statesman who earned respect of everybody who conducted business with him," (p. 17). Remember. Nyerere is one of the greatest presidents Africa has ever produced as we have seen above in his chapter. Thanks to divide and rule that created tribal acrimony in Nigeria, Balewa became the first victim of this crime in Nigeria. Grant, *et al.,* (2014) observe that "Sir Abubakar Tafawa Balewa, fell victim to the nation's persistent tribal animosity after ruling for five tempestuous years," (p. 30). As it was in the case of the DRC, Nigeria became weak for a democratic government to rule after the sudden death of Sir Balewa. The same occurred in the neighbouring Ghana not to mention other post-colonial African nations such as Burundi, Rwanda and Uganda, among others, that became the victims of tribal animosity as colonial monsters created and planted it.

This volume has proposed many yardsticks to evaluate who were the best or worst African leaders and rulers respectively. One of those qualities is the unification of Africa as the means of having a united and strong Africa. Balewa (cited in Padelford 1964) says that his country stood for a pragmatic united Africa that would be based on agreement to certain essentials, (p. 532). This is the language that Lumumba, Nkrumah and Nyerere, *inter alia,* used in defining their policies *vis-a-vis* the unification of Africa. It is not an accident that Balewa took such a stand. Just like any Pan Africanist, he knew the danger such words posed to the imperialists that wanted to see Africa fragmented as they concocted it to be for the purpose of weakening and exploiting it. Balewa too knew how vulnerable he was thanks to his stance as far as the unification of Africa is concerned. However, there are those who think Balewa signed his death warrant for trusting British colonial rule that wanted him to be its extension in Nigeria. Nkrumah cited in Padelfold (Ibid) notes that "what Sir Abubaker and his government succeeded to do was an artificial stage created to suit the needs of twentieth century imperialism," (p. 16). One would argue that Balewa would not impress Nkrumah due to the fact that he hated communism openly despite sharing the same vision and dream of unifying Africa. Apart from his detestation to communism, Balewa was not a bad administrator of public business, especially at the time all African countries were divided right in the middle by the cold war. So, too, such allegations prove how African leaders even those we hold high became the victims of divide and rule based on the *realpolitik* and geopolitics of the time whereby either one allied with the East or the West up until the Non-Aligned Movement (NAM) was formed in Belgrade Yugoslavia in September, 1961, (Nixon, 2016, p. 154). I understand, just like Balewa, Nkrumah was accused of heavy-handedness in his administration during his tenure as president of Ghana. Despite being the best administrator of public business, even Nyerere was accused of the vice. I am not trying to be devil's advocate. It is obvious; nobody is an angel, particularly in such cutthroat politics.

The blame game resulting from divide and rule has gone on almost in all African countries facing ethnic and sectarian conflicts. In Nigeria, for example, when Biafra sought to secede from Nigeria, it was blamed on being used by communists. Those who created the mess in Nigeria were the first to either blame or jump into the bandwagon to *resolve* the conflict. Such mentality of blaming those in ethnoconflicts can be seen in the words of Post (1968) who blames Nigeria for being as sick as Congo (Kinshasa) he refers to as "the sick man of Africa," (p. 26). Post is accusing Nigeria of ethnoconflicts without mentioning the British that created them. This has been the take of the world in blaming victims alone without including those who invented divide and rule which caused all these conflicts.

To the contrary, Post (Ibid) goes on showing how British created all ethnoconflicts Nigeria has ever experienced noting that:

When Britain carved out Nigeria for itself it created, in the words of one of the more enlightened colonial experts 'perhaps the most artificial of the many administrative units created in the course of the European occupation of Africa," (p. 27).

Post shows the illogicality ethnoconflicts draw even for those analysing them. He started by blaming Nigeria for its failure that borders it with another failed state of the time, the DRC (then Congo Kinshasa before it was renamed Zaire then the DRC). Post realises his mistake of hurling insults at, and blaming Nigeria so as to note that Britain is the one that created such an artificial political entity to foster its interests even after attaining independence as it has ever been for many African countries. Aghedo (2014) concurs with Post arguing that "the colonial state was largely created to serve the economic interests of the imperialists, helping to ensure law and order and guarantee an environment that enabled the colonialists to expand their interests," (p. 2). Such adherence to law and order would have been impossible without divide and rule. Aghedo goes far deeper so as to connect Boko Haram, an Islamic fundamentalist terrorist group operating currently in Nigeria, Chad and Cameroon, to divide and rule whereby Muslims in Nigeria were left out of colonial education system so as to become disgruntled after independence. Aghedo (Ibid) argues that the foot soldiers of the group have been the unemployed, poor and uneducated, especially from the "Kanuri nationality," (p. 5). Again, looking at how Boko Haram insurgence is misconstrued as an Islamic move against Christian and secular government, one may *essentiellement* underscore how divide and rule is safely and elusively still entrenched in Nigeria's ethnoconflicts. Whatever definition Boko Haram will be given, and whatever ideology it will use, the truth remains that it is an offshoot of divisive policies British colonial administration left behind in Nigeria after creating divide-and-rule stratagem.

Whereas British colonisers used one communities against others based on their ethnic history, they expanded the practice so as to include more elements as Christopher (1988) notes that it surpassed the simple Christian-Heathen or English-foreigner dichotomy replacing it with "ever more elaborate classifications as governments divided and re-divided populations into discrete groups, on the basis of linguistics, religion, ethnicity and skin colour," (p. 233). Instead of dividing Nigeria along tribal lines, colonisers divided it along religion and region even though tribalism still does exist in Nigeria.

To know who Abubakar Tafawa Balewa actually was his first speech as the Prime Minister of Nigeria may shed light on the person. He made this speech to the nation in September 1957 as he accepted his new appointment and outlined the political future of Nigeria he wanted to manage and build.

This has been a great day for Nigeria, and, as the first Prime Minister of the Federation of Nigeria, I am proud to speak to my fellow-countrymen tonight. I am proud, and I am humble, too, when I think of the enormous responsibility which has been placed upon me, and my colleagues.

Today, we have set out on the last stage of our journey to Independence, and the next three years will see the culmination of a process which has been gathering momentum year by year, and will see us reaping the harvest of what we have sown. The success of the harvest will depend upon us, and that is why I am glad to speak to you tonight. Everyone of us has his part to play in the work of preparing Nigeria for Independence on the 2nd of April, 1960.

I want everyone in Nigeria to realise that this is no easy task, and it cannot be performed by the Federal and Regional Ministers and legislators alone. It is a task for everyone of you because it is only by the personal effort of each individual that Independence for the Federation can become a reality in 1960.

We have declared our intention of attaining Independence for the Federation on the 2nd of April, 1960, and if we wish to take our place among the responsible nations of the world, we must make every effort to see that this aim is achieved, and achieved with an international reputation for good internal government.

Nigeria has now reached a critical stage in her history. We must seize the opportunity which has been offered to us to show that we are able to manage our own affairs properly. Every Nigerian, whatever his status, and whatever his religion, has his or her share to contribute to this crucial task. I appeal to all my countrymen and women to cooperate with me and my colleagues to create a better understanding among our peoples, to establish mutual respect, and trust, among all our tribal groups, and to unite in working together for the common cause, the cause for which no sacrifice will be too great.

I am convinced, and I want you also to be convinced, that the future of this vast country must depend, in the main, on the efforts of ourselves to help ourselves. This we cannot do if we do not work together in unity. Indeed, unity today is our greatest concern, and it is the duty off everyone of us to work so that we may strengthen it. This morning I said in the House of Representatives that bitterness due to political differences would carry Nigeria nowhere, and I appealed to the political leaders throughout the country to control their party extremists. To you who are listening tonight I repeat that appeal—Let us put away bitterness and go forward in friendship to Independence.

To further this overriding need for unity, my colleagues in the Council of Ministers and I have decided to give the country a lead by inviting the leaders of the Action Group to form with us a truly National Government composed of members of the main parties in the Country, and here I must pay tribute to Dr Azikiwe, to Chief Awolowo, Dr Endeley and to the leader of my own party, the Sardauna of Sokoto, for supporting me in this decision. I and my Colleagues of the N.C.N.C. and N.P.C. bold out our hands in welcome to the Action Group members of the Council and I promise you that we shall do our utmost to ensure that the deliberations of the Council are held in an atmosphere devoid of strife and narrow party prejudice.

And now I would like to say a word to the civil service. We are grateful to all the civil servants, through whose work the country has reached the present stage of political development. I know that every constitutional advance puts a great strain on the civil service. Not only is there additional work to be done, but some officers find it hard to accept the new changes, but I must emphasize that Nigeria has today taken another important step forward, and if we are to succeed we must have the loyalty of all Nigerian and expatriate officers in this vital period before self-government is achieved. I should like to reassure all our expatriate staff of our continued Sincerity in the pledges given over the last few years and to promise them that they need have no fears about their future. Their aim and our aim remains what it has always been—the welfare and prosperity of Nigeria. Our political advance will be of no value if it is not supported by economic progress. It is therefore most important that the development plans throughout the country should be carried out with vigour in order that we may have a proper financial standing when, in three years' time, we ask the world to regard us as an independent self-governing nation.

I would like to remind you of what a great American once said. It was this, 'United we stand, divided we fall'. This statement is as true for Nigeria today as it has been for any other country. The peoples of Nigeria must be united to enable this country to play a full part in shaping the destiny of mankind. On no account should we allow the selfish ambitions of individuals to jeopardise the peace of the thirty-three million law-abiding people of Nigeria. It is the duty of all of us to work for unity and encourage members of all our communities to live together in peace and harmony. The way to do this is to create understanding, mutual respect and trust. It is important that we should first show respect to each other before asking the world to respect us.

Well—it is time for me to wish you good night, but first I would Once more tell you how absolutely vital it is for your future and the future Nigeria which your children will inherit that, during this interim period before Independence we should be united. Let us be honest with ourselves, and let us be sincere—we know what we want, and we are sure that we can get it, and get it at the right time, provided we are not delayed by selfish quarrels. At a time like this, we must all turn our minds to Almighty God and seek His guidance and assistance—by His grace, we shall succeed.

Source: Nigerian National Press, Ltd., 1964. - See more at: http://www.blackpast.org/1957-abubakar-tafawa-balewa-first-speech-prime-minister#sthash.dWYfmmTv.dpuf

Special tributes

There is no way one can write the history of the liberation of Nigeria without mentioning those who contributed immensely.

Those are Dr. Nnandi Azikiwe, as an editor of the *African Morning Post*, he used his pen to liberate his people. Also, Obafemi Awolowo played a great role in the liberation of Nigeria. No words can agreeably define Ken Saro Wiwa who fought for the second liberation of Nigeria so as to be hanged for his fiery opposition to dictatorship.

Chapter 7

Was Ahidjo Unsung Hero?

Figure 10: Ahmadou B. Ahidjo Cameroon's 1st President (image courtesy of BBC Afrique)

Ahmadou Babatoura Ahidjo (24 August, 1924–30 November, 1989) is Cameroonian founding father who ruled from 5 May, 1960 to 6 November, 1982 (Nyamndi, 2009). Under his watch, the country saw relative peace even thereafter despite rampant corruption his successor, Paul Biya who is among long–time serving presidents in Africa has always presided over. To the contrary, Ahidjo presided over what Pondi (1997) calls "a commonwealth of nations." Apart from unifying two Cameroons, another nugget that Ahidjo left is the fact that he wrote books just like other founders of his time which is missing now. Some of his books, among others, are *Contribution à la construction nationale, Ahidjo, Ahmadou. Anthologie des discours, 1957-1979,* and "*La pensée politique d'Ahmadou Ahidjo.* On top of that, Ahidjo is commended for reunifying Cameroon. Fonlon (1963; 1965 cited in Awasom 2000) idealised Cameroon under Ahidjo as "the crucible of African unity," in which according to Ahmadou Ahidjo and John Ngu Foncha, stood tall as the architects of reunification," (p. 91) also see Mbaku 2004. However, there are those who see the unification of Cameroon as plebiscite of the United Nations but not the idea of the founders. Awasom (2002) is in dissonance with Fonlon maintaining that "neither Foncha nor Ahidjo originated the reunification ideology, but the two statesmen ended up being taken its hostages," (p. 428). Whether the unification of Cameroon was Ahidjo's and Foncha's project or UN's, it remains to be said that it has been successful where many failed despite having simmering differences between the two Cameroons as Fonka (1999) says that Anglophones and Francophones "are still strange bedfellows," (p. 292); also see Ambe (2004); Besong (2005); and Achankeng (2015). So, too, despite whatever controversies, it is a fact that Ahidjo launched, executed and presided over the whole project of unifying Cameroon. And indeed, when it comes to the vision of unifying Africa, the Cameroonian union still has a lot to offer as per Ahidjo's vision. Dibussi Tande (2006 cited in Nfi 2013) quotes Ahidjo saying that:

> Reuniting today people of both French and English expression, Cameroon will be a veritable laboratory for an African Union which will unite people who speak two languages. She will be a bridge between these two Africans, and her role can only be increased in forthcoming African Assemblies, (p. 126).

Arguably, it needed a good and focused administrator of the business of the state to underscore such palms. Due to this grand vision of the reunification of Africa, Awasom (Ibid) observes that:

> The Organization of African Unity (OAU) rewarded the Cameroon nation for its peculiar Pan-African posture by naming two Secretary Generals from Cameroon: Nzo Ekanghaki (1972-1974) and William Eteki Mboumoua (1974-1978)," (p. 92).

Essentially, since the OAU was formed in on 25 May, 1963 in Addis Ababa, Ethiopia, apart from Cameroon, no country has ever produced two Secretary Generals. Also, no country has ever produced two secretary generals who run the organisation consecutively as it is in the case of Cameroon. Once again, this proves how Ahidjo contributed immensely to the vision of the unification of Africa despite the fact that it has never been achieved thanks to the ongoing divide and rule as copied by many African rulers who took over after the founders exited a political scene in Africa. Furthermore, Ahidjo was ahead of his time. When some African countries that colonial monsters cobbled together aimed at creating and fuel tribal animosity—as it was the case of the neighbouring Nigeria—were at loggerheads, Ahidjo envisaged the federation of Cameroon. Moreover, this was done just soon after acquiring independence the time at which many founders were still learning how to rule their newly-independent countries.

To the contrary, other founders their colonial masters used as indirect rulers of their countries, Ahidjo was the person who would unequivocally say no to colonial monsters as he did. Pondi (Ibid) notes that "Ahidjo took a series of bold steps that contributed to establish Cameroon's independent status *vis-à-vis* Paris," (p. 566). At the time, such "bold steps' taken by a newly-independent country were not heard of in many African countries. Some who became bold such as Lumumba were killed even before bracing themselves in the seat of power. If they were any bold steps that had already been taken, they were only taken by Guinean founding father Ahmed Sekou Toure who refused to take orders from Paris simply because his country was receiving some handouts from France in the name of aid. Furthermore, Ahidjo did not support any cessation in Africa. Pondi (op.cit.) goes on noting that "Yaoundé flatly refused to support the cause of Biafra despite personal pressure from General De Gaulle himself" whom many leaders of French ex-colonies feared the most. This shows the spirit of the unification of Africa apart the independent mind that Ahidjo had. However, after vacating the office, his successor Paul Biya reversed almost everything as far as acrimony between Cameroon and France is concerned. Getney (1983 cited in Berry, *et al.*, (1983) discloses that Biya chose France as his principal economic partner, (p. 3). This is normal. Sometimes, when a lion dies, rats can eat its buckskin.

Despite performing well, Ahidjo had a dark side. His administration attracted fundamentally mixed feelings and reactions as far as democracy is concerned. Again, due to the cold war politics and *realpolitik* of the time, nobody would expect Ahidjo to have been an exception to the general rule by embarking on a different type of democracy from the one many of his colleagues practiced at the time.

Bridge (1987) notes that Ahidjo did not stomach opposing views, something his successor expanded on (p. 40) so as to end up turning Cameroon into his private estate he can mismanage as he deems fit. Comparably, Ahidjo performed better than his successor. The way he calibrated and configured Cameroon made it what it actually is today. Despite accusations that Ahidjo was not truly a democrat, the country was relatively peaceable compared to its neighbours such as Nigeria that experienced and evidenced many bouts of military takeovers for a long time. To the contrary, Eckert (1999) notes that under Ahidjo's tyranny the government machinery was omnipresent in order to quash any form of political opposition and expression was censored, (p. 289). Ironically, despite taking such stern measures, Ahidjo ended up being forced to relinquish power by his prime minister, the current president Paul Biya who has not changed anything for the better, except exacerbating the situation as far as mismanaging the state business is concerned. In spite of all this, the country is still peaceable thanks to the political infrastructure that Ahidjo left in place. Cameroon has never experienced any coup or any mass actions. This is subject to discussion whether it is because of the peaceability of Cameroonians or fear of the brutality the government can unleash shall they take on it.

Despite his wanting qualities regarding true democracy, one thing that makes Ahidjo a good manager but not the best is the fact that he was able to unify British and French Cameroons to form one country the United Republic of Cameroon on June, 2nd, 1972, (Stark 1976, p. 423). Given that the reunification of Africa is the only recipe that is missing in making Africa better, whoever subscribed to or attempted to unite it or his country with another, will always be recommended for setting the tone for a full-fledge unification of Africa. There are some reasons why such a bold steps, *inter alia*, that Ahidjo took, makes him better than those who brutalised and robbed their country so as to end up in chaos after they were unseated. We are not trying to justify Ahidjo's bad acts. Sometimes, the truth about true Ahidjo's rule depends on which side of the divide–among Cameroonians–one belongs. Again, when it comes to any force that can redirect Africa to its rightful path of desired unification, there is no way we can ignore it. United we stand; and divided we fall. The sage has it. Ahidjo is commended for having reached this milestone when some of regions and politicians vigorously failed. The reunification of Cameroon that was, essentially a hunch and step towards realigning Africa to head for its true nature before it was divided by colonial monsters, gives Ahidjo a niche in the list of good managers of Africa's business. Being able to unify such two colonies with precariously different languages, geographical positions as well as two different colonial monsters to get a very peaceable country is indeed recommendable.

Ahidjo's legacy

Apart from being a founding father, Ahidjo will be remembered as the person who unified Cameroon despite some shortfalls. Nyamnjoh and Fokwang (2005) note that "President Ahmadou Ahidjo, came to epitomise national unity and modernization" (p. 254) not only politically but also musically. As well, Ahidjo did not rob his country just like those who succeeded him. Ahidjo gets another accolade of being able to let power go when feuds between him and his successor Biya, ultimately ensued and surfaced to the fore. If Ahidjo were a power monger and power-crazy monster, he would have stood his ground something that would have divided the country given that both protagonists had huge following in Cameroon's politics. Again, Ahidjo decided to avoid authoring a cliffhanger that would have paralysed and polarised the country unnecessarily. Furthermore, Ahidjo would have caused a lot of troubles if he clung to power; and feuded over it. Looking at the time he spent in power, he definitely must have people who were ready to back him either for personal or national interests. Again, sensing what squabbling would cause to his country, Ahidjo decided to let go leaving power to Biya—a long time kleptocrat—that pulled Cameroon back despite its peaceability.

Chapter 8

Senghor the Debatable Philosopher

"The nature of being, contrary to what people say, is not to persevere in being, but as Teilhard de Chardin wrote, to reach for the higher being, fullness where his happiness resides. But, since the universe is united, leaving from the God source and ending up in the God centre, to attain the universe while re-establishing the troubled order, while reinforcing the weakened force, it is to reinforce oneself by reaching God through human society," Leopold Sedar Senghor (1977 cited in Champion, (2010, p. 11).

Figure 11: Leopold S. Senghor Senegal's 1st President (image courtesy of AFP)

Leopold Sedar Senghor (9th October, 1906–20th December, 2001) was the first president of Senegal who was renowned for his philosophy of negritude which means blackness (Adejumo 2016, p. 2). Also, Senghor is a distinguished writer who contributed to African literature immensely. He is the first African professor to become president who ruled responsibly by the standards of the time. The

New York Times (December 21ˢᵗ, 2001) writes that "among African leaders, Mr. Senghor was the chief theoretician of négritude, or "blackness," his definition for the common culture and spiritual heritage of the black peoples of Africa. In one of his earliest poems, "Totem"" (page not provided). As it was for the leaders of his time, Senghor was not only president but also a thinker who articulated his philosophy so that those he led could grasp what he wanted to do for his country. Despite being president, Senghor still wrote just like any writer could do. He wrote introductions for other authors who asked him to do so despite being president. This is encouraging *vis-à-vis* his enthusiasm about education.

At the time Senghor was in power, some, if not all, African leaders, at least, wrote books or articles in the newspapers as the means of communicating their ideas to their people and the world in general. However, as the time went by, the culture for presidents to write books died, largely after African leaders started to use their offices as the spoons for raking money that made them tycoons who got in power promising to serve the people. Instead of serving the people, they used, abused and robbed them wantonly. Unlike corrupt, venal and myopic rulers, Senghor did not use his power or people to become well-heeled just like Houphouët-Boigny and Mobutu among others. Experience shows that most of African leaders who followed socialism were less corrupt compared to capitalistic ones. Cohen (1972) maintains that "some African leaders, notably Senghor, have, however, attempted to generalise the description of such societies to presignify the achievement of a continent-wide socialism," (p. 231). Their belief was based on the equality and sameness of Africa as a whole. You can look at Senghor, Kaunda, Nyerere, and Sekou Toure. They had their burdens but not personal greed for wealth.

Unlike vocal leaders such as Lumumba, Nkrumah and Nyerere who shaped the future of Africa, especially on the quest for the unification of Africa, Senghor did not become as instrumental as those mentioned colleagues were. He became more famous in literature than in the politics of Africa at the time. Arguably, his vision of the nation was narrower than what Nkrumah and Nyerere envisaged. Senghor (1974) for example, says that, for him, the nation to be a "truly nation" must have personality of its own, (p. 191). This statement depicts a small nation that is Senegal but not a super nation of Africa due to the fact that Senghor was responding to the question: Can we hear something literary from Senegal? Had he had Africa in his mind, this question was suitable for him to cross the borders, and expand it to encompass the whole continent. But Senghor did not do so. Therefore, by having a narrow view of the nation as opposed to the larger Africa minimised his influence in uniting Africa. Nobody can tell why Senghor–despite being highly educated and a philosopher, of course–limited himself to local politics while the needs of the time for Africa were, *inter alia,* about the unification of Africa which aimed at forming a very influential and powerful continental country that would rival other continents. Senghor (1961) goes further arguing that Senegal has a privileged geographical position due to the fact that the city of Dakar is the gate to south Atlantic, and its political position is special, (p. 242). This is not the language of the unifier. His words do not link Africa with the world. Instead, they do so for Senegal only. If Nkrumah and Nyerere were asked the same question, obviously, their answers would expand from their countries so as to cover the entire continent.

Despite his narrow view that made him concentrate greatly on the business of his country as opposed to the business of the continent, Senghor was still the best manager of the business of his country. One of the qualifications that put him in the category of the best African managers of state business is the fact that he was the first African president to willingly relinquish power; and thereby enhance swift power transition in his country the precedent others followed. Senghor relinquished presidential power on December 31st, 1980 after ruling the country for twenty years. Like Nyerere, he then was 63 years which is relatively a young age compared to Senegal's third president, Abdulaye Wade, who came to power at the age of 74. Secondly, after Senghor willingly relinquished power, his country remained stable different from others that fell in bedlam after their long-time rulers either died or were flushed out of office. Senghor's *Wikipedia* notes that he was the first person of African descent to earn a PhD in French. Although such a high degree in French had nothing to do with helping Africa, especially due to the fact that the one who earned it did not use it to disclose the secrets he knew about France, it might have had a big impact on Senghor who seemed to ally himself more to France than to Africa. For, Senghor did not end up with earning the highest degree in French; but also became a French citizen. After acquiring French citizenship in 1932, despite his honesty, Senghor still represented his country France in Senegal as he reciprocated by representing Senegal in France. Such a binary duality is naturally controversial; and it can minimize the affiliation of whoever plays such double roles. At the time Senghor took another citizenship, such a move was more of a divisive tactic by colonial monsters which also was seen; and intended to fool Africans so that they could perceive themselves to be better or more superior than other Africans who did not have dual citizenship. It was a divide and rule based on fake identity that affected somebody's personality and trust among his people. Being a double agent has its consequences. For, there is no way one person can serve two masters at the same time. Sometimes, you can view Senghor as French go-between if not betrayer. All depends on how you analyse him and conceptualise his deeds and stances. Being an academic, Senghor had what it takes to dictate African issues and politics had he been free from French carryovers if not hangovers. Nonetheless, he lost this golden chance that would have placed him higher in the good management and service of Africa. For, he had what it takes to do so just like Julius Nyerere, Kwame Nkrumah even Kenneth Kaunda did *vis-a-vis* the unification of Africa which is significant and important in this volume. Due to this weakness, this is why Senghor's contribution was vital; but not revered just like those of the above mentioned doyens of the liberation and unification of Africa were.

What's more, Senghor had already taught at the university; and had already published profusely and extensively. Therefore, if Senghor decided to exploit this avenue, he would have contributed greatly to the continent. One may argue; despite being an academic, author and a good manager, Senghor seemed to care a lot more about his personal glory encapsulated in Senegal than that of his continent. Also, his weakness namely not to use his skills for the unification of Africa, shows how academics, sometimes, are not good at politics. Again, who knows? Maybe, Senghor wanted to link France and Senegal for the benefit of the country which was counterproductive to the benefit of Africa even Senegal. Whatever his vision in this dualism was, it is obvious that it was contradictory to the goal of uniting Africa.

You can see cultural confusion or philosophic *hermaphroditic* nature–which, if you like, is a deficit in Senghor's approach, especially in analysing and intellectualising some of his thoughts and acts. For example Senghor (1974) maintains that:

If we consider the example of the black Africa, the first among these values, which is of philosophic nature, is that for all black people, the soul is incarnated within the body and more generally the spirit within the matter. In other words the matter and the spirit are in a dialectical relationship, bearing in mind that it was the spirit which first informed the matter, (p. 270).

If we face it, the first question Senghor would have to grapple with is: Was his spirit the same with the one he propounded? Was what he propounded practical for Africans? Who gained from it between Senghor and his country? It defies logic for person who was teaching others to be Africans in mind and spirit to have a second spirit, French one. One would argue that Senghor had cultural trinity; namely African mind, African heritage and French spirit in one matter (his body) which creates a controversy and confusion not only for a reader but also for the philosopher himself. In a sense, if you compare Senghor, his philosophy to Nyerere and his philosophy or Kaunda with his philosophy even doyens like Plato, you find that something was amiss in Senghor's philosophy. While the philosophers mentioned above preached and lived their philosophies, Senghor did not. If Senghor wanted to live negritude, he had to divorce his alliance with France. He would have denounced his French citizenship something he did not do. It surprises to find that such a highly person did not ask himself why it was possible for the president of Senegal to become a French citizen but not the president of France to become the citizen of Senegal as well. The evidence is glaringly clear that when Senghor willingly relinquished power, he exiled to, or he went back to France where he died instead of staying in Senegal, just like any retired statesman, to guide those who took over from him (Campion 2010, p. 4). Experience shows that many Africans go back to their home place when they retire. This is what Nyerere did. So, too Kaunda did and Mandela too. Despite staying in their countries, the above mentioned leaders were too close to their villages than their capital cities after retiring, especially Nyerere more than anybody.

Importantly, we must challenge and hold Senghor accountable at a personal level, as an individual academic, philosopher and politician. However, as president, he was not accused of pilfering his country just like bad managers did. This trait awards Senghor the accolade of being one of the best managers of public affairs in Africa however narrow minded as he was *vis-à-vis* the unification of Africa. It is imperative to underscore that Senghor was not an angel but a "sinner' who was trying as Mandela would put it. It is important that Senghor did not hide his weakness in hypocritical draperies. He wrote whatever he thought; and made it public for others to conceptualise, analyse and carp which is good.

Senghor's poem: *who killed him*, Senghor (1974) may shed light on the man and the confusion he was grippingly facing.

Senghor writes:
Who killed him?
O who killed him
The man with dark skin,
Handsome in the arena
And handsome with eyes closed? (p. 271).

One may say that this man–Senghor is talking about is, ironically, Senghor himself; and it was he who was killed by modernity or aping French culture, on the one hand, while he was glorifying African culture which is a contradiction due to colonial juxtaposition to the two, on the other hand. Philosophically speaking, Senghor's poem shows a person with an unsettled mind who seeks to know who he actually is. Again, this is philosophy. When it comes to public management, at least, Senghor tried; and performed better than many African leaders of his time.

Furthermore, you can see how trapped and confused Senghor was in his own words cited in Skurnik (1965) who notes that:

Along with other Africans being educated in France, Senghor had been taught that, as an African, his mind was *tabula rasa*. Hence he was, at first, ready and willingly to be impregnated with French civilisation. As Senghor later expressed it noting that their "ambition was to become carbon copies of the colonizers namely "black-skinned Frenchmen," (p. 350).

This also raises many questions about Senghor. Again, given that we are analysing his managerial skills regarding public business, his literary works need another rostrum so to speak. However, Oguejiofor (2009 cited in Chimuka 2012) differs sharply from Skurnik observing that:

Senghor's concept of negritude is centred on the misunderstanding or misrepresentation of the African and his heritage, a situation that has since imposed enormous burden on all aspects of his life. It is against this background that negritude becomes a philosophy with clear aims, in particular, the aims of furnishing a corrective measure and of contributing to the amelioration of a state of affairs that has obviously uncomfortable consequences. By this character, negritude aligns itself neatly with the rest of contemporary African philosophy, which seeks to use philosophical reflections as an avenue toward improving the lot of battered Africans, (p. 68).

Therefore, when we argue that French culture is the one that killed that man (Senghor), we may be right or wrong depending on how one looks at, and analyses Senghor and his philosophy. We can expand on Senghor's quest-cum-question of seeking to know who killed that *man*, to cover all these–who coincidentally happen to be men due to our patriarchal system–who ruined Africa. We can arguably get the answers as to who killed a *man* in all those we thought were brilliant leaders that turned out to be letdowns such as, Robert Mugabe, Felix Houphouët-Boigny, *inter alia,* that we will discuss in the section of bad managers that mismanaged the affairs of their countries, in trying to explain why Africa is where it is. Senghor goes on unearthing who he actually was however controversial as it may seem. Senghor (1961) argues that:

As the peoples of French cultural background and language evolve in this manner, the Community will become the same fruitful means of cooperation that the Commonwealth became among the states which are the descendants of British Empire. The new bridges and Europe will be built without mental reservations on the side about colonial domination and without fears in Europe that she is about to be colonized in turn by former colonies, (p. 241).

As argued above, Senghor is like an adopted son who does not want to break away from his abusing foster parents. There is no way one can interweave Senghor argument and strike balance due to the fact that Africa's and West's interests and needs were antagonistic and diametrically opposite. Even in his definition of the people, especially Africans, if you may, Senghor does not touch on their African culture, language and heritage. Instead, he bundles them together along English and French background and languages as if African background and languages are nonexistent. Such flaws can show us who killed the *man* that Senghor wants to know however we do not know what he would have done with that killer if at all he was in bed with him. As a *dead man*, Senghor was trying to revivify the dead who happens to be Senghor himself.

The thing is; Senghor tried to articulate his philosophy however he did not live it just like others. This makes him better than those who did not propound any philosophy or those who came up with harangued and confused philosophies such as *Houphouetism* and *Mobutuism* that ended up being a melange of impracticable and inconceivable disastrous potpourris.

Despite propounding the philosophy of negritude, Senghor did not popularise it by applying it to the whole continent. Skurnik (1965) notes that Senghor's negritude was a method and myth (p. 349) that poses the series of interconnectedness; assumptions which sought to explain the nature and direction of history to serve as a framework for blossoming Africa. As a method, Skurnik (Ibid) argues that Senghor negritude "provides instruments with which to assert and develop material and ideal values of Africa," (Ibid). So, by laying down the philosophical underpinnings by which one would approach socialism, African socialism, Senghor contributed a lot academically despite his personal silence about the unification of Africa creates controversy about his seriousness and belief in what he wrote. Also, one would argue that despite espousing blackness, Senghor was but a cultural mongrel that pooled French and African cultures together something that is, as mentioned above, difficult to reconcile. It is as if Senghor was serving two masters namely negritude and assimilation, French system of turning Africans into French so that they could be used well to run colonial interests in their independent countries and in France. Whereas assimilation was aimed at creating *good boys* before the eyes of colonisers, African negritude was supposed to create *rebels* who would mercilessly take on their masters had it been clearly articulated and exercised.

Essentially, despite his meme, his silence about the unification of Africa denied him a very nice niche in the process and the history of unifying Africa. Again, considering that Senghor was a French citizen, it was a little bit harder for him to carry on such a mission knowing that his other country (French) did not endorse such a commitment. Despite having no political clout on the concept of unifying Africa, Senghor contributed immensely to the awakening of Africans towards self-rule and self-actualisation. His philosophy of negritude contributed a lot academically. Nonetheless, there were some barriers to his philosophy given that it was directed–and of course–benefited a small clique of academics who were not all politicians.

When it comes to economic policies, Senghor proved to be a good manager. Senghor proved to be the master of the art of management and administration for his skilful navigation of religious and cultural differences in Senegal. Fatton (1986) notes that "there was also the Muslim dissatisfaction with both the Senghor inspired *Code de la Famille* adopted in 1972 the increasingly secular behaviour of the urban ruling class," (p. 67). Being a Christian ruling a country with majority Muslims, it needed more skills and vision so to speak. Senghor's strength was basically his ability in exploiting a *maraboutic* clique that he inherited from colonial monsters. Beck (2001) notes that:

As in urban areas, the clientelist networks of ethnic and religious leaders in rural Senegal co-exist with a civil society composed of various voluntary associations, including literacy groups, women's associations, youth groups, and economic interest groups,"(p. 606).

We can argue that Senghor bought in the existing system to see to it that his country enjoyed its independence peacefully. With such a traditional system, social cohesion in the country was robust. Villallon (1999) argues that religious institution in the form of Muslim Sufi orders, were an integral feature of Senegal's stable and relatively democratic socio-political system, (p. 129). This informs us that Senghor was not a tribal lord or a religious fanatic who would favour his co-religionists as he vexed his opponents. Such an argument can be supported by the fact that Muslims still felt justice was done to them despite having a Christian president something that is even harder in many African countries today after many years of independence and sectarian animosities resulting from the ever changing Islam. Maybe, due to the tricky nature of tribal Senegal, it became harder for Senghor to concentrate on Africa. However, if Africa were united, tribal animosities would vanish.

The question that boggles the mind is why didn't Senghor use his fame and influence to champion and execute African union? Was it because he was satisfied with the fame he got in literature or was he busy to manage and control the situation in his country with a very complicated composition of Christians, Muslims and traditional rulers?

> *"(Of the « three musketeers » that we were, Léon Damas, Aimé Césaire and myself, it's Léon Damas, the first to announce négritude with a collection of poems that carried, appropriately, the title of Pigments. Because that poetry conserves all the qualities of black art: symbolic images and rhythm made of asymmetrical parallelisms, but also humour. The black humour, black mark, being reaction and other side of the real: life),"* Leopold Sedar Senghor (1978 cited in Olankule (year not provided. p. 3).

Senghor's legacy
Leopold Sedar Senghor will be remembered as an intellectual politician who relinquished power willingly, and who maintained the unity of his country. His literary works will–forever–be referred to

vis-a-vis the emancipation of an Africa culturally. Selfless as he was, Senghor did not face any allegations of robbing his people.

His weakness, as aforementioned, is his silence about the unification of Africa due to his tunnel vision and narrow view of the concept of the nation.

Chapter 9

Mandela the Peace Maker-cum- *réconciliateur*

"During my lifetime I have dedicated myself to this struggle of the African people. I have fought against white domination, and I have fought against black domination. I have cherished the ideal of a democratic and free society in which all persons live together in harmony and with equal opportunities. It is an ideal which I hope to live for and to achieve. But if needs be, it is an ideal for which I am prepared to die, Nelson Mandela, before the Pretoria Supreme Court," 20 April 1964, Adapted from African National Congress (ANC) website.

Figure 12: Nelson L. Mandela South Africa's 1 st President (image courtesy of Global Research)

No other person Africa has recently produced that would be more revered, loved and ranked higher than Nelson Lolihlahla Mandela (18th July, 1918–5th December, 2013). Only two African personalities can match with Mandela. These are ancient Egyptian King Tutankhamen and ancient Egyptian Queen Neferneferuaten Nefertiti. The difference between the two and Mandela is the fact that the former seem to be numinous while Mandela is not. Nonetheless, Mandela was not loved and revered by chance. He tortuously worked and–for a long time–toiled and suffered for such a station in life. The Apartheid regime in South Africa jailed him for 27 years for fighting for freedom, justice, equality and human rights in the country from 1963 to 1991. Mandela is an African politician who served a longer jail term than anybody. So, too, he is the prisoner that served longer term who became the head of the state. Mathematically speaking, Mandela went into jail when he was 44 and came out when he was 71.

True, when it comes to Mandela, one does not need sources to introduce him to the readership. Mandela was well known all over the world due to his plight, as prisoner, that he turned into presidency. So, too, Mandela was revered and loved because of his down-to-earth comportment. However, the academic tenets require that whoever makes a claim must substantiate it by providing evidence in order to have validity apart from enabling the readership to educate themselves even more about the matter claimed or unpacked. Mandela was a normal human who had more wherewithal than many had. We will honour academic traditions by treating Mandela just like any other human beings as he would like to be treated had he been alive. Was Columbus (year not provided) adumbrates on the case that saw Mandela spending most of his youth and adulthood behind bars noting that the "dramatic final statement from the dock, concluding that the ideal of a democratic and free society ... is an ideal for which I am prepared to die" (p. 581) Mandela told the court. It needed conviction, vision, and above all, the courage of the mad for Mandela to take such a stance while he actually knew its consequences which he was wholeheartedly ready to bear. Many people, particularly autocratic rulers fear death. Refer to many bunkers many rulers spent millions of dollars constructing so as to be used if anything happens. Libyan former strongman, Muamar Gaddafi, or former Germany mass murders, Adolf Hitler, provide ideal examples. They built many bunkers geared by fear. But for Mandela this was not the case. The BBC (25 August, 2011) reported that "the rebel fighters have been breaking into the complex tunnel system underneath the compound, searching for Col Gaddafi and his fighters," also see Fukuyama (2004, p. 19). Rulers who constructed bunkers under their state houses show how they were afraid of death. For Mandela, death was not the end but the means as aforementioned Samora Machel would argue. *Hommage* a Nelson Mandela called him *témoigné l'historique* or "a historical testimony" (p. 2) while one choir in *isiZulu*, one of major languages spoken in South Africa, referred to Mandela as *akekho afana naye* namely there is nobody like him or he is unique. And indeed, when it comes to managing state business, Mandela was above reproach; nobody would cast any doubts about him.

For the love of his country and justice, to Mandela, dying while fighting to topple Apartheid regime was more meaningful than living under its tentacles and criminality. Mandela was a person of his own world who knew what he was made for. Selfless and tireless, Mandela changed the way the world used to think about reconciliation and forgiveness among other things that he did in his life time. He changed the course of history once and for all. We–in Peace and Conflict studies–take and uphold Mandela, Mohandas Gandhi and Martin Luther King Jr. as the pillars-cum-beacons of justice that the world is currently enjoying as far as peaceful means of dealing with conflict are concerned. They brought a new spirit of nonviolence that saw a transformed world that used to be trapped in long-drawn-out conflicts. While Gandhi and Luther Jr. paid with their blood, Mandela paid with his family, freedom and children by being behind bars for over two decades. If he had wanted to betray his people in order to be released, even being offered power, he would have had done so. But he did not. Mandela goes down as an African politician who spent longer time in prison than any other who truly forgave those who jailed him. What strikes is the fact that if Mandela had decided to compromise his conscience, he would have had been released earlier. But he decided not. For him, the freedom of his people was better and more meaningful than his own life, his family and personal enjoyment in life. So, when he said he was ready to die for the cause he believed in, Mandela, apart from knowing the consequences, was willingly prepared to do so. And indeed, he did.

Exemplary deeds and torturous experiences of the above mentioned persons who changed the course of the history of the world typify a unique type of humans that were ready to lay their lives down for the emancipation of others. What makes them even special is the fact that they knew and accepted the price of their acts and stances heroically and willingly. What makes Mandela's case interesting is the fact that—as a lawyer by trade—he knew too well that he was facing one sentence as far as his charges were concerned, capital sentence. However, later, his death sentence was commuted to life imprisonment whose border and capital sentence is arguably slight given that the person who receives life imprisonment dies behind bars. As a father and a married person at such a young age, if Mandela were chickenhearted, would have had opted to be compromised so that he could join and cherish a young wife and look after his young family. He did not shilly-shally, or opt for any solution other than the total, and true liberation of his country including his tormentors. Mandela (1962 cited in Simon and Schuster 2012) says "if I had my time over I would do the same again. So would any man who dares call himself a man," (p. 4). Such words cannot come out of the mouth of a coward or a pretender. They are the words of the man whose heart fears nothing but fear itself. They are the words of the man whose spiritual resolve is as tough as old boots. Mandela did not only face a jail term. He, so, too, faced intimidations and temptations to compromise his course. Tiffen (year not provided) notes that "while Mandela's willingness to negotiate was widely lauded, equally important and rarely noted were the times and issues on which he refused to compromise," (page not provided). No doubts that the Apartheid regime feared Mandela. Therefore, if there was any way it could compromise him it *sans doute* would. One may ask: Why didn't Apartheid kill Mandela who was already sentenced to death. It is simple that executing Mandela would have lit a powder keg that South Africa had already become at the time Mandela was captured and jailed.

Mandela is an exemplary person whose deeds acted as the archetypal bonfires of politics, *realpolitik* and history of the modern world. Despite leaving his indelible marks on our modern world, Mandela will always be treasured as a big lesson that many generations, especially of those facing injustice will refer to and learn from altogether. Such behaviour gives Mandela high grades in managing the affairs of his state.

Although many African leaders, principally those who performed well and did a lot to their countries are honoured as the best managers of the affairs of their countries, nobody can rival or be at par with Mandela. While many founding fathers are haunted by their one-party autocracy, Mandela did not introduce or participate in a one-party rule. While his colleagues faced allegations of overstaying in power, Mandela left earlier than any African leader had ever done. For, he left at the time many people were asking him to soldier on; but he flatly refused. Mandela fought for the freedom of his countries from the mid-fifties. Again, he was delayed to join his colleague founding fathers due to being imprisoned for a long time. While all founding fathers fought colonialism without dismantling it, Mandela single-handedly brought down Apartheid rule at the time and manner nobody would have expected or dreamed of. Ingenious and humble as he was, Mandela did not even accept the credit for what he did so as to change the world's political landscape and history. This shows a very humble manager whose success is not his alone but of the people. Despite getting in power late as the head of state, Mandela will be remembered as a stalwart that worked earth; and left such a unique legacy all over the world. While many African founding fathers were famously known and revered locally, Mandela was a creature of a different planet. Arguably, no African or African leader has ever become more famous than Mandela up until this time. Even Tutankhamen, the legendary Egyptian Pharaoh is not as famous as Mandela was. Many still find it unique and harder even to understand how a person who was unjustly jailed for 27 years would forgive his jailers and share power with them. This unique and exceptional trait makes the liberation of South Africa synonymous with Mandela.

As the best manager of public affairs, Mandela refused to amass wealthy or create cult-reverence. Due to how highly he was regarded, had Mandela wanted to create a cult, he would easily have done so. If he, also, wanted to die in office he would. All the same, apart from abhorring being worshiped, Mandela refused to become power sick so as to die in office even when the constitution allowed him to do so. He served only one term in office while the constitution of South Africa stipulates that the president can serve for two terms. What makes Mandela even more unique is his ability to put the interests of the people forward. Knowing the type of the country he inherited from Apartheid system, Mandela initiated reconciliation, forgiveness and restorative justice to cure a highly racially-divided country. He formed the Truth and Reconciliation Commission (TRC) whose works and findings are now the subjects of reference almost in many conflicts around the world. Tutu (2007) notes that:

> With the eyes of the world on this country–and under the leadership of then President Nelson Mandela, a living icon of magnanimity and humanity–the people of South Africa initiated the Truth and Reconciliation Commission, eschewing revenge and violence in favour of truth and forgiveness and, ultimately, the reconstruction of our country, (p. 7).

Indeed, apart from establishing the TRC, South Africa was able to start the continuum of divorcing its past by embarking on true but challenging reconciliation that Mandela and Frederik Wilhelm de Klerk started so as to share power as they prepared the country for the first democratic elections that saw Mandela becoming the first South Africa president. Since then, two more African presidents (Thabo Mbeki and Jacob Zuma) took the office of the president and continued from where Mandela ended as the CEO of the country. What a vision! Mandela's vision and calibre awarded him an international recognition not to mention winning the prestigious Noble Prize in 1993 which he willingly shared with his archfoe-turned friend, de Klerk. Apart from being the point of reference, Mandela was a world's statesman who was respected and welcomed by many powerful leaders of the world as their senior and role model. The *Telegraph* (6 December, 2003) quoted US president Barack Obama–at his funeral as saying "and like so many around the globe, I cannot fully imagine my own life without the example that Nelson Mandela set." These are the words of the president of the most powerful country on earth whose life was touched by Mandela's spirit and behaviour.

The *Telegraph* (Ibid) went on quoting many world leaders as they eulogised Mandela during his funeral in his home town of Qunu where his remains were put to rest. Australian then Prime Minister, Tony Abort, had this to say "Nelson Mandela was one of the great figures of Africa, arguably one of the great figures of the last century." Mandela's fame did not end up with politicians only. Academics as well had something to say about this humble man. Klerk (2003) notes that "at the end of the last millennium there was

116

a felt journalistic need to pick a "man of the century", and one of the names that kept cropping up was that of Nelson Lolihlahla Mandela," (p. 322). No doubt, Mandela was this man of the century due to his role in pulling down the Apartheid regime, and his spirit of forgiveness based on reconciliation that saw South Africa achieving what has never before been achieved in the shortest time possible. Many were shocked to see Mandela initiating such efforts of forgiving those who, hunted him down, tortured and jailed him for a long time, not to forget, killing thousands of his people simply because they demanded their God-given rights. If Mandela were a bad and ill-judged manager, surely, he would have embarked on retribution that would have set South Africa on fire. But he did not even exclude his jailers and tormentors from the government he formed soon after being released from jail. Even after he won with landslide victory, Mandela did not use his power to hunt down those who were openly known to be his tormentors and enemies. Even those he forgot did not expect it to happen as it happened. Selfless, humble and wise as he was, Mandela foresaw the danger the country faced, especially when we consider the fact that South Africa was evolving from long-time gross and systemic violations of human rights that Apartheid regime perpetrated against indigenous South Africa. Mandela, therefore, wholeheartedly, and straightforwardly, attended to the needs of the country and its people without discriminating against anybody at this hour of need. Such unique and exceptional qualities put Mandela among the top best managers of Africa. Desmond Tutu quoted in Klerk (Ibid) had this to say when he was asked to define Mandela. He said that "he's God's gift to South Africa and he is our gift to the world," (p. 325). And indeed, by deeds and words, Mandela was but a gift to the world that Africa gave to the world.

Arguably, Mandela is the only African leader who was known all over the world due to his contribution to liberation of South Africa coupled with his spirit of forgiveness and reconciliation. In conflict and peace studies, Mandela is like a model or an encyclopaedia on forgiveness and reconciliation. If anything, Mandela is the best of the best in the management of the business of the state. After sacrificing all his youth for his country, many would think—after being released from jail where he spent most of his adult life before becoming president–Mandela would have wanted to redress himself by robbing public coffers. Many would think Mandela would cling to power so as to die in office simply because he contributed incalculably to the freedom of South Africa. Others would think it was his right to help himself from public coffers just like Jomo Kenyatta did after getting in power. Again, none of the two happened. For, Mandela did not cling to power or rob public coffers. His belief is that he did what he was supposed to do. His words quoted Schuster (Ibid) above show this. Mandela is quoted as saying that "if I had my time over I would do the same again. So would any man who dares call himself a man." When it comes to accountability, Mandela was second to none. The *Economist* (2013, p. 1 cited in Qureshi, 2014) noted that:

> Towards the end of Mandela's incarceration–through to the abolition of Apartheid–fortunes did reverse slightly, but by now the disparity had grown so large that it barely made a dent. Income growth improved substantially for all South Africans after his 1994 election victory, but sufficiently more so for whites, and the balance has been disproportionately weighted in their favour–and increasingly that of Asian South Africans–since he stepped down in 1999, (p. 2).

For a country that had been under an unequal and a racist system for generations to have even such "fortune reverse" needed a leader with a vision and a mission altogether. Economic, issues, especially land redistribution show how complicated reconciliation can be particularly when some issues are not addressed well. Land issues in South Africa are as old as the country itself. However, Mandela relinquished power and died without addressing these thorny issues. Again, he tried to lay the foundations for future governments to address them. Mandela's vision was clear that if South Africa is not reconciled, it would not be able to bring its citizens to the round table and sort out their differences; and thereby address their needs as a country and a society. Essentially, such undertakings Mandela embarked on asked for the moral imagination and divine naivety to reconcile South Africa through web making and web watching with serendipity on the sideways, (Lederach, 1995) one would argue, mainly when we consider the fact that south Africa was for many generations racially divided based on the policy of Apartheid. Such risk taking for peace and reconciliation brings us to another important element of conflict resolution whereby the charisma and vision of a leader, or leaders, matters a lot in helping us predict where the conflict can go. Gibson (2004) notes that:

> Mandela's continuous pleas for tolerance and reconciliation—not to mention his well-publicized donning of a rugby shirt (the sport of choice among whites)—have undoubtedly contributed to more benign racial attitudes among whites, (p. 99).

So, the new South Africa embarked on Social justice which is defined as "a perceived fairness of the division of rewards and burdens in the society" (Hulbert, 2011, p. 62) in putting some measures in place. However, the look of things on the ground tells a different story. Basically, social justice is about equal, equitable and fair division of rights, responsibility, and rewards in the society. Therefore, South Africa embarked on what Hulbert (2011) notes in defining social justice as "a set of ideas, values and social practices to ensure that all person or groups enjoy economic security…future generations" (p. 59). If anything, this is what Mandela envisaged and wanted to achieve namely a united, equitable and democratic South Africa and its neighbours. Again, economic security in the country and in the region is still far from being realised. Instead, South Africa is suffering from economic insecurity to the extent that poor South Africans are now attacking other Africans from neighbouring countries simply because they believe they are the authors of their suffering. Luckily, Mandela is not there to evidence such a shame. It becomes even grave to note that South Africa is under the president who can be hijacked by Indian conmen. Refer to Gupta family scandal in South Africa in which President Jacob Zuma is untidily entrapped in. The *BBC* (21 January, 2015) noted that "the power lies with the Gupta family. So you really have a president who is indebted to a particular clique." Here the president means Zuma. Remember this is the president accused of raping a daughter of his friend before impregnating another not to mention other corruption charges.

Mandela was not concerned with peace in South Africa only. His mission was to see to it that the entire region lives peacefully as

Zurcher, *et al.,* (2013) note that after the new government came to power, it stopped aiding RENAMO rebel group in neighbouring Mozambique which contributed to peace in Mozambique, (p. 119). Also, the end of Apartheid had a sort of *domino effects* on other countries such as Angola and Namibia which Zurcher, *et al.,* say that peace deals and negotiations in these countries, "could not have been achieved without the fall of Apartheid regime in South Africa," (p. 17). This is exactly what happened. For, the RENAMO came to the negotiation table to talk peace instead of waging a gruesome and losing war that was mostly funded by Apartheid that was no more. So, Apartheid regime did not only affect peace and economies of South Africa but it also affected the whole region. Mandela's ripple effects were all over the place in the region.

Arguably, peace in the world was Mandela's mission to the world. For, soon after retiring, he presided over Burundi peace Agreement taking over from the first chair of negotiations Tanzanian former president Julius Nyerere who then passed on. For the first time, Burundi, after many years of infighting among different factions, enjoyed peace. Khadiagala cited in Lieberfeld (2003) notes that "in Burundi, Mandela did not hesitate to use blunt language to berate the Burundian parties "for failing their people by lacking the commitment and urgency to end the war," (p. 242). Lieberfeld adds that Mandela threatened to resign as a facilitator had Burundian fighting factions refused to reach a peace agreement. His pressure yields fruits. For, in 2000 Burundian warring cliques reached a peace agreement that saw the formation of a transition government. Mandela invited about 50 African and Western leaders to witness a signing ceremony. Despite commanding such huge veneration Mandela did not impose his will on others. He was a good listener who spoke his mind clearly and openly. He took no offence for being faulted. Instead, he was a good learner who wanted everybody to air his views. However, Mandela was not easy to cow or take for a ride. Whenever anything went wrong, he would reprimand or say it openly. For example, Mandela was infuriated by the tendency of some Burundian offshoots who wanted to delay the process so that they could spend much time enjoying *per diems* and chauffeur-driven cars.

Apart from championing peace, Mandela had another feather in his cap. He campaigned against HIV/AIDS even when his successor, Mbeki took a different stance about the existence of the endemic disease. The *BBC* (30 July, 2004) notes that "he continued to initiate campaigns to fight against HIV/AIDS and he would invite tycoons on trips to rural areas and delicately manipulate them into pledging money to build schools and clinics." Mandela was especially touched when his first born son, Makgatho died of HIV on 6 January, 2005. Like Kaunda, Mandela did not conceal the truth that his son died of HIV whose victims were, and are still traumatised and being stigmatised in many countries in Africa. For the president who has all privileges, Mandela would have opted to not divulge the cause of the death of his son. Also, dying of HIV is still seen as something shamefully and sinful in many African societies. Again, as a leader, parent, and a straightforward person, Mandela decided to divulge everything in order to help his people to understand how HIV does not select when it comes to claiming its victims.

Although Mandela is no more, he left a very admirable legacy; and the record he set will take many years and generation to break. The words of Germany Chancellor, Angela Merkel suffice to echo what Mandela lived and died for. The *Telegraph* (6 December, 2003) quoted Merkel at Mandela's funeral as saying that:

His name will always be associated with the fight against the oppression of his people and with overcoming the apartheid regime. Not even years in prison could break Nelson Mandela or make him bitter-a new, better South Africa eventually emerged out of his message of reconciliation ... Nelson Mandela's shining example and his political legacy of non-violence and the condemnation of all forms of racism will continue to inspire people around the world for many years to come.

Again, it is not easy to condense the deeds, and words of Nelson Mandela in one chapter or two. So, too, much have already been said and written about him. Suffice it to say, Mandela was the greatest manager Africa has ever had who was ahead of his time. Meticulous, honest and selfless as he was, Mandela proved to live what he preached. His legacy leaves the world with a lot to learn, emulate, and above all, treasure as a true son of Africa who contributed immensely to the wellbeing of Africa and the world at large.

Mandela's words suffice to summarise him and his mission when it comes to liberating Africa without looking at the colour, creed or history of a person. Contrary to many who brought shame to Africa, Mandela brought humongous fame. His legacy belongs to all Africans. Mandela set a unique precedent that proves wrong all those who thought that nothing good and prominent could come from Africa. A true son of Africa that epitomised African ways of life, Mandela will always be remembered and treasured as a person who changed the course of the history of the world by giving it an alternative way of doing this as far as coexistence, peace, interdependence; and above all, justice and equality are concerned. Among all managers we have discussed in this volume, Mandela is number one despite coming into the big picture latterly. His life and deeds rekindled Africa's hope that yet another important son or daughter of the continent can be sired by an African son so as to be birthed by an African daughter. Mandela said many precious words. We have decided to use his words to conclude our discussion on him.

"I would say that the whole life of any thinking African in this country is driven continuously to a conflict between his conscience on the one hand and the law on the other…The law as it is applied, the law as it has been developed over a long period of history, and especially the law as it is written by the Nationalist Government is law which in our view is immoral, unjust and intolerable. Our consciences dictate that we must protest against it, that we must oppose it and that we must attempt to alter it." Nelson Mandela, 1962, adapted from Bukurura, (2003).

Mandela's legacy
As a humble and conscionable person, Mandela will be remembered for his simplicity and openness among countless qualities he had. He used to say that he was not an angel but a sinner who was trying. Above all, Mandela set the tone, and the pace in visualising a peaceful world. His reconciliatory approach informs us that even protracted conflicts are resolvable if there is a genuine and unshakable resolve and commitment to truly do so. It was like a daydreaming to think that, first of all, Apartheid would be pulled

down in our lifetime; and secondly, that whites and indigenous Africans in South Africa would be reconciled so as to live together as one rainbow nation as Tutu coined it. When it comes to democracy, Mandela was second to none. He believed in the rule of law that empowers and incorporates all stakeholders which is opposed to the awkward tendency of many African leaders who think they are the ones who were created to rule others. His early exodus from office set another precedent that everybody can rule. Mandela did not see any logic in extending his rule or clinging to power just like corrupt and myopic rulers who tamper with the constitutions of their countries to remain in power illegally. Leaving back a very cohesive and transiting country adds another accolade to Mandela.

Mandela has another nugget. He is among a few African leaders who did not keep any vengeance or chip on his shoulder against his enemies. So, too, Mandela becomes an exception to the general rule in that when he died he distributed his estate so as to cover his family, friends, institutions and his Foundation's workers something that had never been heard of before. We know many presidents who died and left their estates in the hands of their family members who also kept the size and value of those estates a top secret due to the fact that many of them were obtained illegally through robbing the *hoi polloi* in their countries.

More importantly, President Mandela was not a hands-on president at any time, (de Klerk 1993 during interview with John Carlin). Mandela was a democrat *per se*. No doubt about this as his chapter indicates. Despite being an iconic figure respected all over the world, Mandela did not use his stature to bully others. He was ready to criticise, be criticised, faulted, and above all, he accommodated the view of others even if they were different from his. Mandela was not a power-hungry monster or a know-it-all type of a leader and person. He ruled by allowing others to contribute to the process as a means of agreeably reaching consensus and owning the process equally.

Mandela's weakness is that he was unmovable when he believed in something. Again, whether this is a weakness or strength, it depends on how it is used.

Special tributes

The history of a free South Africa cannot be completed without acknowledging and mentioning the names of other freedom fighters who, along with Mandela, sacrificed immensely to see to it that the country became independent. Those are, *inter alia*, Govan Mbeki, father to former president Thabo Mvuyelwa Mbeki, Walter Sisulu, Steve Biko, Solomon Mahlangu, Desmond Tutu, Albert Luthuli, Raymond Mhlaba, Elias Motsoaledi, Ahmed Kathrada, Denis Goldberg and Wilton Mkwayi. Their sacrifices were the water that nourished the struggle that gave birth to the current South Africa we have and cherish today. At various levels, and in different capacities and at times, these icons played an important role in wrestling South Africa from the crawls of Apartheid. South African women and men too played a very decisive role to see to it that they wrestled their countries from Apartheid. They suffered a lot of discrimination, especially black South Africans.

Chapter 10

De Klerk the Risk Taker Who Pulled Apartheid Down

"A key leadership factor is the ability to inspire your followers to accept your vision of the future. Some of the followers of the ruling National Party were not prepared to take the risks involved in a radical change of course - even though they could see the breakers smashing on the reefs ahead. It was the task of the party's leadership to assure them that there were other courses that could effectively protect their core interests, while at the same time affording full political rights to all South Africans. We explored the possibilities of power sharing; of constitutional guarantees; of the devolution of power," FW de Klerk in de Klerk (2002, p. 611).

Figure 13: FW.de Klerk South Africa's last Apartheid President (image courtesy of eNCA)

Despite being a horribly deplorable and despicable system of management of state business, Apartheid had good and bad people in its ranks. Frederik Wilhelm "FW" de Klerk (18 March 1936), the last Prime Minister of South African Apartheid, and the vice president of the transition government that saw a democratically-elected government in South Africa in 1994 is one of those who managed Apartheid. De Klerk is credited for having helped in pulling down the Apartheid regime in South Africa. This act gives him a credit of being a creative manager who constructively turned the waves against Apartheid so as to win a place in the club of a few best African managers of the business of the state. However, it must be noted; de Klerk had to make a U-turn to reach his success as a manager of state business. Such undertakings needed a risk taker and a visionary altogether. Try to imagine the person who was born and raised under such a system that inculcated fear of indigenous among Boers. Arguably, taking such measures needed extra abilities of visualising and conceptualising the future of the country. It needed a person who did not look at his personal gains but the one who looked at larger interests of the country. De clerk is essentially an exception to the general rule as far as good management of state business and democracy are concerned. Notwithstanding from Nyerere (*Ujamaa*), Kaunda (Humanism), Khama (*Paso ya batho* or rule of the people) and many more whose administrations were shaped by their environment, de Klerk came from a dictatorial and racist background that he later successfully defeated and completely destroyed. This gives him kudos as liberalist who evolved from a conservative society. For any person to escape from the captivity, entrapment and lulls of her or his past, such a person really needs extra efforts and soul-searching that, nonetheless, many do not have. If anything, this is the same situation de Klerk encountered when he was trying to agree with the ANC to abandon Apartheid once and for all. To get a glimpse of who de Klerk actually is, we need to delve into his history without forgetting the politics, geopolitics and *realpolitik* of the time whereby the cold war was officially coming to its end. One can argue that de Klerk was a quick learner who saw it coming. Thus, he skilfully and successfully avoided it so as to end up making history along doyens such as Mandela, and his comrades. Either way, de Klerk had the tools, discretionary power, and support to either derail or execute the process. He, however, chose to be part and parcel of a noble history of Africa as far as Apartheid and liberation of South Africa are concerned.

Again, taking such measures did not only need a thinker and a quick learner but also a person who believes in what he does. Yet again, who is de Klerk? Kofoed and Ingarvasson (year not provided) note that:

FW de Klerk was born and raised in an environment deeply connected with the Afrikaner nationalist sphere that created and implemented the segregating racist system named apartheid. He followed in his father's footsteps, started a political career and worked his way up on the ranks of the National Party hierarchy, (p. 2).

By all standards, de Klerk was not a simple and light person *vis-à-vis* Apartheid history and machinery. He was a heavyweight who was a very product of this system despite its brutality and illogicality; that he later courageously and heroically helped to pull down. He was one of a few privileged and the product of the system he was born to benefit from and defend. Again, as said above, after a long soul-searching rooted in the vision of the new future South Africa that would accommodate all South Africans equally and equitably though theoretically, de Klerk decided to read the writing on the wall. Kofoed and Ingavarsson (Ibid) note that de Klerk was de Klerk was "a conservative hardliner, a guardian of the prevailing system that showed no ambition of reforms," (p. 2). Certainly, de Klerk was arguably still a hawk yet during the last years of Apartheid. Like a Biblical Paul, it can be argued that de Klerk *saw the light; and heard and heeded the voice* so as to eminently secure a niche in the list of the best managers Africa has ever had despite his dark past under Apartheid. De Klerk is credited for being behind the destruction of nuclear weaponry that the Western countries had given South Africa as symbol and tool of power it would use to intimidate others in the region. Sometimes, I wonder; what would have happened if de Klerk and Mandela were born in the Middle East. When it comes to doing away with nukes, Robinson and Boutwell (1996) note that "early in 1990, however, South African government, under the reformist leader F.W. de Klerk, unilaterally chose to destroy its nuclear weaponry" (p. 601) which, of course, was a danger-cum-threat not only to the southern African region but to Africa in general. Such a move needed the courage of the mad and unflinchingly true commitment to a peaceful future of the country despite evolving from chaos and inequality. If de Klerk were a chicken-hearted manager of public business, he would have clung to nukes that he would have used as a bargaining chip during the negotiations that brought down Apartheid; and thereby propelled South Africa to true and exceptional democracy. But he did not. He trusted Mandela and their visions seem to be the same for their country. Truly, de Klerk beat swords into ploughshares *vis-a-vis* nukes. It is sad that countries with nuclear weapons did not learn from South Africa.

A few can see and do things the way de Klerk did. For a person whose bread and prestigious station in life came from the Apartheid, it was not easy or normal to cut the hands that used to feed him since he was a baby. Again, what do you do if you find that the same hands that used to feed you are rotten and chopping them may help to keep you alive rather than clinging to them and die and rot with them pointlessly? If anything, this is the real situation de Klerk was faced with when he entered into negotiations with Mandela that resulted in the demise of Apartheid; and, in this manner, gave birth to a brand new South Africa. People make history but history does not make them. By facing stark reality, de Klerk made history, noble history. It needed a daring spirit and conviction for de Klerk to timely divorce, and, ultimately, breakaway from the stuff hardliner Boers were made of. So, too, it begs for political precision-cum-maturity to attempt such a thing leave alone doing it. Verily, this shows how de Klerk was not afraid of changes which many hardliners hated and feared the most. Again, what geared de Klerk to rebel against his past? De Klerk (2003 cited in Machel, 2003) answers this question saying that:

> We have done all this because we prefer peace to war. We have taken the positions we have, not to oppose or support any country, nor to seek any glory. We have done what we have because, as South Africans and Africans, we know the pain of war and the immeasurable value of peace, (p. 3).

Such utterances show a peace lover-cum-peacemaker *per se* who, ironically, used to use violence to achieve his goals. Progressive changing as opposed to conservatism is one of the assets for a good manager of the business of the state. Because without reading the signs of time, one makes the same mistakes expecting different results something de Klerk skilfully and timely avoided. Byrne, *et al.,* (2000) make a claim that F.W. de Clerk's speech "Red Friday" to the South African Parliament changed the dynamics of the conflict in

South Africa so as to attract Non-Governmental Organisations (NGOs) to form what was later known as Community Conflict Resolution Service. In the end, Mandela and de Clerk saw a new South African that became a reference point in many ethnopolitical conflicts around the globe, (p. 157).

Under de Klerk's watch, the world woke up to a poser when he unexpectedly announced the release the icon of South African struggle for independence, Nelson Rolihlahla Mandela who had been behind bars for over twenty seven years for political crimes. Nonetheless, this achievement did not come easily, especially at such volatile times of the history of a sharply divided South Africa. Had it not been for de Klerk and Mandela's creativity, impartiality and ability to agree to coexist, South Africa would still be under cold-blooded Apartheid regime up until now. Many years had lapsed now since the conflict started as the African National Congress (ANC) chaperoned, and chaired by Mandela waged one of the fiercest wars for many years. True, the history of racially-instigated animosity was clear and open for both de Klerk and Mandela but not to their supporters or parties. Yet, as good managers, they were able to overcome it within a very short time. A good manager is the one who uses his skills, power, and talents to make life much easier for those who entrusted him public office than otherwise. If anything, this is what de Klerk did despite the danger he faced from inside and outside of his party and government altogether. The move to free South Africa from the grip of Apartheid was extremely dangerous and treacherous, specifically for de Klerk not to mention Mandela. Not all followers in both sides of the divide fully subscribed to or made sense of the process. Radicals within the National Party (NP) as well as in the ANC did not want to hear anything that would bring sanity in South Africa based on give-and-take principles of negotiations and reconciliation. There are spoilers in every conflict. Again, de Klerk and Mandela kept an open eye on them so as to keep tabs on them; and thereby bring about true change in South Africa. Their belief was that—for their part—Boers would mismanage and plunder the country forever while indigenous thought they would militarily or violently wrestle the country from Boers at one time. While spoilers looked at a winner-takes-it-all opportunity, de Klerk and Mandela looked at coexistence and interdependence as the citizens of one country.

Arguably, in de Klerk's eyes and mind, things were, and looked totally different. He strongly and practically believed that compromise would be reached through negotiations based on give-and-take principles something Mandela reciprocated to positively during and after the negotiations that give birth to a rainbow nation. Such an apogee begged for creativity, vision, and above all, risk taking for the two leaders. This is the point at which the rope breaks. It is the point at which all managerial skills are strictly needed and applied. When such a thing happens, what are in the minds of the persons or managers who apply such managerial skills are the results or product of the gamble. Victory-cum-possibility is the only thing they envisage and seek. It is the hardest time one can evidence and endure as a manager. It is as hard as it is for an expectant mother in labour room. I do not want to step into de Klerk's or Mandela's shoes to watch the clock ticking waiting for the reaction of the people without knowing which way the gamble will turn to or go. But surely, in the minds of two leaders, what was going on is hard to imagine and stomach.

True, de Klerk needed to have the chutzpah of the mad to face his fundamentalists and intransigent colleagues in his own establishment. A good manager is the one who reads the writings on the wall based on the signs of time, and thereby, takes decisive actions based on good timing and good judgement. Due to his vision, de Klerk envisioned what many did not. He skilfully articulated his vision and stayed put even when many were trying to sabotage the process as Shepherd (1994) notes that at the time security forces- through the acts of omission or commission– fuelled the problem, (p. 40). Knowing that the wind of change was sweeping across South Africa, de Klerk committedly decided to follow the flow without *wuwei* or opposing. He knew too well that opposing the flow of the wave of change that was sweeping across South Africa would have rocked the boat; and thereby destroyed everything. Failure to nicely interpret the situation would have caused the organisation to end up in trouble. If anything, this is something de Klerk's vision averted skilfully and timely altogether. The way de Klerk and Mandela constructively transformed the conflict left a precedent that nothing is forever under the Sun. They strove to find what united them as they ignored what divided them. Creativity is an important element in any negotiation as a managerial skill; while trying to find opportunities in the conflict is another. So, too, de Klerk and Mandela's demeanours speak to the fact that even enemies can become best friends and vice versa. This is a human nature. De Klerk managerial skills and good management can be seen in the words of Glad and Blanton (1997) who say that "the revolution that these men have helped bring about through democratic and peaceful means goes beyond simply the calling of people to a higher mission or emancipation of a polity from an authoritarian and discriminatory regime," (p. 565). Without the calling for peace, South Africa under Apartheid was like powder keg waiting to explode. It needed cool heads and big hearts to peacefully handle and steer it before causing tremors that would be felt all over the region and the world in general. With grand vision, de Klerk and Mandela sacrificed everything for the good of all people of South Africa. To see how big de Klerk's vision was, he was quoted by the *Guardian* (February 11th, 2015) saying that Apartheid was wrong and morally unjustifiable.

Such an admission–that the system he presided over was wrong–needed trustworthiness, farsightedness, steadfastness and courage due to the fact that not all in his party and government supported the demise of Apartheid. Why was de Klerk different from other Apartheid leaders? The *CNN* (December 6, 2013) notes that "de Klerk recognized the urgent need to bring the black majority into the political process, and most party moderates agreed with him in principle." When we talk of grand vision this is exactly the one. For any good thinker, time for Apartheid regime was up and the game, too, was up. At the time, Apartheid has already lost some backing from its prominent and reliable allies due to the pressure abroad and back home. The United States, for example, was facing immense pressure from civic movements urging it to stop cooperating with Apartheid regime in South Africa. Dobris (1986); Grossman and Sharpe (1986); and Arnold and Hammond (1994) note that investing in South Africa was creating controversies to Western countries. Thus, divestment was the way to go.

And to be safer for whoever presided over the regime, he had to let go so as to enjoy stable and perpetual peace. Sometimes, good management is about taking risk. This actually is what de Klerk did.

For, there were some fears that the ANC would embark on retributory spree after coming to power. Therefore, de Klerk needed firm guarantee so as to assure his colleagues that there would not be any retribution or witch-hunting in the new South Africa. Mandela did this well by assuring de Klerk that he was not a person of revenge who would seek to revisit the past as far as Apartheid was concerned. From the day go, Mandela was a futurist who wanted to nurse the wounds that South African had sustained under Apartheid. Under Mandela's grand vision and wisdom, there was no retribution of any kind. So, such a gamble paid nicely for not only for Mandela but also for de Klerk and South Africa differently from any would have expected. It takes two to tango. Had things gone wrong, definitely, de Klerk and Mandela would have paid high price.

Arguably, even if things took a different turn to the worse, blaming de Klerk and Mandela would have been unfair given that they offered what they had for the good of the whole country and its people. Before blaming the duo, one needs to ask her or himself: "What would I have done differently if I were in their shoes at such time and space?" It is easy to blame others without reflecting on ourselves; and what we would have done if we were the duo. There was nothing personal in their project of inventing a rainbow nation. Arguably, in their minds, de Klerk and Mandela saw only South Africa for all South Africans indigenous and Boers. As said that it needed the courage of the mad to take such a risk. A person like de Klerk was brought up to believe that Boers were better than indigenous South Africans; and had the right to lord it over them. To make such a U-turn, for him, needed both courage and vision among other qualities fitting to take on the task as challenging and as complicated as it was. De Klerk did what failed people regarded eminently such as Gandhi who openly discriminated against Africa when he was fighting for Indian rights under apartheid. Gandhi (cited in Stone 1990) says:

Your Lordship's petitioners have noticed with shame and sorrow the zealous attempts made to compare your Petitioners with the natives of South Africa [and] beg to draw your Lordship's attention to the anomaly that the [Franchise Amendment Bill] would rank the Indian lower than the rawest native, (1, pp. 122 and 124), (p. 724).

Letting Apartheid go under, for de Klerk, did not only evoke fear of retribution but also the fear assassination of those who espoused the idea. In this list of assassins' targets were Mandela and de Klerk on the top of the list. https://www.youtube.com/watch?v=JtPiq-oIgsk

Just like Mandela—who also had his burden in his establishment— de Klerk knew the very risk he was taking and the gamble he was making. Again, he wholeheartedly took it and was ready to pay the price if need be. Yes, he was ready for whatever even if it meant to die for what he envisioned and believed in. You can see this vision in de Klerk's word cited in Norval (1998) maintains that "we are all the children of our times and the product of the cultural and political circumstances into which we were born and with which we grew up, (p. 256). This was an admission of what moulded him. Yet again, he rebelled against it for the love of his country. Despite his colour, when it comes to who truly loves South Africa, de Klerk is one of those whose love for their country is unquestionably unconditional or fake. It is very real; and it can be seen through his work of demolishing Apartheid. No doubt about this. If it were not his love for the country, de Klerk had what it takes to cling to Apartheid not just because he had the instruments of power but because this is what he was brought up to do. Again, he rebelled against the system that created him. He recreated it in a very acceptable and respectable fashion. He still had immense support from outside, especially from some Western countries that became Apartheid's life line after some countries boycotted it.

Furthermore, de Klerk knew that after handing over power, he would become vulnerable due to the fact that he would not have power to constitute or influence the new government which was likely to be formed by an indigenous South African as it turned out to be. Nonetheless, de Klerk did not fear what would happen to him or his people. Rather, he truly trusted Mandela. Instead of labouring under fear, de Klerk focused on reconciliation and working together. He knew that there would be formed the Truth and Reconciliation Commission (TRC) that would look into the past with the aim of reconciling the two parties to conflict so as to forge ahead together as a nation. And indeed, even when he was summoned before the TRC that Archbishop Desmond Tutu, chaired, de Klerk appeared and adduced his evidence freely and truthfully. De Klerk is a lawyer who knows well what happened during the Nuremberg trials whereby Nazi officials were found guilty and heavily punished. Yet for him, it was come whatever may; South Africa is above personal interests one may argue. Graybill (1998) maintains that in 1996, de Klerk admitted that his party committed crimes and all those responsible with committing cold-blooded crimes were supposed to be punished, (p. 106). Once again, such a stand needs the courage of the mad and grand vision; not to forget selflessness and readiness to take responsibility as the means of reconciling and appreciating the victims.

De Klerk's words used to sum up the discussion on him can give you more about the man.

> *"When I explain the process of change, I'm not trying to justify apartheid. I've come to the conclusion that apartheid was wrong, that it was morally unjustifiable, and therefore it had to be changed, and I'm not justifying in any way the wrongs which took place and which were done to the majority of people living in South Africa in the period of apartheid and separate development,"* de Klerk, the *Guardian*, (11 February, 2015).

De Klerk's legacy

F.W. De Klerk will always be remembered for his progressive vision that enabled him to see an equal and equitable South Africa based on merit but not the pigments of one's skin colour, particularly at the time most of his colleagues were entrapped in fear and suspicions. Along Mandela, de Klerk heroically and truthfully took the road many hate and fear to tread on. His contribution to the freedom of South Africa is immense and unique. He stood at the time when many of his white compatriots cowered. He took all blames for *betraying* their course and their system of Apartheid. He embraced and envisaged what many in his party were unable to see and conceptualises; let alone facing. Importantly, he stood on the right side of history at the right time with the right intention and vision.

The history of South Africa was mainly authored by resilient normal South Africans who suffered under white rule for many decades. It is their efforts and supports that enhance what we are celebrating today *vis-à-vis* South Africa. They have all reasons and moral ground to celebrate and walk thumbs up. We salute South African men and women, especially black and pay tribute to them too. They verily deserve it.

Chapter 11

Khama True Democrat Who Negotiated Best Deals

"For many African countries independence came only after a struggle which sometimes, as in Kenya, involved violence. Botswana's political independence was peacefully negotiated. Our struggle is the struggle to make a reality of that political independence, and it is this struggle on which we are now wholeheartedly engaged. The methods of this struggle differ from those of the struggle for independence. Our revolution is peacefully and positive in its goals. But it is none the less real for consisting of small victories over the ever-present enemies - poverty, ignorance and disease. Nor do we regard it as a struggle for ourselves alone, but a contribution by the establishment of self-determination and non-racial democracy throughout Southern Africa,"
Sir Seretse Khama, 1970 in Khama (1970, p. 7).

Figure 14: Sir Seretse GM. Khama Botswana 1st President (image courtesy of YouTube)

Sir Seretse Khama (July 1, 1921–July 13, 1980) was the first president of Botswana. He died in office on July 13, 1980 after serving his country as president for 14 years from 30 September, 1966–13 July, 1980, (Wikipedia). Sir Khama was a true democrat that was born in a royal family (Henderson, 1990, p. 27) who refused to become a king of his country due to having a bigger dream of liberating it from British rule. Also, Sir Khama believed in, and espoused democracy even at the time democracy was not a big talk of the day in Botswana and Africa in general. There were two reasons why he would have succeeded to become a king. Firstly, his people were ready to have him as their king given that his royal family had produced kings earlier. Secondly, under the cold war *realpolitik*, it was easier for him to do as pleased provided his actions would not disturb the stability of the country; and thus hinder or endanger the interests of colonial monsters. If a goon like Jean-Bedel Bokassa (CAR) did installed himself as an emperor, what would stop Sir Khama from becoming the king? If kings in the neighbouring Lesotho and Swaziland prevailed up to this date, what would have stood in Sir Khama's way had he wanted? This shows how Sir Khama espoused and valued democracy more than anything knowing that the bright future of his country would heavily depend on democratic rule but not kinghood. Such a move needs a selfless person who puts other ahead of his personal interests. By so doing therefore, Sir Khama secures a place in a club of a select few African leaders who managed their country competently and well.

What inspires even more is the fact that Sir Khama chose the harder way of getting power through the ballot box nonetheless. Arguably, Sir Khama did not choose democratic way without knowing its pros and cons. Being an educated person, he knew everything. Yet for the better future of his country, Sir Khama took this less-travelled road toward to democracy, in particular at the time democracy had not roots in Africa as a whole. For a privileged person of his time–to choose such a harder way–Khama proved to have had more managerial qualities and skills *vis-a-vis* good management. For, Sir Khama had a *carte blanche* that would enable him to become a king just like Mswati III of Swaziland. If anything, this is one of the qualities that make Sir Khama a good manager among a few Africa ever had as we will see later. Arguably, Sir Khama drew from Botswana's democratic traditions which put it ahead of many African countries as Khama (1970) notes that Botswana's democracy was basically established in the concept of *"Paso ya batho ka batho*, which means "rule of the people by the people" (p. 6), or *gosi ke kgosi ko batho* which means "a chief is only a chief through the people," (p. 7). Interestingly, Setswana, Botswana's language beats many African languages for having its own words that have to do with democracy which in many African languages is just borrowed from colonial languages. Once again, this shows that democracy is not a new concept in Botswana along with languages such as *isiZulu*, one of the biggest languages spoken in South Africa, in which democracy means *yeningi*. Setswana portrays a society that has been with the culture of democracy rooted in its traditions since time immemorial. For example, in the biggest African language, Kiswahili, the meaning of democracy is *demokrasia*. In another big language in Africa, Hausa from Nigeria, the meaning of democracy is *dimokuradiyya* which are directed taken from English. In other words—it can be argued that—it is wrong to teach democracy to Botswana or other African societies that practiced it before the coming of colonial monsters. I think this is why Botswana successfully practiced multiparty politics since its independence while other Africa countries except the Gambia were under one-party dictatorships.

Apart from building a flourishing democracy, Sir Khama built strong foundations for the economy of Botswana. He negotiated a good deal *vis-à-vis* investing in diamond mining. Comparably, like the Lee Kuan Yew, the founding father of Malaysia, Sir Khama steered his country to prosperity. Due to Sir Khama's personal contribution, Taylor (2005) argues that Sir Khama turned Botswana into "a relative backwater of the British Empire," (p. 45) which is very truly unique compared to other African countries whose resources became a curse. Ndikumana, *et al.,* (2009 note that Sir Khama propelled Botswana to becoming "one the highest economic growth rates in the world combined with a stable and democratic political system," (p. 141). Due to this success where many failed Cook and Sarkin (2010) give Botswana a moniker of "the African miracle," (p. 454) which it arguably is up until now. I think; it is out of love and probity that an individual can have a lot of positive impacts on the organisation he or she manages. This is the case with Sir Khama's managerial style and skills. And indeed, unlike other African countries endowed with immense quantities of minerals, Botswana has always benefited from its diamonds while other African countries have always suffered a lot of exploitation so that their resources turned out to be a curse but not a blessing. You can see this in Nigeria with its huge oil reserves that have never translated into improving the lives of the common Nigerians. So, too, you can see this in the Democratic Republic of Congo (DRC), and partly Tanzania and other countries whose people are still wallowing in abject poverty despite sitting on immense resources that a kit and caboodle of powerful criminals rob and mismanage. If anything, once again, such a trait secures a niche for Sir Khama in the club of a few best managers of Africa.

Essentially, Sir Khama's style of managing public business is still logical even today. Africa still can learn from such a good manager in order to turn things around instead of putting much emphasis and belief on dependency that has—for a long time—forced it to depend on in begging and borrowing from its former colonial monsters. For Sir Khama, as well as it was for Kaunda, it was harder to run a country accountably and successfully while sharing borders with the then South African Apartheid regime. Even after his death many years ago, Sir Khama still influences policies and politics in Botswana as Macartney (1969) notes that "the BDP colossus, under the leadership of Seretse Khama, still commands centre stage in a country about to be catapulted into the 20th century,"(p. 30). Such an argument may be seen as an old one thanks to the time it was made. Yet, looking at Botswana in the 21st century, it still is credibly credited for its success resulting from Khama's great role and vision in laying the foundations for the country. Up until now, Khama's contribution as a good manager of state business is unique and instrumental altogether. Sir Khama was a visionary leader of his time as Gillet (1973) notes that "Sir Seretse Khama will take a high position in Tswana history alongside with Khama III, because of him he could see and adapt to the pressure of a changing wold," (p. 185). Being able to foreknow the future is one of the assets a good manager must equip her- or himself with, especially in the ever quickly changing world. To understand what this means, try to imagine what happened to rulers who came and ruled for a long time after him such as Muamar Gaddafi (Libya), Zine El Abidine Ben Ali (Tunisia) and

Hosni Mubarak (Egypt) whose regimes were pulled down as they clung to power without knowing that things had changed.

True, under the foundations that Sir Khama laid down, Botswana is comparably the only country in Africa that has been under successful multiparty democracy since it gained independence in 1966. However, the Gambia did the same since independence although not so vibrantly and successfully as it is the case of Botswana. While Gambia suffers from mismanagement under the current dictator, Botswana has been going from strength to strength democratically and economically altogether. So, too, Botswana is the most stable country economically and politically. Compared to many Africa countries that got their independence shortly before Botswana, the country has always been idyllic as far as shriving democracy is concerned. Botswana came to the limelight after the discovery of diamond. Before then, even colonial monsters did not prefer to colonise it. Cook (Ibid) notes that it was the behest of "two paramount chiefs—Khama and Setshele—who were seeking protection from the Boers 'imminent plans to expand northwards from South Africa" (p. 460) that convinced the British to colonise Botswana. The reason is so clear that Botswana had nothing to offer to colonial monsters what, essentially, they were looking for namely resources. Again, after the De Beers, a South African mining company, discovered diamonds in the late 1960s in Orapa (Mzumara 2012), the Government Of Botswana (GOB) used such resources wisely as Cook (op.cit.) notes that Botswana's leadership has ensured that it has utilised the wealth afforded by its natural resources wisely and accomplished great economic feats, (p. 464). Again, it should be noted as Cook and Sarkin go on arguing that Botswana still suffers from having economic gap among its citizens however. San people are not treated equally to Tswana something that puts Botswana to the task of arresting such an anomaly. Maybe, this can be regarded as one of Sir Khama's failure. However, if we compare Sir Khama's fortes and shortfalls, the former becomes evident.

Sir Khama's vision was not only confined to Botswana but to Africa in general as he said in his speech cited in Henderson (1974) that Botswana's struggle for independence did not mean to acquire independence for Botswana only but also to see to it that non-racial democracy established "throughout Southern Africa,"(p. 39). For the country whose economy depended on Apartheid South Africa that is next door, such a stance needed some sort of courage, grand vision and selfness. Sir Khama's vision does not only stop on "Southern Africa" but also on Africa at large. Khama (1971) notes that when he agitated for unity, it was not like the one of the United States of Africa that the founders envisaged it. His was the more of the unity based on diversity that would still respect individuality based on freedom and its limitations, (p. 25).

Once again, Sir Khama proves what a thinker, a non-rigid thinker that he was. For, his statement was to the effect that the modality of unifying Africa had to be changed or advanced to suit the needs of the day by exploiting all differences, diversity and challenges individual African countries faced. He did not want to ape the Unites States model of unity. Instead, he wanted African countries to come up with a unity that suits their needs and aspirations. In other words, Sir Khama wanted to divorce himself from the manner and pace in which the Pan Africanists did things. He wanted things to be done in new way by underscoring new challenges that Africa faced at the time. Sir Khama argument of faulting the founding fathers of the unification of Africa shows him as a thinker who does not subscribe to everything without analysing, and if possible, critiquing it. It needed a lot of confidence and academic clout to fault the likes of Marcus Garvey, Kwame Nkrumah and Julius Nyerere, among others, who championed the unification of Africa based on US model. A good manager should be able to change; and do things in different manners based on the challenge he or she has at hand. Arguably, Sir Khama had underscored the failure of African unity so as to need to change tacks in order to realise this grand vision-cum-dream that would see Africa liberated completely economically, politically and socially. To take on political giants such as Nkrumah, Nyerere and others who espoused the United States of Africa, also, needed extra quality and courage. Do not wonder to find that the word courage is used many times. It is because of the issue, Sir Khama took on as a young manager compared to the doyens of the liberation of Africa as mentioned above. Without courage and deeper knowledge, it was next to never for Sir Khama to challenge the doyens of the unification of Africa. Once again, this can show you the type of a competent and courageous manager that Sir Khama was. We have shown the role of courage on the stance that Sir Khama took against racist Apartheid regime in the neighbouring South Africa. Divulgating his stance publicly was a dangerous thing next to committing suicide to do for a leader of a small country like Botswana given that Apartheid had the wherewithal to plot against him. Yet, he did not cower or hide his position.

Furthermore, when it comes to the threat that Apartheid South Africa posed to Botswana, it did not only come from Apartheid South Africa but also Portuguese colonial regimes in other neighbouring countries as Good (2008) notes that geographically, Botswana was almost completely surrounded by the hostile South Africa, South-West Africa (Namibia), and Rhodesia not to mention Angola and Mozambique which were under Portuguese just next door, (p. 750).

For such a poor and young country, to take such a stance that was openly against two colonial monsters in the region, begged for a courageous and visionary leader who was ready to make a sacrifice for others. Looking at Botswana's military capabilities and the size of the country, Sir Khama made a very bold decision to fully support the liberation of the above mentioned countries. Had he been myopic and selfish, he would have had taken a soft stance just like Dr. Hastings Kamuzu Banda in Malawi who was always in bed with colonial regimes in the region. Such bold political gait by Sir Khama, once again, puts him in the club of the best managers of Africa. Sir Khama articulated his vision by analysing the situation. He goes on noting that he feared "a new danger that Africa may once again divide itself in "moderate" and "radical" groupings, (p. 26). Such a warning was rarely heard from many African leaders due to the fact that most of them were good subscribers to the politics of division that assured them of the opportunity of remaining in power for a long time thanks to dividing their people. As a small country with immense diamond reserves, Botswana would have shied away from the concept of unifying Africa for the fear of being swallowed or being forced to share its resources with others. But this was not the case. There are many examples of divisive politics such as it was in Kenya, Nigeria and Uganda to mention but a few at the time.

Thanks to Sir Khama's grand vision on democracy and economy which enabled his successor, Sir Quett Masire, to inherit a stable country he steered up until he willingly retired after serving for over ten years in office in which he won elections. So, too, Sir Masire left behind a very vibrant economy that was even more expanded and advanced than he received it from his predecessor. Noting that he had served for long time, Sir Masire decided to retire; and thereafter those who followed served two terms only. Sir Masire left behind a very strong country with sustainable social cohesion that has gone on undisturbed ever since thanks to unshakable foundations that Sir Khama laid down.

"Our principles then are democracy which in our main language Setswana is rendered by IIPUSO ya batho ka batho", or rule of the people by the people, and development which we translate in Setswana as "ditiro tsa ditlhabalolo "which means literally" work for development", a significant rendering as I am sure you will agree. Our third principle is self-reliance which is variously expressed on Setswana and illustrated by numerous Setswana idioms of long-standing and our fourth principle unity, which is also expressed in Setswana by a number of words and idioms, each with its particular shade of meaning," Sir Seretse Khama, (1970).

Khama's legacy

As noted above, Sir Khama left a very stable country both economically and politically. His vision of Botswana has made it what it is today, an exception to the general rule in Africa as far as good governance is concerned. His estate has never faced any allegations directed to Sir Khama's implicating him with amassing any wealth made by means of robbing the public coffers. No allegations of land grabbing or any malpractices under the watch of Sir Khama have ever surfaced. Nothing puts Sir Khama ahead of many African managers of state business like wisely bargaining a good deal with foreign mining companies. Botswana benefits more from diamond—one of its major resources—than many African countries with resources due to Sir Khama's vision and power of bargaining. Had he wanted to be compromised for private interests, he would. But instead, he put forward the interests of his country. When we talk of good management of public affairs, such a manager is a point of reference.

Chapter 12

Jawara the Unionist and Moderate Democrat

"It is now accepted in many African circles that our experiments with different development strategies have not resulted in any appreciable improvement in the lives of our people. In fact, according to the recent Economic Commission of Africa (ECA) report, even as a number of poor is set to decrease by 2000, the total is expected to increase in Sub-Saharan Africa. It is now becoming increasingly apparent that the response to the gloomy prospect could not lie in only more international assistance, but in a self-generated restructuring of our own political and economic and institutions," Sir Dawda Jawara 1992 in Jawara (1992.p. 37).

Figure 15: Sir Dawda K. Jawara Gambia's 1st President (image courtesy of BBC)

Despite manning a relatively small and poor country, Sir Dawda Kairaba Jawara (May 16, 1924) the first president of the Gambia, left an indelible mark in managing state business. Sir Jawara ruled Gambia from 24 April, 1970–22 July, 1994. He was overthrown in a bloodless coup that was led by the current ruler Yahya Jammeh.

145

Compared to many African leaders of his time, Sir Jawara was a progressive leader who promoted some human rights at the very time some other leaders in Africa were suppressing or ignoring them. Although Sir Jawara was blamed for ruling under one party system for a long time, after he was deposed, he was remembered, especially after the government that took over from his became more brutal and monocratic than what Gambians expected. It was too late though. Although Sir Jawara wanted to return to power, it was too little too late. There was no way Sir Jawara would be reinstated to carry on with his plans that saw relative peace and tranquillity in the country however liminal it may be viewed today. Sir Jawara did not go under without a fight however. He was not gun-shy when it came to defending his and his country's rights. For, after being overthrown, he petitioned to the African Union (AU) as Ondikalu (2008) notes that:

In a later case brought by deposed Gambian President Dawda Jawara, the Commission concluded that a 'military *coup d'état* was, therefore, a grave violation of the right of Gambian people to freely choose their government as enshrined in Article 20 (1) of the (African) Charter, (p. 2).

This is very true as it later happened when the Organisation of African Unity (OAU) banned coups which are against one of citizens' democratic rights of selecting a person they want to run their affairs.

By seeking legal remedies instead of plotting to overthrow the government, Sir Jawara, once again, proved how he believed in the rule of law. Furthermore, Saungweme (2007) argues that:

In two cases brought by the former president of the Gambia, Dawda K. Jawara, the African Commission on Human and Peoples Rights stated that unconstitutional changes of government violate the individual rights of people to free expression, assembly and participation in their government, as well as the collective right of peoples to self-determination, (p. 10).

Once more, this shows how Jawara believed in freedom of expression. If he had curtailed it, he would not have guts to champion it before the international body as he did. However, he failed; Sir Jawara set a precedent as a deposed leader who tried legal means to restore sanity and human rights in his country. It was not heard of for any deposed African leader to petition such an international legal instrument seeking the remedies for his country and for himself as a normal citizen but not a former head of the state. What's more, Sir Jawara did not petition for the sake of his power but instead, he did so for the sake of democracy even if it meant for another person to be elected to the office of the president. For, the new government had already banned him from participating in any elections in Gambia due to the fear it has about Sir Jawara. The new government knew too well that if it allowed him to compete in any democratic elections, either he would win or become a threat to the *status quo*. Apart from that, believing in regional and Africa integration, even after being overthrown, Sir Jawara was still active in regional politics as the *Foroyaa* Newspaper (4 February, 2007) reported that Sir Jawara and Gambia felt honoured to head ECOWAS delegation in Nigeria soon before elections. Sir Jawara was responding to a question that wanted him to assess the preliminary development for elections in Nigeria.

This shows how acceptable and strong Sir Jawara was in the politics of his country and in the region. Thanks to his legacy, Sir Jawara became instrumental even after being overthrown something that is rare for many deposed leaders in Africa. His political legacy was as attractive as that of Zambia's found father, Kenneth Kaunda whom citizens wanted to return to politics after his successors proved to be a hyena in sheep's clothing and a liability. As noted earlier, Kaunda refused by reminding Zambia how they were the ones who voted him out even when he told them that he felt like going on leading them. It was too late, wink wink, nudge nudge. This shows how democracy was one of Sir Jawara's aspirations as a president and a citizen of his country. He believed in democratic means of getting to power. However, Sir Jawara did not espouse democracy alone. He, too, wanted to build an educated country as Njie and Fye (1989) note that primary school enrolments increased by 174 per cent between 1976 and 1986, and secondary enrolments by 123 per cent between 1976 and 1988. At the same time, the population had also grown dramatically. Whereas in 1973 the population was estimated at just

493,000, by 1989 it was estimated at 822,000, (p. 62). Such an increase in literacy, especially for a poor country like Gambia, did not rain from the skies. There was a committed government behind it. And this government was under Jawara. While many rulers of the time invested heavily on means of clinging to power, especially through keeping their army happy and loyal, Jawara invested heavily on education to see to it that the country is becoming self-sufficient intellectually. Any good manager, particularly of the state invests heavily on human development. Such a mission, among others, won Jawara a place in good managers' slot in managing the business of state. Moreover, when it comes to education, Jawara valued it not by only offering it but also doing something about it. Like many founders, Sir Jawara did not shy away from writing books. The *Point Online* (April 9, 2010) notes that "the first president of The Gambia, Alhaji Sir Dawda Kairaba Jawara has made history again by becoming the first Gambian statesman to write and publish an autobiography." What makes Sir Jawara's move of writing a book remarkable is the fact that he did so at the old age not to mention being an exception to the general rule to the current crop of Africa rulers who do not write books even read. Again, his autobiography is not the only intellectual work that Sir Jawara wrote. He has a couple of academic works under his belt. Again, for an octogenarian like Sir Jawara, to write a tome of 500 pages is not a joke or any easy thing to do at such an age. At his age, many become senile, thus, writing such a tome proves how mentally stronger Sir Jawara still is. Furthermore, it needs commitment and endurance due to the fact that age has already taken a toll on the health of the person. Against all odds, Sir Jawara defied age impediments and wrote a tome that many people of his age cannot write currently. For, it needs commitment and his standard of discipline to pen such a tome. Also, this shows that Sir Jawara is still reading something that is amiss among many of our current rulers who like to spend time either doing private business or globetrotting without caring about the burden they put on their poor taxpayers. Ironically, Sir Jawara's book *Kairaba* was launched by Yahya Jammeh who toppled him; and who has no guts to write anything. This shows how Jammeh needs Sir Jawara to legalise his vicious rule. Looking at how pathetic insane Jammeh is, if Sir Jawara had any skeletons in his closet, he would not have enjoyed the peace he has enjoyed since returning from exile in Britain.

Additionally, after being overthrown, Sir Jawara fled to Senegal, and thereafter to Britain where he stayed for a while before returning home and leading a normal life. Due to his good management skills, Sir Jawara was able to return home even after being exiled for seven years. Ever since, he has been in his home town Barajally. Unmistakeably, if Sir Jawara had any cloud lingering over his head, he would have been charged for whatever crimes given that it was an in-thing in Africa for successors to charge their predecessors after overthrowing them. It is only his wife who ironically tainted his image after being charged for defrauding authorities in the UK at the tune of £20,000. However, British authorities granted her asylum after SAS saved her from West Africa and brought her to UK. The *Daily Mail* (5 September, 2015) notes that "Lady Njaimeh Jawara, 65, was ordered to wear an electronic tag after admitting over-claiming housing benefit, council tax and pension credits." However bad this may seem, it proves that Sir Jawara did not rob his country. For, if he did, his wife would not have claimed more benefits. She would have been spending her husband's or her wealth as it currently is with the wives of Sani Abacha, Charles Taylor, Joseph Mobutu and others who robbed their countries or allowed their wives to enrich themselves on the their backs by using the office of the president which has become a norm in Africa currently; whereby first ladies are robbing their countries by forming phony companies known as Non-Governmental Organizations (NGOs) which they use to rake money in simply because they are the wives of the presidents.

Once again, this proves how competent and diligent Sir Jawara was in running the business of the state. Sir Jawara was one of a few moderate democrats in Africa of his time who won many terms in office. Clague, *et al.,* (1999) observe that Sir Dawda Jawara led Gambia from 1962 through 1992, winning re-election in several meaningful elections, (p. 190). However, it must be understood that when we say that Sir Jawara was a moderate democrat, it means so at his time when many African countries were comparably under one-party dictatorship not to mention coups that saw many founders go under or being murdered by the regimes that took over after them. There were only two countries in Africa namely Botswana and the

Gambia that had multiparty elections since they gained their independence in 1966 and 1962 respectively. Coincidentally all these two countries were led by president with the title Sir. However weak such elections may be deemed, especially in the Gambia as opposed to Botswana, at least, there were democratic processes that involved many competitors. What taints the image of Sir Jawara, in this sense, is the fact that running the state for many terms is an anomaly in modern democracies; however it was normal at the time Sir Jawara came to power. Again, Sir Jawara receives accolades for doing things differently from others at the time. Despite being the longest serving president in Africa at the time he was toppled, Sir Jawara maintained the position of being a democratic leader. Saine (1997) maintains that Sir Jawara was at the time a longest president who continuously survived multiparty democracy in Africa, (p. 555). So, when it comes to who was a true democrat among African leaders of the time, Jawara beat all of them followed by Leopold Sedar Senghor and Abdul Diouf (Senegal), Ahmadou Ahidjo (Cameroon), Julius Nyerere (Tanzania), Kenneth Kaunda (Zambia) Sir Quett Masire (Botswana), Olusegun Obasanjo (Nigeria) and Nelson Mandela (South Africa) among others. Reisman (1994) notes that "the Gambia had been one of Africa's few successful multiparty democracies since Sir Dawda Jawara won the presidency in 1970 in the nation's first post-independence democratic elections," (p. 797). We know that those elections were not as transparent as current democratic criteria require. Comparably, they were more important than where there was none.

Sir Jawara is one of a few African founders who was overthrown and remained in his country as a free man. All this can be attributed to his rule that was seen as less corrupt, peaceful and a little bit democratic. As indicated above, he, too, did not use his office for his personal enrichment. Sir Jawara did not allow even his wife to use his power to mint and print money just like modern first ladies that have become bedroom presidents. This is why he is featuring in the list of the best African managers who served their countries diligently and altruistically. Although his vision of Africa might be seen as narrow, Sir Jawara once attempted to unite his country with Senegal. The *New York Times* (November 16, 1981) reported that Sir Dawda Jawara formally united his small West African nation with Senegal. However, this union known as Senegambia was ephemeral, it still is self-explanatory. Nonetheless, the *New York Times* went on showing why Sir Jawara decided to unite his country with Senegal. It notes that "it came less than four months after Senegalese troops helped Sir Dawda foil a coup attempt." So, one can say that this short-lived union was enhanced by coup attempt. Sir Jawara was very right. For, after colonial monsters partitioned and divided Africa, they wanted it to become weak and vulnerable. So, whoever that tried to counter such desperation the colonial monsters created, that person was, in a sense, decolonising his country. So, too, the unification of Africa, or some African countries, was a good attempt to lessen the danger the colonial monsters created for their advantage. Despite that, Sir Jawara goes down as a president who tried to unite Africa. Even if you look at what led to the break of the Senegambia confederation or union, you find that Sir Jawara is irreproachable. Saine (2000) notes that the said short-gun confederacy was marred with fear and controversies, particularly over issues to do with rotating presidency which Sir Jawara espoused as opposed to his counterpart, Abdou Diouf of Senegal opposed, (p. 75).

Trying to enter confederacy or union or any arrangement of this nature geared by the fear of insecurity is a normal thing, especially for tiny country like Gambia. Even the famous union of Tanganyika and Zanzibar that has stood–the test of time–was solicited based on security reasons, mainly bumping up the security for both parties to this union. Even the one we agitate that African countries should enter is aimed at enhancing security and cooperation of member countries. However, when it comes to Senegambian experiment, Gambia had valid reasons that created fear, particularly when Senegal's president showed openly that he wanted to remain president without rotating presidency. I do not know the arrangement between the two countries. Again, rotating presidency of the union would have offered assurance to a junior partner like Gambia. Further, it would be indifferent for Sir Jawara not to cool down after the threat of *coup d'état* to re-evaluate everything he had entered with Senegal. Understandably, fear of one another is a common thing in any marriage. However, as the days go–due to, or if, those entering the marriage are committed and willing–such fears dissipate; and trust and cooperation crop up instead.

151

What happened in the case of Senegambia is totally antithetic to what transpired in Tanganyika and Zanzibar regarding the treatment of parties to the unions. For, while Senegambia was entered after suppressing coup attempt, the Tanzania one experienced an army mutiny just a week after being entered as Reisman (Ibid) notes that in January 1964, one week after a revolution in neighbouring Zanzibar, Tanganyika's small army mutinied," (p. 796). Either Senegambia was a result of Sir Jawara's survival or visionary get-up-and-go; it still goes in the annals of history that he tried to take Africa back where it was before 1884 when colonial Europe divided it to what it is today.

When it comes to managing the economy, Sir Jawara was better than many leaders of his time. Clague, *et al.,* (Ibid) note that after conducting a research in various countries in the world that the data indicate a substantial upward trend in the contract-intensive money ratio from 1969 to 1990 (consistent with the general stability of the regime) that is interrupted in the 1978-82 period, (p. 9). This is another feather in Sir Jawara's cap.

"Certainly one cannot divorce it from the nature of The Gambia and from our history. The fact is that our Party, the PPP, has, right from its inception in 1959, drawn up a constitution which emphasises democracy and human rights, and even though these had not been fashionable in Africa, particularly from the time most African countries were achieving their independence (Ghana in the late '50s and many others in the '60s), we steadfastly tried to adhere to these principles. It has not been easy, but we have, as you have said, maintained them up to the present day. Of course we have every reason to believe now that this is the correct path and we will continue along it," Sir Dawda Jawara, 1990 in EC Courier, (N° 119 Jan - Feb. 1990).

Jawara's legacy

Despite ruling for many years, Sir Jawara managed his country well. Even after being overthrown, he has been able to live in the country without facing any criminal charges resulting from corruption. So, too, Sir Jawara left a functioning democracy that his successor destroyed. Sir Jawara, as indicated above, became instrumental in regional affairs and international arena. He is still respected as a patriotic statesman. Importantly, to have the guts to write a tome at old age is another nugget if not a bonus. His love of education still goes on even at an eleventh hour. Such an undertaking, apart from being a motivation for other African leaders and rulers, acts as a catalytic agent for other people to write books and value education, thus investing in it.

Chapter 13

Sankara, Another Martyr Who Promised a lot for Africa

"You cannot carry out fundamental change without a certain amount of madness. In this case, it comes from nonconformity, the courage to turn your back on the old formulas, the courage to invent the future. It took the madmen of yesterday for us to be able to act with extreme clarity today. I want to be one of those madmen. We must dare to invent the future," Sankara, 1985 cited in the *Guardian* (15 October, 2008).

Figure 16: Thomas I. Sankara Burkinabe revolutionary President (image Daily Mail)

There are a few good African leaders of post-post-colonial era. However, only one leader stands out. This is none other than the late

Thomas Isidore Noel Sankara (21 December, 1949–15 October, 1987). Born from a humble family, Sankara became the toast of the town after seizing power in the then Upper Volta (now Burkina Faso) on 4 August, 1983; thereby becoming president up to 15 October, 1987 when he was tragically killed in the *coup d'état* his most trusted friend, Blaise Compaore staged. Sankara was too honest and too obsessed with his vision of decolonising his country so much that he was not able to see the enemies that congregated at the table with him. Therefore, his zeal and openness made him potentially an easy target for his enemies. This is natural to humans, especially when one wants to do something he or she thinks to be very important. Like Dedan Kimathi, Kenyan Mau Mau leader; and Patrice Lumumba of DRC that we have discussed above, Sankara was betrayed; and thereby killed by the person whom he wrongly trusted the most, Blaise Compaore. Wilkins (1989) notes that on Thursday October 15, 1987 when president Sankara was shot, along with thirteen others, just outside the *Conseil d'Etente*, the central parliament. The presidential post was immediately claimed and taken by Sankara's right-hand man Captain Blaise Compaore, (p. 375).

If there is anything at which Sankara beat other African leaders was nothing but his zeal and commitment to *invent the future* as he divorced *old formulas*. So, too, Sankara was too open. He did not conceal what he wanted to do and what his dreams for and about Africa were. Arguably, being neophyte and inexperienced–which he once admitted publicly–took a toll on his vision so as to be used by his nemeses to easily and quickly finish him. Despite those weaknesses, no leader has ever expressly and ebulliently articulated his vision like Sankara; chiefly when we consider the fact that he was not highly educated. Sometimes, one can say that the luck of academic sophistication, also, contributed to his fall. He was neither a hypocrite nor a cunning fox or snake but a neophyte. What made him a threat to most African political dinosaurs; and the interests of the big guys, thus susceptible is the fact that he wanted to divorce old formulas and old solutions so as to embark on a search for new answers and alternative for Africa. This deportment made him fair game not only for imperialists but also their stooges such as Ivorian first president, Felix Houphouët-Boigny and Malian Moussa Traore who openly showed aversion of Sankara. Many old guards did not like Sankara and what he stood for. Some felt like Sankara was stealing thunder from them apart from being a threat to their corrupt and ham-fisted regimes. They were afraid that the example he would set would motivate their citizens to ask why their countries were not performing as good as Burkina Faso under Sankara's watch and vision was. So, his was death either caused by imperialists or their agents or both as it happened when his most trusted friend Blaise Compaore was assigned to carry on the plot. The *Guardian* (15 October, 2008) notes that "Compaoré is widely suspected to have ordered Sankara's murder in order to do the French and regional dictators a favour." How thoughtless is this? How could a true leader do colonialists a favour by sacrificing his brothers and sisters after killing their leader? Despite doing such a dirty job, Compaore did not understand how he also endangered his own life. After being booted out of power, France that used him did not even welcome him just like it did to Mobutu after exploiting him for a long time. France abandoned all stooges it once used. You can see this in the way it maltreated Bokassa after being pulled down. Essentially, when somebody uses you to commit buffoonery, that person cannot respect or value you. What a lesson for those who betray their countries and people to serve colonial interests!

Certainly, the biggest sin that those fallen heroes, namely Lumumba and Sankara above, committed is nothing but to wrongly think that everybody around them had love and commitment to their causes of stimulating the brains of Africans to take their destiny in their hands. Swahili sage has it that in the entourage of the crocodiles must have some monitor lizards in it too. Unfortunately for Lumumba and Sankara and Africa, they did not look over shoulder which helped their betrayers to stab them in the back. Although the world has known Compaore Sankara's murderer because he benefited from it, there are other conspirators along with him. Skinner (1988) argues that Captain Thomas Sankara was assassinated on 15 October 1987 under the instructions and wishes of Captain Blaise Compaore, Major Jean-Baptiste Lingani, and Captain Henri Zongo (p. 437) not to forget Ivorian president Houphouët-Boigny whom France used to finish the business *neutralising* Sankara. And this is not the end of the story. Compaore's death was a grand scheme that involved rich countries, mainly Burkina Faso's former colonial monster, France and other Western countries that were afraid of seeing Africa freeing itself from their fangs after starting depending on itself. Now it is history that Sankara was betrayed by his best friends who willingly offered themselves to the imperialists to be used to do their dirty laundry. Again, there is a lesson. Since African countries acquired independence, their former colonial monsters did not let them go as they wrongly thought. This propensity of wanting to keep on exploiting and dividing Africa has since gone on. Again, how many have gotten the lesson so as to take precautions *vis-a-vis* betrayals geared by power hunger and greed?

Just as it was in the case of Mobutu, the West installed Compaore headed by France in order to derail Sankara's drive that aimed at freeing Burkina Faso from colonial grip which would have been a catalytic agent to other African countries. If Sankara had lived to fulfil his vision and dreams, Africa would not be the same. For, Sankara's ripple effects would have engulfed and swallowed Africa like a bush fire. Sankara's death was made in Paris; and French former president Francois Mitterrand is said to be behind it, (Harsch, 2014). Like Lumumba who dressed down Belgian colonial monster during independence ceremony by breaking the protocol, Sankara did exactly the same in the presence of Mitterrand. Skinner (1988) argues that when François Mitterrand visited Sankara in November 1987, Sankara broke protocol by haranguing him about France's foreign policy *vis-à-vis* South Africa, Angola and Chad, (pp. 447-448). Skinner goes on saying that due to the infatuation Sankara caused, Mitterrand had to abandon the remarks he had prepared so as to delve into lecturing the guests on the complexity of world affairs as a response to Sankara he regarded as child to him.

If anything, no unforgivable sin that Sankara committed like humiliating a colonial monster, especially the president of France before the public. Therefore, from there, Sankara's fate was sealed. What was left is nothing but the execution of the plot. Additionally, Sankara's policies seemed to have liberated Burkina Faso from dependence on France. Within a short time he was at helms, Sankara motivated his people to produce for their consumption which set them away from their former colonial monsters. Sankara wanted to teach his people how to fish instead of giving them a fish the same way colonial monsters have always kept on doing to their former colonies. They do not like to teach them how to fish for fear that the will become truly independent. Imperialists did not want his ideas to spread across Africa. If he had succeeded, it means Africa would have divorced its colonial monsters; and thereby became self-sufficient which is detrimental not only to the economies of the individual countries but the whole capitalist system. It is sad that many African leaders were not bold and brave enough to pick up from where Sankara left and propel Africa to prosperity. Up until now, Africa has not gotten another Sankara. It is only recently that Sankara-like president—that we will discuss later—surfaced in Tanzania.

Due to his love of decolonisation and fight against corruption, Sankara created many enemies within and outside his country and in the ranks especially. Some of the measures that Sankara took, although won him the place in the best managers of Africa, left him with many enemies including those he trusted the most. Like Mobutu, Compaore provides an ideal example of how the best friend can become the worst enemy as far as greed and myopia are concerned, particularly if this friend is a straight partner. Skinner (Ibid) notes that Sankara was not ready to spend 60 per cent of Burkina Faso's income paying civil servants who comprised of 0.3 the population while the rest of the population—especially at the time Burkina Faso was hit by famine—while the majority were suffering and dying. Skinner (op.cit.) argues that Sankara viewed as a sin for a few to have champagne while the majority had water, (p. 441). Going on serving just a fraction of the population of his country was totally unfair and immoral in Sankara's eyes. He thus, decided to cut down public servants' salaries which created more enemies. Essentially, Sankara was ahead of his time due to the fact that Africa has become poorer and poorer due to wasting a lot of revenues in paying bureaucrats who happen to be corrupt and good thieves in public offices. The West has always been at home with this criminality on top of supporting corrupt regimes, toppling the visionary and responsible regimes that were not ready to vend their people knowing the repercussions of such a phenomenon. Western countries know that African countries cannot develop in such a manner in which a big chunk of the revenues is spent on administrational services. They know too well the type of the people they created. They know how African governments are a loss-making project they created and left abaft to do their show. Sankara wanted to change this. And doing so would mean that African countries had to become independent; thus, irreproachable and uncontrollable by the West.

There is more evidence that implicates the West to be behind the death of Sankara just like that of Lumumba. Interestingly, much of the evidence can be derived from Western media just as the *Guardian* (15 October, 2008) discloses that:

> Like Patrice Lumumba–an earlier principled political leader who was a violent casualty of the cold war–Sankara proved to be a creative and unconventional politician. He wanted to a chart a "third way," separate from the interests of the major powers (in his case, France, the Soviet Union and the United States).

The *Guardian* shows that there was no safe alliance for Sankara. Sometimes, imperialists cooperate, mostly when their heinous interests are threatened as it is the case of Sankara and Lumumba. One would ask: If Sankara's, just like Lumumba's, sin was to align himself with the opposite side when Lumumba was assassinated the USSR knew what would befall him. But it did not act or come to his aid. It was obvious that those Sankara wrongly thought were his friends would not help him at the hour of need given that his plans and policies were opposed to theirs. Jaffre (2011) notes that:

> Thomas Sankara, among other priorities, focused on agriculture and farmers to stimulate national revival. He sought to create an internal market for a variety of consumer goods accessible to the masses and meet the greatest number of basic needs. He promoted women's emancipation and changes in men's attitudes toward women. He took a patriotic approach to managing public funds, campaigning against debt and the impoverishment of Africa, and agitating for internationalism that challenged the subordination of Africa by the global economic system. In short, he took on many radical initiatives that confronted the norms of the global system. He quickly alienated himself from local, regional and international supporters, especially from within his own backyard in Francafrique.

As argued above, Sankara was hated by both internal and external enemies because he wanted to set an example that would stop Africa's dependency on the West once and for all by sensitising his people to work on their problems as an example for the whole Africa. Western countries did not like Sankara to use his country as an economic laboratory whose results would sweepingly affect the whole continent they have held at ransom since they introduced colonialism. Further, Sankara wanted to build confidence that would dispel the myth by introducing new "answers based on new formulas" that would discourage Africans from depending on handouts and degradation wantonly. Apart from inventing the future, Sankara wanted to invent a new Africa that would solve its problems and abhor dependency and beggarliness that have, for a long time, inundated the minds of many Africans elites and *hoi polloi* that they cannot survive without the help of the West, the god-turned *saviour*. Sankara wanted to challenge the dominant narrative that has hijacked Africans so as to treat them like androids for generations.

Jaffre (2009) discloses that renamed Upper Volta Burkina Faso, meaning 'land of the honourable'. He argues that Sankara wanted to avoid foreign dictates as he refused aid from the IMF and the World Bank. He argues that Burkina Faso was semi-arid, hungry, and indebted; and had one of the highest infant mortality rates, with no hope of going it alone. Furthermore, Jaffre argues that Sankara had to fight desertification, achieve food self-sufficiency, and provide healthcare. Sankara's motto was 'two meals a day and ten litres of water a day for all every day'. Again, Sankara wanted his country to produce what it eats and eat what it produced "without unnecessary imports and military purchases, end waste, privilege and corruption, (page not provided).

Sankara led by examples. For example, like Nkrumah, Sankara wanted Africa to have its own club which would match with the doctrine of cartelization of its products which the ever-exploitative West would not endorse. Although many academics and analysts tend to think that Sankara did not know his fate, he actually knew it too well; and, like Lumumba, he was ready to pay the price. In the concluding speech he made to the African Union Organisation, he saw it coming; and stood to be counted just like Plato who said that one must die for the Truth. Sankara was one in a few who stood and paid for the Truth even if it needed him to die as he did. Furthermore, Sankara has another credit that many Africans do not have. He is the only African leader who tried to take on gender inequality as it is entrenched in colonial and African patriarchal cultures. He questioned the logic behind men being on top of women; and did something about it by empowering women as well as men. Nobody has ever, and ever since, attempted this experiment. He became the first leader in the world to champion the rights of women. He ordered men to do women's chores so that they can see first-hand how harder it is to be treated like that.

Given that the East and the West have always banked on mythical but unfair and exploitative relationship with Africa, whoever tried or wanted to debunk such a myth was their enemy number one. Thus, he was to be eliminated at all costs, and by all means as it was in the Sankara's case. Sometimes, the West and East cooperate when it comes to destroying the enemy who threatens their interests. Lumumba's assassination provides an idea example of this dichotomous relationship. Moreover, Sankara truly abhorred injustice. For example, he did not find any logic in paying debts to ex-colonial monsters whose economies depend heavily on offering loans to poor African countries that would—in the future—pay back ten folds as it currently is, thus pauperising these countries. Sankara viewed debts as one of the factors that have always created more harm to African countries even more so as to become more dependent and controlled than even before these countries acquired independence. Such dependency has furthered exploitation and neocolonialism and neo-imperialism. Sankara's vision was so simple. If we pay them we will die while they will not die if we do not pay them the loans. It appeals morally and logically that a pauper will die if he or she commits suicide of denying what he or she depends on to pay a tycoon who does not need what the pauper pays her or him. After uttering such sacrilegious words, the West was at work to see to it that Sankara goes under. Baker (2002) notes that "in Burkina Faso under Thomas Sankara (1983–7), a structural adjustment programme modelled on that of the IMF created considerable discontent in urban areas and arguably led to Sankara's downfall, (p. 69). Again, despite this open secret, many African countries—as of

162

today–still allow such denting neoliberal policies to keep on destroying their economies and their people for fear of being toppled like Sankara. For how long will Africa languish in this mess and why?

To show the way and how pragmatic Sankara was, he did what he said and said what he did. He did not want to preach water and drink wine. The *Guardian* (15 October, 2008) discloses that Sankara discouraged the extravagances that came with government office and encouraged others to do the same. He earned a small salary ($450 a month), refused to have his picture displayed in public buildings, and forbade the uses of chauffeur-driven Mercedes and first class airline tickets by his ministers and senior civil servants. Essentially, this is what new Tanzania's president Dr. John Pombe Magufuli is doing currently. Sankara went further declaring his assets as he wanted his comrades to do the same. Some (1990, 65–68 cited in Jaffre 2014) notes that:

> At the last cabinet meeting the day before the coup, Sankara pushed for adoption of a code of conduct for everyone holding high state office Ernest Nongma Oue´draogo, a cousin of Sankara who was then interior minister, later recalled that Compaore´, already 'not very enthusiastic about the struggle against corruption', was additionally unhappy that he had to publicly declare his assets. According to Oue´draogo, Compaore´ was subsequently 'reproached for having hidden certain properties of his wife, such as a massive gold clock given to her by President Houphouet-Boigny of Cote d'Ivoire, in whose family she was raised (author's interview, Ouagadougou, 4 March 1999).

With such a greedy mongrel in the fold, Sankara was to die. Like Jude Iscariot to Jesus, Sankara either was in bed or was dancing with a devil. Differently from Jesus, Sankara had no any God's preferential room of being brought back to life after dying. Sankara was larger than life. No way can words deliver him to readership as he actually was despite his life being cut short. To enjoy more of Sankara, please read his following iconic speech to his colleague African leaders as presented *mutatis mutandis*. To view and listen to this iconic speech please click this link https://www.youtube.com/watch?v=DfzoToJEnu8. For those conversant with French can also watch this clip to know who actually Sankara was. https://www.youtube.com/watch?v=bfesorqV1To Speech was given at the African Unity Organisation (OAU) Conference, Addis Ababa Ethiopia, and July 29, 1987.

Mr. President;
Heads of delegations:

I would like at this moment for us to take up the other question that plagues us, the question of debt, the question of Africa's economic situation. As much as peace, resolving this is an important condition for our survival. That is why I thought I should impose a few additional minutes on you, so we could take this up....

We believe analysis of the debt should begin with its roots. The roots of the debt go back to the beginning of colonialism. Those who lent us the money were those who colonized us. They were the same people who ran our states and our economies. It was the colonizers who put Africa into debt to the financiers—their brothers and cousins. This debt has nothing to do with us. That's why we cannot pay for it.

The debt is another form of neocolonialism, one in which the colonialists have transformed themselves into technical assistants. Actually, it would be more accurate to say technical assassins. They're the ones who advised us on sources of financing, on underwriters of loans. As if there were men whose loans are enough to create development in other people's countries. These underwriters were recommended to us, suggested to us. They gave us enticing financial documents and presentations. We took on loans of fifty years, sixty years, and even longer. That is, we were led to commit our peoples for fifty years and more.

The debt in its present form is a cleverly organized reconquest of Africa under which our growth and development are regulated by stages and norms totally alien to us. It is a reconquest that turns each of us into a financial slave—or just plain slave—of those who had the opportunity, the craftiness, the deceitfulness to invest funds in our countries that we are obliged to repay. Some tell us to pay the debt. This is not a moral question. Paying or not paying is not a question of so-called honour at all.

Mr. President:

We listened and applauded to the prime minister of Norway when she spoke right here. She said, and she's a European, that the debt as a whole cannot be repaid. The debt cannot be repaid, first of all, because, if we don't pay, the lenders won't die. Of that you can be sure. On the other hand, if we do pay, we are the ones who will die. Of that you can be equally sure. Those who led us into debt were gambling, as if they were in a casino. As long as they were winning, there was no problem. Now that they're losing their bets, they demand repayment. There is talk of a crisis. No, Mr. President.

They gambled. They lost. Those are the rules of the game. Life goes on. [Applause]

We cannot repay the debt because we have nothing to pay it with. We cannot repay the debt because, on the contrary, the others owe us something that the greatest riches can never repay—a debt of blood. It is our blood that was shed.

People talk of the Marshall Plan, which rebuilt the economy of Europe. Bur they don't mention the African Plan, which enabled Hitler's hordes at a time when their economies were under siege, their stability threatened. Who saved Europe? It was Africa. There is very little talk about that. There is so little talk that we can't become accomplices ourselves of this ungrateful silence. If others can't sing our praise, we have the duty, at the very least, to point out that our fathers were courageous and that our veteran fighter saved Europe and ultimately allowed the world to rid itself of Nazism.

The debt is also a product of confrontations. When people talk to us today about economic crisis, they forget to mention that the crisis didn't appear overnight. It has been with us for a long time, and it will deepen more and more as the popular masses become increasingly aware of their rights in face of the exploiters.

There is a crisis today because the masses refuse to allow wealth to be concentrated in the hands of a few individuals. There is a crisis because a few individuals hold colossal sums of money in foreign banks—enough to develop Africa. There is a crisis because in face of these individual fortunes, whose owners we can name, the popular masses refuse to live in ghettos and slums. There is a crisis because people everywhere refuse to stay in Soweto when Johannesburg is directly opposite to them. That is, there is a struggle, and the deepening of this struggle leads to worries among the holders of financial power.

They ask us today to collaborate in the search for stability. Stability to the benefit of the holders of financial power. Stability to the detriment of the popular masses. No, we can't be accomplices of this. No, we can't go along with those who suck the blood of our peoples and who live off the sweat of our peoples. We can't go along with their murderous ventures.

165

Mr. President:

We hear talk of clubs—the Club of Rome, the Club of Paris, the Club of Everywhere. We hear talk of the Group of Five, of Seven, of the Group of Ten, perhaps the Group of One Hundred. Who knows what else? It's normal that we too have our own club, our own group. Starting today, let's make Addis Ababa a similar seat, the centre from which will come a breath of fresh air, the Club of Addis Ababa. We have the duty to create the united front of Addis Ababa against the debt. This is the only way we can say today that by refusing to pay, we're not setting out on a course of war but, on the contrary, a fraternal course of explaining the facts as they are.

What's more, the popular masses of Europe are not opposed to the popular masses of Africa. Those who want to exploit Africa are the same ones as those who exploit Europe. We have a common enemy. Our Club of Addis Ababa must tell both sides that the debt cannot be paid. When we say the debt cannot be paid we are in no way against morality, dignity, or respect for one's word. It's our view that we don't have the same morals as the other side. The rich and the poor don't share the same morals. The Bible and the Koran can't serve in the same way those who exploit the people and those who are exploited. There will have to be two editions of the Bible and two editions of the Koran. [Applause]

We can't accept their morals. We can't accept their talking to us about dignity. We can't accept their talking to us about the merits of those who pay and about a loss of confidence in those who don't pay. On the contrary, we must explain that it's normal these days to favour the view that the richest people are the biggest thieves. A poor man who steals commits no more than larceny, a petty crime, just to survive, out of necessity. The rich are the ones who rob the tax revenue and customs duties. They are the ones who exploit the people.

Mr. President:

My proposal does not aim simply to provoke or to create a spectacle. I am trying to say what each of us thinks and hopes for. Who here doesn't want to see the debt written off, pure and simple? Anyone who doesn't want that can leave, take his plane, and go directly to the World Bank to pay it off. [Applause] I hope you don't take the proposal from Burkina Faso as something coming from immature youth, who have no experience. I also hope you don't think only revolutionaries speak in that manner. I hope you acknowledge that it's simply a matter of objectivity and of duty.

I can give you examples of both revolutionaries and non-revolutionaries, of both young and old, who have called for not paying the debt. I could mention Fidel Castro, for example. He has said not to pay. He's not my age, even if he is a revolutionary. François Mitterrand has also said the African countries cannot pay, the poor countries cannot pay. I could cite the madam prime minister of Norway, I don't know her age, and I would hesitate to ask. *[Laughter and applause]* I could also cite President Félix Houphouët- Boigny. He isn't my age. But he has officially and publicly declared that, at least as far as his country is concerned, the debt cannot be paid. Now, the Ivory Coast is counted as one of the wealthier countries in Africa, at least in French-speaking Africa. That's why; moreover, it's no surprise that it no longer pay its dues here. *[Applause]*

Mr. President:

This is not a provocation. I hope you can very wisely offer us solutions. I hope our conference sees the necessity of stating clearly that we cannot pay the debt. Not in a warmongering or warlike spirit. This is to avoid our going off to be killed one at a time. If Burkina Faso alone were to refuse to pay the debt, I wouldn't be at the next conference. On the other hand, with the support of all, which I greatly need *[Applause]*, with the support of all, we can avoid paying. And if we can avoid paying, we can devote our meagre resources to our development.

I would like to close by saying that when we tell countries we're not going to pay the debt, we can assure them that what is saved won't be spent on prestige projects. We don't want any more of those. What is saved will be used for development. IN particular we will avoid going into debt to buy arms. Because an African country that buys arms can only be doing so to use them against an African country. What African country here can arm itself to defend against the nuclear bomb? No country is capable of that, from the best armed to the least armed. Every time and African country buys a weapon; it's for the use against another African country. It's not for the use against a European country. It's not for the use against an Asian country. So in preparing the resolution on the debt we must also find a solution to the question of armaments.

I am a soldier, and I carry a gun. But Mr. President, I wish we would disarm. Because I carry the only weapon I own. Others have camouflaged the weapons they own. *[Laughter and applause]* So dear brothers, with everyone's support we can make peace at home.

We can use Africa's immense latent resources to develop the continent, because our soil and subsoil are rich. We have the means to do that and we have an immense market, a vast market from north to south, east to west. We have sufficient intellectual capacities to create technology and science, or at least to adopt it wherever we find it.

Mr. President:

Let's assemble this united front if Addis Ababa against the debt. Let's organize so that beginning in Addis Ababa we make the decision to limit the arms race between weak and poor countries. The clubs and swords we buy are of no use. Let's make sure that the African market is a market for Africans. Let's produce in Africa, transform in Africa, consume in Africa. Produce what we need and consume what we produce, in place of importing it.

Burkina Faso has come to show you the cotton produced in Burkina Faso, woven in Burkina Faso, sewn in Burkina Faso to clothe the Burkinabè. My delegation and I were clothed by our weavers, our peasants. Not a single thread comes from Europe or America. [Applause] I'm not here to put on a fashion show; I simply want to say that we should undertake to live as Africans. It is the only way to live free and to live in dignity.

Thank you, Mr. President
Homeland or death, we will win!
Worst and venal rulers

Most of African monsters survived the purge by the mass because leaders of two camps, the capitalist West and communist/socialist East stood by them. Under the cold war, no citizens would successfully take on their rulers. This is why; we state this from the outset of this section so that the readers could know it. Under the cold war, barbarity, and gross violations of human rights were tolerated as long as those committing them were able and ready to supply needed resources to the two camps. Such clientele relationship caused a lot of problems for many African countries. Fundamentally, many notorious and corrupt regimes were sustained by their Western or Western masters. An ideal example of this notorious relationship can be drawn from Zaire (now the Democratic Republic of Congo-DRC) whose notorious dictator Joseph Desire Mobutu was installed and sustained by the Central Intelligence Agency (CIA). Whenever he robbed, ruined and tortured Congolese, he knew too well that nobody would topple him.

Sankara's legacy
In sum, this is Thomas Sankara who was baptised Che Guevara of Africa. Again, Sankara's death did not only affect his country alone

168

but also the whole continent at large. For the short time he was in power, he was ebullient enough to articulate his vision and views which–if were put at work by African leaders–Africa would have not been as desperate as it is over twenty years after Sankara's death. That is one thing. Another thing that is an important lesson that Sankara taught us that education is not only obtained through attaining many diplomas or spending lengthy terms in classrooms. The world is a good class if one observing it and decides to learn; and thereby put in practices what is learned. Fearlessness and learning from one's experience–as it was Sankara's case–can be a very good school, tool and a good source of knowledge based on practicality and applicability. Thirdly, the death of Sankara has, ever since, proved that many African leaders are weaklings that are afraid of travelling the less travelled road Sankara willingly decided to take. Fourth, there is yet another lesson that, if African leaders decide to shed their ignorance and fear, chances of cutting the shackles they have willingly been in are high. Although Sankara is dead–wherever he is–must be laughing at our rulers as he feels sorry for poor Africans that have been hijacked by venal and corrupt rulers who have refused to learn even trying things. What has never been clear is the reason why our rulers do not want to learn while Burkina Faso was able to reach food self-sufficiency within just four years under Sankara. Again, why should they do so while self-sufficiency of their countries–for many–will deny them leftovers they receive without thinking or working from their masters? Many use dependency as an opportunity for them to spend time and begging instead of working. If there is an African leader who was supposed to be like Sankara is none other than Samora Machel of Mozambique who died tragically two years after Sankara. Although a little bit slower, Machel had what it takes to transform Mozambique hugely.

Among African best managers, Sankara can claim a high position due to the fact that:

Firstly, he served for a short time–just four years–yet, he attained great success that many would not achieve even after being in power for over forty years. Secondly, Sankara showed an ideological-roadmap about what he believed in. Thirdly, Sankara pragmatically lived according to what he preached. Fourthly, Sankara was able to mobilise and motivate his people to use whatever resources under their disposal to solve their problems by themselves without necessarily resorting into begging as it is pointlessly a norm in many African countries. One of his mammoth successes was being able to organise vaccination that saw over 2,000,000 citizens vaccinated in 15 days (Jeffre 2010) which impressed the World Health Organization (WHO) to applaud Sankara's efforts for attaining such a milestone within a short time. Fourthly, Sankara was able to reach food self-sufficiency not to mention being able to build the railway without depending on foreign aid or experts. Fifthly, Sankara was able to run a country for four years without borrowing which is different from many African governments that are ran by donors. This means, if Sankara would have ruled even for only ten years, Burkina Faso would have changed tremendously.

Above all, Sankara will be remembered for being a president who did not rob his people. Instead, he was toppled simply because he wanted to stamp out misuses and embezzlement of public funds, not to mention beggarliness and borrowing. Sankara was the first African president to stop using gas guzzlers as a way of cutting down useless expenditures; and thereby reducing the burden many African governments place on their poor taxpayers. Sankara preached water and drank water contrary to most of his colleagues who preached water and drank wine. His acts and words are what he lived. Another thing that differentiates Sankara from other African presidents is the fact that he wanted his people to divorce dependency; and, instead, rely on themselves. He is the only African president who dared the International Financial Institutions (IFIs) by actions and words. Sankara will be remembered for his openness, steadfastness and, above all, his meticulousness and hardworking among others. As a man of the people, Sankara wanted Africa to take a leaf from his government *vis-à-vis* true decolonisation of the continent as the preparations for it to take its destiny in its hands.

Most importantly, Sankara left a legacy that, if Africans get good leaders, just like any other human beings endowed with high brains, are able to develop their continent without necessarily depending on begging or being given handouts. Sankara proved that principally, what is lacking now–in Africa–is a visionary, trustworthy, abler and competent leadership. Moreover, Sankara proved beyond any doubt that youths–if they are trusted and supported–can do things differently from old guards; and thereby usher development and prosperity in their countries. It is ironic that most of African rulers are old guards with frozen ideas that are incapable of helping either their countries or the continent.

Chapter 14

Magufuli a Promising Palooka-cum-*Bulldozer*

How come tusks are impounded in China or Europe while they passed at Dar es Salaam Port? Something should be done to make sure that this situation does not recur," Dr. John P. Magufuli, *allafrica* (25 November, 2015).

Figure 17: Dr. John P. Magufuli Tanzania's 5th President who poses to change the country (image courtesy of allafrica.com)

Dr. John Pombe Magufuli was born in Chato, Kagera on the shores of Lake Nyanza on 29 October, 1959. His parents took him to the seminary school aimed at enabling him to go into Roman Catholic priesthood; but later, Magufuli rebelled and went to finish his secondary school at a private secondary school. A teacher by professional, Magufuli pursued his diploma in Education; and later became a chemistry teacher. Thereafter, he joined the University of Dar es Salaam (UDSM) where he obtained a bachelor in Science before proceeding to obtain a Masters, and then, a PhD in chemistry at the same university.

After becoming president; and showing his vision to his country, many people started saying that they could see the spirit of the founder of Tanzania, the late Mwalimu Julius Kambarage Nyerere, coming back through Magufuli. However, it is too early to compare the two; there are some similarities between the twosomes. Like

Magufuli, Nyerere was a teacher who was born in the same region on the shores of Lake Nyanza. They all went to missionary schools however Nyerere did not aim at becoming a priest like the former. The *Citizen* (21 February, 2016) had this to say about Magufuli in conjunction with Nyerere (after his choice, Benjamin Mkapa betrayed him):

> Mwalimu hinted that, a serious person who really hates corruption can be seen from his face. His words must match with his appearance as he utters his words. President Magufuli's words do match his facial expression-at least this far, three months since he ascended to office.

It seems. Nyerere's prediction has become a reality after 17 years of making it. This becomes evident due to the fact that, currently, in Tanzania, Magufuli is the second adored president after Nyerere whose governance left a very shimmering legacy in managing public undertakings. Despite being a palooka in politics, Magufuli has already created a niche for himself within a short time in office. His seriousness about transparency, accountability, and responsibility, among others, has made Magufuli the darling of poor Tanzanians who have much trust in him. While almost all of his three predecessors created banditry economy in Tanzania, Magufuli, just like Nyerere, wants to turn things around. Being a long time senior minister without any cloud of corruption allegations makes him the right guy who can take on the systemic decadence without any fear of being haunted and hunted by his dirty past.

Practically, Magufuli is a crop of the new-generation of African leaders who shows that Africa still has some people with probity, patriotism, selflessness and true vision. Contrary from others regarded as young leaders in Africa, Magufuli–within a short time in office–has outshone many African leaders of his age even younger than him such as Hailemariam Desalegn Boshe (Ethiopia), Joseph Kabila (DRC), Yahya Jammeh (The Gambia), Uhuru Kenyatta (Kenya), Faure Gnassingbe Eyadema (Togo), Ali Bongo (Gabon), and Filipe Nyusi (Mozambique). Magufuli is relatively new in office. Despite that Magufuli has taken the world by storm. And this is why such a political rookie is appearing in the list of the Best African Managers even before completing his first term in office. Again, all depends on how Magufuli will stay steady and focused on his new type of leadership-cum-vision. Thanks to Magufuli's style of leadership, he has made Tanzania to have two best managers in this book along with South Africa as opposed to Kenya that has two worst Managers in the same.

After being sworn in as Tanzania's fifth president, Magufuli initiated concerted plans to revamp the economy of the country by fiercely and truthfully taking on mega corruption, instilling discipline in public services, introducing fiscal discipline and, above all, restoring the dignity of the *hoi polloi*. Arguably, this is why we have skipped three presidents who followed after the first president as a way of acknowledging Magufuli's good start in the politics of managing public affairs in Africa. We are sure the challenge Magufuli poses to other do-nothing or corrupt rulers in Africa is huge. The motivation his leadership provides to *hoi polloi*–if other negatively affected people nicely worked on it–is likely to change African continent a great deal. Africa has many Magufuli save that they are not easy to find due to the fact that many ruling parties do not like them in power. Even the coming of Magufuli is like an accident for the ruling party in Tanzania that was forced to sponsor him after noting the heat of the opposition.

While his predecessor, Jakaya Kikwete was renowned for unnecessarily globetrotting under the pretext of begging, doing nothing, and putting the country on the *autopilot*, Magufuli saw to it that no public officials are allowed to globetrot as they were used or abused their subjects was a norm under Kikwete. Magufuli seems to have learned from the weaknesses of his three predecessors renowned for hand-off sort of administration. Before Magufuli bursting onto the scene, politically, power and public services in Tanzania had become a conduit for robbing the public. Since the first government exited office, Tanzanians became like orphans who were abused and used by rulers and their cronies to get rich quickly. Magufuli seems to have put a stop on this anomaly at least for the time being. Currently, everybody respects everybody; and somewhat justice and sanity in public offices are slowly returning. This is why Magufuli is seen as a leader but not a ruler who uses power for self-enriching without forgetting his praise singers. Essentially, Magufuli's first act that reverberated all over the world is his cancellation of Independence or Uhuru Day celebrations which would have burnt Tshs. 6bn pointlessly. Instead of allowing the high and mighty celebrates, he ordered that money be spent on constructing one section of a major road in the capital, Dar es Salaam. Magufuli (quoted in Pereira year not provided) says "it is so shameful that we are spending huge amounts of money to celebrate 54 years of independence when our people are dying of cholera," (p. 4). Once again, Magufuli seems to understand the problems many poor Tanzanians face. He knows them too well. He is the son of the pauper who has never forgotten where he came from. Looking at how rotten Tanzania was, saying such words needed true love, patriotism and the courage of the mad. As if that was not enough, Magufuli ordered Tanzanians to spend Independence Day celebrations cleaning their streets which he partook of as the *BBC* (9 December, 2015) notes that "Mr Magufuli picked up rubbish from the street outside State House as part of the scheme, which he had ordered to replace Independence Day celebrations." Magufuli's vision that some analysts called the *magufulification* of the economies of their countries (*New Zimbabwe*, 10 January, 2016) did not end up suspending Independence Day merriments. The *Daily Nation* (29 February, 2016) reported that "hospital stores have been replenished and new equipment bought, under-performing administrators sacked, easy government lunches scrapped, and unnecessary travel banned. Magufuli went on stopping the newly-elected Members of Parliament (MPs) in Tanzania from conducting what they usually called congratulatory parties for their victory. These parties would have consumed Tshs. 250 million. Magufuli was quoted as saying that the MPs should spend only Tshs 15 million; and the rest was spent on buying beds and mattresses for patients who were sleeping on the floor at the Muhimbili National Hospital (MNH).

Magufuli's style of leadership has attracted many people all over the world, particularly in the East African region where many citizens wanted their leaders to rule like Magufuli by downsizing their huge government the same way Magufuli did by forming a 34 members cabinet led by 19 ministers and 15 deputies contrary to that of his predecessor that was comprised of cabinet comprised 29 ministers and 31 deputies, (*Citizen*, 10 December, 2015). As if this was not enough, Magufuli's steadfastness almost in all spheres has attracted many observers. Just like any fantastically corrupt African country– to borrow Britain Prime Minister's words when informing the Queen about corruption rates in Afghanistan and Nigeria (*BBC*, 10 May, 2016)–Tanzania is facing endemic poaching in which elephants and rhinos are paying the price heavily. Magufuli's approach is likely to reverse the situation. Kideghesho (2016) notes that "the approach of the fifth phase government under the leadership of Dr John P. Magufuli, fostering accountability and good governance, is the right direction to changing the current scenario," (p. 379). Once again, this shows how Magufuli is the force to reckon with regarding administrating public affairs.

Magufuli did not end up with downsizing his government. He went ahead putting a stop to embezzlement of public fund by sacking many bigwigs who were accused of graft. The heads of the Tanzania Revenue Authority (TRA), the Prevention and Combating Corruption Bureau (PCCB), The Tanzania Harbours Authority (THA), and the MNH, *inter alia,* were fired due to their poor performance. It took a long time for Tanzania to become such corrupt. However, Magufuli's actions show that if those who are the helms decide, corruption can be defeated. Further, the challenges that Magufuli is facing now do not only dwell on corruption but also other areas. Tanzania currently is a narco-state. Many Tanzanians are waiting to see what Magufuli will do in dealing with drug trafficking which has become endemic in many countries in Africa. His predecessor, Kikwete, once admitted to have been given the list of drug barons. But, he did not arrest even a single one. Why? Eglert (2008) notes that some high-ranking politicians in Tanzania are implicated in drug trafficking, (p. 84); and this may be the reasons why the authorities did not arrest the problem. Eglert cites an example of Member of Parliament who implicated bigwigs to end up dying mysteriously; and since she died, nothing has ever been done even to know the cause of her sudden death.

Notwithstanding, after being sworn in as the fifth president of Tanzania, Magufuli stole thunder internationally. The *DW* (12 February, 2016) reported that when Magufuli marked 100 days in office on Saturday, February 12 of the same year had clamped down on Tanzania's political elite apart from giving up some of his own presidential perks. The paper went further noting that Magufuli had cancelled what he thought were unnecessary flights and downsized delegations for international trips. None of his predecessors had ever given up some of his perks. Instead, they kept on increasing their pecks wantonly even when the economy was tanking. Additionally, Magufuli did not allow his wife, the first lady, to form a phoney company aka Non-Governmental Organisation (NGO) that the wives of his two predecessors, Benjamin Mkapa and Kikwete, used to make suspicious wealth. Neither has his son, daughter, brother nor sister been seen riding on his shoulders just like the above mentioned predecessors since Magufuli came to power. Essentially, what makes Magufuli fundamentally different from many African rulers is the fact that he is a leader who speaks the language of a common person in the streets of Tanzania.

Although Magufuli is not an economist, he seems to score high economically. He recently announced that his government is going to review the salaries bigwigs take home. He wants the salaries that correspond with the real situation. He too proposed to reduce unnecessary taxes, especially for poor people as he refuses to offer tax exemptions to the rich who, in a word, ruined Tanzania despite having huge reserves of minerals and other resources. According to the Comptroller and Audit General (CAG) report 2016/07, Tanzania lost over Tshs. that the TRA did not collect thanks to inept leadership of his predecessor (*Citizen*, 26 April, 2016). How many schools could such amount construct in such a poor country had there been abler leadership to collect this money? Interestingly, Magufuli told his people that he is not ready to go cap in hand begging just like his predecessors used to do. And this–for a competent manager of public affairs–makes sense, in the main when we consider the fact that what is lost is bigger than what is begged. Again, by refusing to go self-dressing down begging, Magufuli proves to be different from other African rulers who have turned begging into a booming business through which they get some cuts to stash abroad. He shows the vision of using the available resources to develop his country. Magufuli categorically tells Tanzanians that the era of graft as usual is long gone. He does whatever he does fearlessly knowing the danger of doing so. This is why he always asks for Tanzanians to pray for him due to the fact that he knows the danger he faces and the sacrifice he has made to his country.

As noted above, Magufuli is a new rookie in political scene–who is equated to the giants like Nyerere–that has attracted much attention even academically. Girling (year not provided) observes that Magufuli's victory poised to more transparent and accountable governance which "marked desire to return to the founding principles of Nyerere, also known for his modest lifestyle," (p. 3).

And indeed, due to his fearless style, Magufuli has been nicknamed "Bulldozer" that fears nobody. He seems to be an antithesis of his immediate predecessor who was baptised Vasco da Gama because of globetrotting instead of remaining in office to serve the people. This is why when Magufuli and his predecessor were compared in the period of six months soon after they ascended to power; Magufuli had travelled only once as opposed to his predecessor who had already made ten foreign trips outside the country in his 100 days in office. While many current African rulers are in power to make many blunders, Magufuli has started in the right direction. Shall he not change or being discouraged or sabotaged, chances of reinventing Africa are high. Again, given that Magufuli has been in power for months–despite receiving many accolades– there is no way we can write his legacy the same way we have done about and for others. Many academics that will have the chance to write about his legacy will have a lot to note for the future generation. However, it must be said. If Africa could have at least ten Magufuli, the dream of freeing Africa economically, reunifying it, and stopping it from begging and misusing its resources can be easily realised. Again, Magufuli has already made an indelible mark on the politics of Africa as far as the management of public affairs is concerned. The precedent he has already set–if it is well studied and understood–is likely to move Africa forward more than any time in its history.

When it comes to Magufuli's legacy, nobody can write it now. He is like the first chapter in the tome. More time and much are still waited to be done so as to contemplate about writing his legacy. Situationally, shall he remain on course, Magufuli is likely to write a new and unique history of Africa that will add up to what doyens like Machel, Mandela Nkrumah, Nyerere, and Sankara left. Like a morning shooting star, Magufuli–if he fulfils his mission–is likely to change the way the West looks down at Africa. It is sad that he is a loner in this reinvention and redefinition of Africa. For, one who follows very, very far abaft is Kagame whose tampering with the constitution deprived him the accolade and wand he had as far as reinventing and redefining Africa is concerned. Magufuli–who burst onto the scene in his unique way–is somebody whose legacy will contribute immensely conditionally that he stays on course. Shall his mission succeed; Magufuli is likely to create a new paradigm shift as with regard to the future of Africa.

In sum, when it comes to the crop of Magufuli type of leaders is rare to find, particularly at this very time Africa has been cascading to dictatorship, stinking corruption, nihilism, myopia, egoism and other vices that have always kept Africa abaft in meaningful development. Many African countries are still hunting for their Magufulis. Indeed, time will tell when it comes to the legacy of Dr. John Pombe Magufuli.

Chapter 15

Kenyatta a Land Grabber Who Got Away with Murder

"Our country today is in a bad state for its land is full of fools- and fools in a country delay the independence of its people. K.A.U. seeks to remedy this situation and I tell you now it despises thieving, robbery and murder for these practices ruin our country. I say this because if one man steals, or two men steal, there are people sitting close by lapping up information, who say the whole tribe is bad because a theft has been committed. Those people are wrecking our chances of advancement," Kenyatta, 1952 adapted from Kenyatta and Halsall (1998).

Figure 18: Jomo Kenyatta Kenya's 1st President (image courtesy of Swahili hub)

Mzee Jomo Kenyatta (20th October, 1891–22nd August, 1978) the first president of Kenya, was a shrewd politician who evolved and rose from ashes to glory. Kenyatta's life before becoming president is so controversial and murky in that it, sometimes, becomes too good to be true. Kenyatta's truly history evaded many so to speak. For, it has a lot of missing links. Growing up in such a situation, Kenyatta did many jobs to survive. However, his, cunning behaviour, resilience and ambitions enable him to aim higher, and later, succeed in life. He started his life as water metre reader, then, he exiled himself to Russia, thereafter to England before going back to Kenya where colonial authorities detained him for his activism, largely being linked to Mau Mau, a Kenyan movement, that swore to topple British rule in the country. Notably, despite being credited to have links with Mau Mau uprisings in Kenya, Kenyatta spent much time abroad enjoying himself while the actual movers and shakers of Kenya's struggle for liberation were either killed or suffering in jails if not in the forests. If history is well rewritten, there is no Mau Mau without the late Field Marshall Dedan Kimathi whom Kenyatta betrayed as we will later see.

Due to his ebullience and *hoopla*, when Kenyatta became Prime Minister of Kenya, hopes were high. He seemed to be an ideal choice of a leader that would launch and usher his country into the future after suffering from civil war and colonialism for a long time. Nevertheless, as the time went by, Kenyatta slowly proved to be a different person that Kenyans did not know, more of a liability than an asset. His dark shadow showed a monster whose rust for wealth was unmatchable. We will see a true Kenyatta, especially at grabbing land later– the one that used his office to rip the country off. Kenyatta made sure that he grabbed big parcels of land and amassed a lot of wealth so as to leave abaft a very well-heeled family. When describing Kenyatta's family, the *Daily Nation* (20 February, 2014) reported that "going by the rankings of the New World Wealth report, the family can be ranked among cent millionaires, whose wealth range between $100 million and $1 billion." The family talked about is Kenyatta's family. The paper went on saying that when it comes to the size that Kenyatta's family owns is subject to speculations. Interestingly, despite Kenyatta's family sitting on such humungous wealth made by means of robbing the country, Kenyans had the guts of voting his son-cum-heir, Uhuru, to become their president in 2013 in controversial elections.

Kenyatta ran and presided over the most ludicrously brutal and corrupt regime among the first crop of African post-colonial leaders. Gray and MacPherson (2001) note that "President Kenyatta also tacitly encouraged a chain of events that imposed two burdens on

182

Kenya's economy" (p. 5) through normalising corruption; and allowing foreign companies to bribe Kenyan politicians. And indeed, this is very true due to the fact that Kenyatta grabbed land almost everywhere in the country; and used to reward loyalty. So, too, under Kenyatta's watch, some of his detractors or those he thought to be his opponents went missing so as–for some–to be found dead. The first casualty was Pio Gama Pinto (March 31th, 1927–February 25th, 1965) whose death was known to Kenyatta's government as Durrani (2008) notes that "it is generally believed that those in senior position in the Government were involved in, or were aware of, the plot to assassinate Pinto," (p. 211). Durrani purposely, but shrewdly, uses those in "senior position" not the one with the most senior position to imply one person who at the time was President Kenyatta. "Those" can stand for the power whereby president always uses "we" instead of "I" as the symbol of power which in English is known as majestic qualification. As for Pinto, being vocal and seemingly progressive, he posed a looming danger to the powers that be as far as the economy of Kenya–the economy that was indeed, ran criminally–was concerned. Therefore, the need to get rid of him was imminent; and he had to be eliminated. Much since has not been written about Pinto however.

The second casualty was Thomas Joseph Odhiambo "Tom" Mboya (15th August, 1930–5th July, 1969) who was short at point blank on 15th July, 1969–almost four years after Gama was gunned down–when he was walking in the street. Mboya will be remembered as a person who changed the world by affecting the history of racism in the US and the world in general. For, he is the one who engineered and supervised the exercise of airlifting some Kenyans to go for high education in the US among who was Barack Obama Sr. the father of US's first Afro-American president, Barack Obama in 1959. Mboya's friendship with former US president J.F. Kennedy who offered to help some African students to acquire higher education in the US was the force behind this project. Why was Mboya assassinated? Oculi (2011) answers the question noting that Mboya was killed due to posing danger to Kenyatta; thereby "his ethnic Luo people saw his death as the culmination of a Kikuyu plot to block his ambition to succeed the ailing Kenyatta," (p. 22). Such a claim is obvious that Kenyatta was behind the whole plot. However, those who see

Kenyatta as an ideal leader may maintain that he, as a person, had nothing to do with the assassinations save that the buck stops with him due to being president. As Oculi alludes, the death of Mboya was about the succession politics after the death of Kenyatta. We can say that Kenyatta's inner sanctum is responsible for the assassination of Mboya. It is not easy to exactly pinpoint at who order the two killings above. So, too, it must be noted that such a systemic elimination of opponents will feature in the regime that took over after the death of Kenyatta. The chain of reactions did not end up here. The regimes that took over from Kenyatta's would replicate the same with the bigger magnitude so as to cost the lives of hundreds of innocent Kenyans. We will see this later.

The third victim of Kenyatta assassination policies was his tribesman Josiah Mwangi Kariuki (21st March, 1929–2nd March, 1975) who opposed Kenyatta's rust for grabbing land. Githongo (Year not provided) notes that Kariuki was brutally murdered on 2nd March, 1975 during Kenyatta's regime for rubbing the government the wrong way for matters of social justice, (p. 334); also see Ajulu (2002); Kagwanja (2005); and wa Mutonya (2013). Despite such assassinations and land grabbing, there are some close friends and associates who exonerated Kenyatta from being behind these assassinations due to old age that circumstantially rendered him incapable of running the country. Even if Kenyatta's consigliore were behind such killings given that the old man did not run the show, Kenyatta will take a hit. As it was in the case of Mboya even Gama, under such murky circumstances, who actually ordered the killings will not be known. However, under vicarious liability or inattention, whatever that was done under his watch—weather he ordered it or not—Kenyatta will bear the brunt for it. This is what leadership is all about; and this is why leaders must be responsible and accountable for whatever they do or order to be done underscoring that whatever happens under their watch is perceived to have come from them. A good and competent manager would not wait at the helms like Kenyatta did for a long time while knowing he was incapable of running the business of the state. He would hand over power to others knowing that he was incapable of running the business of the state for whatever reasons be they incapability or the lapse of time just as Leopold Sedar Senghor (Senegal) and Nyerere (Tanzania) willing did even if they were still capable of running their countries competently.

Arguably, trying to exonerate Kenyatta based on being senile does not hold water. Why waiting up until things go wrong if Kenyatta were a good manager? Kenyatta will always be blamed on the deaths of his opponents even if he did not order them personally. As indicated above, vicarious liability, in Africa, can be summaries in the fact that when a dog bites somebody, the owner of the dog is always blamed and held accountable. This being the case, there is a rationale in blaming Kenyatta for the deaths of his opponents. Tactically, and out of affiliation, it is easy to exonerate Kenyatta from the assassinations of his opponents. However, it is hard to do the same *vis-à-vis* land grabbing that Kenyatta and his colleagues were involved in which became a permanent scar on Kenya. Big parcels of land that Kenyatta left to his family will always bemoan whoever tries to exonerate Kenyatta from this crime resulting from greed and abuses of power. A shaky foundation that Kenyatta laid down for the country will always disturb Kenya if nothing is done to alleviate the situation by calibrating it. You can see this in the 2007's chaos from rigged elections whose major causes were revolving around the history of land grabbing and unfair land distribution which created tribal animosity. What came to be known as the Post-Election Violence (PEV) happened because there were segments of Kenyans that felt that their land illegally, and under tribalism went to Kenyatta's community, Kikuyu. Arguably, the PEV revolved around land redistribution as it was maliciously done in the past under Kenyatta's watch. We have tried to clarify this in length given that Kenyatta is still regarded as the father of the nation. So, dealing with such a person needs extra care due to the followership he commands not to forget the millions of those who think they benefited or still benefit from his tribal politics even if they did not.

Although Kenyatta surrounded himself with his homeboys—or call them courtiers or bootlickers—he still did not want anybody to challenge his *diktat* or authority even if such a person hailed from his community as it is in the case of Kariuki who ended being assassinated. Gathogo (Year not provided) notes that "JM's political philosophy and belief that the Kenyatta Government had hijacked the aspirations of the freedom struggle that the Mau Mau freedom fighters staged. Kariuki's apparent ambition for leadership won him true enemies within the ruling clique," (p. 335). Gathogo goes on arguing that JM was the first Kenyan politician to surrender the land so that it could be redistributed to landless Kenyans something Kenyatta and his toadies–who later were known as "Mount Kenya Mafia" (Wanyeki, 2010, p. 92) under Mwai Kibaki–did not approve of or subscribe to openly. Kariuki, therefore, was regarded as a grand *provocateur* whose stand would antagonise people with Kenyatta's regime. Therefore, he had to be eliminated as the means of avoiding the danger he posed to the regime. Before Kenyatta's eyes, this was unacceptable. Firstly, Kariuki challenged Kenyatta's *diktat*. Secondly, he created an unnecessary danger for himself and the country. Thirdly, Kariuki refused to partake of the sin of land grabbing that the *head priest* and those surrounding the *altare* were committing. Therefore, he had to be eliminated as soon as possible by all means and at any cost. Arguably, nothing would have irked Kenyatta and his courtiers like his statement that "…we do not want a country of ten millionaires and ten million beggars…," (p. 335) which Kariuki skilfully articulated in his quest of seeing social and economic justice for all Kenyans.

True, Kenyatta monkeyed with the system so as to get away with murder even after dying. For, up until now, most Kenyans are still afraid of openly accusing Kenyatta of what he did even posthumously. They are not even ready to confront his estate to demand that their land and property be returned to them. It is only in academia where the dark side of Kenyatta is exposed as the above mentioned academics show. But, despite all, the trail still goes on tracing Kenyatta in ruining Kenya using cronyism, tribalism and nepotism. Oculi (2011) notes that "… in 1976 Kenyatta ruled with 50 per cent of provincial administrators drawn from the Kikuyu ethnic group" (p. 17). Such a rule cannot stop leaving such a bad legacy of a divided and exploited society that Kenya has been ever since Kenyatta to the present under another Kenyatta.

Kenyatta, as argued hitherto, was a very controversial person. He could talk right and walk left. For example, Kenyatta cited in Mazrui (1973) maintains that "Europeans told us to shut our eyes to pray and say Amen, when our eyes were shut, and while our eyes were shut, they took our land," (p. 669). Ironically however, the same

Kenyatta who was complaining about Europeans' land grab became more of a land grabber than those he accuses. While European colonial monsters used religion to grab Kenya's land, Kenyatta used politics to commit the same crime at bigger magnitude than those he accuses. Médard (2010) notes that Kenyatta and his associates used *Africanisation* as a ploy to own land as they accumulated wealth the same token Kenyatta's successor, Daniel arap Moi used even though at less magnitude, (p. 19).

Despite such exploitation, Kenyatta went on exploiting Kenya even posthumously. His remains were embalmed and preserved for the future generations to see. Is there anything that Kenyatta has done that deserves to burn billions of shilling preserving his remains Kenyan poor taxpayers cough to keep such evil historic relics? With such a stinking legacy it, sometimes, becomes difficult to gauge what Kenyatta's remains have been kept for. Arguably, if preserving the remains of the founders of the nations were something important, Africa has only four personalities whose remains were supposed to be preserved for the coming generations to see and study. Those are Nelson Mandela, Patrice Lumumba, Julius Nyerere and Thomas Sankara. For, they did not betray their conscience or people just like the failed and the worst managers of Africa did. Ironically, the bodies of Lumumba and Sankara either were destroyed or buried without any honour. If things were to go the way some of the victims like, there are people whose dead bodies would be flogged, mainly those who robbed their countries. Kenyatta's tentacles were not only extended over land but also over anything that made sense to Kenya. Like any dictator, Kenyatta made sure that his name was on everything. It is not a hidden secret in Kenya to find that streets, universities, hospitals and whatnots carry his name and some his son's and wife's which his successor, Moi emulated and exploited religiously.

If we face it, when it comes to who actually championed the politics of freedom in Kenya, Kenyatta misses out of the bigger picture. For, in 1929 the KCA sent Kenyatta to London to lobby on its behalf with regard to Kikuyu tribal land affairs. So, you can see that Kenyatta's activism primarily was tribal but not national which makes him a tribal lord. While he was abroad living his life, some Kenyan activists, prominent ones being Marshall Dedan Kimathi,

Harry Thuku, Jaramogi Oginga Odinga, Tom Mboya, Masinde Muliro, James Gichuru and others decided that enough was enough. Sometimes, one can argue that of all mentioned above liberations fighters in Kenya, Kimathi was like Mandela in South Africa. However, this liberation icon was betrayed by Kenyatta. Mnthali (2014) puts it that "in Petals of Blood the various shades of the new entrepreneurial class who are the tempters in Dedan Kimathi are now in Blue Hills, an exclusive suburb in which they spend their 'useful' lives in prayer, business deals and cocktail parties," (p. 98). What a betrayal. It does not need more words to explain. However, we will do our work to explore it even more by adducing more evidence. Otenyo (2004) maintains that Kenyatta's government betrayed Mau heroes while it ironically rewarded loyalists, (p. 76). On his side, Mnthali goes on noting that Names like that of Jomo Kenyatta and Waiyaki are accidentally in the history and Kenyan institution while real those who truly fought for the independence of Kenya are dubiously left out, (p. 98).

Interestingly, even after Kenyatta *brought* independence, as Kenyans like to say, he kept betraying Kimathi. One living example is the maltreatment of his widow who came back to limelight when Nelson Mandela visited Kenya and asked the whereabouts of Kimathi's widow. The *Daily Nation* (December 8, 2013) had this to report quoting Kimathi's widow as saying that she met Mandela at Jomo Kenyatta International Airport either in 2005 or 2006 where he sighed looked unbelievably after being introduced as the wife of Dedan Kimathi whom he affectionately and quickly hugged and introduced to his wife (Graca Machel)."

To see clearly how Kimathi was betrayed even posthumously by those he helped to get in power, the *Daily Nation* (Ibid) goes on citing Mrs Kimathi saying she had only heard in the news that Mandela was visiting Kenya. Thus, she had to struggle to meet him since he had all along expressed desire to meet Kimathi's family. This is why Mandela looked at Kimathi's widow who happened to be a freedom fighter too "unbelievably" as Mrs. Kimathi nicely puts it. While Kenyatta's administration and those that succeeded him betrayed and ignored Kimathi's contribution to the liberation of Kenya, Mandela did not betray him. The *Daily Nation* (June 14, 2013) notes that "when he visited Kenya in July 1990, shortly after he was released from imprisonment, he inquired about the location of the grave of Field Marshall Dedan Kimathi." Maybe, Mandela thought that Kimathi's grave was in Heroes Acre while nobody bothered to locate it or force colonial monsters to divulge where they buried Kimathi. Again, why did Kenyatta betray Kimathi just like Mobutu Sese Seko did to Patrice Lumumba or Compaore did Sankara? Lonsdale (1990) provides an answer noting that Kenyatta had enjoyed the best of British civilisation, including a course at the London School of Economics (LSE) and the love of an English wife, (p. 8).

In other words, Kimathi's betrayal was engineered by British colonial monsters which make Kenyatta a caricature they used just like Hastings Kamuzu Banda, Mobutu, Idi Amin and many more that Africa evidenced soon after the independence. Instead of preserving Kimathi's remains, Kenyans are burning money on preserving the remains of one of those who betrayed them and Kimathi. Sadly though, almost all governments that came after Kenyatta maintained this betrayal. Mandela underscored this as the *Daily Nation* (Ibid) quotes him standing in front of a giant portrait of former Kenyatta's protégé and successor, Moi saying that "it is an honour for any freedom fighter to pay respect to such heroes" whose graves are unmarked or unknown while their betrayers had monuments erected for them. Although Mandela's plea was not a jeremiad, it had huge impacts on those whom he targeted. The paper says that Mandela's words did not augur well with Moi. *Daily Nation* notes that the speech irked and became a major embarrassment to Moi who, like his predecessor "had refused to publicly acknowledge the Mau Mau as national heroes and Kimathi as a legendary figure who inspired other freedom fighters in Africa."

Even after Kimathi was murdered by British colonial rule, Kenyatta did not lead the struggle. Santilli (1977) maintains that Harry Thuku is the one who formed the first African nationalistic in Kenya in mid-1921-the East African Association that in 1924 the Kikuyu Central Association (KCA) replaced so as by 1939 to have a paid membership over 7, 000, (p. 144).

Fundamentally, those who ignited the sparks of the quest for freedom are not the ones who received the independence. For, when Kenyatta returned back, he was welcomed, just like Hastings Kamuzu Banda in Malawi was, to join the movement. Being an

African who lived in Europe for a long time, his colleagues thought he knew more about Europe than they did. They, therefore, invited him to become their leader. Henceforth, Kenyatta has been in the picture even posthumously due to the fact that as we write this book, his son is the fourth president of Kenya. Kenyatta became Kenya's Prime Minister on 1 June, 1963–12 December, 1964 before amending the constitution that enabled him to assume the title of president after Kenya became a republic. He ruled until 22 August, 1978 when he died naturally in a sleep in the city of Mombasa he liked to go for vacations.

Due to the old age, and being a *tribal chief*, Kenyatta used to rule hands-off by letting his mostly Kikuyu young Turks–as they were known then, to do the rest of the job of managing Kenya–while he only remain a figurehead president ruling Kenya. Given that Britain had huge investment in Kenya, it highly protected Kenyatta's rule. So, nobody would even bother to think about toppling Kenyatta at this time. Kenyatta made sure that his masters', personal interests and those of his inner sanctum were protected.

Fundamentally, he used land to reward those surrounding him something that made them become accomplices to the crime Kenyatta was committing. As indicated above, Kenyatta is renowned for land grabbing. Until his death, Kenyatta has parcels of land almost everywhere in Kenya. There are some speculations that Kenyatta grabbed land so much that he left to his family the land as big as one of Kenyan provinces, Nyanza region. Acquaah-Gaisie (2008) reveals that "Jomo Kenyatta, and his family amassed a large fortune in land, precious gems, ivory and casinos during his rule from 1963 to 1978," (pp. 3-4). Such findings are in tandem with the findings of the government commissions that looked into the issue of land grabbing involving the first family. The *Daily Nation* (May 21, 2013) quoted the report by the Truth Justice and Reconciliation Commission (TJRC) that was formed by the government under the pressure of the new constitution of Kenya maintaining that "President Kenyatta's direct engagement in irregular land allocations compromised his position to prevent or remedy similar cases of land grabbing by his close associates," (p. 1). Such findings were not new to Kenyans who knew Kenyatta and his courtiers, friends and associates as good land grabbers. Klopp (2000) notes that "Kenyatta used the former settler land as patronage to solidify his support and build alliances, and many former loyalists became prominent in the new KANU government," (p. 16). So, you can see how endemic land grabbing was under Kenyatta who used it as means of wining loyalty and rewarding the loyalists, family and friends. Even today many years after Kenyatta, land grabbing has remained a thorny issue due to the fact that even the regimes that came after Kenyatta did exactly what he did. Under Moi whom we will discuss later, everything remained the same as far as land grabbing was concerned. Under his *Fuata Nyayo* or *Follow the Footsteps* incubus-like slogan, Moi hypnotised many thereby grabbing land; and naming many hallmarks of the country after himself just exactly the same as Kenyatta did. Another report by another commission famously known as Ndungu Commission came up with the same findings where presidential powers were used to grab land and reward loyalists and friends. Southall (2005) quotes the report maintaining that there was found to have been widespread abuse of presidential discretion with regard to unalienated urban land whereby both Presidents Kenyatta and Moi were implicated for granting land to individuals against public interests simply because they wanted to gain political mileage even by breaking the law, (p. 145).

A competent and a good manager of state business cannot involve herself or himself in favouritism and nepotism or tribalism. For the best managers as we have seen many above, independence of their countries meant emancipating their people from diseases, exploitation, humiliation, ignorance, injustices and poverty while for bad managers, independence was nothing but, it-is-our-turn-to-eat business. By appropriating land to himself and his consigliore, Kenyatta acted exactly the same like those he unseated. Instead of serving the people, Kenyatta used them to acquire and amass wealth to himself and his courtiers who in the main were his Kikuyu tribesmen and a few non-Kikuyu who were ready to toe the line as it was for Moi. As indicated above, it goes without saying that Kenyatta's legacy of land grabbing has gone on affecting Kenya even posthumously as it was evidenced in 2007 during the PEV mentioned above. Many would agree with me that if Kenyatta were a good and competent manager of public affairs, he would not have amassed wealth and grabbed land. Instead, he would have done like Nyerere in the neighbouring Tanzania who nationalised land and redistributed equally to Tanzanians without allocating anything more to himself or his tribesmen or friends. Typically, Kenyatta created a very obnoxious capitalist country in which the gap between poor and rich was huge and has gone on becoming even bigger. Kenyatta created a cabal of *les petites bourgeoisies* that has always enjoyed the fruits of freedom while the majority is still suffering the same way it was during colonial times. A good manager would have considered the danger such wealth gap poses to the country.

> *"In the early year of European colonisation many white men, especially missionaries, landed in Africa with preconceived ideas of what they would find there and how they would deal with the situation. As far as religion was concerned an African was regarded as a clean slate on which anything could be written. He was supposed to take wholeheartedly all religious dogmas of white man and keep them sacred and unchallenged, no matter how alien to African mode of life. The European based their assumption on conviction that everything the African did or thought was evil,"* Kenyatta, 1938 in Kenyatta (2015, p. 185).

Kenyatta's legacy
One of Kenyatta's legacies is land grabbing that enabled him to amass thousands of acres all over Kenya. Kenya–just like Namibia, Zimbabwe and South Africa–is a time-ticking bomb waiting to explode as far as land disputes are concerned. Kenyatta left behind a very wealthy family as indicated above in terms of money and land. This is true. For, some media have alluded onto this. For example, the *Mavulture* notes that "according to some estimates, the Kenyatta family is reputed to control about 500,000 acres." How many acres does Kenyatta family sit on? Nobody can exactly tell. What is obvious is that the Kenyatta family has more land swathes than it needs, especially in a country in which landlessness is ubiquitous. A good manager would have had considered others instead of stealing from them. A good manager is considerate; and does justice.

Another legacy that Kenyatta left–which was copied and perfected by his successor–is making sure, as aforementioned, that his name is on everything. Kenyatta's name is on the currency, universities, hospitals, streets, roads, airports and many more. So, too, Kenyatta left a sharply divided country along tribal lines which resulted into the PEV 2007-08 whereby over a thousand innocent Kenyans lost their lives not to mention thousands whom became Internally Displaced Persons (IDPs) up until now. Another legacy as far as Kenyatta is concerned is that he left his humble disciple Moi, who stepped in his footsteps under *Fuata Nyayo* philosophy. Moi, as we will see in his legacy, perfected the copy-and-paste art almost in everything. Essentially, Kenya has never had a good copycat like Moi. Although Kenyatta did not create a cult like Mobutu and Houphouët-Boigny, he was all over the place as far as Kenya is concerned. More importantly, Kenyatta has a legacy of being the only African ruler whose body was mummified which makes him go on burdening Kenyan poor taxpayers. His remains are guarded twenty-four hours. So, too, the government spends a lot of tax payers' money on keeping his remains. Although Kenyatta died a long time ago, his legacy of land grabbing and amassing ill-gotten wealth will always caught up with him if not haunt his family and his estate. This crime is unexorcisable.

Special tributes

Although Jomo Kenyatta is regarded as the founding father of Kenya, there are other personalities who contributed even more immensely to the independence of Kenya than Kenyatta himself. Those are Dedan Kimathi, who was murdered by British colonial administration, Bildad Kaggia, Kung'u Karumba, Fred Kubai, Paul Ngei, and Achieng' Oneko who with Kenyatta were known as "the Kapenguria six" (Odari, 2011, p. 4) due to being tried at Kapenguria before being jailed in Northern Kenya thereafter for opposing colonial regime in Kenya. There others who also contributed immensely such as Odinga Oginga, Tom Odhiambo Mboya, Harry Thuku, Martin Shikuku, Ronald Ngala, Masinde Muliro, Argwigs Kodhek, Koitalel arap Samoei, Esau Khamati Oriedo, Mekatilili wa Menza, Pio Gama Pinto and Jean Marie Seroney among others. There sacrifices will always be honoured and remembered by Kenyans. For, it is through their commitment that Kenya became independent after a very long time bloody struggle for independence.

'Well, I mean .. they're different, ain't they?'

Chapter 16

Mobutu the Monster that Ruined the DRC

"There is a story about Zairean President Mobutu Sese Seko which sums up the arrogance and gall required to ransack your homeland and not lose a night's sleep. In an interview on American television the President was asked about the size of his personal fortune. Could he personally pay off his country's multi-billion dollar debt? President Mobutu answered that theoretically that was possible - but how could he be sure he would ever get his money back?" The *Independent* (16 May, 1997).

Figure 19: Joseph D. Mobutu DRC's kleptocratic President (image courtesy of RDA)

195

Joseph Desire Mobutu, later, Mobutu Sese Seko (14 October, 1930–7 September, 1997) is among the most ruthless and corrupt rulers of the monstrosity nature Africa has ever had. When it comes to corruption, comparably, Mobutu was but a monster whose size can be compared to that of amegalodon, the biggest whale said to have been bigger than the current type we know. He can be ranked high among worst managers Africa has ever has in running the business of the state. Ruthless and cunning as he was, Mobutu, indeed, used his showmanship, braggadocios buffoonery and eccentricity to fool everybody himself included. With the help of the West, Mobutu was able to manipulate Congolese so as to get away with murder after messing and vending the country—he turned into his private estate he would mismanage as he deemed fit—for over thirty years. Unpredictable as he was, Mobutu became famous for all wrong reasons. Like Attila the Hun, the most successful barbarian rulers of the Hunnic Empire, Mobutu was one of the most disastrous barbarous rulers the world has ever seen in modern time. He robbed and traumatised his people without any sense of humanity. Apart from immensely robbing the country, Mobutu is alleged to have been behind the assassination of the first Congolese Prime Minister Patrice Lumumba whom he killed under the conspiracy with and orders of the Central Intelligence Agency (CIA). Like, Houphouët-Boigny, Kamuzu Banda and Kenyatta, Mobutu is one of the first corrupt crop of Africa's post-colonial rulers whose legacy will always be synonymous with kleptocracy and brutality. Pusillanimously and callously, Mobutu became a symbol of infamy and corruption *per se*. Olaka-Onyango (1995) defines Mobutu as the dinosaur of African politics that effectively ruled the DRC for over thirty years after assassinating Lumumba, (p. 2). Apart from being the creature and agent of the West–just like any thuggish dictators–Mobutu epitomises the hypocrisy and the duplicity of the so-called the civilised international community that awarded him a *carte blanche* to rob and ruin the DRC, then Zaire. The hypocrisy and duplicity– Western countries have always applied on Africa–can be seen in the fact that Mobutu was able to squander billions of dollars while poor Congolese were dying of preventable and treatable diseases; and nobody objected or condemned this criminality. Again, the reasons for such silence are obvious that Mobutu was installed by the same West to run the show of plundering and hijacking the DRC for the benefits of Western countries. Ironically, even the *champions* of democracy in the world did not bother to remind Mobutu of democracy or human rights. Neither did they talk about the rule of law or good governance. For them, the rule of law and good governance made sense only when a ruler was carrying their orders and serving their interests even at the expense of the citizens of her or his country. Instead of reminding or reprimanding Mobutu, the West kept mum and went on doing the business of plundering Congo wantonly and pointlessly. Essentially, the *champions* of democracy of the world were, instead, in bed happily raping the DRC as pleased as Mobutu held it. For over three decades, Mobutu cuckolded Congolese and the world by playing many roles in his comedies all aimed at keeping his grip on power. For a long time, and big time, of course, as aforementioned, Mobutu succeeded in duping everybody himself included.

Again, how did Mobutu come to power in the first place? Betchtolshmeir (2012) notes that on the 25th November, 1965 Mobutu, the colonel, staged a bloodless coup to take charge of the political turmoil in independent Congo and established one of the most brutal and corrupt dictatorship in the modern African history,

(p. 3); also see Romaldi (2010); De Rezende (2012); and; Grisse (2011) after betraying Lumumba who had appointed him his chief of staff. Although Betcholshmeir calls Mobutu's *coup d'état* bloodless, what happened before and thereafter was real bloody. The killing of Lumumba and his two compatriots disputes the assertion that Mobutu's coup was bloodless. Although the number of those who were killed in this coup can be seen as small, if we consider the weight of these personalities and the fact that their blood was spilled, the coup was bloody. After bracing himself in power, the situation seemed to come to normalcy. Arguably, in the beginning–after the CIA installed him–Mobutu seemed to be a promising leader who skilfully articulated his vision for the country so as to convincingly dupe many people at home and abroad. Being Lumumba's right-hand man added up to the hope of Congolese and the world before knowing the horrid truth that Mobutu betrayed; and later brutally assassinated his boss, Lumumba. In his early days in power, Mobutu was seen as a fitting substitute for Lumumba, the man he assassinated so as to snatch power and abuse it thereafter for over three decades. This is why, at the time, Mobutu could be seen with gurus of African politics such as Nyerere and others. No wonder this is why Mobutu would dine and wine with the founders of the Organisation for African Unity (OAU) whenever he happened to attend its annual conferences as the cover photo indicates. Mobutu, however, seemed to charm them at the time hoping that he would be one of them in their quest of liberating Africa.

It took some time for some of the founders to unearth the true Kafkaesque Mobutu so as to start avoiding him. Mobutu perfected the art of deception. This is a very important point to make. Archival photographs show Mobutu with the best managers such as Nyerere which may be seen as an antithesis. Again, in building the monument of history, some contradictions are inevitable. Humans are capable of knowing and appreciating the person today but incapable of foreseeing the changes in the same person may cease to be a better person to end up becoming worse one in the future. Frederik Willem de Klerk, Apartheid's last prime minister in South Africa provides a very ideal example as we have seen it above. Before dismantling Apartheid, de Klerk would not dine and wine with any serious African leader. But after bringing the Apartheid regime down, the same de Klerk became the darling and the most trusted African statesman just the same way Mobutu changed from a leader to a monster. Nelson Mandela, South Africa's founding father, was once branded a terrorist who ended up having a cup of tea and parties in the White House after engineering; and supervising the demise of Apartheid. Therefore, those who will notice this contrast of history making must underscore its nature in that things and people can change from one condition to another or others time after time. And this is normal. Always, the process of history making has many ups and downs and twists and turns. Not all bricks that build history are casted into a blazing furnace. Some happen to be even ice cubes like Mobutu, and some are rocks such as, *inter alia*, Nkrumah and Nyerere were. Despite being sworn enemies–due to the interests of their countries–you would see Idi Amin and Nyerere posing for a photo ops as heads of states when they met at the then East African Community (EAC) conferences. African sage has it that you can choose a friend but you cannot choose a neighbour. This is how politics behaves and works. Sometimes, leaders have to put their personal or ideological enmities and stand together in some issues and podia as heads of states even if they do not like each other.

Nonetheless, nothing is forever under the Sun. For, slowly and chronically–after power climbed into his head, plus the pressure from his cloners–Mobutu started to disclose and display his true self so as to cascade into a venal dictator who ruined Congo big time. Arguably, Mobutu robbed, ruined, and above all, killed innocent people as pleased; and nobody would touch him provided that the West was getting what it wanted from the DRC. Being a project the West enacted before the DRC became independent known as Manhattan Project as we have seen above in the discourse about Lumumba, Mobutu was untouchably beyond reproach at his halcyon days as a stooge of the West. The West saw to it that Mobutu survived whatever attempts that were made to topple or kill him. Who wants his lapdog to be harmed? Through, "state terrorism backed by the military" (Emizet 2000, p. 203), Mobutu was able to lord it over Congolese for over three decades while enjoying financial, military and technical assistance from the US and other Western countries which would not *bug* him given that whatever Mobutu did helped them to get what they wanted from him. By safeguarding the interests

199

of his masters and cloners, however detrimental such interests were for the Congolese, Mobutu was not a danger compared to those who inclined to the communist East. So, too, Mobutu was safer than those who refused to be in bed with the West. This East-West acrimony sustained many dictators who knew that by subscribing to it, they would survive and thrive. Furthermore, the West had to fill Mobutu's vaults with monies knowledgeably that he would turn such monies into his private wealth. They, too well, knew all the monies they pushed into Mobutu's hands would end up being stashed in their capitals; and when the right times arrive, after getting rid of him, the same would retrieve their monies to top up the money they would have already made through robbing the DRC. For example, nobody can tell exactly what happened to the billions–billions of dollars whose sum has never been known; and maybe, will never be known– that Mobutu robbed from the people of the DRC. It is easy to trace the genesis of Mobutu's rule and the source of the Mobutu-US *marriage of convenience* that followed after being installed. Ray (2000) observes that the Mobutu era began with unwavering U.S. support, financial and military in which as from 1965 to 1991 he received more than $1.5 billion in U.S. economic and military aid which in return, U.S. multinationals increased their share of the ownership of Zaire's fabulous mineral wealth, (p. 2).

This amount of money is humongous by all standards if we consider the time at which it was availed to Mobutu. MacGinty and Williams (2009) trace where this money went maintaining that Mobutu and Ferdinand Marco, former Philippines president, robbed their countries of approximately $ 50 billion, (p. 36). And if such an amount were spent wisely on public services, the DRC would not have been in the quagmire it is in now. Again, all this money either ended in Mobutu's many offshore accounts or was spend on protecting Mobutu's kleptoratic regime.

In other words, Mobutu traded his people to the West in exchange of favours and protection with impunity and brutality. The West sustained his venal regime, as noted above, by providing technical and military capabilities, training for his henchmen and intelligence on top of providing administrational wherewithal for Mobutu to heinously and brutally run the DRC as a private property. Ndikumana and Boyce (1998) note that during his dictatorship, Zaire accumulated a public external debt of roughly $14 billion while Mobutu and his associates extracted wealth from the country. They add that by 1990, real capital flight from Zaire amounted to $12 billion. With imputed interest earnings, the accumulated stock of Zairian flight capital was nearly $18 billion, (p. 165).

If you trace where the money made out of capital flight went, you will obviously find that it ended in Western banks. Acquaah-Gaisie (Ibid) observes that President Mobutu's fortune approached $5,000 million in a Swiss Bank account, a fortune larger than Zaire's $4,400 million foreign debt… The President's official salary alone amounted to 17% of the annual budget, while the country's foreign debt amounted to 70% of the GNP, (p. 4). What makes Mobutu's criminality interesting is the fact that it was done openly. His life style was an open secret to everybody. He openly lived large while Congolese were dying of preventable and treatable diseases not to mention the lack of infrastructure and other social services the government was duty-bound to provide.

Apart from robbing the money that donors offered him, Mobutu allowed Western companies to extract as many resources as they deemed fit provided that their countries were assuring him of protection. If anything, this macabre trade in minerals (and other resources) in exchange for human rights and other favours is the only secret that helped and enhanced Mobutu to cling to power for a long time just like Omar Bongo, Theodoro Obiang Nguema, Yoweri Museveni, Gnassingbe Eyadema, Joseph Kabila and many more who ruined their countries while the West stood by and watched. Such negligence and double standard have been going on for generations in African countries ruled by corrupt rulers such as Mobutu and other mentioned above. Is there any sin on earth that deserves condemnations and punishment like this really? The West cannot pretend that it did not know how people were living in beastly conditions in these countries. But geared by their hidden interests, the West still pretends to hear or see nothing as far as plundering Africa is concerned. A wise monkey sees nothing, does nothing and says nothing. What would the West do while these venal dictators were safeguarding and promoting its interests in their countries? Interestingly, when dictators rob their countries and terrorise, and kill innocent citizens, the West does not call them names. They do not make any efforts whatsoever to even partially admit their guilty and complicity wherever everybody knows the role they played in sustaining such murderous regimes. Normally, the West just waits for the right moment and time to show how to kill a thieving dog. Once such brainless criminal it was in love with fall from grace, the West becomes the first to denounce, disown and call them names such as refer to them as dictators without putting in mind that they are the ones who cloned, launched and protected most of them simply because they were easy to fool, use, abuse and dupe. Before being overthrown, no Western country dared to call Mobutu a dictator. Arguably, West's protectionism to African criminals in power like those mentioned above, among others, has either diluted or put the meaning of democracy to disrepute. Ironically, despite all examples of fallen dictators that the West cloned and thereafter disowned after becoming a liability, still many African potentates trust the West so as to stash looted money or invest it in bogus things such as villas, expensive yachts, cars, ranches and other nonsensical investments in their capital cities.

One wonders how the West would still dole out monies and pour some aid in the DRC while they actually knew that the same monies and aid would end up in Mobutu's pockets as military and technical aid would be used to terrorise Congolese. One of the groups that Mobutu used to lord it over Congolese is the Division *Speciale Presidentielle* (DSP) that he trusted and remunerated the most. Again, what would the West worry about while the same money was stashed back to its capitals as indicated above? Western countries knew the type of the game they were playing; and the type of the stooges they were using namely abusing and dealing with gullible African dictators. When Mobutu was flushed out, the whole humongous amount of money he had already stole ended up in Western banks; and sadly for the DRC, nobody has the power or means to retrieve it. So, in simple parlance, one can comfortably say that Western countries used Dracula Mobutu and the likes to rob their people and deposit to their banks wrongly thinking they own the monies they illegally acquired while in reality they actually did not own even a penny. If there is anything that many African thieves who stash money in banks abroad own is nothing but pieces of papers issued by those banks. So, too, such robbers have a small window of withdrawing a few dollars from their accounts whenever they needed them provided that they must be in power. Western banks attach strings on their accounts so as to end up owning the said money as it is in the case of Mobutu. Another undeniable thing that the likes of Mobutu owned is nothing but the guilty or robbing their own people so as to end being demonised by those who used them to commit such a crime. Other things African thieves in power were able to own from the money they squandered are nonsensical things such as jewels, ranches, expensive cars, yachts, mansions which also ended up in the hands of the same Western countries or being vandalised if they were in their countries. Apart from Mobutu, Bokassa provides a precisely good example not to mention Abacha. They robbed their countries and ended up getting nothing but blames. Bokassa robbed his country and stashed the money in France where he flew to after being toppled. After noticing that Bokassa had no more power, France forced him to live like a rascal that was later forced to return to his country and face the long arm of the law.

Essentially, the West was using Mobutu like a caricature they would manipulate any way at any time they wanted to. Like it was for Idi Amin, the West knew Mobutu's myopia, greed and weakness which they fully exploited at the detriment of Congolese people who are now facing debts to pay after Mobutu incurred them. Mobutu, too, thought he was using the West unbeknown that he, indeed, was being abused let alone being used. True, what was going on at this time period between the twosomes is nothing but the *marriage of cons* in which every con believes he or she is using another without underscoring that the situation is vice versa by nature. Arguably, the West—in this game of con—was able to outsmart Mobutu at the time he needed it the most. For, even when he was toppled, they did not provide asylum to him something that forced him to die and be buried in Morocco. By and large, many African rulers who ruined their countries were, or will be abused in this way. Ironically, despite evidencing what happened to Mobutu and his loot, more many are still robbing public confers; and stashing the monies to the same capitals in Western countries. Thoughtless as they have always been, it will take time for such thieves in power to realise that they are being used, abused, misused and criminalised.

Being a poor manager, Mobutu, apart from robbing public coffers, he destroyed the economy of the DRC as Brough and Kimenyi (1986) note that:

The dictator of Zaire, President Mobutu, portrays a clear cut example of the extensive inefficiency in appointments. In 1973, Mobutu 'Zairianized' all foreign enterprises, expelled the Asian merchants and Belgian farmers who kept the economy alive, and replaced foreign managers with low skilled Africans, most of whom were his close friends and relatives, (p. 38).

Again, all depends on how one looks at it. Whether foreigners that Amin and Mobutu expelled were sustaining the economies of Uganda and Zaire is arguably subject to discussion. Those who see such foreigners, who, in the main, are in bed with corrupt rulers, see nothing wrong with expelling them, mainly if we consider how despots use them to rob their countries. Experience shows that such dictators expelled those foreigners not for the love of their people but, instead, they used it as a way of duping their citizens to think that they loved them. When Amin expelled Asians who were regarded as ticks to the economy of Uganda, many people were duped to think that his intention was to uplift Africans whom most of those expelled Asians exploited and discriminated against as it has been going on in the countries were they were not expelled. This trend still goes on in many African countries where Asians are seen as conspirators with venal despots to dupe and rob them. And indeed, in some cases are. Given that when the European colonial monsters brought such foreigners to Africa, it used them to rob Africans of their produces not to mention being implicated in many scandals such as the Goldenberg and Radar scandals in Kenya and Tanzania respectively even after African countries acquired their independence.

Michel (1999) observes that "Mobutu *a été l'otage des Américains et des Belges, c'est évident. Mais il s'est affranchi de cette tutelle. Il a joué les Américains contre les Belges, les Français contre les Américains,* etc., (p. 4) literary, "Mobutu is a hostage of American and Belgians, this is evident. But he is an emancipated slave of this tutorial. He is now playing Americans against Belgians, French against Americans etc." If anything, this is the same hoax former Ivorian dictator Laurent Gbagbo tried to use against Ivorian former colonial power, France to end up ricocheting and kicking him out of power.

Acquaah-Gaisie (op.cit.) discerns that once Mobutu bragged in a 1984 CBS "60 Minutes" profile that together with his family and friends, Mobutu owned more than 26 properties in Belgium, France and elsewhere. They included a 15-acre beach resort, orchards and a vineyard in Portugal, a 32-room Villa les Miguettes in Savigny, Switzerland, and a 16th-century castle in Spain. Mobutu also owned property in Brazil, Senegal, Morocco and Ivory Coast, (p. 4).

Just like other powerful African thieves, it is not easy to gauge as to how much money Mobutu robbed the DRC. It must be noted emphatically that when we talk of how much Mobutu robbed the DRC it does not include the amount his cronies, masters and whatnot robbed under his negligent and corrupt rule. We are not talking about humungous amount of money in billions of dollars that Western countries made in this marriage of convenience. We are not talking about the danger such money caused as far as post-Mobutu-era conflicts are concerned in the DRC and the region in general. We are not talking about destructive policies such a fool introduced to his country whose population was left to fend for itself while their resources were plundered on the broad daylight. When we talk about how much Mobutu and his cronies stole, we are not talking about billions multinational corporations evaded in terms of tax. Neither do we are talking about billions of dollars that was siphoned out of the DRC by the way of capital flight thanks to having no stable, accountable and competent government to manage country's resources. Ndikumana (2003) observes that after taking over, Mobutu moulded a scheme, in the mid-1970s, which promoted a cult of personality aimed at entrenching his absolutism that existed for over thirty years thereafter, (p. 15). Under this cult, Mobutu became everything in everything, and above all, the sole *protector* of the DRC. However, Mobutu ironically ended up ruining the DRC. To crown it all, Mobutu called his irrational philosophy *Mobutuism* which kept changing names every moment. It started as *Mobutuism* then was transmuted to *Zairinisation* which later was called *authentiste* or authenticity. It is argued that Mobutu used this flimflam in order to

205

offer citizenship to Rwandese he used as his allies at his time as van Acker (2000) notes that Mobutu offered Rwandan descent that had obtained the Zairian nationality under the 1972 law on nationality (later repealed) to end up becoming his "staunchest political allies at the time. These 'Banyarwanda' consequently became the main political beneficiaries of the 'zairinization'" (p. 10).

So, what was known as *Zairinization* was nothing but a ploy for Mobutu to reward loyalty; even offering citizenship to foreigners and thereby cling to power. Despite being empty of philosophical underpinnings, *Mobutuism* was nothing but personal shibboleth engrained in his party, the *Mouvement Populaire de la Révolution* (MPR) all aimed at hypnotising Congolese that Mobutu was a thinker while he was but a hare-brained fool. Furthermore, *Mobutuism* was nothing but thuggery and trickery stuff aimed at assuring Congolese that their ruler had good plans and programs for them. Callaghy (1984, p. 6 cited in White 2005) sums Mobutu's philosophy and manoeuvres and manipulation as thus:

> The Mobutu regime has a vague and eclectic legitimating "mentality"—an eclectic and often haphazard blend of ambiguous, fluctuating, and often derivative legitimating formulas or doctrines (as opposed to a coherent ideology)—which includes notions from liberal democracy, revolutionary populism, even socialism. Above all, however, it is organic-statist in orientation, drawing on traditional African notions of community, equity, authority, and power, particularly pre-colonial concepts of kingship, chiefship, and the "big man," (p. 67).

To be precise, when it comes to what was known as *Mobutuism*, everything ended up being a chicanery but not a philosophy. Naturally, philosophy does not come out of aping or copying. Again, sensing how doyens such as Julius Nyerere of the neighbouring Tanzania who was regarded as a philosopher king were coming up with new philosophies and new ideas, Mobutu jumped into the bandwagon without anything in his machinery and toolbox. Those who remember how Mobutu became everything in everything will remember how musicians in the DRC were coerced, bought or manipulated to compose songs to emulate and glorify Mobutu. Some did so in order to get closer to the *king* or out of fear of reprisal; while others did so in attempting to survive under the tyrant as it has been in many African countries. White (2008) maintains that Mobutu was so fond of saying that "happy are those who sing and dance" (p. 24) but not those who are able to question; also see Grice 2011). This was like anaesthetic overdose that Mobutu and his spin-doctors administered to the whole country whose hypnotising power and effects enabled Mobutu to rule unchallenged for over three decades of destruction and suffering. The *New York Times* (17 May, 1997) says that Mobutu used his cunny courtship of Western support topped up with extravagance as it was displayed in his emblematic leopard-skin cap and carved wooden sceptre topped with an eagle left Zaire teetering on the brink of economic collapse not to mention his cult personality forced Zairians to refer to him as president or *chef de l'état* but not by his name.

Furthermore, Mobutu manipulatively invested in music in order to give the population something to ease their frustration and angers towards his autocratic and thievish rule for over thirty years of mismanagement of the DRC. Again, if one asks: what for? Mobutu's ploy-cum-abracadabra did not only charm Congolese but it did also charm the West. Evidently, despite embarking on such macabre politics of the cultism, the *champions* of democracy turned a blind eye provided they were getting what they wanted in this scheme that ousted Lumumba who was seen as an obstacle by all means. Gordon (2009) discloses that from the 1960s through the 1980s, U.S. policy in DR Congo was shaped by the cold war needs that entailed support of Mobutu, (p. 1368). So, what mattered most in this exploitative and abusive relationship between Mobutu and the US was nothing but countering the effects of communism which meant sacrificing human rights which the US has always prodded to many countries all over the world. Again, this is where the hypocrisy of the West is unleashed and unveiled to its full force and dangers. As if this was not enough, Mobutu allowed his intelligence, police and military officers to spin dangerously and do whatever they deemed fit. They robbed mugged, solicited bribes and terrorised people in order to instil fear in them not to mention making a kill without doing anything as per their duties. Despite all atrocities this terrorist regime committed, yet again, the West was comfortably doing business with Mobutu. Justice was aborted. It was not here or there. It was business as usual of ransacking and fleecing the DRC in spite of the dirty and openly evident criminal nature of Mobutu regime. Despite this tragedy—the one that the West caused the DRC by instating Mobutu— nobody talks about redressing the people who suffered for long under Mobutu regime in the post-Mobutu era. Once again, this puts the West to disrepute and shame altogether. As it was for Amin in Uganda and Jean-Bedel Bokassa in the CAR, Western countries have closed the files; and gone ahead with other missions of the same nature as we can evidence this phenomenon in Equatorial Guinea and Gabon to mention but a few of the countries that are being raped by dictators backed and supported by the West.

To mismanage the country swiftly even more, Mobutu invented another scheme based on dressing code. Congolese were forbidden from wearing Western suits. Instead, they were required to wear Congolese or African fashions. Once again, Mobutu, as a *bon chef* or a great leader as he preferred to be referred to, was on the frontline waging wars against cultural imperialism. Ironically, instead of investing on building textiles so that Africans could wear African clothes, he allowed second-hand clothes in the country. Ironically, instead of encouraging Congolese to produce cotton, he encouraged them to embark on fashion competitions of which were more French than Congolese. With his *bling- bling* and other nonsensical gadgets such as calved wooden walking sticks, Leopold skins and whatnot, Mobutu was seen as a cultural emancipator while in real sense he was a mere parodist hoodwinking them to remain in power. Again, despite all sideshows, Mobutu used French, a Western language to popularise his ideas, as he left Congolese musicians use Western guitars and other musical instruments. What a contradiction-cum-confusion! Had he embarked on Nyerere's introduction of Swahili as a national language of Tanzania and Africa in general, at least, he would have made a point successfully. Despite being a lunatic, at heart, Mobutu regarded himself as a genius whose intellect, ironically, performed well in destroying his country and his people.

Typically, Mobutu was a very controversial character next to a madman. He abolished European names, yet, he remained a catholic who, later, went to the Vatican to bless his second marriage! This move, however—the media did not take on it extensively like the change of names—put the Roman Catholic in disrepute as well. For, it was in bed with a conman who would manipulate anything to his advantage. Changing colonial names would make sense if the one doing so abandoned all colonial faiths and practices. Ironically, Mobutu liked to spend much time in Europe shopping and squandering taxpayers' hard-earned money not to mention stashing billions and purchasing mansions there while the DRC was turned into an island due to the lack of connective infrastructure. The DRC is only African country that has never been connected through roads and other infrastructure. Mobutu did so deliberately in order to tighten a grip on power through rule-and-divide-and-suffocate approach.

Arguably, apart from being a crook, Mobutu, his courtiers and his allies were but letdowns not only to the people of Congo but the entire world, especially that of democrats. The death of Lumumba was not only a blow to the DRC but also to democracy, particularly, if we consider what followed in the CAR, Togo, Uganda, Ethiopia, Ghana, Nigeria, and elsewhere in Africa. Once again, post-colonial Congo epitomises the dark days of abducted and raped independence. For, its true leader was killed under the orders of the West and the one who took over instead of becoming a leader became a leading thief who saw to it that his country was robbed to prosper his cloners as his countrymen and women cascaded into stinking poverty wantonly. Mobutu was a very hare-brained person suffering from *small-man syndrome* who goes down to the annals of the history of Africa as a fool that was able to spent millions of dollar hiring Concorde to take him and his goons to do shopping in New York not to mention other trips he made to other Western capital cities. Despite being manufactured and mostly owned by France, no French president had the guts to use Concorde as pleased the same way Mobutu did with his courtiers and goons renting it even for delivering birthday cakes. To quench his inferiority complex and mania, Mobutu once ordered Concorde to take off from his home village of Gbadolite (which is now in ruins) to New York just for a joyride. As any inferior small-man-self-turned-into-big man, like Felix Houphouët-Boigny's Yamoussoukro and Omar Bongo's

Bongoville, Mobutu turned his Gbadolite village into a town with all amenities many provincial headquarters in the then Zaire lacked simply because it was the place where he was born. This is not, in any sense, a managerial logical undertaking. However, Mobutu fell short of making Gbadolite a capital like his counterpart Houphouët-Boigny did. The *Guardian* (10 February, 2015) reports that "it [*Gbadolite- these words are ours*] was an African Versailles," says politician Albert Moleka, who reckons how US$400m was spent and recalls how in 1985 France's Gaston Lenôtre, the leading pastry chef in the world, "flew in on Concorde with a birthday cake for Mobutu." This is the only known incident that robbed Congolese people of millions of dollars. What of unknown incidents for the whole 32 years this fool spent in power? The *Black History* (2012) reports that Mobutu's construction of a US$500 million dollar palace in his ancestral village of Gbadolite that has been called the "Versailles of the Jungle. His son-in-law estimated that Mobutu and his entourage would run through 10,000 bottles of Laurent Perrier pink champagne a year."

However, Mobutu knew the comportment of his people. He used this knowledge to lord it over them easily for many years as Gould (1980 cited in Ikome, 2008) notes that Mobutu used to constantly flatter Congolese either through praises or publicly criticising corrupt members of his inner sanctum while he secretly neutralised those who opposed his rule, (pp. 24-25).

To get away with murder, Mobutu allowed every Congolese to fend for her-, or himself by all means legal and illegal. Corruption—of course, which the citizens were forced committed alongside with their rulers—surged at all levels. Basically, Mobutu created a corrupt country in which systemic corruption was institutionalised so as to make everybody culpable. Arguably, there were systemic, macro-, meso-, and micro levels of venality all over the country under Mobutu's regime. Sadly however, even the governments that took over from Mobutu replicated the same something that is still going on costing the DRC dearly up until now. By all standards, Mobutu presided over a failed, fake, wobbly and fraud state save that due to the politics of the day, he was able to survive by conning his unwary people who would have easily toppled him had they known what was behind the curtain as it was for Gaddafi not to mention US's backing.

Like a hyena's fete, Mobutu liked living large. He used to invite his cronies many times to enjoy his ill-gotten opulence while his people were suffering. Heartless, brutal, myopic and greedy as he was, just like Felix Houphouët-Boigny (Ivory Coast), Omar Bongo (Gabon), Kamuzu Banda (Malawi) Jomo Kenyatta (Kenya) and Gnassingbe Eyadema (Togo), Mobutu plundered the DRC for a long time up until he was booted out. The *realpolitik* of the time was that either one was with the West or with the East in this allegiance that acted as a protective gear for the person. Under Mobutu, the DRC was an anarchic and failed state by all standards saves that the presence of the West saved it from being declared and presumed so. What helped to maintain tranquillity was nothing but fear that the regime instilled in its people. There is saying that where law ends tyranny begins. This is the only way one can easily describe Mobutu's corrupt and ridiculous regime.

As argued above, nothing is forever under the Sun. The year 1997 marked the time for Mobutu to pack and vanish forever from the scene he manipulated for a long period of time. May 16, 1997 will always remain one of the most important days to the Congolese. For, it is the day a ragtag army supported by Burundi, Rwanda and Uganda led by Laurent Desire Kabila flushed Mobutu out. Thereafter, he fled to Togo then Morocco where he died on September 7th of the same year. Once again, the world evidenced the disgraceful fall of the dictator renowned for sideshows, corruption and brutality. When Mobutu was pulled down, Congolese and the world at large were elated and relieved. Again, no sooner had Kabila took over than the cracks started to appear. For, Kabila would become another dictator who did not stay longer though. He was mysteriously killed in office on 16th January, 2001. Due to the duplicitous and shaky system Kabila inherited without changing it, it enabled his neophyte son Joseph Kabange Kabila to take from where his father left. Thanks to the delicacy and want of the system, Kabila's son was propelled to power; thereby inheriting his father's presidency in order to keep his father's loosely movement in power. He hitherto went on mismanaging the country for a long time just like Mobutu did however with different style and magnitude. Like Ali Bongo and Faure Eyadema, Kabila came to power not just because he was qualified or supported by the people. Instead, Kabila came to power simply because he was the son of former president Kabila. After the fall of Mobutu from grace, many thought that the DRC will get a reprieve. However, what happened is nothing but changing one dictator to another. As it has happened in many countries that were under brutal dictatorship for a long time, the DRC has since never recovered from corruption, dictatorship and above all, it still lacks of true democracy.

In sum, the assassination of Lumumba became a curse that has since been eating the DRC. For, despite toppling Mobutu's regime, the situation did not improve for a common man and woman in the country. What happened is but changing the eaters who go on eating as ferociously as those they kicked out of power. However, the DRC is not out of woods yet. For, Gray and McPherson (2001) note that "though Africa's greatest kleptocrat, Mobutu, has departed, there are still many lesser Mobutus," (p. 31); also see Nyanchama (2006). Although we tend to blame everything on Mobutu which is the right thing to do due the role he played in plundering his country, the DRC was hijacked by the US and the West for their hidden and heinous interests. Mobutu's sin was conspiring and accepting to become a stooge. To know more, and see how Mobutu ruined his country watch this *youtube* clip
https://www.youtube.com/watch?v=nJ93UkBc8Bw

Given that Mobutu, just like Bokassa, had nothing substantial to teach the world, we thought it makes sense for the reader to know how his high life ended antithetically. We will not allow him to wind his discussion by speaking himself just like other managers we have discussed. Let us make an exception to the general rule by letting somebody talk on his behalf. There is a lesson for our thievish rulers in; that when they die, the money they stashed abroad is eaten by their masters and some are buried like paupers as Muchie and Tutieri (2011) note that:

> Mobutu oversaw the plundering of the Congo for thirty years, but according to a Congolese medical doctor I had an opportunity to meet and discuss in South Africa, he died with the embarrassment that there was no money to buy the appropriate sized coffin to bury him. One wonders where did all the money stashed in Swiss banks go and the houses I saw are Mobutu's from Geneva to the Riviera, where did they all vanish? Neither

Mobutu's family nor the people of the Congo got anything. The coffin for Mobutu has to be bought by the King of Morocco according to my informant. This is how the Economist and other commentaries try to capture his dastardly legacies: "Mobutu inherited the Belgian Congo; the empire created by King Leopold of the Belgians, and treated it similarly. They both created gargantuan fantasies for themselves out of its vast wealth and neither had the slightest concern for the inhabitants, (p. 8).

Mobutu's legacy

If there is any legacy that Mobutu left to his country is nothing but a time-ticking bomb—next to a chaotic failed state—that exploded after he was dislodged from power on 7 September, 1997. Thereafter, the DRC became a powder keg that produced many violent conflicts that have been going on since Mobutu was forced to flee the country. The DRC, since then, has experienced a very sharp slump economically and politically without any prospects of improving due to the fact that the followed governments did almost the same, plundering and doing nothing else. It becomes difficult to exactly limn the size of the injuries Mobutu caused his country. The dent that Mobutu's mismanagement caused to the country will take generations to overcome. Due to such stinking legacy, even calling your dog Mobutu is like abusing it. For Mobutu is but a very ugly face of Africa historically next to slavery and colonialism. Kleptomaniacal as he always was, Mobutu wantonly robbed and mismanaged the DRC at unimaginable proportions. He turned such a humongous country—that is endowed with immense resources—into his private estate; for him and his cronies to plunder. However, there is a lesson from Mobutu's thuggery; in that, the West protected, and benefited from his regime for over three decades that have turned out to be a nightmare for Congolese people. So, too, Mobutu will be remembered, though negatively, for having divided the country geographically after he failed to invest in infrastructure. He left none or dilapidated infrastructure that colonial monsters built all over the country which looks like a bunch of manmade island thanks to being unconnected to each other. Importantly, after Mobutu was kicked out, he left a country without any sound and reliable machinery to run it. Thus, when he left, the country fell in more chaos after the regime that took over from him failed Congolese people miserably. Like any other country that was under the dictator for a long time, even today the DRC is still suffering in a post-Mobutu era whereby power is still in the hands of a bunch of corrupt elites with no any plans whatsoever to revamp it; and propel it to prosperity.

Arguably, Mobutu left a vile country politically. White (2005) maintains that "long before Mobutu passed away, the Zairian state had already been diagnosed as chronically ill," (p. 66) like Mobutu himself was in his last days. Due to his maladroitness and ravenousness, Mobutu has one big relic which is being one of big thieves Africa has ever had and seen. As any dupe manning a parasitic regime, Mobutu robbed his country and hid the money in foreign banks abroad. There are some rumours that he died somewhat a bankrupt man just like Bokassa. After power slinked from his hands, the banks turned tables on him so as to deny him access to his accounts.

So, too, Mobutu left a very paralysed and divided country with lack of almost everything material and moral. Immense resources—the DRC is endowed with although not benefiting from them—have turned out to be a curse instead of becoming a blessing.

Unsurprisingly, the DRC has always bled to death due to its abundant resources whereby "rich reserves of coltan (a mineral used in mobile phones) have fed war in, (Hartford and Klein, 2005, p. 1) since the country gained its independence in 1960 which makes the DRC a cockpit of conflicts that have destabilised security in the region; also see Guenther (2008); Basedau and Mehler (2005); and Ross (2004).

True, live by sword, die by sword. Mobutu toppled Lumumba to end up being toppled by Laurent Desire Kabila who however did not rule longer before being gunned down in office. Who would believe that a creature like Mobutu who spent money as if it was water from the ocean would die in such a condition? Sometimes, divine intervention does work in order to give others a lesson not to replicate the same buffoonery other foolishly and blindly committed. Those who want to avoid turning their countries into fool's paradise by answering the question: "If it was so easy to get rid of Mobutu, then what exactly had been keeping him in power (White 2005, p. 66) other than being in bed with the West?" The answer to this question is not as simple as one may think. Although there is no way one can exonerate Mobutu or convict him alone without his conspirators, African leaders need to question their consciences as far as power is concerned. In doing so, one has to examine the demeanour and integrity of the best managers discussed before the worst ones. Citizens, too, are partly to blame for not doing their homework well to know why buffoons like Mobutu were able to take them for a ride for a long time without being booted out.

Mobutu goes down to the annals of history as a heartless criminal who would vend his people to any bidder provided that he pushes a bill or coin into his hands. Lucky for him, he was able to survive thanks to the politics of the cold war. Once, the iron curtain fell, Mobutu was abandoned and left to fend for himself something he was not used to. He thus, went under easily leaving abaft a very paralysed and diseased country that fell into chaos thereafter. Like Belgian colonial monster king Leopold who sold Congolese to Western pharmaceutical companies, under the leadership of Hilary Koprowoski, (Curtis 1992; and Hooper 2001) to use them as guinea pigs in 1950s, Mobutu would do the same shall there be any money to be made. The difference however is that Mobutu had a very developed economy to plunder and exploit. What an avaricious ogre that Mobutu was. Sometimes, the difference between that bastard king Leopold II and Mobutu is basically the pigments of their colour and time differences. When it comes to atrocities, another difference is that Leopold was brutalising the people he was not related to while Mobutu was hawking his own brothers and sisters. The consequences of this are the fact that Mobutu died in Morocco and was buried by a handful of relatives. If you compare Mobutu's burial with Mandela's or Nyerere's, you can see how corruption and mismanagement of public business do not pay at all. For the person of Mobutu's stature–who was in national and international limelight big time–to be buried like a dog, is not a good legacy. In African culture, the last send-off is something to live and die for. Mobutu will be remembered as a big thief that Africa has ever had apart from being a dictator and a stooge of the West who would do anything to remain in power. The greatest lesson from Mobutu's dogly life is for African elites and politicians to put their acts together and do things differently aimed at reversing the detrimental situation that Africa has been in.

Figure 20: Gbadolite's ruins (image courtesy of Le Congolais)

PREMIER VOL DIRECT

PARIS - GBADOLITE
VOL AF 839E - 16 JUILLET 1989
Concorde F8TSD

Figure 21: Mobutu's relics (image source Concorde)

Chapter 17

Bokassa a Stupid and Vampiric "Emperor"

"Toward the end of his life, Mr. Bokassa returned to the intense religion of his youth, praying several times a day with a well-thumbed Bible. The former Emperor, long known for his high living, told a recent visitor that he had renounced alcohol and sexual relations for several years," the *New York Times*, November 5, 1996.

Figure 22: Jean B .Bokassa CAR's 2nd President (image the courtesy of BBC)

As mentioned heretofore, Africa has had many dictators benign and brutal sane and insane. Jean-Bedel Bokassa (JJB) aka Salah Eddine Ahmed Bokassa (22nd February, 1921–3rd November, 1996) was among them the most, ludicrous, injudicious and freak African ruler, a self-proclaimed emperor who seemed to be more a megalomaniac and harlequin than anything Africa has ever seen before and thereafter. After taking power from his distant cousin, David Dacko, Central African Republic (CAR) first president, Bokassa became a military ruler just before he later installed himself the emperor of the CAR. Reno (1998) notes that:

The life of Jean-Bedel Bokassa, who became president of the Central African Republic (CAR) in 1966 (the emperor from 1976-1979) is subject of Brian Titley's book the *Dark Age: The Political Odyssey of emperor Bokassa,* (p. 501).

This shows how gullible and injudicious the man was. Why did Bokassa decide to crown himself an emperor in the country that did not have a culture of having kings and emperors? It is simple. Thanks to colonial legacy, that caused by rickety mind, Bokassa used to worship French emperor Napoleon Bonaparte. He therefore wanted to emulate him by proclaiming himself an emperor. Once more, this shows how ridiculously confused and controversial Bokassa was. For, before crowning himself an emperor, Bokassa had declared himself to be the president for life something Idi Amin and Hastings Kamuzu Banda did. It became difficult to know which was which between president for life and emperor. For, Bokassa ended up overthrowing himself to become a political pye-dog if not a mongrel. This can show the readers how gullible and mentally unstable Bokassa was. For the love of; and greed for power, Bokassa would do anything to make sure he stays in power. This is why he decided to call himself Salah Eddine, after Selahedînê Eyûbî, an Arab warrior and the founder of Ayuyubid dynasty in the Seventeenth century. More confusion regarding Bokassa can be noticed due to the fact that Selahedine and Napoleon were two different things from two different worlds and times. Even their ruling styles were different not to mention their nationality, timeframe and tactics as far as power is concerned.

Again, who actually was Bokassa; and what did his rule bring to the CAR? Ghura and Benoit (2004) answer this question observing that Bokassa declared himself president for life in 1972 while in 1997 he proclaimed himself emperor the same year the economy was declining so as to force him to become more repressive and brutal after the dwindling of foreign aid, (p. 10).

By declaring himself life president, Bokassa was breaking one of the fundamental pillars of good management which always comes from the people. This means that, despite whatever evaluation would have been made on how the manager of state business performed, employers—who in this case are the citizens—had no right to fire their

218

manager. In other words, Bokassa stole the firm from the owners by declaring himself life president. Dearborn (1986) argues that Bokassa would be equated to Amin when it comes to brutality associated with their rule, (p. 326).

Bokassa's overbearingness did not end up with his brutality but also with his myopia and eccentricity. For, when he crowned himself emperor, Bokassa spent the fortune of his poor country wantonly. Jallow, *et al.,* (2014) note Bokassa, just like any dictator suffered from "the small man syndrome," an acute sense of smallness and inadequacy that so starkly contrasts with the fact of being head of state as to be painfully obsessive," (p.14). So, too, Mobutu and Banda, among others, suffered from the same syndrome that forced them to do things that no sane manager of state affairs can attempt leave alone doing. Power for them was a means of compensating their internalised anomalies resulting from the small-man syndrome. Jallow, *et al.,* (Ibid) go on disclosing that Bokassa hired the French firm of Guiselin, which had embroidered Napoleon's uniforms, to design a coronation negligee with 2,000,000 pearls and crystal beads for US$145,000. He drew up a list of earls and dukes, imported white horses from Belgium to pull his coach to the cathedral and spent US$2 million for a crown topped by a 138-carat diamond. All this seemed a bit lavish for a Texas-sized country with only 170 miles of paved roads and a per capita income of US$250. The *BBC* (2 January, 2009) reported that Bokassa had to ruin public coffers spending tens of millions of dollars staging a lavish and ludicrous coronation for himself as he wore costumes styled on Napoleon riding in a carriage flanked by soldiers dressed as 19th Century French cavalrymen. How much did Bokassa burn on the day of his sham coronation will never be known given that there was no way he would have been audited while he had all discretionary power under his disposal to use and abuse as pleased. Ayittey (1987) notes that suffering from "so-too-must-we" syndrome Bokassa spent 20 percent of the GNP of the Central African Republic (US$20 million) crowning himself "emperor" to prove that, like France, black Africa can produce emperors, (p. 202).

Bokassa did not only squander CAR's fortune but also robbed it; and stashed it abroad. Like, Mobutu and other thieves, he preferred to stash the stolen money to Europe, especially France, his colonial master. Like all foolish African thieves, Bokassa believed that his loot would be safer without knowing the double standard of his conspirators as the *BBC* (12 January, 2011) notes that "a French chateau that once belonged to African dictator Jean-Bedel Bokassa has sold for 915,000 euros (£760,000)." Who would think that an emperor would fail to maintain one chateau? Again, suffering from "bumbling buffoon" syndrome, the condition that turns a person into a joker, any unthinkable is possible. What happened, however, has a very big lesson for other present African dictators. After being overthrown, Bokassa had no more meaning or value for his colonial monsters. So, they offered him asylum to end up turning against him; and thereby torture him so as to force him to return to the CAR where he was condemned to death. Despite all this, there are still other stupid rulers who rob their countries and stash money in Europe without underscoring the fact that—once they are out of power—those they wrongly and blindly thought were their friends turn table on them; and thereby rob them the way they robbed their countries. Indeed, a fool is the one that is bitten twice in the same hole, Swahili proverb has it. Or once bitten, twice shy as an English proverb puts it. Bokassa lived in France as pauper who could not pay even for his property as the *BBC* (Ibid) that quoted one of Bokassa's daughters, Marie-France, as saying that Bokassa's family did not have the money to maintain the property.

We are trying to organise all these sources to show the readership why Africa is poor today. From our findings, we can argue that Africa is poor because of the worst managers just like the one in this chapter. Unfortunately, there were, and there still are many venal rulers and their courtiers, doing the same business as usual while poor African taxpayers are dying of preventable and treatable diseases. Again, why hasn't the situation changed even after African countries got independence over five decades ago? The answer is simple that our former colonial monsters cheated us. They said; they ostensibly gave us freedom. However they did so with one hand and took it with the other almost in all African countries. To perfect this art of deceit even more, the colonial monsters used our own brothers and sisters to rob us. This is why Africans need to fight for their true independence afresh. All countries that corrupt dictators abused and extravagated–which, indeed, are many in Africa–have never become independent at all.

For a sane person with just common sense, the extravagance that Bokassa and others committed would have left him with wretched guts. Again, for megalomaniacs like Bokassa, Mobutu, Houphouët-Boigny, Gaddafi and many more, such extravagance was a worthy thing for them to do. For example, on top of selling his own people, Bokassa, just like Amin, was a Casanova who was busy flirting with women so as to let the country be robbed as Lamb (1983, p. 50 cited in Jallow, *et al*, 2014) notes that he had "a huge fortune and immense power, so many decorations that he needed a specially made jacket to display them all, and a fine family numbering nine wives and thirty legitimate children," (Ibid). To keep such a family using taxpayers' money also has its negative implications on the economy. If we gauge how many such womanisers–Africa has ever had or still has in power; and how much they burnt–we can get another reason why Africa is poor. Additionally, if we consider the percentage of country's income big and do-nothing governments do in Africa, we get more of the bigger picture as to why Africa has always been poor. However, the *BBC* (2 January, 2009) quoted Bokassa's son Jean-Serge Bokassa as saying that his father, with about 50 kids, was very affectionate and loved children a lot. When it comes to how many children Bokassa exactly had, nobody can exactly tell as it was for Amin and Mobutu. With "a small man" syndrome, such demagogues liked to father as many children as they could as a way of assuring themselves of dominance even if doing so meant depriving the majority their basic human rights.

Apart from having and keeping a big family, Bokassa was foolishly extravagant. For example, he hired French poets to perform on his coronation day. How would, a sane man in his sense hire French poets and musicians to sing praise for him as if African does not have poets and musicians? Additionally, Bokassa hired French musicians not to mention a tailor who went away with $ 72,400 for just making one coronation gown. The *World History* wrote, "Lanvin made the empress's coronation gown for a $72.400 bill," not to include over $ 5 million that was spent on jewels for the occasion. A good manager would have considered his people before burning such humongous amount of money in such a laughable occasion. The day

Bokassa crowned himself emperor was so extravagant so much that some of the guests of honour such as the then president of French Valéry Giscard d'Estaing decided not to participate despite being behind the making of the tyrant. The *worldhistory* goes on observing that "his fellow emperors, Japan's Hirohito and Iran's Shah Reza Pahlavi, were the first to be invited, but they declined." However, there are some who responded positively and attended the coronation of Bokassa which the *Telegram* (April 23, 2014) noted that it echoed how men camouflage brutality with beauty, like colourful spiders. The paper went on disclosing that Bokassa was crowned in an elaborate ceremony attended by statesmen and cardinals, surrounded by guards on horseback, layered in red ermine and accompanied by a son in a crisp white uniform who at one point, fell asleep on his oversized throne. The paper concluded that roughly a third of the country's entire budget went on the coronation.

What must be clearly known is the fact that megalomaniacs like Bokassa were kept in power by those who hypocritically pretend to be the world's guardians of human rights and the harbingers of thievish and gullible civilisation. When France authorities found that Bokassa was no longer useful for them, they decided to have him disposed just the same the Americans did with Mobutu, and the British with Amin to mention a few. So, those who wrongly think that such criminals abused their countries wantonly as pleased simply because their people were afraid of pulling them down misconstrue and misrepresent the real situation to their advantage however there are some truth that the citizens are partly to blame for not taking on their dictators. This is why it becomes imminently crucial for the victims of such countries to think about seeking redress from such imperial powers that made a lot of wealth using such stupid rulers. Given that a colonial project was a crime, time for African countries to agitate for redress is now, especially after getting evidence on how the West sustained all carbuncular regimes that destroyed Africa. For, the colonial monsters plundered everything without investing in these countries. If there is anything they invested in these countries is nothing but division that left many countries polarised along tribalism and elitism.

Like Houphouët-Boigny, Bokassa erected a cathedral, the *Notre-Dame de* Bangui Cathedral whose inauguration was, ironically, presided over by Pope Paul VI. While Bokassa was doing all this, the CAR did not have even a worthy University or a Referral Hospital. Paradoxically, while Bokassa was burning millions of dollars, there are some assumptions that such phoney projects received financing from Western banks knowingly that such undertakings were but loss-making white elephants as Ayittey (2002) underscores that "even Jean-Bedel Bokassa's coronation and Felix Houphouët-Boigny's basilica had Western financiers," (p. 8). Is it being indifferent for countries that received such loans and finance under mad rulers to abscond from paying such monies? Morally speaking, this is the only right thing one can do and everyone can accept without any regret or conditions. Sankara quoted above agitating that African countries should not pay such loans still makes sense even today many years after his death. For, it defies logic even of the mad man to loan money for the construction of the church while everything is clear that the church does not produce anything material save for the offerings that end up being eaten by church leaders. While such accomplices–that ruined Africa in complicity with our mad dogs as George H. Bush would call them–stand in the agora saying Africa is poor because of bad policies. Sadly however, such hypocrites exclude themselves from the sin of pauperising Africa as if they did not engineer and man everything! Mhango (2015) insists that African countries need to reunite and demand redress for the losses and suffering they endured during slavery and colonial era not to mention neocolonialism that sustained African thieves. If we face it, countries like the DRC, the CAR, Ivory Coast, Malawi, Congo, Uganda and many more that suffered hugely under Western-pampered-tin-pot dictators and thieves are not supposed to pay any loan that was extended to known criminals such as Bokassa. If there would have been any means of forcing all financiers that supported phony and loss-making projects to come and pull down the ruins of their projects such as the basilicas and cathedrals and cities in the jungles such as Gbadolite in the DRC, so be it. For, they intentionally, greedily and illegally backed losing horses on top of already robbing the countries they need to hang by demanding more monies. If there would be any just international institution or system, what such banks and financiers are supposed to do is redress millions of victims.

It does not make any sense even to a mentally-sick person for financiers of such white elephants to have any right whatsoever, legally and morally to demand CAR's paupers to pay for projects that were purposely aimed at ruining their lives as they did. Asking them to pay is but ruining them for yet another time. Doing so is but adding salt to injury something that can create anger; and set the country on fire shall people become aware of the whole truth and what they are supposed to do as sane humans. Even those demanding to be paid are as mentally sick as those they financed to have their people ripped off. Fortunately, despite all this extravagance, Bokassa died a pauper after losing everything along with his power. He spent years in France where life was not so promising. He ended up licking his vomits by returning home to face the wrath of his victims and the long hand of the law. Gathogo (year not provided) notes that Emperor Bokassa's bizarre return to the CAR, in full knowledge of what fate awaited him, argues strongly for some kind of supernatural intervention. For, the vengeful souls of the violated children dragged him back from the security of his French asylum, (p. 342). Swahili sage has it that whenever you leave a thorn in the farm, it will one day hurt you.

Despite Bokassa authoring a very good version for African dictators and thieves to learn from, many fell in the same trap as Bokassa fell in. A few years thereafter, Nigerian strong man Sani Abacha died suddenly in office. After his death, his dirty linens were on the agora. It came to light that he had stashed billions of dollars abroad. Also, former Libyan strong man Muamar Gaddafi–who pretended to be a brotherly leader, apart from financing many mosques all over Africa–is said to have stashed billions of dollars abroad. Africa still has many suckers who rob their people and stash the loots abroad without taking a lesson from the already fallen dictators. It is a matter of time that many hidden thieves in power will be ashamedly unearthed soon after they die like in the case of Bokassa and others mentioned above, or after being overthrown. As Gathogo rightly mentions above, it needs supernatural intervention to unearth African strong men's netherworld. Again, should Africa wait for the supernatural intervention to rid itself of the thieves in power? However, the said divine-intervention, sometimes, does not intervene like it was in the cases of Omar Bongo, Gnassingbe

Eyadema, Jomo Kenyatta, and Felix Houphouët-Boigny who died in power or many more that are still at large? Africa needs to wake up and take on its robbers in power instead of waiting for the divine-intervention.

Bokassa's legacy

Bokassa's legacy, just like for any gorilla, is the shame and loss he caused to his country which he suffered as well after trying to live in exile in France after losing hold of power. His life and those of his family members were not that impressive. Financial problems hit them harder. However, such a life in France had a very good lesson that once a dictator falls from the grace, those who used him tip him as well so as to end up becoming a laughingstock to his victims as it was in the case of Bokassa who died a desolately poor, and crestfallen person that once deceived himself to be an emperor. Ill-reputed as Bokassa ending was, maybe, just maybe, would send signals to other daydreamers in power like him.

Apart from leaving behind an impoverished country, Bokassa left dilapidated and undeveloped infrastructure. If there is anything that Bokassa left behind apart from shame to his country is nothing but his *black elephant* , the *Cathedrale Notre-Dame* of our Lady of Immaculate in Bangui which he unnecessarily built while the country was taking a tumble into abject poverty. Being one of the worst managers of his country, Bokassa will be remembered for having caused miseries and indignation to his country. Like Mobutu, Bokassa was buried like an infant by a handful of chagrined mourners as if he had never been the head of state. Again, what importance did Bokassa have so as to deserve a very sound and deservedly send-off? He acted like a dog so as to be buried like a dog. Live by sword, died by sword. There are many lessons for the likes to learn from the death of such corrupt and stinking dictators.

"Every time we have a problem, the French have to come and meddle. Finally, you have to ask yourself, are we independent, or are we not? Jean-Bedel Bokassa," New York Times (November 5, 1996).

Figure 23: Cathederale Notre-Dame of Our Lady Immaculate Bangui (image courtesy of American. Pink)

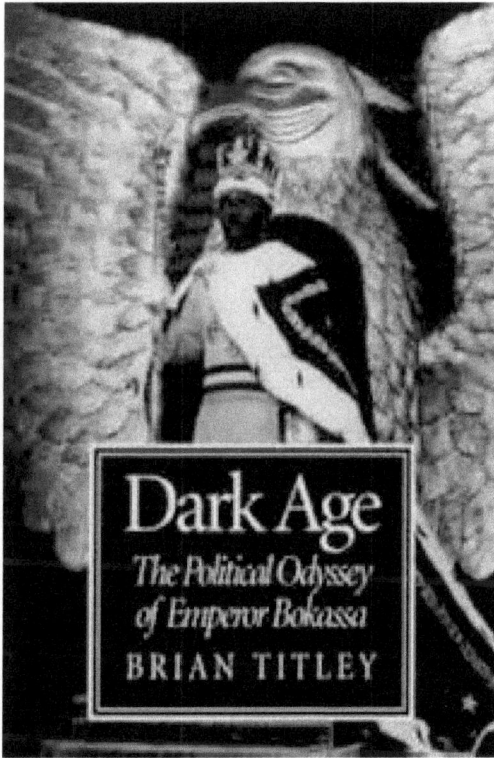

Figure 24: (image courtesy of amazon)

Chapter 18

Bongo the Turncoat That Influenced France

"From the time of independences until the end of the Cold War, in spite of the participation of a considerable number of African states in the non-aligned movement, everyone in fact chose to align with one or another of the two major blocks," Omar Bongo

Source: http://www.azquotes.com/author/1635-Omar_Bongo

Figure 25: Omar Bongo Gabon's corrupt president (image courtesy of AFP)

As mentioned above, "small-man syndrome" left Africa paralysed due to the fact that it claimed many victims as far as African dictators are concerned. Arguably, Albert Bongo Ondimba (30 December, 1935–8 June, 2009), later, Omar Bongo was another monster that was suffering from the *big man syndrome* that was struggling by all means to become big man in the continent which dictators surely later became at the expenses of pauperised citizens of their countries. Myopic, short and a midget as Bongo was, he liked bigger and taller things from cars, building to women. For, his last wife, Edith Sassou-Nguesso, was taller and younger than himself. Unfortunately for him though, due to being myopic and megalomaniac, Bongo spent much of the wealth of his country made from gas irresponsibly and unreasonably.

Bongo came into the limelight after winning the trust of the Gabonese founding father, Leon M'ba (9 February, 1902–27 November, 1967) who appointed him prime minister. Mba died in office in 1967 paving the way for Bongo to inherit presidency thereafter up until 2009 when he, too, died in office. After Bongo's natural death, his son Ali was sworn in as president to inherit his father's office. At the time of his death, Bongo was Africa's longest-serving president followed by Libyan strongman Muamar Gaddafi. Had Bongo been a wise and responsible manager of public affairs, he would have left behind a very shinning legacy just like Botswana's Sir Seretse Khama due to the fact that Bongo was ruling a very rich country with a small population as Legault (2008) notes that the small African country of Gabon illustrates the new state of affairs. With a population of 1.4million, Gabon is situated right on the equator; and has an incomparable wealth of natural resources, including petroleum, manganese, uranium, and diamonds, (p. 40).

For such a small population, one would think that Gabonese would live better lives. However, Gabonese are not benefiting from or enjoying their resources as it is supposed to be. Instead, Bongo's family and his courtiers are the ones who are enjoying after mismanaging these resources for over forty years.

Through deception, manipulations and tempering with the constitution, Bongo was able to get away with murder until death did him part with his beloved power he enjoyed for over four decades so as to once become the longest president in the continent. Like any African thief in power, Bongo was sustained by the West which he allowed to self-serve from Gabon's immense resources. Vencovsky (2007) notes that "Gabon's Omar Bongo came to power in 1967; and he then was the continent's longest-serving leader," (p. 17). As argued above, Bongo did not stay in power just because Gabonese wanted him to. He used his power to lord it over them so as to rule them unconstitutionally for over forty years. All in all, his strength came from Gabonese former colonial monster, France which he paid by befriending its presidents who used to be on his payroll as Legault (2008) argues that "president Omar Bongo, who ruled Gabon for the last 40 years with the support of the French government, despite evidence of misappropriation of funds, shows the hypocrisy of the situation," (p. 42). With such paternalistic and clientele arrangements known as support aimed at exploiting one country for the benefit of another, can we really say that Africa has ever been independent and free from its colonial bloodsuckers? Thanks to the cold war politics of the day, the West, particularly, France supported Bongo for two reasons. Firstly, the capitalist West loved dictators who could easily fleece their countries for its advantage. Secondly, for the capitalist West, it was better to have dictators and thieves in power than having diligent leaders who would easily be swung to join the communist East. If anything, this is the secret, *inter alia,* that—for a long time—maintained many dictators such as Mobutu, Amin, Compaore, Moi, Barre, you name it that Africa has ever had. Without unearthing and documenting their history and the role they played in hijacking Africa's development and future, we will not be doing justice to ourselves as a people. Unless we do this, we will be able to show next generations where things went wrong so that they can avoid committing the same mistakes we committed as a people. Academics need to make things right by exploring; and documenting the true history of Africa in order to counter fake and biased history that the colonial monsters wrote with prejudgments. Shillington, (2012) argues that these racist prejudices seriously impeded the study and writing of the history of African history (p. 2) which resulted into serious distortion of the facts. Among the subjects of African history is Bongo who along with other thieves ruined not only Gabon but Africa as well.

Nothing busied Bongo like securing more friends in French state house. Sometimes, things would take a bad turn so as to force Bongo to dig deeper in his pocket to make sure he survived the wind of change as it was in 1998. Marchal (1998) maintains that election that were due to take place in Gabon in spring 1998 might have sparked off incidents in the region. Therefore, Bongo could not be sure that he would be guaranteed the same support and freedom accorded him by his friends in Paris in the elections of 1993 and 1996," (p. 363).

This means; Bongo had to sell more of his country in order to illegally remain in power which he did so as to die in power nine years thereafter. Despite all woes, Bongo prevailed after manipulating the electoral system that was laden with his courtiers as Magaloni (2007) notes that after announcing the introduction of multi-party elections in 1990, Bongo, since then, had been able to rule despite constant allegations of election rigging and intimidation of opposition which despite the fact that the more than six opposition parties announced the formation of a united front, the Coordination of Democratic Opposition (COD), it failed to unite behind a single candidate, allowing president Bongo to re-elect himself in 1992 over thirteen competitors by a narrow 51.18% of the vote, (p. 3).

Bongo was not alone in this game of deceit. His friend Mobutu and his father-in-law, Denis Sassou-Nguesso (who despite being eight years younger, consented to marrying his daughter, Dr. Edith Lucie, to Bongo did the same. He did not want to lose his power. Therefore, he had to trade his daughter so as to secure assistance that would enable him to cling to power. On top of using France to support his regime, Bongo used his courtiers at home to gain political legality under democracy as it was introduced by their master, the West, to fool citizens under venal dictators just like Bongo. Essentially, the introduction of democracy to Africa early in the 1990s was a ploy the West used to disencumber itself of some of its unproductive allies on the one hand and gaining leverage from the population in the continent on the other hand. So, too, the reintroduction of democracy was aimed at reducing tensions in the continent without considering economic burden it unleashed to poor taxpayers who finance the same democracy to end up legalising dictatorship be it one-man or one-party democracy. For, the change of guards—especially uncooperative ones—was aimed at installing new ones so that the West could go on with business as usual. Mhango (2015) queries the logic for poor countries to burn billions of dollars in elections that would bring just the same while social services such as health, education and infrastructure are in bad shape. He goes on questioning the rationale for the Western countries to fund some of the elections in poor countries. Mhango concludes arguing that who pays the piper calls the tune. Thus, the West fund elections to get their people in power that would protect their interests. And when poor taxpayers fund their elections end up ruining their treasuries to get just the same. This is true given that in the countries where long-time dictators such as Bongo protect the interests of the West such as Congo, Uganda, and Equatorial Guinea, democracy has never been preferred. No way can democracy make sense in the countries whose presidents have been in power for more than ten years.

Bongo is renowned for misusing the resources and wealth of this tiny-oil-producing nation. Rumours have it that Bongo was a chief financier of French elections. He used Gabonese wealth to commit all types of crimes in order to remain in power. Even if it needed to kill, or send someone to exile or eliminate anybody he deemed to be an obstacle to his power, he would do so without hesitating or caring about human values. Eko (2007) notes that in February 2002, Michel Ongoudou Loundah, editor of La Griffe (The Claw) "an irreverent, satirical newspaper based in Libreville, Gabon, Africa, survived a kidnapping and murder attempt" (p. 219) simply because he satirised the big man. Eko goes on disclosing that the whole editorial staff of the newspaper was banned from practicing journalism as a result of this sin they committed to the big man of Gabon. So, apart from exiling, killing and torturing, Bongo was good at silencing detractors and journalists among other. All he wanted–just like any tin pot dictator would want–is to look good even if the truth says contrary. Eko (Ibid) makes more damning allegations as far as Bongo reign of terror is concerned arguing that "those who did not toe the official line risked arrest, banishment or death. The tightly controlled media became the main instrument for sustaining authoritarian regimes marked by ubiquitous cults of personality," (p. 221). Can such a person in power be a good manager of state affairs while he actually is a threat to others and their freedoms? How can one become a good manager of state affairs without allowing others to evaluate his works? While Bongo did not allow his people to evaluate him, foreign media were out of his reproach. The *New York Times* (June 8, 2009) had this to say when Bongo died of what is said to be a long time cancer that his spin doctors used to deny:

Mr. Bongo, a disciple of the first generation of African leaders, came to power in 1967, when Lyndon B. Johnson was still president. He presided over an oil boom that fuelled an extravagant lifestyle for him and his family—dozens of luxurious properties in and around Paris, a $500 million presidential palace, fancy cars. But the tide of money did little to lift his country of 1.5 million people out of chronic poverty.

Just like any self-seeking thief, Bongo's wealth and happiness were more important than those of Gabonese. With presidency and France's support, Bongo has the wherewithal to weather whatever resistance or threat. He, therefore, did not waste time investing in his country. Instead, he spent Gabonese fortunes on buying mansions and villas in Europe and financing his friends 'campaigns' in Élysée palace in exchange for protection that assured his stay in power. It reached the point at which Bongo and French politicians became yin yang in that their survival mutually depended on each other.

As said heretofore, knowing that Bongo was their stooge, some Western leaders would not even influence their media to stop them from telling the truth about their ally in crime. For the *Economist* (June 18th, 2009) wrote that Bongo made no distinction between Gabon and his private property. After ruling for 42 years he became Gabon. The paper goes on noting that it was therefore perfectly natural that an oil company granted a large concession for coastal drilling, had slip him regular suitcases stuffed with cash. It was natural that $2.6m in aid money should be used to decorate his private jet, that government funds should pay for the Italian marble cladding his palace, and that his wife Edith's sea-blue Maybach, in which she was driven round Paris, should be paid for with a cheque drawn on the Gabonese treasury. Of the US$130m in his personal accounts at Citibank in New York, it was probable—though Citibank never asked, and nobody ever managed to pin a charge on him—that much of it was derived from the GDP of his country.

Suffering from a *small-man syndrome*, like Jomo Kenyatta and his successor Daniel arap Moi in Kenya and elsewhere in Africa, Bongo made sure that money was spent on his monuments as the *Guardian* (5 May, 2008) notes that "there are many ways of measuring Omar Bongo's rule. One of which was to count the monuments: the Omar Bongo Triumphal Boulevard, the Senate Palace Omar Bongo, and the university, football stadium, gymnasium and military hospital that all bear his name. The *Economist* (Ibid) went on disclosing how rich Bongo and his family were. It wrote in 2007, French prosecutors found the Bongo family owned 33 properties in France alone, including a $27m villa. At the same time, Ali-Ben Bongo's wife, Inge, appeared on a US reality television show, Really Rich Real Estate, shopping for a $25m mansion in California.

Again, when it comes to Bongo's wealth made by fleecing his country, what the *Guardian* exposed is but the tip of the iceberg. How did Bongo and his courtiers make their wealth? The *Guardian* (Ibid) discloses that there was no way one would discuss any business in Gabon without knowing a minister or any person with surname Bongo. This means that Gabon was turned into Bongo and family private estate. It was an unforgivable sin in Gabon to disclose Bongo's wealth. According to the *New York Time* (12 March, 2008) which quoted local sources in Gabon, wrote in 2008 that Gabonese authorities banned a private newspaper for republishing a report on President Omar Bongo's private wealth in France. The original story appeared in French daily, the *Le Monde* at the end of January of the same year. This shows how illicitly the said wealth was obtained. Suffering from a small-man syndrome, if Bongo's wealth were legally obtained, he would have liked it to be publicised so that he can be respected. But given that the said wealth was obtained illegally, disclosing it was a sin that the authorities in Gabon would not make do with or ignore or pardon. Arguably, Bongo and his courtiers turned a rich country like Gabon into a fragile state which Makochekanwa and Kwaramba (2009, p. 4 cited in Mawere, 2013), defines as one in which "the state power is unable and/or unwilling to deliver core functions to the majority of its people: security, protection of property rights, basic public services and essential infrastructure," (pp. 2-3) wantonly due to his greed and myopia.

Almost all dictators fear one thing, death. Sometimes, they do not believe that they would die. Like his counterpart Gnassingbe Eyadema in Togo who passed on two years before Bongo; or Papa Doc in Haiti; or Kabila, when Bongo died, his beloved power remained in his line. For, as noted above, it was peacefully transferred to his son Ali.

Arguably, Bongo was a very lucky dictator who died in power peacefully despite all crimes he committed to his country. Again, the history of Africa will never treat him generously due to the fact that his role in plundering his country is something no sane person can overlook or ignore. Like other thieves, Bongo's name will be synonymous with mismanagement of public office, theft of public funds, dictatorship, ineptness, and above all, the underdevelopment of his country and Africa at large. Bongo epitomises the extension of colonialism carried out by black colonialists on behalf of their white masters that installed them in power to sabotage and exploit Africa. So, too, Bongo characterises French and Western double standards, dependency, and above all, the thuggish nature in dealing with African countries. Again, there is a very good lesson from Bongo's legacy in that Africa needs to fight for true independence by getting rid of itself of thieves in power. It is unfortunate though, despite all such dirty linens to be put on the agora, Africans still fear and trust their thieves in power. This needs to change urgently shall Africa aspire to forge ahead decently and realistically. While other dictators such as Gaddafi, Hosni Mubarak and Mobutu failed to pass their power on to their children, Bongo successfully did. It does not cross the mind to gauge and get the logic–for example–of allowing sons of dictators to inherit their fathers' offices and estates while they belong to the people. We evidenced this in the DRC, Gabon, and Togo. Why?

Bongo's legacy

Differently from many of his type, Bongo was able to manipulatively create a system that enabled his son, Ali to inherit his presidency. Like father like son. When Ali ascended to power, he duped Gabonese that he would redistribute some of his holdings–he inherited from his father–to them without telling how it was made and how big it was. The *New York Times* (18 August, 2015) wrote "one of Africa's wealthiest presidents said this week that he was giving up at least some of his holdings." Another Bongo's hallmark was endemic corruption, theft and mismanagement to the extent that, from time to time, during his presidency, French politicians turned him into a cash cow which makes him another bumbling imbecile with power in his hands that would not use his head well. Many still wonder. If Bongo was sane, how would he finance France's politics while the majority of his people were wallowing in poverty?

Special tributes

The history of Gabon makes no sense without mentioning its founder, Leo M'ba who overthrew Paul Marie Indjendjet Gondjout to become the first Prime Minister of Gabon.

Figure 26: Bongo's caricature (image courtesy of MAGIXL)

Chapter 19

Amin a *Bumbling Buffoon* Britain Cloned

"In any country there must be people who have to die. They are the sacrifices any nation has to make to achieve law and order" Idi Amin.
Source:
http://www.brainyquote.com/quotes/authors/i/idi_amin.h
tml#fHRzctc4BFlePXeO.99

Figure 27: Idi Amin, Uganda's brutal President (image courtesy of AP)

General Idi Amin Dada (1923-28–16 August, 2003) angered and shocked many when he staged a successful and bloodless *coup d'état* in 1971 toppling Uganda's founding father Milton Obote who was attending a commonwealth Conference in Singapore. Gullible, illiterate, heartless and eccentric, Amin, just like Joseph Desire Mobutu, was a product of the cold war *realpolitik* of the time. After taking over, Amin Ugandans who were tired of Obote whose rule had already started to show some cracks as far as power abuse is concerned acclaimed him as a liberator without knowing he would become an antithesis of what they thought. For a few months after the coup, some unsuspecting Ugandans were elated to have been gotten rid of Obote without reckoning that another ogre was bursting onto the scene to, later, mercilessly butcher and terrorise them wantonly for nearly a decade. Mamdani (2009) maintains that in 1979, he began to realise that whatever they made of Amin's brutality, "the Ugandan people experienced the Asian expulsion of 1972—and not the formal handover in 1962—as the dawn of true independence," (p. 3).

This is how controversial Amin was. For Ugandans, especially those who benefited from nepotism and allowing the army to do as pleased saw Amin as a hero; while, to the contrary, to his victims he was but a vampire hell-bent to destroy the country and its people as he did for eight years he was in power. Obwona (2001) refers to Amin's rule period as an "economic war" arguing that the said period was marked by the "Economic War" of 1972, which resulted in the expulsion of the British-Asians, expropriation of the assets and businesses of foreign investors mostly Asians and eventual collapse of the industrial and commercial sectors, (page not provided). The expulsion of Asians who were British citizens angered Britain that–along with the West–helped Amin to come to power. However, Amin knew how to play his game. He had already befriended rich Saudi house in Saudi Arabia and Libyan former strongman Muamar Gaddafi under the banner of Islam. What is clear is that Amin, sometimes, had very healthy relationship with the West especially Britain. As the time went by and Amin showed his true colour–like it was with Museveni and Rwanda's Paul Kagame later–he lost leverage from Britain as the BBC (1 January, 2005) notes that "by the end of his reign Amin had fallen out with Britain and given himself the title of Conqueror of the British Empire in Africa in general and Uganda in particular." Basically, the relationship between Amin and the West was nothing but the nap of two strange bedfellows in the same bed in which everyone was scheming to stab another in the back shall the opportune time avail itself.

Arguably, those who cloned Amin wanted a stooge they could use and misuse to counter Obote's socialist inclination. Amin was a creature and a product of colonial and capitalistic legacy in Africa. David Martin cited in Mazrui (1977) defines Amin noting that, "… he was the type of material the British officers like in the ranks– physically large at six feet four inches and uneducated," (p. 190). Amin himself admits his illiteracy and poverty as the motivations that pushed him to join the military. *Brainyquote* quotes Amin saying, "I was a good soldier in the British Army. I was born in a very, very poor family. And I enlisted to escape hunger. But my officers were Scottish and they loved me. The Scots are good, you know." Amin was dead right. For, Britain was the first country to recognise him soon after ousting Obote. Quoting the Library of Congress, *Uganda Forum.org* notes that quickly, Britain, Israel and the US recognised his government while to the contrary, Presidents Julius Nyerere of Tanzania, Kenneth Kaunda of Zambia, Jomo Kenyatta of Kenya, and the Organization of African Unity (OAU) initially refused to accept the legitimacy of the new military government. *Forum.org* tosses on noting that Nyerere, in particular, opposed Amin's regime, and he offered hospitality to the exiled Obote, facilitating his attempts to raise a force and return to power.

Furthermore, Amin's former military boss, Major Ian Grahame in the King's African Rifles (KAR), described him to be as strong as an ox something that made him a perfect choice for brutalising his people. Additionally, Amin was purely illiterate. Therefore, his cloners thought he would receive orders without questioning. So, too, thanks to being an illiterate, Amin would create many enemies within the ranks so as to heavily depend on his cloners. Furthermore, Amin was a "heavyweight boxing champion 1951-1960," the *CNN* (June 8, 2011) the title he held without being beaten. Being so mechanical and illiterate, Amin became an ideal choice for colonial monsters to do their dirty laundry. His intimidating and bullish physique enabled him to join colonial army, the KAR, wherefrom Amin went on to become a colonel in Uganda's first Defence Forces that was formed after gaining independence. Essentially, those who cloned and installed Amin wanted a bullish and rancorous 'buffoon' as Nyerere used to refer to him, or *bumbling buffoon,* as once the *BBC* referred to him, who could be busy womanising and fooling around not to forget terrorising his population so that it can toe the line for his cloners to easily exploitation, rape and rob his country. And indeed, Amin was exactly that. Like another military goon, Bokassa in the CAR, Amin had many wives and many children which awarded him a title of *Big Dad* as he liked to be referred to among many titles he ridiculously added to his name.

All started on the day Uganda became independent. Sadly though, even after Uganda became independent, Obote re-enacted the same colonial mentality of preferring an illiterate soldier from his region to become his chief of the Defence Forces believing that he would not overthrow him. The *BBC* (16 August, 2003) notes that "Amin was appointed head of the army and navy under President Milton Obote in 1966, but overthrew Mr Obote five years later and declared himself president for life." After appointing him, Obote used Amin to settle scores with his enemies of whom some used to be Amin's friends. One of them was King Mutesa who was later attacked by Amin as Mazrui (Ibid) notes that "in 1966, after independence, an occasion arose when Idi Amin was given orders by Prime Minister Milton Obote to attack Mutesa's palace," (p. 194). Just like the British colonial monsters, Obote saw a tool in Amin that he could use against his nemeses without reckoning that when you teach a dog to eat eggs it likely ends up eating your own chickens. Even in the neighbouring Tanzania, Mwl. Julius Nyerere preferred to appoint illiterate Chiefs of Defence Forces from his region throughout his twenty-four years administration. Again, this was like an in-thing in Africa. This is why illiterates like Togolese former dictator, Gnassingbe Eyadema and many military men in Nigeria were able to come to power before and thereafter. You can see this currently in Rwanda and Uganda among other African countries where the Chiefs of the Defence Forces–however, they are not illiterates–are from president's communities.

Ironically, even when Amin started showing his true colour as a coldblooded killer, the so-called civilised world–which had cloned him–turned a blind eye and a deaf ear. Amin is one of African rulers renowned for having committed massacres of thousands of innocent Ugandans–who died peacefully in South Africa–without being brought to book. Due to being an exception to the general rule, some writers, even academics equate him with Hitler (see Melady and Melady, 1977). However, such a claim is controversial and an exaggeration if we consider how pathetic and lethal Hitler was. Arguably, comparing the person who massacred thousands with the one who slaughtered millions, sometimes, can be an overstatement. Again, what this comparison shows is that brutality and mass murder were something new to Africa. This is why we cannot historically mention even five Africans who massacred big numbers of their people compare to Europe, Asia and America. What needs to be made clear is that, apart from being ignored by the West when Amin was massacring Ugandans, there are countries that actively helped and supported him. The regimes in Libya and Saudi Arabia offered him a lot of money that enabled him to survive financially, especially after the world woke up from the slumber and conspiracy on Uganda so as to shun him. Again, it was too little too late. Amin was not badly affected due to the fact that he had already secured another lifeline in Libya and Saudi Arabia.

Sometimes, I wonder why the international community that enabled Jews to claim compensation after being gas chambered by Hitler failed to force such regimes mentioned above to redress Amin's victims and Uganda in general. Every now and then, hither is whither racism and conspiracy against Africa are intentionally and internationally displayed vividly. If the international community were fair, Amin's victims would have been redressed and would have had a special International Day for their commemoration as reminder to the world that conspiracy to commit crimes against humanity is evil. Ironically, despite the conspiracy and silence that enable Amin to kill thousands of innocent Ugandans as pleased, those who cloned, launched and sustained him have never been put to shame or faced any criminal liability for the crimes they committed against innocent Ugandans. So, we can openly and comfortably argue that among other reasons of exposing such autocratic and inhuman regimes is to link their masters and abettors to the crimes many African dictators and criminals committed aided and supported by Western and other powers.

According to the *BBC* (16 August, 2003) when reporting the death of Amin, it estimated that "up to 400,000 people are believed to have been killed under his rule." The exact number of Ugandans Amin butchered has remained a mystery due to the fact that even the same media outlet would contradict itself by giving differing figures such as the *BBC* above offered compared to the ones the same offered on 1 January, 2005 which is quoted as reporting that "by the time of his 1979 overthrow he had been responsible for 300,000 deaths and the economic ruin of his own country. So savage was Amin's rule that the former British foreign secretary Lord Owen suggested assassinating the dictator." What is clear is that Amin brutally, secretly and openly killed many innocent Ugandans. Look at another misnomer. The *CNN* (16 January, 2003) reported that "during his eight-year rule, Ugandans were gripped in a climate of fear as an estimated 500,000 people disappeared or were killed." Sometimes, you wonder how the Western media and, sometimes, the same media house could not get its facts right on the same subject. Is it because some Western media are always in hurry to demonise or sundeck their subjects so as to forget to have and put their facts rightly? The *CNN* went on quoting Amin's friend and former health Minister Henry Kyemba as saying that even Amin does not know how many people he ordered to be executed who littered Uganda with bodies. At least, Kyemba shows how complicated it is to know the actual number of Amin's victims.

Under Amin, many Ugandans paid dearly. We saw that in neighbouring Kenya where two post-colonial administrations killed, exiled and silencing activists and politicians. Differently from Kenya, Amin killed both politicians and civilians. Prominent people who were killed under Amin are, *inter alia,* Chief Justice of Uganda Benedict Kiwanuka and Archbishop Janan Luwum, not to mention ministers who differed with Amin. The Ugandan *Daily Monitor* (16 February, 2015) reported some people testified to have seen the archbishop Luwum and the two cabinet ministers, Erinayo Wilson Oryema and Charles Oboth Ofumbi, were being taken away in a Land Rover. The next day, a government spokesperson claimed that Archbishop Luwum had died in a car accident.

As quoted above, for Amin, death for some people was inevitable as far as maintaining fear and order were concerned. He used death as a means of eliminating enemies and sending a warning to others who had not fallen in his traps. In one of many YouTube clips Amin once said that some people had to die so as to maintain peace and order in the country. Due to being an illiterate, mechanical and sadistic—it obviously seems—law did not make sense for Amin as means of maintaining peace and order in the country.

When it comes to brutality that Amin applied in killing his nemeses—real and unreal—Amin was second to none in Africa. Nothing was a simple solution for Amin like killing. It was as easy as winking. Ofkansy (1996 cited in Quinn 2004) notes that "the tactics

Amin used against his adversaries defy description. He did not merely order his henchmen to kill people but also encouraged them to subject their victims to unspeakable atrocities after they were dead, (p. 402). Ever since its independence, arguably, Uganda has always encountered one calamity after another. From the outset, Uganda's first president Obote seemed to be unprepared to rule diligently. His irresponsibility is among the reasons that created opportune for the West to clone Amin; and thereafter back to topple him. After Amin toppling Obote, Ugandans wrongly thought they might get a reprieve. It did not come to be. Yet, more was to come. For, even after the Tanzania People Defence Force (TPDF) toppled and expelled Amin, Ugandans did not get what they expected. Quinn (2004) explains why saying that "in the case of Uganda in 1986, Museveni's government was simply seen as the next in a series of military coups, a military government fighting to hold on to what legitimacy it could," (p. 406). And truly, before long, Museveni proved to be another power grabber who stretched out, and metamorphosed his regime from one shape to another and from one phase to another. The *BBC* (27 July, 1999) notes that "now Uganda's destiny lies with an altogether different kind of strongman-Yoweri Museveni, a guerrilla commander turned statesman," who is hell-bent to cling to power at all cost.

As argued above, Amin killed whomever he perceived to be his enemy. Therefore, after eliminating Obote's associates who were not lucky to have escaped, civilians, politicians and academics followed suit. Knowing how academics unearth and criticise malpractices in the upper echelons of power, Amin did not spare them. He saw them as enemies that were supposed to be eliminated for him to rule for a long time and comfortably. Essentially, the role academics played in criticising Amin along the media and Non-Governmental Organisations (NGOs) guaranteed and warranted Amin the reasons to hunt them down; and thereby kill academics and intellectuals for two reasons. Firstly, Amin did not like, in any way, the way they told him the truth such as restoring human rights. And secondly, being an illiterate, Amin had a phobia *vis-a-vis* intellectuals whom he regarded as being arrogant, smart and nonconforming. Mazrui (2003) notes that after a military coup occurred in January 1971 and brought Idi Amin into power, within eight years of brutal dictatorship followed.

Mazrui notes that the Vice-Chancellor of Makerere–Frank Kalimuzo–was abducted in broad daylight from the campus and a similar fate befell the judicially courageous Chief Justice of Uganda, Benedicto Kiwanuka. Mazrui notes that after the above deaths, "the scintillating intellectual voices of Uganda either fell silent or went into exile. Before long I too packed my bags and left my beloved Makerere," (p. 137). This is what Uganda went on under Amin as the international community watched.

Mazrui (Ibid) links Amin's death of intellectualism to Daniel arap Moi's in neighbouring Kenya as he praises Obote's and Nyerere's tolerance of the same. However, it should be noted that Obote's tolerance did not go on for the all times he was in power like it was Nyerere's. Cohn (1998) notes that "the Amin-Obote period of terror and destruction set Uganda back more than the fifteen years that it lasted," (p. 102). There is no way one can describe Amin without touching on Obote and vice versa. When it comes to ruining Uganda, the duo is like yin yang arguably. And for Uganda, this has been a prolongation of suffering. As indicated in the former chapters, Africans–in various countries under corrupt and dictatorial regimes–tried to resist such brutal regimes but there were no international pressure towards such regimes. You can see how international pressure and support help in toppling dictators by revisiting what happened in Egypt in 2010 when mass actions resulted into the toppling of Egypt's long-time Strongman, Hosni Mubarak. The situation was the same in the neighbouring Libya where a long-time demagogue, Muamar Gaddafi was toppled; and later killed by the mob a year subsequently. So, many African dictators descended hard on their people knowing that there was nobody who would hold them accountable. The situation was different from what we now have whereby such brutal rulers can be indicted by the International Criminal Court (ICC). However, some academics such as Murithi (2013, p. 8) view such a move as the conduit of promoting neo-imperialism under the gaze of protecting human rights. It depends on how one looks at the role the ICC is likely to play in ridding Africa of dictators and human rights violators it currently has. When it comes to Amin's reign of terror, even the countries we see today pretending to champion some selected human rights, did not interfere for fear of spoiling their relationship with the regime that used to supply them with what they wanted. The easy way of putting this across is to simply state that it was an international conspiracy based on political sellout that ruined and held Africa at ransom for many years. Such negligence–that international community has committed for many times and years–needs to be documented, and condemned altogether. For, it is a part of African history those who authored it do not like to tell accurately and rightly.

Interestingly, despite being sponsored by British to topple Obote–which of course was a punishment for aligning with communists–when Amin showed his true colours, the British were the first to jump the smoking gun though in vain. They thought they would use Amin without being aware that he, as well, wanted to use them. What do you expect when two conmen are involved in business? At a personal level, Amin is the only dictator who was not accused of robbing his country. This is ironic and startling so to speak. Again, give the devil its due. Amin was a murderer but not a thief thanks to not being implicated in or accused of any corruption. Amin's rule came to end in 1979 when the TPDF invaded Uganda after Amin claimed a part of Tanzania to be Ugandan. Despite getting military and financial supports from Libya and Saudi Arabia, the TPDF dislodged him. Luckily for him, Amin fled Uganda for the fear of being caught by the TPDF to end up in exile in Saudi Arabia where he lived comfortably up until he naturally died on 16 August, 2003. Like Mobutu whose remains were interred in Morocco, Amin's remains were interred in Saudi Arabia. Arguably, eight years that Amin ruled Uganda marked a very grief and torturous part of the history of this nation. His buffoonery did not only bring shame to Uganda but also to the entire continent. Interestingly, the West that cloned Amin has recently produced satirical films about him trying to show the world how evil Amin was without including its own part of the plot to destabilise and exploit Africa using black colonialists. Just like other stinking dictators, Amin became famous for the wrong reasons. His brutality and inanity awarded him a place in the history of Africa and the world. This is Amin the world knows for his bad management of public affairs. Let us conclude Amin's sickening history with his own quote that implicates the West.

"I love the Americans. They are my best friend," Amin.
http://www.brainyquote.com/quotes/authors/i/idi_amin.html
#D2B8Ik3lWlMmfjYD.99

Amin's legacy

Like Adolf Hitler, Pol Pot, Nikita Khrushchev and other coldblooded killers, Amin will always be remembered—as said above—for the wrong reasons. He will be remembered as a mass murderer that evaded the long arm of law; and died peacefully in exile. As a shame to Uganda and African in general, Amin's major legacy is being what British called a *bumbling buffoon* who abused the office of the president. Amin's major hallmarks are nothing but brutality, insanity, and above all, unpredictability. So, too, Amin's legacy unearthed Western double standard, especially during the cold war whereby the West would support any butcherer, criminal or mentally-sick person in order to avoid communism. The fear of communism, arguably, turned the West into irrational next to mentally-sick creature. Amin's punitive and double-faced marriage with Britain will always haunt Britain forever. So, too, the countries such as Libya and Saudi Arabia that used to support Amin after the West abandoned him make a good legacy of how Africa is viewed by these countries. If the international system were based on justice, such countries, along with Amin's Western friends and backers are supposed to redress Ugandans for the pains and sufferings they endured and went through under Amin's murderous regime whose lifeline was nothing but the supports these countries extended to Amin.

Special tributes

Uganda's history cannot be completed without mentioning and honouring those who died in Amin's hands. Archbishop Janan Luwum who stood his ground against Amin's barbarity shed his blood for the emancipation of Uganda. So, too, Dr. Benedict Kiwanuka, Joseph Mubiru, Frank Kalimuzo, Byron Kawadwa, Erinayo Wilson Oryema, and Charles Oboth Ofumbi among many whom Amin killed. Also, tributes go to those who stood against Amin and survived such as Henry Kyemba who penned a book, *The State of Blood* that shamed and slammed Amin's regime, Mwl Julius Nyerere, the TPDF and Festo Kivengere whose book *I love Idi Amin*

248

dressed Amin down even more, among others. So, too, special tributes go to all Ugandans who–for eight years–endured Amin's tyrannical rule.

Figure 28: Amin's caricature (image courtesy of everysparrowfall)

250

Chapter 20

Houphouët-Boigny a Ruthless and Mystique Crocodile

"If we are naive enough to cut ourselves off from the West, we will be invaded by the Chinese and Soviet Russia," Houphouët-Boigny cited in Pondi (1989).

Figure 29: Felix Houphouet-Boigny Ivorian 1st President (image courtesy of AFP)

Félix Houphouët-Boigny, a typical tribal chief whom "the French called 'the Sage of Africa'" *New Statesman* (23 October, 2008) was born on 18 October, 1905 and died in office on 7 December, 1993. Houphouët-Boigny was the first Ivorian president, who corruptly and venally ruled the country for thirty three years from 3 November, 1960 to 7 December, 1993, when he died in office (Kirwin, 2006); also see Akindes, 2004b, p. 7). Like Mobutu with his village of Gbadolite, or Jean-Bedel Bokassa with his *Cathedrale de* Notre-Dame Bangui, Houphouët-Boigny decided to transform his village into a city he wanted to become the capital city of Ivory Coast in vain.

251

Among many things, Houphouët-Boigny built a mega Basilica so big that it dwarfs St. Peter Basilica in Vatican which is the headquarters of Catholicism. While the best African managers such as Julius Nyerere (Tanzania) left shinning legacies such as providing social services, Houphouët-Boigny left what was later known as a *black elephant* of a basilica and a town he was born in. Isaksson (2015) notes that in the early 1980s, Houphouët-Boigny made his birthplace Yamoussoukro, the onetime little more than an agricultural village, the capital of Ivory Coast that soon boasted an artificial lake with crocodiles, a six-lane highway, an airport that could land a Concorde, and perhaps most notably, the world's largest church–the Basilica of Our Lady of Peace, (p. 1).

Despite erecting such a humongous basilica, Houphouët-Boigny was not truly a religious man whose power was supped to depend on God to whom he devoted the church. When it comes to religious belief, Houphouët-Boigny was more of a mongrel than a believer. The *New Statesman* (23 October, 2008) notes:

Now I was on my way to discover what had become of the Catholic basilica in the African bush, as well as the rest of Houphouët-Boigny's legacy, reptiles included. In the early 1980s, V S Naipaul came here, a visit that produced his celebrated essay "The Crocodiles of Yamoussoukro", published in 1987. Naipaul was quite complimentary about Houphouët-Boigny's rule, and thought the crocs seemed to symbolise his mystique and power over his people.

Thanks to his madness, Houphouët-Boigny's crocodiles used to feed on chickens those looking after them supplied. Arguably, Houphouët-Boigny was but a crocodile that was devouring his people by robbing them while shedding crocodile tears. Houphouët-Boigny, like Bongo, Eyadema and Kenyatta, was lucky –he peacefully died in office–without facing the music for the crimes he committed to his country, people and Africa. While the majority of Ivoirians were suffering from poverty, ignorance and preventable and treatable diseases, Houphouët-Boigny had the guts to shell out millions of dollars to finance his white elephant, the basilica in his village of Yamoussoukro. A competent manager of public business cannot think about let alone committing such misappropriation of public funds. Ironically, the French called him a *sage of Africa* as if he truly was. Was he a sage of Africa or a bogus Oldman of Africa? If Africa needed sages, they were Mandela, Kaunda, Machel, Sir Khama Nkrumah and Nyerere among a few at the time. If Houphouët-Boigny were a good manager of public affairs, how would he burn such money on nonsensical things that his people did not, and will not need or benefit from? As noted earlier, Houphouët-Boigny's basilica project did not lack Western funders. You wonder how Ivoirians could pay such a debt that ended up in what many called a *black elephant*. Isaksson (2015) equates Houphouët-Boigny's Basilica to Egyptian pharaohs who spent their fortunes on expensive buildings so as to pointlessly end up in penury that marked the end of the African most ancient and the greatest civilisation. A competent and sane manager of state affairs cannot squander resources financing such a project that has nothing to contribute to the wellbeing of the people. Like Muamar Gaddafi who used to fund mosques in various African countries without even considering religious compositions of these countries, Houphouët-Boigny did not bother to consider the fact that Ivory Coast consists of Christian, Muslims and traditionalists. For him, building the basilica in his village, just like Mobutu did, was the best thing compared to other amenities such as schools, hospital, universities and roads that his people needed the most. Even if he had constructed some, it would have made more sense to construct more than wasting money on the basilica that has nothing to offer to the country. If you ask for the rationale of choosing Yamoussoukro to be the capital of Ivory Coast while it had already had a well-established Abidjan as its capital, you end up wondering. Hill (year not provided) notes that "Felix Houphouët-Boigny chose the town for the site because it was his birthplace and in over a quarter of a century only one pope stayed at the villa, and that was once and for a day," (p. 8). Such a project only made sense to an insane megalomaniac, but not a sane person. How can a sane man embark on such a loss-making project, especially at the expense of the people while Ivoirians, at the time, were suffering from hunger? (Also see Mhango, 2015).

Another reason from Houphouët-Boigny managerial skills, maybe, can be the fact that his philosophy of "Houphouetism gives preference to the individual rather than to the citizen" (Akindes 2004b, p. 12); therefore, that individual was to be himself first before others. This is contrary to Ubuntu, African great philosophy mostly practised by Bantu in East, Central and South African regions, which argues that 'I am human because I belong' (Tutu cited in Swanson, 2008, p. 54). Furthermore, Houphouët-Boigny's philosophy does not recognise citizenship; instead it just considers an individual without looking at her or his legality of being where the person is. Arguably, considering an individual by ignoring her or his legality of being where that person is means that someone has no sense of nation which to such a person, a personal glory seems to be better than the national one, which is in our sense, is African but not otherwise. We are trying to avoid generalising everything to avoid non-African to come and plunder our continent under such infamy philosophies. Akindes (Ibid) goes on showing how the so-called *Houphouetism* was nothing but an empty and poor harangue noting that was best understood as a set of structuring principles and practices in various way which function as a system of reference based on political culture which is socially recognised but not intellectualised, (p. 7).

However organised the philosophy it might be regarded, if it cannot be conceptualised it means it is obsolete, wanting and bankrupt. And this is very true *vis-à-vis Houphouetism* due to the fact that no academic sources showing Houphouët-Boigny articulating his philosophy the same ways gurus such as Julius Nyerere (*Ujamaa na Kujitegemea* or socialism and self-reliance), Leopold Sedar Senghor (Negritude), and Kenneth Kaunda (Humanism) were articulated and experimented. Essentially, the product of *Houphoutism*, just like any of this type propounded by a decadent ruler, resulted to creating a venal and corrupt society in which everybody was plundering whatever was left for one to plunder after elites plundered almost everything. And, Houphouët-Boigny was at home with this destruction of his country. Arguably, this is why many rotten African despots survived. They allowed their people to become petty thieves so as to generally make the whole system corrupt and self-serving at the detriment of the poor majority in many countries; otherwise, there were no way thieves such as Houphouët-Boigny and others, mentioned above, would have survived for a long time without being pulled down. They made their innocent citizens accomplices in their netherworlds.

Furthermore, what is referred to as *Houphoutism* has no difference from another hotchpotch known as *Mobutuism* which, Jackson & Rosberg (1982, p. 172 cited in Ikome, 2008) defines as, "the promotion of the state party, the MPR, as the central political agency of the state; and the pursuit of cultural and psychological decolonisation embodied in his policy of authenticity," (p. 24). During Mobutu's reign of terror, *Mobutuism* became a cliché wantonly simply because Mobutu was in power orchestrating and choreographing everything to this advantage in manipulating Congolese people. We have proved above that Mobutuism was nothing but abracadabra that did not make any sense due to its results. How could Mobutu decolonise his people while he was a stooge of the same colonial system he was serving unapologetically? Did he want to stamp colonial toxicity out of the head of his people while he was pumping more lethal one? There is no way a hyena can teach any goat cleanliness while it is itself filth. Our understanding of the philosophy is that it must be general covering vast space and matters.

Fundamentally, if *Mobutuism* was about promoting his own former autocratic and corrupt party, it fails the test academically. Although Houphouët-Boigny was a medical assistant by trade, nobody knows why he failed to articulate his philosophy just like another medical assistant-turned politician, Patrice Lumumba, eloquently did. At Houphouët-Boigny's time, being a medical assistant was a very high level of education. If he were a good manager of state affairs, his level of education would have enabled him to see through his philosophy successfully. Maybe, due to the lack of philosophical underpinnings, clarity and hunch, anybody would interpret and use *Houphouetism* for whatever reason noble and evil. One of those who screwed this philosophy up is none but foreigners. This is why according to Jean-Noel Loucou (1996 cited in Akindes, op.cit.) argues that "foreigners occupy dominant, sometimes hegemonic, situation in the Ivorian economy," (p. 13). Essentially, this has been the real situation in many African post-colonial countries. When Mobutu wanted to offer citizenships to the so-called his Banyarwanda, he invoked *Zairinisation* under his

Mobutuism. Normally, corrupt dictators like to use foreigners in terrorising their citizens due to the fact that foreigners are easy to get rid of or threaten when they tend to misbehave. As long as the foreigners toed the line under whatever corrupt regime, they were at liberty to operate as pleased. People from the East and South African regions know this too well as we will see in Kenya. Foreigners–who were able to please and praise rulers–were allowed access to everything they needed if it came at the detriment of the citizens. For instance, Houphouët-Boigny quoted in Babo (2013), due to ignoring the rights of the citizens, "declared that 'land belongs to the person who works it'," (p. 104). For the leader whose country was just evolving from colonialism, such a declaration is but committing suttee, especially for poor people of that country. If such a leader was a pro-unification of Africa, such a stance would make more sense. Furthermore, had Houphouët-Boigny had his people at heart and in mind, he would have underscored the fact that he inherited a country with many French exploiters than any other in West Africa. Given that he would benefit from using foreigners, Houphouët-Boigny did not bother with or see the importance of empowering his people. Instead, he invited immigrants to produce, exploit and use whenever internal dissent rose. Parenti (2008) notes that Houphouët-Boigny invited in hundreds of thousands of Muslim farmers from neighbouring Mali and Burkina Faso to grow cocoa; and they produced abundant and profitable crops, and Ivory Coast became one of the region's more prosperous and stable countries; however But the newcomers were not given citizenship, identity papers or legal rights, (page not provided).

Arguably, Houphouët-Boigny did not only exploit Ivoirians but also foreigners from poor neighbouring countries in his cocoa production which the Parenti calls blood chocolate.

More importantly, Houphouët-Boigny was irresponsible as far as land policies were concerned. In many countries, land is a very thorny issue whose entitlement is only for the citizens first but not everybody who can work it. Due to such *tummy politics or siasa za tumbo or politics of the belly (la politique du ventre)*, the situation was worse in the DRC, Kenya, Ivory Coast and Malawi and Tanzania after Nyerere, where foreigners still control the economies of these countries. To see how Houphouët-Boigny's heart was not in Africa, at the time the

256

Organisation of African Unity (OAU) unequivocally passed the resolution to apply sanctions against Apartheid South Africa, Houphouët-Boigny cited in Preiss (1973) said he wished to open talks with this country (South Africa)," (p. 6) while the resolution was to shun the regime. This shows how Houphouët-Boigny did not only betray and sell his own people but also all Africans.

When it comes to economic total deprivation of their citizens, many African venal rulers did not enable their people to own and run the economies of their countries. They feared that they would become so powerful that they would overthrow them or prevent their governments from exploiting and bullying them wantonly. Those who did not bother with economies such as Mobutu did not develop important sectors such as education, health and infrastructure. Thus, such criminals conspired with foreigners in robbing their countries pointlessly. African corrupt rulers loved to be in bed with foreign thieves due to the fact that it made them safer from the eyes of their people. Foreigners whose bond with venal rulers was like yin and yang would not divulge the secrets of their partners in crime. Whenever scandals surfaced so as to threaten unearthing their dirty linens, African rulers extradited the foreigners either to keep their secrets or avoid criminal liability not to mention the public wrath. So, too, it was not easy to threaten or control the citizens especially in crime. To be safer and sure, African thievish rulers invented foreigners to run their business which they copied from their colonial monsters who brought foreigners to act as middlemen during their rule. In East and South Africa, the British colonial monsters brought Indians to do the same. This is why Houphouët-Boigny appointed a Lebanese, Pierre Fakhoury to build his now ghostly basilica instead of using Ivorian architects despite the fact that Lebanese, just like any other foreign economic immigrants in Africa, are always not ready to integrate with and assimilate to African society due to their racism. So, too, it is a fact that, for foreigners, distancing themselves from their hosts keeps their secrets safe. Bierwirth (1999) alludes that "unwilling to assimilate to African society, but unable to gain acceptance in European colonial society, Lebanese immigrants remained a group apart," (p. 79). For corrupt rulers such as Houphouët-Boigny, refusing to assimilate with African society was a good and safe thing. For, with such uncooperative relationship, there was no way such foreigners would sell their secrets to their people whom they are not connected to or integrated with.

Arguably, many African despots survived the wrath of the people so as to cling to power for long due to three major reasons namely: First, some used foreigners in exploiting and robbing their countries as indicated above in the case of Houphouët-Boigny. Secondly, some used rule and divide after turning divide and rule upside down as it was in the case of Mobutu who used many opportunistic politicians to form bogus political parties while they were in his payroll so as to deceive and divide his people along fake ideological lines. Third, some used tribalism by favouring the people from their communities as opposed to other communities. This strategy worked perfectly due to the fact that those who were favoured were hated by those who were not favoured. Therefore, for venal African rulers to survive, they needed to maintain division and hatred between them and artificially-cloned enemies of their colleague citizens. Kenyatta was good at this. Obote tried it but its repercussions were not good. Museveni perfected it—and for a long time—it has worked to his advantage. When it comes to Houphouët-Boigny, he almost used all three methods at once to cling to, and thereby, remain in power for a long time. On top of the three divisive methods, add the fourth one which is protection from former colonial monsters. Apart from using the above methods, Houphouët-Boigny was almost everything in everything in Ivory Coast. He appointed himself or his courtiers and stooges to all crucial positions. Ikome (2008) names Bedel Bokassa, Mobutu, Houphouët-Boigny and Eyadema projected as one of the rulers who projected themselves as 'fathers' of their nations, simply because they held the positions of heads of state, heads of government, commanders-in-chief of their national armies and security forces and also serving as the repository of the judiciary, (p. 16).

Arguably, whenever an individual be he a king, president or a queen controls all arms of the states, ends up being above the law, and thus becomes the *guardian* of the nation. Such a person tries to convince everybody that he or she is the one who stabilises the country. He or she conceals all bad things such as tokenism, tribalism, nepotism, nihilism, and whatnot to project her/ or himself as a competent leader while in actual sense is a failed person. Mhango

(2015) discusses the anomalies and dangers of allowing one person to be above the law. If anything, this is what Houphouët-Boigny did. He was above the law, thus, he became irreproachable and untouchable as far as criminal and civil liabilities are concerned. By having demigods such as Houphouët-Boigny above the law, many African countries paid dearly including Ivory Coast as indicated above *vis-à-vis* commuting Yamoussoukro into a useless and unused capital city to suit the interests of one demigod. Houphouët-Boigny created what Salem (1975 cited in Woods, 1988) calls the dependence on "patron-client or ethnic networks, (p. 105). This is the very system the majority Ivoirians had to overcome in dealing with the state whose "narrow-minded, ethnic conscious political elites" (Badmus 2009, p. 45) were given a privilege of milking them even when the majority was starving and wallowing in manmade poverty. Indeed, just like any tin-pot dictator, Houphouët-Boigny's death culminated into the division of the country between Christian South and Muslim North that saw many people killed and others displaced. Narrow-minded elites started fighting over who should become president soon after Houphouët-Boigny died; also see Daddieh 2001. We allude hereunder on how Kenya neared bankruptcy after an Indian conman duped former president Moi and his vice president Professor George Saitoti so as to ruin the treasury under the *Goldenberg project* that intended to produce gold while Kenya does not have even a single gold mine. All was possible simply because the president was above the law in Kenya.

Again, with all such failures in Ivory Coast under Houphouët-Boigny, France called the sage of Africa as if Africa did not have sages. What for? In African, even in English sense, the sage is a wise person, be he or she old or young. Referring to Houphouët-Boigny as an African sage simply because he was good stooge who would protect foreign interests as he squandered the interests of the people is an insult to Africa as whole. Essentially, insulting Africa by referring to its dictators and thieves as progressive, liberators, guardians and whatnot has always been one of the strategies and the ruses the West has used to dupe their population. For common Ivoirians, Houphouët-Boigny was a bad manager of state affairs just like any person in power. This is that. Even when it came to African unity or cooperation, Woronoff (1972) notes that Houphouët-

Boigny rejected nonalignment and Third World solidarity as he opted for close cooperation with the former colonial master, France, (p. 52) which was itself a betrayal in which he was on a collision course with Nkrumah by which the latter alleged "to have escaped an assassination attempt" (Hagberg and Tengan 2000, p. 10) arguing that it resulted from Houphouët-Boigny-Nkrumah rivalry over Upper Volta whose president Yameogo played one against another. The scrimmage between Houphouët-Boigny and Nkrumah was but war of giants. While Nkrumah believed in persuasion, Houphouët-Boigny believed in elimination. It was like the confrontation between a crocodile and a golden lion. When a lion is in the forest, no animal can easily defeat it just like when the crocodile in the water. However, Nkrumah impacts on the tussle were liminal due to the fact that he was overthrown; and later, died before achieving his goal of decolonising and unifying Africa. Inversely from the crocodile, the lion roars without making its tussle secret while the crocodile may kill and still shed tears. This is actually how Houphouët-Boigny-Nkrumah acrimony ended whereby the crocodile won while the lion lost it flatly. Houphouët-Boigny made sure that he put a spoke in Nkrumah wheel the same he did with Sankara later however at different magnitude and style.

However, Houphouët-Boigny was not only an obstacle to African unity but also an obstacle to his own country's development. To show how much Houphouët-Boigny destroyed the economy of his country by spending millions of dollars on the *new* capital, the *New Statesman* (2008) notes that "even by the time Houphouët-Boigny died in 1993, Yamoussoukro remained a capital in name only. None of the government or judicial institutions had moved from Abidjan." Israel did not commute Bethlehem to its capital despite being the place where Jesus, Judeo-Christians' noblest person, was born. In spite of all eccentricity, Gaddafi did not make Sirte, his home town, Libya's capital city. So, too, Napoleon Bonaparte did not turn his home village of Ajaccio into the capital of France so did Benito Mussolini *vis-à-vis* his home town of Preddapio. Even the most mentally sick Bokassa did not turn his M'Baka village–despite producing two president himself and David Dacko, his cousin, the founding father of CAR–into a the capital of *ephemeral empire*. So, what Houphouët-Boigny saw as a vision for his country was nothing but wastage of money just for self-aggrandisement. We were talking about US$ millions the basilica sank. How much money did the whole Yamoussoukro project sink if we consider all posh buildings, airport, roads and whatnots? When we argue that such managers of state affairs who invest in such loss-making projects are mentally sick, we do not mean to affront them or their people. This is what their works tell us, and this, essentially, is how we interpret them. How Bongoville, Gbadolite, Yamoussoukro or Bokassa's *cathedrale de Notre Dame* can make sense, especially to whoever bothers to care a little bit about the plight of the continent whose governments depend on handouts from their former colonial monsters and other rich countries? How do you interpret such monumental projects when you consider many poor people African countries have that are literary hanged as they are forced to pick up the tab? How much would such a project have provided to such people if the mangers of their affairs were sane and competent people? What makes such projects liabilities is the fact that, differently from Egyptian pharaohs whose monuments led to their failure, they do not attract tourists just like the pyramids in Egypt do. Instead, like it currently is in Gbadolite, such projects become so unproductive that they attract wild animals only but not humans. They need a lot of money to maintain not to mention repairs and whatnots. No investors are interested in investing in them knowing how risky such projects can be. Take, for instance, airports in Gbadolite and Yamoussoukro that were capable of handling the Concorde. What are they doing now apart from rotting? How much money spent on them would have delivered to the people of these two countries? How many roads and railways would have such money financed? These are the questions the best managers asked themselves before sinking money into mega-megalomaniac projects.

Like any other dictator, Houphouët-Boigny turned Ivory Coast into a private estate wantonly. Despite such liberty of extravagating public money and resources in his country, Houphouët-Boigny was not even satisfied. He wanted all Africa to be misruled and mismanaged the same way he did Ivory Coast. This is why he is accused of being behind the toppling, and later, the assassination of Thomas Sankara, former Burkina Faso president when he wanted to pragmatically decolonise his people so that they could part ways with dependence and beggarliness. Wilkins (1989) argues that "Ivorian President and 'wise man' Houphouet-Boigny was accused of setting up the coup and financing it, while Blaise Compaore was labelled a liar, a murderer and a puppet of Houphouet," (p. 378).

Going back to the basilica in Yamoussoukro, how much money did this *black elephant* burn from public coffers? Blay-Amihere (1990) answers noting that "his latest claim to 'fame' is the building of Vatican-like basilica estimated to have cost US$ 400m at his hometown of Yamoussu-krom," (p. 26). Despite burning such huge amount of money, once, the West fooled and praised Ivory Coast as an economic success story, (see Bartlett 1990). For the West, taking loans that would be paid later with high interests without considering negative impacts on the citizens was a good thing to do so as to become an "economic success story." Was it really an economic success story really or an insult to the intelligence of the Ivoirians?

> *"On my visits to America, I discovered that the old Marxist dictum, "From each according to his abilities, to each according to his needs," was probably more in force in America-that holy of holies of capitalism-than in any other country in the world,"* Houphouët-Boigny.
> *Source:*
> http://www.azquotes.com/author/50105Felix_Houphouet_Boigny

Houphouët-Boigny's legacy

Although a legacy is something that person leaves behind after he or she completes a certain job or dies, some legacies are stinky and worse. Houphouët-Boigny's legacy is as well stinky and abhorring. Apart from leaving the *black elephants* behind, nothing substantially as far as good management of public affairs is concerned that Houphouët-Boigny left to his country. As argued above, after Houphouët-Boigny dying in office, due to having no self-sustaining political foundation, Ivory Coast cascaded into chaos that culminated in division and civil war that cost the country heavily. Houphouët-Boigny goes down as a very extravagant and undisciplined manager of state affairs as far as misspending public funds is concerned. His other *black elephant* is the town of Yamoussoukro, his home village he wanted to commute to a capital city to no avail. Apart from squandering public funds, George Ayyiteh (2002 cited in Lawal 2007) notes that Houphouët-Boigny robbed Ivory Coast at the tune of US$6 billion, (p. 4). If Ayyiteh's figure is the one to go by, adding it to the billions of dollar spent on his Basilica and his village, chances that Houphouët-Boigny may become the president who stole much more money than any African president are high. As chance has it, sometimes, divine intervention does work in averting dangers. It seems. Houphouët-Boigny, despite having children, did not have any competent son to groom to take power after him just like other dictators did. So, thankfully his death closed the curtain of *Houphouetism* in Ivory Coast's history.

Chapter 21

Mugabe a Hero Who Became a Villain

"I will never order the war veterans to retreat from the farms they are on (...) what are we supposed to do? (...) Fold our arms and say "Ah, you are the ordained ones by the Almighty, by virtue of your white skin and by virtue of your being British, royal blood every one of you, we will not touch your land." No. The end has come; land will now come to the people," Robert Mugabe, on 3 May, 2000 [Sic] cited in Chiumbu, (2004, p. 32).

Figure 30: Robert Mugabe Zimbabwe long-time President (image courtesy of Mail & Guardian)

Dr. Robert Gabriel Mugabe (February 21st, 1924–present) is one of African long-serving rulers. He is one of living three African second-generation-founding fathers along with Sam Nujoma (Namibia) and James Mancham (Seychelles). Mugabe was born in Kutama Jesuit Mission in the Zvimba District northwest of Salisbury (now Harare), in Southern Rhodesia (now Zimbabwe). Like Kenneth Kaunda Zambia's founding father, Mugabe was born to a Malawian father, Gabriel Masuzyo Matibili, and a Shona mother, Bona Shoniwa. It is not known how he got the name of Mugabe instead of Matibili and why he preferred the former to the latter as his surname. Mugabe is the second generation founding fathers who became the founding father of Zimbabwe. So, when we say Mugabe is a founding father, he does not belong to the first generation of the founding fathers of the 1960s due to the fact that his country, gained its independence in 1980 five years after Angola and Mozambique and ten years before Namibia. It must be clearly noted that there are two generations of Africa's founding fathers. Only two founding fathers from the first generation are still alive. These are Gambian Sir Jawara, and Kaunda.

Before coming to power, just like Yoweri Museveni (Uganda), and Paul Kagame (Rwanda), Mugabe was a promising leader whose vision was constructive and progressive. Apart from waging a long time war of liberation of Zimbabwe, Mugabe showed all signs of becoming a very good and notable manager of public affairs due to his high education and ebullience. The qualities of being a well-rounded person and normatively level-headed awarded Mugabe a golden opportunity to rub shoulders with, and thereby, *dine and wine* with doyen such as Julius Nyerere (Tanzania), and Kenneth Kaunda (Zambia) among others; who trusted him so as to offer to help him to liberate his country he later sadly turned into a private estate with inexplicable abuses and brutality. Many people in Africa and abroad thought that Mugabe would have learned from such exemplary managers of public affairs how to diligently conduct public business as far as a new Zimbabwe is concerned. Sadly, though, if there is anything Mugabe learned from those doyens is nothing but clinging to power even when his mentors had already changed minds due to the shift in the politics of the time under the cold war. Nyerere and Kaunda ruled their countries under one-party system that enabled them to rule longer than it would have been if they had multiparty politics which recommends two terms of serving in the highest office in the land. Even though, they did not rule for as a long time as Mugabe has already done. At those times, Mugabe was an exemplary manager of the struggle for the liberation of Zimbabwe which he carried on well and successfully. That was then. Mugabe reminds us of Museveni's words which he uttered shortly after seizing power in Uganda in 1986. Museveni said that, "the problem of Africa in general and Uganda in particular is not the people but leaders who want to overstay in power." Museveni's words are still hauntingly true however, especially haunting him. Ironically, Museveni said these factual words before becoming the same problem he was alluding on. It is as if Museveni was lampooning himself. If you ask him today what he meant by then, Museveni will come with a lot of hoo-has if not saying he was quoted out of context. Arguably, it is as if he predicted what himself, and Mugabe, would perfect and become just three decades thereafter. For many years, Museveni has attempted to recant his words to no avail. As Latin sage has it that *Verba volant, scripta manent*, spoken words fly away, written words remain. There is no way one can take it back. Even Museveni's words flew away from his lips so as to try to change them several times to no avail. However, Museveni's words are still written and are rewritten every now and then, particularly when one wants to show how double tongued some of our rulers are. Museveni's words will never fly away from any historical or political discourse. They will not only haunt him but also will be used to judge him as far as integrity is concerned.

More on Mugabe, when it comes to the freedom fighting, the West revered him as opposed to a changed or lost Mugabe that the same West started to revile and demonise—when his sanity reached at its lowest and worst point so as to be compared to Idi Amin, the butcherer of Uganda, who was also equated with Adolf Hitler. Mamdani (2009) notes that:

> What distinguishes Mugabe and Amin from other authoritarian rulers is not their demagoguery but the fact that they projected themselves as champions of mass justice and successfully rallied those to whom justice had been denied by the colonial system," (p. 3).

Ironically, the two ended up pointlessly replicating what they were complaining about. Nonetheless, it can be seen as exaggeration to compare Mugabe to Amin, they have some similarities in that all of them authored the miseries in their countries however at different times and magnitudes. While Amin killed many academics who tried to say to him that things were going wrong, Mugabe sent them packing so as to make Zimbabwe one of African countries with many academics abroad simply because they are not welcome home in their country. While Mugabe used land as his means to cling to power, Amin used shops. They both acquired illegal and detrimental means to cling to power by robbing those they presumed to be foreigners however they were their citizens of foreign pedigree. All of their victims were brought to their countries by colonial monsters either as colonial monsters themselves or agents. Again, laws do not operate retrogressively. If Mugabe is a Malawian by his father's line, and yet he became a true Zimbabwean, what would be wrong with European farmers becoming true Zimbabweans just like him? Swahili sage has it that "the monkey does not see its back." Mugabe fits in this allegory. European farmers became aliens to Zimbabwe simply because they were brought by colonialism the same way his father was brought by joblessness in his native country of Malawi. Again, the difference here is the fact that Malawians were forced to go to Zimbabwe after being exploited at home by colonial rule. Thanks to double standard and power hunger, had Europeans supported Mugabe's carnage, they would not have been branded aliens in the only country they call home even after being forced to pack and go to exile. Unluckily though, Mugabe has been blamed for appropriating the land as if he is alone in this crime. Although Mugabe betrayed Zimbabwe, he, too, was betrayed by British authorities that were supposed to issue some funds for buying back the land in order to be redistributed to landless Zimbabweans. Like Amin who was blamed for butchering Ugandans without blaming the British that propelled him to power, Mugabe has become a scapegoat for Zimbabwe's former colonial monsters.

Incongruously, well-educated and experienced–as he was by then–Mugabe articulated well his vision for Zimbabwe and Africa so much that he impressed many people inside and outside of Africa. For his ebullience, Mugabe was respected and trusted so as to get support from many doyens such as indicated above. But then was then. Again, as the time went by, power corrupted Mugabe so as to become his own antithesis-cum-prisoner who is, ironically, still afraid of relinquishing power for the fear of his haunting past. When such an impasse happens, it forces many to call the qualifications of whomever behind it, be they academic and managerial, into question. What is the rationale of education for a person whose education failed to deliver her or his people? It becomes even more ridiculous than anyone can envisage when the same protagonist becomes the subject of his own prison in that he does not trust the system he created. Many dictators preside over the governments and systems they do not have faith in. When it comes to Mugabe and the way he abusively exploits power, true, absolute power corrupts absolutely. The sage has it rightly. For a well-educated and ebullient person like Mugabe who commanded a very high esteem among African statesmen—especially during the struggle to wrestle Zimbabwe out of Ian Smith's grip—to end up becoming a dictator is an irony to whatever he attained and stood for. Mugabe's high academic qualifications become zilch and a loss if not futile and an anathema for him and his people. Mugabe was not expected to end up becoming a letdown in any sense; if he knew what he was doing which is contrary to what he stood for during liberation struggle in which he promised a bigotry-free society. Again not all analysts blame Mugabe for reclaiming the land that white farms acquired illegally during colonial era. Mamdani (2009) observes that the seizure of white-owned farms by Mugabe's black supporters has been depicted as a form of thuggery, and as a cause of the country's declining production, as if these lands were doomed by black ownership. Mamdani goes on noting that sanctions have been imposed, and opposition groups funded with the explicit aim of unseating him, (p. 3); also see Mlambo 2013).

However, that was that and then. Mamdani (Ibid) argues that Mugabe's policies of land reclamation and denying the opposition the space buttressed by violent supporters had negative impacts on the economy of Zimbabwe due to the sanctions that were slapped on Mugabe.

It becomes harder to understand the rationale behind employing violence, especially for the person who fought for independence in order to bring down Ian Smith's violent regime; and thereby reclaim whatever colonial rule looted from Zimbabweans. This is the way Mugabe looks at the whole conflict. He thinks—by seizing white-owned farms—he was setting right the anomaly that colonialism created in Zimbabwe. This argument holds water however, ironically Mugabe seems to have replicated and committed the same sin under the banner of independence which renders him a violent ruler who is even worse than the one he unseated. It boggles the mind even more to evidence a person—who suffered from racism and barbaric acts based on madness so as to strongly fight against it—to employ the same method in the twenty first century. By specifically targeting European farmers instead of all land owners—including elites who acquired land after independence–makes Mugabe a racist. How many indigenous Zimbabweans own big parcels of land Mugabe included that they got soon after getting power?

Again, is it wrong for them to own land if they got it legally? If the issue is land grabbing resulting from colonialism (Mitchell 2014, p. 567), we think there is no difference between Mugabe and those he took land from even if in the back of their minds they thought they were reclaiming the land that colonial monsters and their agents grabbed from Zimbabweans. Had land reclamation been conducted based on equity, transparency, give-and-take arrangements, maybe, Mugabe would have become a hero like Nyerere who did the same in Tanzania in 1967. How many *hoity toity* own land under the drive of land reclamation that left *hoi polloi* out to go on being landless even after the country many fought for became independent? So, if the issue is land reclamation, even the *hoity toity* who acquired land after getting power must cede their land to the *hoi polloi* in order to set right the anomaly that colonial rule created. Sometimes, however abhorring and horrendous it may seem for one to question the rationale for Mugabe to waste many years in classes while he would end up acting as if he did not see any room known as a classroom for all those years he spent in academic institutions. Had this been the end of Mugabe's fiascos, at least, we would have something to salvage from what is left of Zimbabwe and Mugabe himself. Up until now–Mugabe is still hell-bent to seize more land as long as such a move assures him to remain in power. Further, if we consider Mugabe's old age, there are possibilities that his handlers have hijacked him so as to use him in this show. Considering the mess Mugabe and his kit and caboodle in his ruling party have already created, hijacking each other is the rule of the game. What makes Mugabe's move dangerous is the fact that he seizes the land he uses to reward loyalty in order to remain in power as indicated above whereby the *BBC* (28 February, 2009) had this to report "speaking at a rally to celebrate his 85th birthday, he also promised to push for majority Zimbabwean ownership of companies operating in the country." As argued above, it is sad that we have never studied the brains and the behaviours of dictators so as to know what they are suffering from; and the way their brains work. Arguably, after becoming inebriated by power, Mugabe became very worse as a manager of state affairs who has mismanaged Zimbabwe to the extent that it has lost its power in the southern region. Zimbabwe, arguably, lost its face and position simply because Mugabe failed to address the land issue that emanates from colonial times. Although we may blame everything on Mugabe, Britain deserves a fair share of blames if justice is done. To accurately perceive what we mean, please refer to how Mugabe plunged Zimbabwe into long-time economic miseries wantonly after taking white settlers' farms and distributed them to his courtiers. However, we need to underscore that Mugabe and some Zimbabwe view the issue of land reclamation or whatever you may call it differently. For them, what happened is the natural and legal act of reclaiming their land that white settlers grabbed during the colonial era. We need to call a spade a spade so that we can feel the pinch; and thereby avoid re-enacting the same sin. This becomes even more important when we consider our history of colonisation, exploitation and degradation. Shaw (2003) observes that Zimbabwe inherited a strikingly unequal racially distorted Agricultural system right from the day it became independent in 1980 with approximately 6, 000 white commercial farmers owned I5.5 million Hectares equivalent to 47 per cent of the country's agricultural land, while 8,000 black small-scale commercial farmers owned or leased I-4 million hectares, and 700,000 peasant house-holds occupied I6-4 million hectares under communal tenure, (p. 75).

Looking at the disparity that Mugabe inherited, he had a very good reason to expropriate the farms but not to rob white farmers and create black ones. Importantly, as argued above, it is easier to misconstrue the situation given that Zimbabweans are the ones who nicely know the situation they are facing. Although Mugabe has been condemned for seizing the white-owned farms, he has some sympathisers such as the South African Economic Freedom Fighters (EFF) opposition party. The *Times Live* (03 July, 2015) reported that "Julius Malema sang the praises of Zimbabwean president Robert Mugabe, claiming that the 'true African leader' has never killed any of 'our own people'." Nonetheless, land issues—as it is for Namibia and South Africa—were discussed and agreed upon during the Lancaster conference that culminated into giving Zimbabwe its freedom whereby British government would fund the so-called "willing buyer, willing seller" (Lebert 2003, p. 4) on which it later defaulted. Such a default offered Mugabe a reason to seize farms and use them for his political survival. Also see Deininger (2004); Ntsebeza and Hall (2007); Kamusoko, and Aniya (2007); and Njaya and Mazuru (2010) who argue that British governments did not live up to its promise so as to award Mugabe the reason he utilised to engrain himself in office by using land offers and favours to his friends and courtiers. Obviously, the people he promised land were frustrated as well as Mugabe. The *Guardian* (27 June, 2008) reports:

> In truth, both Mugabe and Britain are guilty of sidelining history in favour of skewed stories which legitimate their own position. Britain reneged on its commitments to the land reform programme claiming that there were "no links to former colonial interests" while concerning itself with the fate of white farmers.

Ironically, despite having once obligingly and contentedly been in bed with Mugabe, British authorities, and the West in general, are leading the choir of demonising their former bedfellow while they share the same blame in the same sinful bed. For a good manager of state affairs, Mugabe would have reckoned with the fact that such partners were trying to use him the same way he thought he was using them. But, instead he trusted them for granted by failing to underscore their hidden motives of exploiting Zimbabwe just like his were. Now everything is on the agora *vis-à-vis* such hypocritical undertakings. I think this is the best thing South African regime and others facing the same debacle must learn from Mugabe; in that land issues are thorny and contentious that need extra cautious to deal with. Even writing about them needs to be balanced and nuanced. Thus, sitting on them is not a solution. Instead, it is but a temporary reprieve for whoever tries to push land issues under the carpet. The consequences resulting from postponing the very problem of land redistribution—as it currently is in Kenya, Namibia and South Africa— are huge and unconcealable or ignorable.

After reckoning with the fact that the British colonial government conned him, Mugabe decided to do things, "his ways" by seizing the farms white farmers grabbed from Africans during colonial era. Notably, from outside we may condemn Mugabe for seizing the farms; Zimbabweans who support Mugabe see this differently. This is why Mugabe has been able to remain in power at his old age. Mugabe fruitlessly applied a tit-for-tat approach the same British colonial monsters applied, grabbing the land. Under "Operation Murambatsvina (Restore Order)," (Kapp 2005, p. 1151) Mugabe decided to grab the land from white farmers without underscoring the fact that the consequences of such a move would bring to the *hoi polloi* of Zimbabwe. There are those who think that for Mugabe, political survival was, and still is, better and more precious than the whole nation. He knew, and still knows that his move was counterproductive to the country however productive to him it may be.

Contrary to South Africa–which is still sitting on land issues– Zimbabwe became poorer than it was before Mugabe expropriating the farms from white farmers forcing some to flee the country; and invest in neighbouring countries such as Mozambique and wherever they were welcome. As a result of this, many Zimbabwean labourers lost their jobs; not to mention food shortage that hit Zimbabwe on top of economic consequences. However, much share of job loss can be attributed to neoliberal policies spearheaded and championed by the IFIs that were introduced in Zimbabwe in the 1990; also see Moyo (2008); Sadomba (2008); and Mamdani (2008). Zimbabwe's economy started to tank and sink as Mugabe went on with his megalomaniac and biased land reclamation that ended up being a disaster resulting from land being used to reward loyalty. Clemens (2005) observes that the economy has contracted in real terms in each of the past five years, inflation is in triple digits, the local currency has lost 99% of its value, and almost half of the country faces food shortages. Unsurprisingly, up to one-quarter of the population has fled the country, (p. 1). When it comes to who benefitted from Mugabe's policies of land reclamation, The *Guardian* (30 November, 2010) notes that:

A "new, well-connected black elite" of about 2,200 people controls nearly 40% of the 14m hectares seized from white farmers, *ZimOnline* found. These range in size from 250 to 4,000 hectares in" the most fertile farming regions in the country.

Despite all these miseries, Mugabe had the guts to say that what he was doing was the right thing to do not only for Zimbabwe but also for other countries with similar problems. Mugabe cited in Bukurura (2003) says that "if the other neighbouring countries have problems similar to the ones we have encountered, why not apply the same solution as Zimbabwe. It is a simple solution," (p. 37). The *Simple solution* Mugabe espouses can be contrary to the wisdom that it's always darkest just before the dawn. Mugabe's vision did do completely reflect on this wisdom. However, for Mugabe, his policies are *right* however destructive they are, and could be emulated by others in the region to where he wants to export them! Interestingly, Mugabe makes his problem a solution to others. Such cannot be a good manager of public affairs. Why export something that has failed to work in your firm? When it comes to managerial skills, the move, among others, that Mugabe made puts him in the list of the worst managers of Africa's resources and its people. However, Africa's resources are still owned and managed by TNCs and MNCs and that is precisely the reason why Zimbabweans and Mugabe decided to challenge. It was a refusal to be a mere superintendent over TNC and MNC capital in Zimbabwe (see *Journal of Pan African Studies*, December, 2015). Had Mugabe not rewarded loyalty and friendship, maybe, we would be talking about a very different story. Many wonder; why Mugabe has remained popular and instrumental in the politics of Zimbabwe. The reason is simple that–despite being accused of all things that saw Zimbabwe cascade economically–Mugabe fought and brought independence. So, too, Mugabe remained loyal to war veterans. This is why they have always been loyal to him. It is the matter of symbiotic relationship based on reciprocity among the parties. When it comes to land reclamation, Mugabe was not the first to attempt to synchronise the issue of land. Nyerere did the same in 1967 when he nationalised all means of production. Nyerere became a genius of management of state business after nationalizing the means of production due to the fact that he did everything selflessly and diligently. However, he was able to succeed due to the fact that there was no way the world would demonised him as it has done to Mugabe thanks to the booming and mushrooming social media the West knows how to use too well to further its interests. What is clearly evident is the fact that Nyerere did not reward his friends as far as material rewards are concerned. He avoided the trap that caught Amin who on 4 August, 1972 expelled Asians and gave their shops to his cronies and friends. As mentioned above however, Amin has never been accused of any embezzlement of public funds or allocating any shop to himself.

How can we evaluate Mugabe? Rotberg (2000) notes that kleptocratic, patrimonial leaders like Mugabe give Africa a bad name and plunged its people into poverty and despair, and incite ethnic conflict, (p. 47). If anything, Rotberg's analysis of Mugabe fits well in explaining who actually Mugabe is and what he did to his country despite the fact that Britain too has a big share of blames for not living up to its promise of buying back the land for the purpose of redistribution. The *New York Times* (19 October, 2003) reported the misappropriation of public funds saying that Mugabe was putting the finishing touches on his own 130,000-square-foot, 25-bedroom retreat north of the capital, a $9 million palace with a Chinese tiled roof and ceilings adorned by the work of Arab craftsmen, (p. 8). This is not a small amount of money for a country whose budget depends on donors. Again, you wonder if the same *New York Times* can put Saudi King's dirty linens the same way it did to Mugabe's. It sometimes becomes difficult to grasp the real truth given that Western media always have their hidden interests when it comes to covering those they deem to be the enemies of the West simply because they refused to be in bed with them in the sin of betraying Africans. So, too, a good manager of state business would not squander such a humungous amount of money while his employers, the people, are dying of preventable and treatable diseases not to mention manmade famine. Mhango (2015) maintains that Mugabe's seizure of farms turned the country that used to be breadbasket case to a bucket case. This is true. Zimbabwe that the world used to know before Mugabe seized the farms is different from the one the world knows today. Zimbabwean dollar that used to be among the strongest currencies in Africa is no more.

To show how bad Mugabe is, as the manager of public business, while he spent such a mammoth amount of money to build his palace–f it is true–his people were going with empty stomachs. He did not care. He used his authority for his benefit and those surrounding him while the Zimbabweans are suffering pointlessly.

Such cannot be a good manager at all. Furthermore, while nonagenarians in other countries such as Botswana, Gambia, Namibia and Zambia who happen to be his peers are happily enjoying retirement benefits, Mugabe is busy plotting how to remain in power. A good manager must retire and must know the time and manner to do so. The fear of retiring even when the body has already informed the person knocks the person out of the list of the best managers of public affairs. While Mugabe is scheming to remain in power, his Gambian counterpart Sir Dawda Jawara is busy selling his biography he authored himself recently not to mention Kaunda who enjoys playing with his grandchildren as he reaps the reward of his services to his country. A good manager of state business must have the strategies of getting in and exiting public services. At such an eleventh hour what can Mugabe do that he did not do when he was able and adorable? Although Mugabe, his handlers and courtiers may fool themselves that power will always be in their hands, one thing is certain that Mugabe's age will soon defeat all of his plans to cling to presidency. To get a flavour of who Mugabe actually is, please read his speech,

I remind you today that our independence followed over 90 years of oppressive settler colonial rule imposed on us in 1890 when the British occupied our country.

Our independence followed years of bitter protracted struggle. Ask yourselves how many had to die for this great day to come...

The bitterness of our colonial experience could have so easily driven us into a pogrom against the white community, most of whom diligently served and sustained UDI [Universal Declaration of Independence - the period of white rule].

Yet our high level of political consciousness soared above bitterness and has long made us see the Rhodesian problem as inhering in a system of racial injustice and not in the colour of the skin of those who manned that system.

Except of course for those who did not know our politics, it came as no surprise that humanism and magnanimity prevailed by way of the policy of national reconciliation which I declared in 1980. That policy proved a wand of peace at home and a priceless export in the region as it found a replay in Namibia and South Africa.

While all within the white community welcomed and benefited from the policy, not all felt the compulsion to reciprocate this gesture of forgiveness, reconciliation

and peace across the colour bar. All the same that policy gave our society the multi-racial character for which Zimbabwe has been applauded.

What we reject is the persistence of vestigial attitudes from the Rhodesian yesteryears, attitudes of a master race, master colour, master owner and master employer. Our whole struggle was a rejection of such imperious attitudes and claims to privilege...

The issue of land remains both emotive and vexed. It has always been so and many will recall that negotiations for independence almost got bogged down over this matter.

Between 1980 and 1995 we were able to resettle 71,000 families on about 3.3m hectares excised from the commercial sector. This was a far cry from the 162,000 families we had hoped to settle on 8 million hectares of land.

We resumed land reforms under what we have termed the second phase and to this day over 2,422 households have been resettled on 66 farms. The second phase of land reforms envisages the excision of about 5 million hectares of land from the commercial sector with 1 million hectares set to be delivered for resettlement every year.

We had hoped that this would start with nearly 1,000 farms which we had designated for acquisition. Sadly this was not to be as the commercial farmers contested the matter in the courts, forcing government to abandon the acquisition process.

The process of land delivery has been both slow and frustrating. Between 1980 and 1990 we were slowed down by the 'willing seller, willing buyer' clause in the Lancaster House constitution.

Equally, the resources which the British and the American governments had pledged to make available at Lancaster House either stopped or were reduced to a trickle.

Even after removing the constitutional barriers we were still faced with the issue of diminishing resources against ever-rising prices.

After 1997, we also had to contend with the reluctance of the new Labour government which did not want to honour commitments made by previous British governments on the land issue.

We also faced farmer resistance, whose manifestations included not just the legal challenges I have already referred to but also resistance to the land clause we had introduced in the rejected draft constitution.

Naturally, this has created frustration leading to the current spate of farm occupations by the war veterans and sporadic clashes in which two lives have regrettably been lost.

We can understand the frustrations of the war veterans, just as we appreciate the pressures faced by the commercial farmers.

Yesterday and today, I have been meeting with the leadership of the farmers and the war veterans so we can reach some understanding. Two weeks ago, I met with the British foreign secretary who suggested Zimbabwe sends a delegation to the United Kingdom to reopen negotiations on land reform.

We should be able to find a way forward but one that recognises the urgent need for land reform. It is the last colonial question, heavily qualifying our sovereignty.

We are determined to resolve it, once and for all.

Let us continue to cherish our independence as well as uphold the principles of our sovereignty. Let us defend our freedom and deliver the benefits of independence to our people.

Happy anniversary.

Source: BBC, 18 April, 2000.

Mugabe's legacy

Apart from destroying Zimbabwe, Mugabe's legacy is likely to be nothing but leaving chaos shall he die in power any time. There are two potential sources of chaos shall Mugabe die now. Firstly, members of his ZANU-PF are likely to fight among themselves over who shall inherit Mugabe's power. Another source is the section of Zimbabweans, especially opposition that will never like to see a post-Mugabe era being manned by his that is accused of being corrupt party apart from messing the country so much that if anything happens to Mugabe, God forbid, chances for Zimbabwe to cascade into chaos are high. However, not all see the situation with the same lenses as the ones we are using here. Mugabe and his party still have followers, mainly those who benefited from his policies. So, how post-Mugabe era will look like is the matter for time to tell. If there is anything that Mugabe has competently created politically is nothing but his powerful wife, Grace whose influence sometimes overshadows her husband's. Refer to how she was accused of throwing out former vice president Joyce Mujuru. For example, when allegations surfaced that Grace hatched a scheme to oust Mujuru so that she can inherit her husband's office, she did not deny. Instead, she admitted squarely how she was legible to become Zimbabwe president. The *Bloomberg* (27 October, 2014) reported that Grace

Mugabe, 49, called on Vice President Joyce Mujuru to resign and indicated that she may seek to succeed her 90-year-old husband when she told a rally on Oct. 23, that "some say I want to be president. Why not? Am I not Zimbabwean, too?" Due to rampant corruption and abuses of public offices in Africa, some first ladies have become the power to reckon with. Using bedroom politics, they have cornered their husbands so as to get away with murder pointlessly.

Another legacy that Mugabe leaves behind is nothing but endemic corruption that traces its root to colonial era, tanking economy, suffering population, and above all, many and stinking skeletons in the closet such as long-time violations of human rights. Zimbabwe has a very huge task ahead if Mugabe, under any circumstances, vacates the office of president. The mess that Mugabe has created will take many years to expunge and rinse out.

Special tributes

When the independence of Zimbabwe is dissected; it cannot be completed without mentioning the name Joshua Mqabuko Nyongolo Nkomo (19 June, 1917–1 July, 1999) the founder of the Zimbabwe African People's Union (ZAPU) which was instrumental in the struggle for the freedom of Zimbabwe. Others are Rekayi Tangwena, Herbert Wiltshire Pfumaindini Chitepo, Ndabaningi Sithole, Edgar Tekere, Enos Nkala, and Maurice Nyagumbo who contributed immensely to the liberation of Zimbabwe that Mugabe and his party ended up hijacking. More importantly, tributes go to Zimbabweans within and outside Zimbabwe who endured the sufferings and tribulations Mugabe's rule enacted.

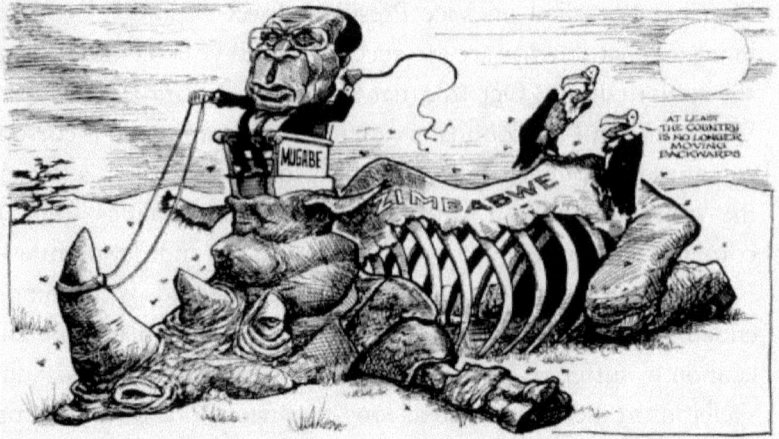

Figure 31: Mugabe's caricature (image courtesy new Rhodesian)

Chapter 22

Moi: A Blind Follower Who Brutalised Kenya

"AIDS is not just a serious threat to our social and economic development, it is a real threat to our very existence .... AIDS has reduced many families to the status of beggars.... No family in Kenya remains untouched by the suffering and death caused by AIDS... the real solution of the spread of AIDS lies within each and every one of us," Daniel arap Moi, 1999 in Ajuando (2004, p. 1).

Figure 6 Daniel arap Moi Kenya's 2nd President (image courtesy of AP)

When former Kenyan president Daniel arap Moi (2nd September, 1924) took the reins of power after the death of Jomo Kenyatta on 22nd August, 1978 till 30th December, 1992), he was not widely known. Despite being a Vice President for over a decade, Kenyan did not expect he would become their president. However, the constitution said so shall anything happen to the President. Again, Moi was Kenyatta's vice president for over 11 years 5 January 1967–22 August, 1978. There are those who thought that Moi's coming would turn things around so as to usher democracy in Kenya. Others saw Moi as Kenyatta's protégé who would not alter anything except extending Kenyatta's maladministration as it came to be thereafter. For those who knew Moi, his ascending to power did not promise anything save maintaining the *status quo*. Lumumba (2011) notes that Kenyatta left the culture of corruption rooted in kleptocratic behaviour was normalised and when Daniel arap Moi took office in 1976 things continued to deteriorate, (p. 43).

Contrary to the belief of many Kenyans, Moi was not among Kenya's pumpkins of the time of who most were Kenyatta's kitchen cabinet members and consigliore. By being the Vice President for a long time, Moi's demeanour had already informed Kenyans what type of the person he was. Many did not even expect Moi would become president of Kenya despite the fact that Kenya's constitution was clear that if president of republic becomes incapable of running the state either from illness, death or anything, his Vice President would be sworn in as President to fill the gap for ninety days before convening elections for a new President. In fact, this is what happened when Kenyatta died in office. So, too, given that Moi got Presidency by the way of filling in the gap after the death of his boss, he had no vows to make good on in the beginning of his Presidency that was expected to end after ninety days. When he became president after serving ninety days the constitution stipulates, many thought Moi would put some democratic rule in place. After Kenyatta's inner sanctum famously known as "Kiamba Mafia" (Adar and Munyae 2001, p. 2) plotted to stop Moi from being sworn-in failed, the constitution prevailed and Moi was sworn-in to serve as president for ninety days according to the period stipulated constitutionally. Moi did not only inherit Presidency but he also inherited Kenyatta's party, the Kenya African National Union (KANU). First of all, Kenyatta inner sanctum wrongly and widely regarded him as a *passing cloud* that ended up hanging over their heads for over two decades. Their assumption that they would wink him out later became a nightmare after Moi mercilessly and systematically purged them one after another. What they did not know is the fact that Moi they used to know, when he was Vice President, proved to be his antithesis. The Moi they had in power as president was different from the one they used to know under Kenyatta. Adar (2000) quotes Moi as saying "when I was Vice-President, I sang like a parrot after Kenyatta; now I am President and you must sing like a parrot after me," (p. 75). Now Moi had power in his hands, the tame and timorous Moi that Kenyatta inner sanctum used to know had escaped whereas the underhand, hardnosed and aggressive Moi took takeover. For, after the Kikuyu clique tried to dislodge Moi failed, he went on tightening his grip on power something they did not expect. He started replacing Kikuyu inner sanctum with his Kalenjin buddies. Arguably, Moi had to do an extra work to see to it he clings to power as Foeken and Dietz (2000) concur arguing that in his first five years the situation was risky but Moi succeeded to manoeuvre it and strengthened his grip on power, (p. 124) which saw him serve for over two decades uninterruptedly. Foeken and Diets go on saying that Moi became more vicious and more suspicious in 1982 when he survived coup attempt on his government. Moi, whom Kenyans had known for four years he had been in power, was gone. In his place came Moi the schemer, eliminator and immoral whose rule was no different from a criminal state. Moi had to mismanage his country in order to survive. Most of his new Kalenjin and Masai buddies used him to become immensely rich. When Moi's corrupt rule is mentioned and the tycoons it produced, apart from Moi himself and his family member, two names namely Professor George Saitoti, Moi's long-time Vice-President and Minister for Finance and Nicholas Biwott, Moi's right-hand man, feature high on the list of those who robbed Kenya; also see Wolf (2006); Holmquist and Ford (1998); and Henderson (2003).

Those who plotted to stop Moi from becoming president had to either keep quiet or face his wrath and purgative actions. For, it downed on them one after another due to the fact that they did not have plan "B" of dislodging Moi from power. The big mistake they committed was but underestimating Moi due to the underdog role he skilfully played under Kenyatta. In the capacity of Vice President under Kenyatta, Moi found himself totally overshadowed by Kenyatta towering image. It seems; Moi was happy and satisfied with it knowing that the old man would die anytime as it happened thereafter. Moi is known to have been a good and smart schemer who kept his cards close to his chest. His unassuming tendency deceived Kenyatta's Kiambaa Mafia and whoever who eyed the presidency after Kenyatta. It was easy for any person to think that Moi was a *passing cloud* as the clique of Kenyatta buddies believed due to his sheepish nature of receiving orders from Kenyatta without necessarily budging. So, too, coming from the minority Kalenjin community, Moi was seen as a rookie who posed no threat despite spending all of his life in cutthroat politics of the then Kenya. He knew what he was doing and when and how to do it when an opportune time arrived. Therefore, patience became another tool that helped Moi to get power from Kenyatta; and thereby cling to it for twenty four years. Another tool that helped Moi is the fact that he did not show his ambitions openly from the beginning. However, those who underestimated Moi erred in that they forgot that he once formed a political party he used as a bargaining chip to join KANU; thereby impressing Kenyatta who ended up appointing him his Vice-President. In spite of that, Moi was seen as a timid person without big dreams as far as power in Kenya was concerned. Again, Kenyatta's inner sanctum erred by failing to read the writing on the wall in that Moi had already shown his edge when he and Ronald Ngala found his opposition party Kenya African Democratic Union (KADU) in 1960. For good a schemer, this would have acted as a wakeup call if not a hunch in analysing, dissecting and planning how to deal with Moi; the man who came to tower over Kenya even more visibly than his mentor-cum-predecessor.

After bracing himself in the power well, Moi used tokenism and nepotism as the two most powerful tools to remove his nemeses and reward loyalty. If anything, this is the skill–he learned from his predecessor–which Moi even perfected more skilfully. It seems that Moi learnt every trick his mentor was using to weather whatever challenges he faced. As you will see later, Moi embarked on eliminating and frustrating his enemies. Out of sheer fear of losing power if not rust for power, like his predecessor, Moi turned his government in a killing machine for detractors and whoever that was perceived as a threat to his grip on power. Moi ruled Kenya ruthlessly with an iron fist for the whole time he was in power minus four years before the coup attempt that changed him for good. After defeating and getting rid of himself of Kenyatta's inner sanctum that wanted to superimpose their person from among themselves for president, Moi stayed put so as to become unwaveringly immovable for over twenty years that followed. So, once again, Kenyans lost the chance for change in almost all aspects of life. To crown it all, Moi came up with his notorious slogan-cum-philosophy of *Fuata Nyayo*, or Follow the footprints or "footsteps" of his predecessor as Abwuza (1990) defines it noting that, *Nyayo* as a slogan-cum-philosophy encompassed and epitomised almost everything under Moi. Abwuza sums up *Nyayo* as a path for economic and betterment that enjoined Kenyans to follow the footsteps of the ancestors (p. 185) in working together for the noble cause of the nation. Ironically, under *Nyayo*, Kenya did not achieve anything as it was envisaged. Kenya did not become better; instead it became even worse than Kenyatta left it. Otenyo, (2004) notes that Moi decided to follow the same strategy which was "to follow in Kenyatta's footsteps" based on a small group of consigliore out of which Kikuyu assemblage lost the position it used to enjoy, (p. 17) under Kenyatta's rule. Instead of improving, the situation worsened to the extent that mega corruption, insecurity, disappearances of nonconforming voices and gross violation of human rights became the hallmarks of Moi's rule of twenty four years he was in power. If we can argue, despite its good spirit, *Nyayo* became another anathema to the Kenyans, especially those who were not related to Moi or those who opposed his barbarity.

Moi, indeed, followed the footprints of his predecessor religiously and zealously to his advantage. For within no time, Moi started to do exactly as Kenyatta did for the entire period he ruled Kenya. He grabbed land; and named almost everything worthwhile after himself. Kenyans used to hear and see Jomo Kenyatta International Airport, University, and Hospitals, streets, Avenues and whatnot not to forget Mama Ngina (Kenyatta's wife) streets and avenues and Uhuru (Kenyatta's son current Kenya President) streets and avenues. Soon–under Moi–Kenyans woke up to evidencing Moi everything. The difference however is that Moi did not name anything after his wife or children. Following the footprints was at work once again to end up after over two decades of corruption, mega theft, intolerance, assassinations you name it. Those who made a goof hoping new breathe would come in ended up disgruntled and dismayed as Anderson (2002) notes that the transition from Kenyatta to Moi era represented a change or more of the same, (p. 17). If anything, Moi's rule was more of a Kenyatta's typical replica if not an identical twin. Gray and MacPherson (2001) note that under Moi Kenya's average per capita economic growth rate during the years

1991–97 was zero, (p. 174) thanks to mismanagement Kenya witnessed then. Arguably, it was obvious that the economy would not do well due to the fact that the country was presided over by one of the most corrupt and autocratic regimes in Africa that was unaccountable to anyone except Moi himself.

In the beginning, Moi retained all of Kenyatta's members of cabinet. Hopes were high that, maybe, he would change or tweak the system that many were fed up with. However, as they days went by, and after learning the rules of the game, Moi started to fill all key positions Kikuyu held under Kenyatta with his Kalenjin tribesmen and women. Nepotism went on save that the difference was that new kids were on the bloc doing the same money-minting-and-printing business. Another notable different from Kenyatta's rule to Moi's is that the latter was a semi illiterate compared to the former who was literate. So, too, most of Moi's inner sanctum were as well less educated compared to Kenyatta's homeboys-cum-home guards.

Moi was seen as a humble servant of people–when he ascended to power–that later on, changed into a monster. However, things changed anecdotally and exponentially, as noted above. In 1982, some army officers tried to take over in a failed military coup that came to define Moi's rule as far as distrust is concerned. Essentially, this coup reinvented Moi, or say, became a turning point that revealed a ruthless Moi that Kenyans did not know of before. For, since 1982, Moi did not trust anybody out of his battery of home boys. In protecting his presidency, Moi did not waiver. His was to purge whoever he thought or deemed to be a threat to his dear power.

Moi's style of rewarding loyalty and cronyism ruined Kenya's economy horrendously. Just like Kenyatta, land and high positions in government became Moi's cards he used to win the game. He kept his card close to his chest so much that he became terribly unpredictable. Moi's managerial skills of state business were very much wanting. Instead of bringing people who entrusted him power together, Moi divided them under what Mhango (2015) calls rule and divide, the tactics many African leaders and rulers use when they get into power. They get power from the people. Then, they use the same power to divide then rule the same people so as to easily weaken their unity that would be used as the sole power to oust them. They just divide them along many artificial lines such as tribalism, regionalism, party affiliations and whatnot. A good manager of public affairs is the one who unitedly involves people in the process instead of sidelining or dividing them aiming at intimidating and weakening them so as to exploit them. Moi lost a very golden chance of turning Kenya into a socio-economic success story after Kenyatta's long time web of venality and impunity in committing crimes ruined it. With highly qualified manpower under his disposal, had Moi been a good manager of state business, he would have reversed the situation which as a result would have enabled him to leave a very shining legacy behind. Again, this did not happen. Moi was concerned with his personal survival even if it meant to come at the cost of the whole nation. Power was everything that Moi knew and wanted. For, Moi instituted *Nyayo* which became everything as far as his rule was concerned. Like any harangued philosophy, *Nyayo* was not well articulated. So, too, *nyayoism* as it was then known did not aim at serving all Kenyans equally and equitably. Instead, it was aimed at serving Moi, his family, associates and cronies. Under Moi, brutality, intimidation and reclusion became the order of the day. Such tendencies distanced him from the majority of Kenyans that he was supposed to collectively mobilise to build their country he ended up destroying. Instead of being trusted and liked, Moi was feared and suspected. However, a few tried to show such tendencies openly for the fear of retribution. Moi coined a saying that his era was the era of "our turn to eat" (Burgess 2010) meaning that under Moi, people from his community, Kalenjin and partly Masai and all those who toed the line, were the ones eligible to come to the table and enjoy the *national cake*. Such exclusionary tactic based on paternalistic relationships badly affected Kenya's economy. The turning point was when a mega scam, Goldenberg, was unearthed in which Moi and his associates were alleged to have robbed Kenya millions of Dollars. Chege (2008) notes that one of the disappointing example was the reaction of the government to the so-called the "Goldenberg scandal, a US$800 million Moi-era scam involving government rebates for fake diamond exports," (p. 129). When this scam surfaced, Kenya's economy had already taken a heavy hit so as to be on the verge of collapsing. Instead of prosecuting those alleged to have been behind the scam, Moi kept quiet. Again, given that he was one of the chief architects and executors of the scam, there was no way Moi would have instituted any charges against the culprits. Once, again, this shows how Moi abused his managerial powers. Instead of instilling accountability and transparency as the virtues any manager of state affairs was expected or required to instil in the organisation, Moi instilled irresponsibility and criminality. Instead of doing what it is that makes the best manager, Moi sought what makes the worst Manager pointlessly. What makes Moi's style of running state business interesting is the fact that, despite favouring the members of his community, he went ahead, hiring academics such as his former Vice President and minister of finance, the late professor George Saitoti to do his dirty laundry. So, too, the culprits in the Golden scam were government senior official so connected that it was hard to differentiate who is who As Kegoro (2003) lists down the names of those behind Goldenberg scandal to include professor George Saitoti (Kenya's long-serving Vice-President), Eric Kotut (then the Governor of the Central Bank of Kenya), E. Owayo (then the Commissioner of Geology and Mines), Wilfred Koinange, (then the Permanent Secretary to the Treasury), James Kanyotu (then the head of Kenya's security intelligence), and Kamlesh Pattni (a Nairobi trader in his early twenties, who was the mastermind of the scams), (p. 141). You can see how messy and big the scam was plus the top brass involved.

In other words, when you look at the positions those alleged to have been behind Goldenberg scam held, you find that it was the inner sanctum of sacred cows, the qualification that insulated them from criminal liability. It was corruption with impunity at best. For a poor country like Kenya whose budget depends on aid, loans and handouts from donors, the amount of money lost to Goldenberg scam is tremendously unforgivable. Some donors stepped in to make sure that those responsible in the commission of the crime were brought to book to no avail. Gathii (1999) notes that "Finland and Norway initiated campaigns in the Nordic countries to stop project funding in Kenya because of official corruption," (p. 409). Despite such efforts, donors, either seemed to get it wrong, or their drive was just aimed at protecting their interests in Kenya. Gathii goes on elucidating that donors put emphasis on structural adjustment and multiparty politics that saw Kenya cascade into the Post-Election

Violence (PEV) of 2007-08 which saw over a thousand innocent Kenyans massacred and other thousands displaced. Arguably, the PEV occurred due to the fact that Kenyatta's and Moi's divisive policies created endemic tribalism, regionalism and cronyism which culminated in hatred and mistrusts among Kenyans. A good manager of state affairs brings prosperity to her or his people but not fracas, chaos and sufferings. So, too, the structural adjustment the donors were advocating did impact well on the economies of African countries in general.

Moi did not favour and reward his friends only but also his family. His Machiavellian family members did not miss out on the high table at which the national cake was eaten. Moi's children became super rich just soon after their father became president. They solicited money from public banks and corporations simply because they had a *carte blanche* for being the children of the strongman. As if allowing his children, friends and family members to illegally enjoy national cake was not enough, Moi was so generous to his guests and levellers. Many people who paid him a courtesy call or who attended his meetings or who just visited him at the state house did not go empty handed. He used to fork money out to whoever that seemed to please him either at his home or in the meetings he used to attend regularly in various parts of Kenya. Moi did not budge when it came to dishing out wads of cash. This speaks to Moi's gross mismanagement the business of the state by trying to make himself look good instead of doing good based on law and expectations of the people who entrusted him their office as their leader. So, too, we can argue that Moi had a culture of keeping money at home instead of keeping it in the bank. What a bad example to the general population? Keeping money at home, apart from being economically unviable, deprived banks the money to keep and circulate. If anything, self-serving is one of the worst thing any manager can do. Essentially, such a manager cannot be credible. Instead of motivating his subjects to use banks services, Moi turned his home into an illegal bank something that denied banks business opportunities. Swahili sage has it that the capon taught chicks to *poop* in the nest.

Luckily for Moi, even after being booted out in 1992, after trying to impose his protégé Uhuru Kenyatta, the son of his predecessor on Kenya without success, the government that took over from him did not prosecute the culprits of many Moi's era including the man himself due to being rotten as well. Once again, Moi was able to survive. The government did not open his closet to see his skeletons in it. As mentioned above, for the new government–under former president Mwai Kibaki–made by a shaky and loose opposition embarked on eating spree under its *it-is-our-turn-to-eat* comportment as Wrong (2009); and Branch (2010) refer to it. What made Moi and his courtiers safer is the fact that the new government was ensnared in scams famous one being Anglo Leasing, (Cockcroft 2010; and Asaala 2010) Kibaki was comfortably at home with graft despite some significant progress in some areas. For, a year and a half that Kibaki had been in power then, Anglo-Leasing graft scandal came to light. Bachelard (2010) discloses Kibaki ended protecting members of his cabinets involved it to mark the end of the anti-corruption crusade, (p. 188). Basically, Kibaki would not do anything to take on Moi's regime given that he was in the same catch-22 situation doing the same business in the same bed. *WikeLeaks'* leaks of 2004 disclose that "in May, 2004, the Kibaki government itself suffered a credibility blow when several of the President's closest advisors were implicated in a 777 million US Dollar corruption scandal known as the Anglo Leasing scandal." Here we talking about over a billion dollars that the two regime robbed Kenya among others.

WikeLeaks points a finger at Philip (Moi's son) who it said had an estimated wealth of approximately $ 770 million and controls more hidden cash than Gideon (another Moi's son), even though significant attention has been directed at the latter, (p. 55). *WikiLeaks* went on disclosing all companies the Moi and associates own. As for Moi, the father, the report lists down 32 companies ran by his other son Gideon while Philip own 10 companies, (Ibid). Moi's associates and consigliore have business empires all over the globe. One wonders. If Moi and associates have such vast business empires worth millions of dollars even billions, how much did Kenyatta regime rob from public coffers? This speaks to why African countries are poor. They are not poor just because Africans do not work hard. They are mismanaged and robbed; and this trend has been going since independence with the exception of a few countries such as Botswana and partly Tanzania under Julius Nyerere. However, this should not be misconstrued as saying that colonial regime were not corrupt. They were corrupt through and through save that there was no way they could be held accountable or could be expected to be accountable while they were in power illegally all over the continent. Furthermore, Moi, a self-declared *professor* of politics or call it *polly tricks*, created and presided over an iceberg-like system which he tried as hard as he could through his propagandas to make Kenyans believe that what they used to see is but the tip of the iceberg. Up until now, nobody knows the size and nature of Moi's iceberg. Using his spin doctors and government machinery, Moi made sure that Kenyans believed that his regime was a rock that nobody would break or shake. So, too, what Kenyans used to see and know about Moi, as far as corruption is concerned, was, once again, just the tip of the iceberg. Unlike other venal dictators like Joseph Mobutu (DRC) and Houphouët-Boigny (Ivory Coast), Moi did not show off quite openly. He cunningly portrayed himself as God-fearing person who never missed a Sunday service. However, he turned out to be a completely different person when it comes to seeking wealth and clinging to power. By being like an iceberg that nobody can know exactly how big it is in the water, Moi was unquestionably unpredictable. This being said, nobody would risk questioning his style, practices, policies or *diktat*. For, Moi used to say that he was as visionary who was as tall as a giraffe. However when it comes to managerial skills and competence, Moi was but a goat. Activists such as Willy Mutunga who went on becoming Kenya's Chief Justice later, Koigi wa Wamwere, George Anyona, John Khaminwa, Laila Odinga, James Orengo, Dr. Gibson Kamau and many more who tried to take on Moi either spent time behind bars or had to go to exile as the only means for them to avoid doing jail terms or face death if not disappearing mysteriously as it was in Kenya then under Moi.

Again, when Moi's regime was kicked out after losing elections in 2002, for Kenyans it was *voila change un fin* or change at last! Moi's regime was hated due to its brutality and secrecy. As noted above, among the tools that Moi used to cling to power is intimidation. Under Moi's regime, every Kenyan who was not from his community or his kitchen party, lived under fear of being apprehended or facing trumped up charges. Everybody was watched. Nobody was safe or sure of seeing the next day. The Intelligence and police machineries were at liberty to apprehend and torture whomever they deemed an enemy of the state. What's more, such organisations took advantage of the *carte blanche* they were given to extort money from innocent people which added more hatred among Kenyans against Moi regime. Whoever that refused to do what he or she was asked to do by police or Intelligence, ended up in troubles; not because he or she had committed any offence. If there was an offence that tortured many innocent Kenyans under Moi is nothing but refusing to cooperate with the state even when it was doing stupid things. Ironically, under Moi, Kenyans were supposed to follow the footprints even if they led to purgatory or hell.

Moi's policies did not only end up with destroying the economy but also saw to it that whoever appeared to threaten his power was destroyed too. Just like in the case of JM Kariuki mentioned above under Kenyatta regime, Robert Ouko, Moi's former minister for international relations, had to pay the price. Makinda (1992) claims that on 13th February, 1990 Ouko disappeared from his home near Western city of Kisumu to be discovered dead and his body charred. The authorities tried to cover up the cause of his death (p. 191). There were rumours that Ouko had some crucial information on corruption. Why was Ouko assassinated? Oculi (2011) answers the question maintaining that Ouko was massacred to avoid succeeding Moi who "had survived a 1982 military coup and whose leadership was associated with Raila Odinga, also a Luo," (p. 22). Inasmuch as I can remember, Kenyans knew who killed Ouko nonetheless, at the time; they would not divulge the names of those who were behind the assassination of Ouko. They knew the culprits too well. Again, dead people tell no tales. Ouko was assassinated; and his death acted as a warning-cum-reminder to whoever thought he or she would attempt, let alone snatching power from Moi and his courtiers most of who were from his Kalenjin community, what would befell her or him. As it was under Kenyatta's state of terror, the death of one famous person silenced many wannabes as far as change was concerned. Generally speaking, the death of Kariuki under Kenyatta, and that of Ouko under Moi, acted as a deterrent.

Actually, due to having bad and inept government, after he exited from power, despite being a semiliterate, Moi has been an influential figure in Kenyan politics ever since. Due to his cunning nature, as mentioned above, he earned a moniker of *professor* of politics, bad politics of course. Some say Moi was smart. For, he made sure that his protégés, namely Uhuru Kenyatta and William Ruto, Kenyan current President and Deputy President respectively, were taking over from Kibaki who later reconciled with Moi so as to allow this to happen. Others saw Moi as a gullible person whose power was used and abused by his consigliore to do as pleased without Moi being aware that he was used. There are those who think that Moi was a good guy whom his consigliore and handlers corrupted or abusively used if not duped. Being the man who wanted to be revered and worshipped, Moi would offer his ear to whoever that told him what he liked and wanted to hear instead of the bitter truth. Such a trait is not the ascription of the best manager of any business or firm. If anything, among reasons that helped manipulators to easily dupe Moi is his love of being respected, loved and listened to. As Moi exited the scene, Kenyans waited for yet another surprise in Moi's successor, Kibaki who was his Vice President once before the falling out of his favour. Kenya was engulfed with euphoria when, at last, Moi's brutal regime unceremoniously and unexpectedly came to an end. Many did not believe that the person who was thought to be a passing cloud–that ended hanging over Kenya for twenty years– would call it a day one day. So, when Moi's regime breathed its last, Kenyans overwhelmingly breathed a sigh of relief. However, their aura and dreams of freedom were enjoyed and felt temporarily. For, it did not live longer before Kibaki showed his true self as far as poor management of state business and abetting corruption are concerned. This shows, once again, how Kenya has been managed or mismanaged since the time it acquired independence on 1st June, 1963.

Come 2012, Moi's acolyte and the son of his predecessor, who happened to be his protégé that failed to succeed him, Uhuru Kenyatta was elected president of Kenya in the elections in which the opposition accused the government of rigging. Due to the fact that Kibaki and Moi had already buried their hatchets, they settled on Kenyatta's son for two different reasons. Moi wanted his mentee and the son of his mentor to become president while Kibaki wanted his tribesman. Given that the country had gone through macabre bloodshed resulting from rigging in 2007/08 that culminated in PEV, international community urged the opposition to settle for give and take for the sake of the peace of the country. By having Kenyatta in office, Moi was safer even than when he was under Kibaki who somewhat seemed to be unpredictable and unreliable the same way Moi was when he was at helms. Knowing how he mismanaged Kenya, Moi tried unsuccessfully to hand the baton over to Kenyatta's son so as to assure himself of protection after exiting power. Being a good schemer; and thanks to corrupt nature of the government of his successor, Moi evolved a winner. For, up until now, Moi has never been brought to justice. And by the look of things and his age, Moi is likely to safely die without being brought to book.

Moi's legacy

As one of the worst managers Africa has ever had, Moi left a very bad legacy. Apart from presiding over the most brutal and corrupt regime, he left a vandalised country after robbing and wrecking it for over two decades. Some his relics, like his predecessor, is his name on many Kenya's hallmarks such as, Moi Teaching and Referral Hospital, Moi Air Base, Moi International Airport, Moi University, and Moi everything meaningful in Kenya, among others. Also, Goldenberg scandal will not only define Moi as a worst manager but will also feature high in Moi's history book. So, too, Moi left a country with malodorous tribalism even though he inherited this vice from his predecessor which he expanded on it so as to entrench it systematically. No way can one complete any analysis about Moi without touching on endemic corruption which, sometimes, can be synonymous with his name, his regime and his legacy. Like any dishonest and nihilistic manager of state business, Moi will be remembered for bad things he did to Kenya and Kenyans, especially the deaths of his opponents not to mention gross violations of human rights and robbing the country in conjunction with Western countries. Under Moi, just like under his predecessor; and successor altogether Ayittey (2002) argues that "over the past few years, Kenya has performed a curious mating ritual with its aid donors," (p. 14). Arguably, Moi became another brand after Kenyatta whose name was almost on everything.

Above all, Moi will be remembered as the man who robbed his country so as to be one of the richest former presidents in Africa after Abacha and Mobutu. If shinning legacy is something to go by,

Moi left nothing but the dimmest legacy and sufferings to his country and its people.

> *"I think it is too much for always trying to undermine the intelligence of the African people. Those who will decide the destiny of Kenya, for instance, or other countries will be the people themselves. I made my point when I was in U.S. So I don't know what is worrying you,"* Daniel arap Moi, 2001.
> *Source:* Archive of the *US Department of State* (May 26, 200).

Special tributes

Kenya has two phases of independence namely the one that its founders championed and fought for and the other that those who opposed Moi's dictatorial rule championed and suffered for. These are Jaramogi Oginga Odinga, Raila Amolo Odinga, Willy Mutunga, George Anyona, Ngugi wa Thiong'o, James Orengo, Abuya Abuya, Koigi Wamwere, Mwachegu wa Mwachofi, Chibule wa Tsuma, Wasike Ndobi and Lawrence Sifuna and many who thankfully survived Moi's reign of terror so as to have left him shaken to the core. We also would like to pay our tributes to Kenyans who–in one way or another–suffered under Moi regime, exclusively those who were tortured and killed at the infamous Nyayo House, the building that Moi used as a centre for *dealing with* and *neutralising* his opponents and enemies.

Figure 33: Moi's caricature (image courtesy of *economist.com)*

Chapter 23

Hijacked Democracy as the Cause of African Political Systemic Failure

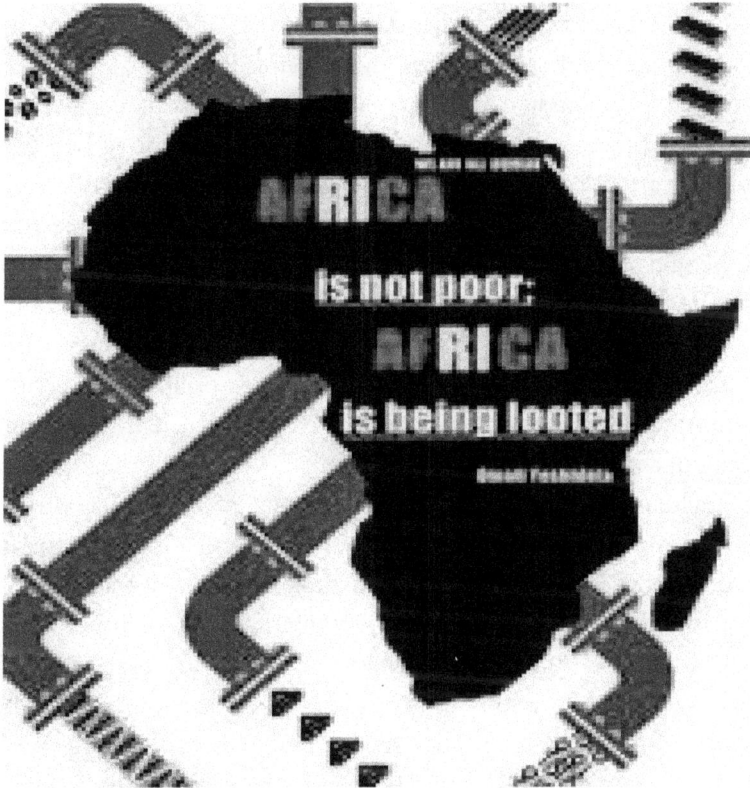

Figure 34: How Africa is robbed by the West and others (image courtesy of pinterest.com)

After exploring individuals *vis-à-vis* managing or mismanaging African public affairs, it is important to look at systemic causes based on the current political dispensation. This is very important. For, it will help us to tackle systemic as well as individual anomalies. For example, after pinning down the causes of Africa's impasse, we will be able to devise the means out of it. This is one of the reasons this volume was written. Arguably, systemic and individual anomalies depend on each other. There cannot be any system without humans to run it.

297

Likewise, there cannot be any success in public affairs without the system to regulate. So, when it comes to running public businesses, there is a marriage between humans and the structures which work interdependently as a system. They interact with each other so as to function swiftly or otherwise all depending on the quality of management. So, to run a country, we need a government. And so, as to have a government to run the country, it must be formed by humans from whom, one becomes the head of the government. As you can see, the head of government is nothing if he or she does not have people to assign tasks her or him with various tasks or solicit advices from. Again, every government is the creature of humans but humans are not the creatures of the government. The government is there to serve the interest of the people but not vice versa, especially if the said government is the government of the people, by the people for the people.

Arguably, since many African countries gained their independence, Africa has gone through many political and economic experiments. However, some gains have been made however liminal they may be. For example, if we compare Africa in the 70s and the 80s when *coup d'états* were rife with today, we find that Africa has gained substantially politically whereby democratic governance is taking roots however slowly. Nonetheless, this is not all that Africa needs. Africa needs to be as democratic just like other Western countries based on its own version of democracy that must aim at serving its needs, aspirations and plans. Africa needs the type of democracy that fits in its environment but not aping Western democracy which has always been used to nurture detrimental and hidden interests and needs of the West. Despite some gains, much still needs to be done. Soon after gaining independence, many African countries were under one-party system for over thirty years namely from 1957–1992 when multiparty politics was introduced to Africa. During the cold war, Western countries did not champion or introduce democracy for the fear of losing allies who would cross the carpet and join the communist east; thus lose resources and strategic positions or endanger the interests the West used to enjoy. Therefore, many African presidents took advantage of this *realpolitik*; and thereby entrenched themselves in power by all means legal and illegal altogether. This is why bad managers of state affairs such as Felix

Houphouët-Boigny, Mobutu Sese Seko, Omar Bongo, Gnassingbe Eyadema and others were able to mismanage their countries for over three decades. The lack of democracy motivated military juntas to topple governments. They knew too well; once one came to power, he would cling to it for as long as he could all depending on the camp one subscribed to or allies himself with. This is why countries like Burundi, Ghana, Nigeria, Mauritania and Uganda suffered many *coups d'états*. Many evil rulers such as Idi Amin, Jean-Bedel Bokassa, Denis Sassou-Nguesso, Theodoro Obiang Nguema, Yahya Jammeh, Sani Abacha and others are the products of this lack of democracy in Africa as it was espoused by the cold war.

However, after military coups started to become a norm, the Organisation of African Unity (OAU) decided to stand up against them. The OAU later succeeded to declare military regimes illegal and unconstitutional. OAU's move against military rule got support from the United Nations (UN). The *IPS* (2 June, 1997) quoted the former UN Secretary General, Kofi Annan, as saying "the will of the people must be the basis of governmental authority in Africa, and governments, duly elected necessary and desirable, is not sufficient. We must also ostracise and isolate putchists." Annan said this when he was attending the OAU conference in Harare Zimbabwe. The OAU had convened its meeting on the heels of military coup in Sierra Leone on 25 May, 1997 which was led by Johnny Paul Koroma. Annan did not only condemn the putchists for this political *faux pas* but also laid down the foundations for what Africa had to expect saying, "Africa can no longer tolerate and accept as a *fait accompli*, coups against elected governments and the illegal seizure of power by military cliques, who sometimes act for sectional interests, sometimes simply for their own." If anything, Anan's remarks were a major boost to Africa. However biased, controversial and unfit the Western democracy is, it has partly enabled Africa to make some gains however not at the magnitude expected for free countries. Africa can use Western democracy to transit to an African oriented democracy conditionally that it should be united first.

After getting rid of military juntas, there is still a lot to be done *vis-a-vis* this ersatz. At least, outlawing coups rescinded the scope and magnitude of their occurrence in Africa. However, there were some exceptions to this general rule, especially in the Central Africa

Republic (CAR) where on 15 March, 2003 General Francois Bozize staged a successful coup that saw democratically elected president, Ange Felix Patasse, ousted from power. As if it was not enough, the military in Guinea, led by Captain Moussa Dadis Camara seized power on 23 December, 2008. Two years later, the military burst onto the scene in Niger. Major Abdoulaye Adamou Harouna staged a successful coup on 18 February, 2010 ousting Mamadou Tanja. However, these two coups did not live longer. They were dislodged; and thereby elected governments were resumed in this country. At least, OAU's drive to purge Africa of military juntas bore fruits. Unfortunately though, the OAU and thereafter the African Unity (AU) has not yet succeeded to put a stop on the regimes that amend their constitutions to remain in power. This needs to be addressed and arrested for democracy to shrive in Africa. Many ruling parties, particularly those that brought independence, temper with the constitutions of their countries and literary stay in power through what we can call *constitutional coup d'états*. This is evident in Angola, Cameroon, Tanzania and Zimbabwe, where ruling parties suffocated opposition parties so as to remain in power for a long time.

Another ruse that the ruling parties use is bribery. Despite outlawing military dictatorship, Africa is still suffering from two categories of setbacks namely; political dictatorship whereby many ruling parties manipulate and rig votes so as to remain in power against the will of the citizens. So, too, Africa is now facing another type of dictatorship which involves some individual presidents who tamper with the constitutions of their countries so as to cling to power. Recent examples from Burundi, the DRC, Rwanda, the Republic of Congo (DRC), Sudan, Togo, and Uganda speak volumes. Some rulers think they are the only ones who are supposedly god sent to run their countries. Such a situation, as it was recently evidenced in Burundi, costs Africa a lot of money and time. For, it is a good source of violent and protracted conflicts. Those clinging to power do so by making sure that the armies in their countries support their move. To secure the guarantee from the armies, resources and public funds are diverted to the armies. Unfortunately, instead of protecting the people and the country, such bribed and compromised armies protect big men; and thereby become their accomplices in mismanaging the business of the state. Rwanda and Uganda provide ideal examples *vis-à-vis* this sort of *coup d'état* carried out systemically based on doctored constitutions.

Furthermore, almost all rulers who want to cling to power make sure that armies are remunerated or bought to see to it that those buying them remain in power as the means of assuring their upper hand in public business. Such an undertaking has caused a lot of sufferings, problems and dissent among the citizens of countries under such dictators. When Burundi's president Pierre Nkurunziza decided to seek the third term in office contrary to the constitution, there occurred some mass actions which caused the deaths of many innocent people. The *Wall Street Journal* (12 December, 2015) quoted unnamed officials saying that eighty-seven people were killed in violence in Burundi when three military installations were attacked by armed men. As indicated above, when an individual supported by a compromised army clings on power, some citizens decide to oppose the move something that causes acrimony between citizens on the one hand and military and police forces on the other hand. This is why, in Burundi, the military and police forces killed tens of innocent people who are opposed to the unconstitutionality of the current government. Essentially, when an individual decides to cling to power, he or she creates hatred from a section of the population. Whoever opposes this criminality becomes fair game. This can be done by way of suppressing dissent voices or eliminating the leaders of the movements that oppose the government as it was in Burundi where journalists, politicians and activists had to flee the country for fear of their lives or be detained or killed simply because they were not in bed with the regime in Bujumbura. Due to frustrations and hatred, some people take the law on their hands so as to attack military installations which triggers the government to unleash repressive measures such as state terrorism against its own citizens. However, we need to be careful. Sometimes, the so-called attacks on military installations are staged; and thus used as a pretext of unleashing terrors all aimed at intimidating and silencing dissent voices. This is what is known as state terror whereby the state uses its military muscles to terrorise the population in order to either silence them or force them to abandon their quest for change or democracy.

More on Burundi, quoting the UN agency, the Kenyan *Daily Nation* (May 12, 2015) reported that since early April 2015 over 50,000 people, mostly women and children, had fled Burundi with at least half of them going to Rwanda. These numbers do not include Internally Displaced People (IDPs) or those whose lives have been negatively affected due to the lack of peace which is needed in carrying out their day-to-day activities such as production, among others. True, the conflict that resulted from power grab in Burundi has dragged on for many months now. After the president succeeded to run for the third term and *won*, he has been using whatever tactics and expenses to remain in power. Unfortunate for Africa, there is no viable mechanism to dislodge him. To us, this is a civil coup. As noted above, some years ago, the AU banned military coups in Africa. However, it seems to have failed short of banning civil coups that politicians carry out by amending the constitution to illegally remain in power. Such a situation is obvious *vis-à-vis* the conflict in, as aforesaid, Burundi where the president changed the constitution to remain in power after many people were killed as they opposed the move. At least, the conflict in Burundi received some condemnations; and the pressure is still exerted on the president to relinquish power to no avail due to the politics and *realpolitik* of the region. Even when we consider Burundi internationally, what does it have to offer so as to be considered the same way crises in Iraq, Syria and elsewhere are dealt with? After all, Burundi is an African country. When it comes to other countries such as the DRC, Gabon, Republic of Congo, Rwanda, Sudan and Uganda, among others, the AU is silent. Why? In other words, the AU has allowed illegal managers of state business to mismanage those countries. Some allege that they brought change and prosperity in their countries as if others cannot bring the same. Nobody is created to rule except when the majority vote her or him to become their leader. While those clinging on power give all such hogwash and pretexts, they forget that the people have the right to choose whomever they want to manage their affairs based on their constitutions and volition but not compulsion or manipulations. People need the manager that they can hold to account instead of the one who superimpose himself on them as it is in countries where presidents have usurped power by amending the constitutions to illegally remain in office mismanaging the countries and abusing power. The person who amends the constitution to remain in power is by all means unaccountable to anybody except the powers that enabled him to do so.

When it comes to political parties that manipulate their electorate and rig votes, the problem is becoming bigger and bigger by days. Currently, some African countries are still ruled by the parties that brought independence even when they are outdated and unpopular. Again, this is not the general rule in all African countries. For example, Botswana, Mozambique and Namibia provide a very different case in that founding parties are still popular. When it comes to Botswana, it provides an ideal example thanks to being a democracy since independence. Countries in which unpopular ruling parties that brought independence are still in power are Angola, Tanzania, South Africa and Zimbabwe, among others. Most of these ruling parties–for many generations they have been in power–have not delivered as they were expected of. Arguably, if there were true democracy in these countries most of these parties would be either in the opposition or in the oblivion. There are ideal examples whereby founding parties were pushed out of politics once and for all after becoming either corrupt or unpopular. Such parties are, *inter alia*, the United National Independence Party (UNIP in Zambia), the Malawi Congress Party (MCP in Malawi), the Kenya African National Union (KANU in Kenya), and the Uganda People's Congress (UPC in Uganda). To the contrary, parties that are still in power since independence are, among others, the Chama Cha Mapinduzi (CCM in Tanzania) which was previously known as Tanganyika African National Union (TANU), the *Rassemblement Démocratique du Peuple Camerounais* (RDPC in Cameroon) which was previously known as the Cameroonian National Union (CNU), the *Frente de Libertação de Moçambique* (FRELIMO in Mozambique), the South West Africa People's Organization (SWAPO in Namibia), the *Movimento Popular de Libertação de Angola* (MPLA in Angola), the African National Congress (ANC in South Africa) and Zimbabwe African National Union–Patriotic Front (ZANU–PF in Zimbabwe). It is only the Botswana Democratic Party (BDP) which, at least, has delivered compared to others. These are the famous ones; and whose rules have ushered in a lot of corruption in their countries despite some gains. Nobody would convincingly say that the parties above have been in power simply because they were legally and truly and democratically elected. They used their powers to allocate resources to themselves so as to use them either to bribe voters and national armies or buy votes not to mention intimidating and suffocating opposition. To get away with murder, many parties weaken the opposition as another way of remaining in power intact. Again, there is a high cost to pay when such parties remain in power. They encourage rent-seeking practices in their ranks so as to raise funds for their survival. In Tanzania, the purchase of military radar provides an ideal example in which government high-ranking officials conspired with businesspeople–local and foreign–to rob poor taxpayers under the ploy of procurement. Experience shows that such graft is committed as means of raising fund for the party if not getting backing from corrupt beneficiaries. So, too, most of mega scandals in Tanzania normally occur close to general elections. This can shows the pattern of corruption with power and power grab in some African countries. In its editorial, the Tanzanian *Guardian* (12 August, 2012) unearthed radar scam in Tanzania noting that on December 4, 2011t same paper reported that three top suspects in the radar scandal who swindled $12 million paid as bribery by BAE Systems are British citizens, currently living comfortably in London, despite the UK pressure for Tanzania to seek prosecutions for bribery in relation to a $44m (£28m) defence equipment deal.

You can clearly see how the price was inflated in this illegal deal. Arguably, the actual price that the radar asked was less than the amount the government of Tanzania bid and purportedly paid. So, too, the West is not spared in such scams in two ways. Firstly, BAE Systems is a Public Limited Company based in Britain. Secondly, much of the money ended up in Switzerland and London as the *Guardian* (Ibid) notes that the architect of this scam, Saileth Vithlani, has been moving between UK and Switzerland since he jumped bail in Dar es Salaam in 2006, despite an international arrest warrant issued by International Police (Interpol). You wonder how Interpol could fail to arrest the culprit whose residences are known. Had this Vithlani been wanted in connection with charges related to terrorism or any aimed at attempting to rob or harm a Western country would be at large? After the media in Britain and Tanzania disclosed the radar scandal, BAE Systems decided to save face. The *BBC* (19 July,

2011) notes that "in a plea bargain with the prosecuting authorities, the Serious Fraud Office, BAE agreed to pay £30m to the Tanzanian people" which however, Tanzanians have never received any cent. Arguably, corruption–involving top-government officials and military procurement–does not end up in Tanzania. In the neighbouring Kenya, Anglo-Leasing scandal sank billions of Kenyan shillings. The *Daily Nation* (23 November, 2015) reported that "Mr Mwiraria is among ten people accused of conspiracy to defraud the government of billions of shillings through dubious contracts for the purchase and installation of security surveillance systems for the Kenya Police." Mwiraria was a Kenya finance minister who was accused along with other officials in this scandal.

When it comes to why Africa has always been mismanaged, one of the reasons is the fact that democracy has always been hijacked by ruling parties despite the fact that some of them are in power after winning sham and rigged elections that gave them the majority control of the government. Amundsen (1999) defines this type of corruption arguing that "political corruption is when political decision-makers use the political power they are armed with, to sustain their power, status and wealth," (p. 3). Amundsen goes on arguing that this type of corruption involves mega scandals in which big amounts of money are made. Essentially, this type of corruption, apart from hurting the country politically, it also hurts it economically. In countries like Tanzania with abundant resources, many investment contracts that the country entered are bogus and lossmaking. Currently, Tanzania produces tons of gold which benefits invests more than citizens so as to become a resource curse that we have discussed above in the case of the DRC as a typical replica of many African countries endowed with resources.

We are talking about political corruption. There are yet other types of corruption resulting from this type of corruption which essentially is the mother of all corruption. Military corruption is another offshoot of political corruption. Politicians, military personnel and industrialists have a sort of mutual interdependence. This is why corruption in many Africa countries has become a norm that is sustained by this tripartite marriage. The top military officers get their cuts through procurement after colluding with either politicians or businesspersons. Essentially, all this draws from the archaic and anarchic world system whereby rich countries produce arms and corruptly sell them to poor countries that use them to hang on power illegally as it has been the case in many African countries currently where many dictators are sustained by the armies and arms. Furthermore, when military officers are involved in corruption as far as procurement is concerned, they end up becoming endemic so that military personnel become government suppliers just as what the *New York Times* (23 November, 2014) reported on Iraq military corruption noting that "one Iraqi general is known as "chicken guy" because of his reputation for selling his soldiers' poultry provisions." Prices are hiked not to mention substandard materials that are procured and supplied. Sometimes, you find that some military officials are the proprietors of the companies they are buying from. To do this well, politicians or officers behind such corruption connive with suppliers who are businesspeople where such suppliers are not military personnel. Mbaku (1994 cited in Mbaku 1996) claims that:

> In many African countries, the armed forces receive a disproportionate share of the public budget. It is argued by many researchers that these post-independence developments have contributed significantly to increased corruption, underdevelopment, and pervasive poverty and deprivation, (page not provided).

Ironically, in many African countries, the budgets of the ministries of defence are made a top secret something that makes it difficult to know how much the military burn and how much they make corruptly. Why and how can one audit such ministries? This speaks volumes that ruling politicians bribe the armies this way. If anything, this is a legalised type of corruption that takes money directly from the budget. In the countries where the budgets of the ministries of defence or security are not disclosed, it means that even the parliaments cannot deliberate on them. Isn't this making parliaments rubber stamps and implicationally conspirators? Isn't this a systemic corruption-cum-failure? When it comes to military corruption—just as it is for other government ministries and departments–Passas (2007) notes that procurement is one of the most vulnerable areas *vis-à-vis* fraud and corruption, (p. 4) in many countries, especially where rent-seeking practices are tolerated as it currently is in many African countries. What transpired recently in Nigeria may show us how security and military corruption is. The *BBC* (1 December, 2015) reported that Nigeria's former national security adviser, Sambo Dasuki, was arrested for allegedly stealing US$2bn (£1.3bn) which was intended to purchase equipment aimed at fighting Boko Haram. If an individual is able to steal such a humongous amount of money, how much money have many military personnel stolen in the entire continent since independence? The *BBC* goes on reporting that Mr Dasuki is accused of awarding phantom contracts to buy 12 helicopters, four fighter jets and ammunition.

In sum, when it comes to the cost of hijacking democracy in Africa, it is mind-bogglingly humongous. Lawal (2007) puts the tug at billions of dollars noting that "according to a United Nations estimate in 1991 alone, more than $200billion in capital was siphoned out of Africa by the ruling elites, (p. 5) which George Ayyiteh (2002 cited in Lawal, Ibid) puts at " more than half of Africa's foreign debt of $300billion." Here we are talking about capital flight without touching on another sacrilege the colonial ruling class in Africa cause their taxpayers.

Chapter 24

Conclusion: Poverty is not an Accident

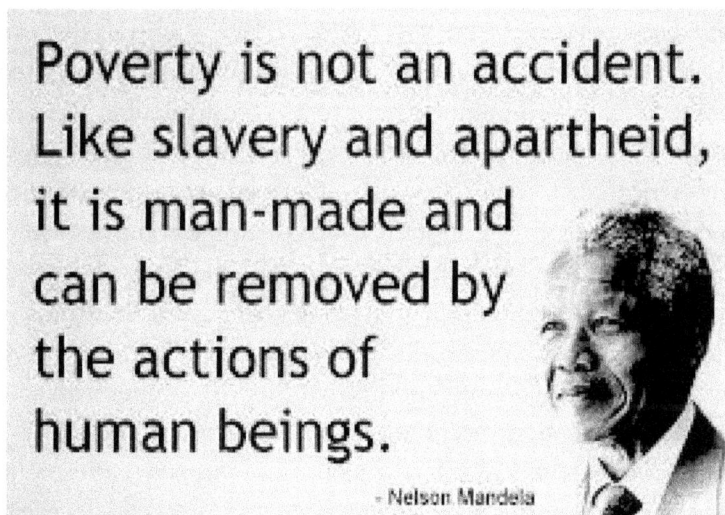

Poverty is not an accident. Like slavery and apartheid, it is man-made and can be removed by the actions of human beings.

- Nelson Mandela

Figure 35: African manmade poverty (image courtesy of poorpeoplequotes.blogspot.com)

It is probable and provable that corrupt and myopic rulers whom the West supported in the seventies and eighties for the purpose of protecting its interests in their countries hijacked Africa. As argued in the introductory party of this volume, it is upon African academics to wage their power—which in this context—the knowledge they have to see to it that they, fearlessly and tirelessly; question the *status quo* which is made of those with political power continentally and globally due to the fact that the duo depend on each other. Academics have all reasons to wage this war to see to it that Africa is wrestled from dirty hands so that it can move forward. We need to make resources available for coming generations. If they use them or do not, it is not our fault. If the West has never stopped accusing Africa of untrue things, why should we stop making our case *vis-à-vis* West's conspiracy against Africa? If the West seems to go on backing such traitors, what else should academics do? Take on them of course. This is a very important war to wage due to the fact that those in power, or those waging political power, control almost everything from private to public space in the society. They preside over organs that enact, amend or repeal laws. However, we must underscore the fact that even our governments are controlled by imperialistic and opportunistic rich countries which influence how our laws should be enacted and applied to suit their interests. For, countries that do not want to comply receive threats of withdrawing aid. Many African rulers control governments which, so too, control all institutions in the countries due to the fact that there is no separation of power in many African countries. They have absolute power over the income and expenditure of the countries which–in some countries–heads of governments do so without being accountable to anybody but to themselves and their masters or sponsors all depending on who enable them to be in power. Such West-cloned rulers have power to even undermine their constitutions that they oft-tamper with so as to remain in office as it recently happened in some Central and East African countries where rulers sought more terms in office contrary to the proviso of the very constitutions they pretend to swear to defend. This coupled with West's perpetual drive to extend colonialism and exploitation in Africa; it conspires with its cloned African conspirators who replaced their colonial monsters under the divide and rule which, as noted above became rule and divide (Mhango 2015). Therefore, whenever we seek to know what left Africa out in cold as far as development is concerned while others where excelling, we must not forget the role African stooges in various state houses played. We must also not shy away from the fact that this heinous method is still at work in a different modality however. We need to challenge the *status quo* at any cost for the good of Africa. So, deciding to go down this rough road needs commitment, readiness, agility and above all, fearlessness. Instead of fearing the organs of the state, we must fear the shame of not using our knowledge to bring about deserved and desired change to our people. So, too, we need to consider how new generations will treat us even if we will not be there. This is very important. Everybody would like to leave behind a very good legacy. However, when it comes to corrupt people, shinning legacy is nothing they bother about given that they are able to serve their greed and criminality. Despite that, just like any other creatures, this is why humans, even animals invest heavily in children. This is why there is no way we can win this war without rewriting our history. History, if used well, is a very powerful weapon for emancipation in that it provides tools and information to those who are the part of the process of emancipation but not those who want to conquer and exploit them as it has been for Africa. For, their future has hanged in the balance for many years. It is time to make sense of our history so that we can use it, among others, to launch our future based on our needs and aspirations as a people.

We need to state it clearly that Africa has nothing to do with, and it will always be exonerated from being the part and parcel of whatever forces that authored the miseries its people are in currently. It is only a few African stooges that have always been used by the West to rob Africa wantonly. What must be done is for Africans to confront those who cloned and nourished these criminals that sold them to their colonial monsters. And nobody can help Africans to do this except their resolve and understanding of their true history. Such undertaking can bear fruits when, and only when, the true history of Africa is written to counter the jaundiced and *doctored* one that the colonial monsters wrote, misconstrued and mispresented to suit their covert and overt interests. And the duty of writing this true and noble history of Africa rests on the shoulders of Africans, especially academics. This way, we can use history as tool for emancipation. Sometime back, somebody was complaining about recipient habit that is endemic and chronic in many African countries. He said that if we do not watch, our children and grand and great grandchildren will urinate on our graves one day. Such a statement irked me terrifically so speak even though it did not formally represent the views of all youths. But as it sank in, I found that the person uttering such words was right due to what he knew and what he did not know *vis-a-vis* the plight and history of Africa. This young person, presumably, looked at the outgoing generation as a foolish and lazy one while it actually is not. What drove this young person to condemn all people collectively, apart from frustration, ignorance about the truth on what actually has been going on in Africa, is the major reason that geared me to write this book, among others. As a parent, an African and an academic, I do not like my kids to have such assumptions or feelings about me and my generation. First of all, it is traumatic experience for both parties namely the current generation and the coming generations. Secondly, it can make young generations believe that this is a normal thing that they have to make do with. Thirdly, such assumptions may lead them to believe that they are inferior before those who make them believe so simply because they are Africans. Fourthly, some of them would end up conspiring—just like our worst managers of state business discussed in this volume—with the forces that have always held Africa at ransom as a way of either individually escaping or communally surrendering themselves thinking it is a norm and a normal thing that their parents lived with. Fifthly, such assumptions may deny them the spirit of rebelling against the present situation that those who authored Africa's miseries would use to their advantage. We need to get into the heart of the matter by making our own case ourselves through exploring and presenting our true history as people and society.

What makes the situation of being undeservedly blamed spooky is the fact that we are collectively accused of, and thereby condemned for not doing something about this criminality that left our continent bankrupt and abaft. To make matters worse—it sadly seems—the young generation is distancing itself from the mess we are in currently. For the fear of such wrong perceptions, I decided to present the situation some of us went through. In essence, this aims at enabling future generations to justly judge us instead of erroneously blaming us for not taking right actions, specifically taking on such autocratic rules that caused almost all miseries Africa is in unjustifiably facing and suffering from. They need to know that—in spite of claiming to be independent—Africa has never been fully independent. Sadly nevertheless, Africa has been subjected to all sorts of experiments all aimed at exploiting its abundant and immense resources. As a deconstructionist, I full understand that it is upon Africa and Africans to pull it out of such a *cul de sac* and bottleneck of being a guinea pig or a *bête noire* any criminal can easily and abusively use. It is conceivable that the task of wrestling Africa from such a pig-headed situation will always be tough and demanding.

It is through *governmentality* (Foucault) or the art of government—or the *ruledmentality* (*this is mine*), or the mentality of the ruled—that Africa was subjected to the guinea pig's role pointlessly. So, it is through unearthing and debunking the mystery and fashion of how our governments are formed, who form them, and above all, how they do it based on our desires and needs. We need to go further and ask: How are–the so-called our governments–managed or manned or *womaned* (to be gender sensitive)? Do they deliver or end up becoming a burden to taxpayers, particularly if we consider the duty of any government on earth? Political scientists and lawyers tell us that the duty of any government is to keep its citizens and their property safe. However, this is not the case in many African countries where the governments are in power only to rob and exploit the citizens. Therefore, it is only through examining the real situation in order to see how we can make things right so that they can rightly work for us all but not for them, or work for a select few in the upper echelons of power as it currently is in many African countries where governments are unimpeachable. We need the system, government and model of the people that are made by the people, for the interests of the people. We need a people-engineered-and-experimented government in Africa. We need the government that has roots in Africa but not America and Europe or anywhere else. Mhango (2015), for example, questions the rationale of putting a mortal above the law. He calls this a disaster that has made it easy for Africa to be exploited and robbed for a long time without awakening. It becomes even more ridiculous when such a mortal put above the law is insane and fraudulent as it was in many *bumbling buffoons* such as, *inter alia,* Amin, Bokassa, Mobutu even Gaddafi. Sadly though, it is only in Africa and in some other emirates, kingdoms, queendoms and the likes where an individual mortal is above the law. I tend to subscribe to Mandela's philosophy when it comes to defining what he was despite being regarded as a creature from another planet. He used to say that he was not an angel but a sinner who was trying to be good or upright. If a person of Mandela's calibre can succumb before such fallibility, what of the mentioned bumbling buffoons? If anything, this is where things started to become cockeyed. Without deconstructing such systems based on the experience we have at hand, there is no way we can avoid the blemishes as people and a society. To do the right thing, is to radically take on such regimes, systems and laws head on so that we can reengineer, recraft, and overhaul our institutions for our own benefits and interests. Again, this is not the end. Our systems depend on global systems. Therefore, shall this succeed; it must lead to taking on global systems too. As indicated above, many venal, autocratic and sitting-duck-like despots and thieves were sustained by the bipolar politics of the time which was acrimoniously polarising so as to accommodate and sustain such illusory, shaky and incompetent regimes provided they were able to blindly serve the interests of those who cloned or compromised them. Most of them were but chicanery. They duped their people using police and armed forces which were unbrave and fraidy-cats. How quick and easy the toppling of Mobutu was speaks volumes. For over three decades, Congolese were held at ransom by cons under pretenders who presented themselves as powerful and able while in actual fact they were but chicken-hearted creatures whose strength were in the confidence game. Due to being made to believe that those who lorded it over them were powerful and able to quash whatever riot or mass actions that would have been taken, our people tolerated weak and shaky rules. Had they known what was behind the curtain, they would not have made do with such chicken-hearted regimes. Therefore, one can comfortably argue that such deception made any reasonable people to think twice before making any move or decision. However, there are some examples of people who daringly tried and failed or succeeded all depending on the type of the rule in place. Therefore, it is not out of the cowardice, fear or inactions of the victims that nursed and nurtured such bad regimes. What transpired in Burkina Faso just recently speaks volume. Apart from the Arab spring which is not African, the Burkinabe showed the way after toppling their long-time thief Blaise Compaore who toppled and assassinated their world-shattering leader, Thomas Sankara. Had Sub-Saharan African (SSA) countries been ready and ripe for taking on their venal dictators, Burkina Faso's precedent would have authored African spring. Again, we need to understand that dictatorship is a global phenomenon in which capitalist countries dictate our dictators who end up dictating us. Sometimes, we need to show the cloners of our dictators that we know what has been going on; and we are not happy about it.

The question why Africa has been maltreated and *maladministered* like an android still lingers. We still need to find more answers for it. This brings us to the superstructure that colonial monsters created and left behind when they purportedly gave freedom to their colonies. No matter what, this dynamic-colonial superstructure that has always been in place is to blame among others for the most of our predicaments. So, rekindling the fire of retrieving and rejuvenating Africa's thew requires us to deconstruct the current superstructure as it was enacted by imperialists in the West. There are some undertakings that we need to purposely and resolutely embark on in order to achieve our goals. In effect, it is this very juncture at which—we need to conceptualise; and apply methods such as reunification of Africa, re-writing Africa's history; reviving Africa's ways of life and other things that are important requirements of the people—Africa can commence the journey to its full emancipation. As for the need to reclaim Africa's lost glory—is still manifestly bemoaning us—we need to fully understand that there is no way Africa can be safe and sound if it will go on being under the current system that depends on the West for almost everything. We need to take a leaf from the best managers and expand on where they left to see to it that the "flickering torch" (Nyerere) that they started should never die. Again, it is squarely upon Africans, especially academics and activists to take the challenge seriously, honestly and pragmatically. Rewriting our history is one of emancipatory methods that will free Africa from dubious and erroneous history that many European fiction writers compiled with malice and then call it the history of Africa. Nyamndi (2009) notes that "the writer of fiction can tap directly from history and produce a historical work, or can rely vicariously on it and author works of high realist content," (p. 5). This is exactly what happened to the true history of Africa that needs to be reclaimed with zeal and recompiled with accuracy without any bias and fallacies in it. Currently, for example, Africa has many literature legendary figures such as the late Chinua Achebe, Wole Soyinka, Ngugi wa Thiong'o, Okot p'Bitek, Mongo Beti, Camara Laye, Ousmane Sembene, Shaban Robert, Peter Abraham and many more who used their education to rebel artistically. Where are African notable historians? If there are there, are they famous? Are their contributions used and honoured in our learning institutions? If yes, how; and if not, why aren't they used? What are we waiting for? I know a few notable historians such as Bethwel Ogot, David Were among others. Where are our famous economists who penned eye-opening pieces apart from Dambisa Moyo? Again, does it mean that there are no other African thinkers that deserve to be in the limelight? The foregoing literati were popularised by the West which hijacked most of them for its interests after they became unwelcomed back home. Africa, now, needs to popularise its academics by intentionally and seriously using their works. The sage has it that charity begins at home. Africa must shy away from deceptions such as *nemo profita in patria sua* namely No one is considered a prophet in his hometown/homeland. In African philosophy it is opposite. Swahili proverb has it that *Nyumbani ni nyumbani hata kama mwituni* or home is home even if it is in the wilderness and *hisani huanzia nyumbani* or charity begins at home. If the prophet is not accepted at home, he or she is not a prophet. To most of African societies, if someone is not accepted at home, either he or she does not belong to that place or there are some unwanted things such a person committed. Thanks to colonial legacy-cum-mentality, many African countries are still using colonial texts in their schools despite being independent for over a decade. Under the No-one-is-considered-a-prophet-in-his hometown/homeland chicanery, Africans faithfully accepted all sort of prophets most of them fake ones such as the IMF and WB that destroyed their economies and wellbeing. We still use colonial languages simply because we refused to agree to have one African language. If there were an African language that is used all over the continent, I would not have bothered to write this volume in English. Again, language has never been a big problem if we agree on how to borrow and modify it. We can take a leaf from English language that has always copied from others. America advanced on English which is not an American language. Africa needs to decolonise its academic regime based on *changing the syllabi* which Mhango (2015) dissects and digest in detail in a chapter bearing the same title in his book *Africa Reunite or Perish*. On their side, African academics need to write as many books on as many subjects as possible. Likewise, on their side, African government should use such literature to liberate their people instead of clinging to fear of the unknown that the West has always taken advantage of. While African academics are not seen thanks to being betrayed by their own countries and governments, Western academics have always churned tons and tons of books on tons of issues and subjects. Shakespeare is more accepted and read by many readers in many African countries than many African authors while what he actually wrote has nothing to do with Africa. The same applies to many Western bigots who intentionally miswrote, misconstrued and misrepresented the history of Africa to suit their heinous interests. Again, due to having corrupt, myopic and clumsy rulers, our academics are not motivated and taken care of. This is why it has always been easy for the West to fish them and lead to what is dichotomously known as the *Brain Drain* which others call *Brain Gain*. How does Africa gain from its brains by slamming the door in their faces? Many African countries are coughing a lot of money to educate their youth abroad where some of them are taught by African professors who would teach them at home if they were motivated and courted to return home. Thanks to corruption, indifference and neglect of professionals, even those educated by their colleagues abroad, sometimes, tend to stay there instead of going back home for the fear of being exploited, ignored, misused and underused.

Given that we are facing the same situation as Africans and academics, we need to do something about this resentful *cul de sac* we are now in academically. Who wants her or his grave to be defecated on by her or his own progenies? Thanks to African culture of repatriating the dead back home, even those sharpening the minds of academics abroad will face the same once they die. To avoid this shame, I think the information contained in this book is helpful to many, especially the youths who did not suffer under the system at the time, to dispel such fear and wrong perceptions; and thereby free most of us from the fear of being dishonoured posthumously. Although African youths may distance themselves from the mess Africa is in, they still are a part and parcel of the problem given that they live under the same corrupt and impotent system that needs to be changed. As youths, they surely have what it takes to take on it. As members of the society, they have an important role to play in doing things differently from how the outgoing generation did. The emancipation of Africa is the duty of every African in Africa and in diaspora. I believe that there are two ways of confronting rotten and superimposed regimes the West has always used to fleece Africa. Firstly, there must be peaceful and mass strategies of bringing them to account before thinking about toppling them through mass actions. Offering bad governments a window to change things acts as a warning to those in power to become aware that those they have bullied and exploited for a long time have awaken; and they need their countries back. It does not make sense to tell the ruled or the oppressed that the countries belong to them whereas, to the contrary, they ironically do not enjoy security and prosperity independence and ownership are supposed to bring to them. Poignantly, many African venal governments dupe their people telling them that their countries are peaceful only because there is no chaos. The absence of war does not necessarily connote peacefulness. Liminal peace is not peace, and of course, protecting people and their property does not end up with normalcy in which many people are going without indispensable amenities and needs. Protecting people is about everything such as having food on the table, getting worthy and meaningful education, jobs, and in fact, being sure about the future of the whole society. Accountability is the only venue through which justice can be delivered to all but not to just a few elites in power.

The second step is to actively take on the regimes that refuse to change or yield to the need and voice of the people as suggested above through offering the window to change. I strongly recommend mass actions against complicity between local and global players as the only practicable and possible means of turning things around in Africa. However, this method failed in many African countries due to the support such venal and brutal regimes got from the West and the East. We learn through our mistakes. When one tries a certain method aimed at achieving desired goals and fails, it does not mean that this is the end of the story. We need to tirelessly practice more resilience and try more methods with which we can change the *status quo* by cultivating and inculcating the spirit of accountability at all levels. Practice, always, makes perfect. So, too, patience is the mother of success. We are the living witnesses of what happened in countries such as Burkina Faso, Egypt, Libya, and Tunisia where long-time dictatorships were pulled down when the citizens decided to say "enough is enough." However desired achievement was not realised in some countries after the process was hijacked thereby ending up creating even greater chaos. Given that Arab spring was not African and for African countries, we can still use Burkina Faso spring which is truly African in that it was not backed by neither the West nor the East. I believe; all African countries are made of citizens who can say enough is enough. Thanks to the genesis of quick and fast means of communication and media, the citizens are able to communicate easily; and quickly decide even without physically meeting to execute whatever mission they decide to. We now have many types of mass media which we can use to bring about changes in our countries. Again, this is not an easy ride. Africa needs to carefully watch its steps due to the fact many media may take this opportunity to further their hidden interests at the detriment of African people. Calhoun (1988, p. 225 cited in Mutz 2001) notes that "most of the information we have about people different from ourselves comes not through any direct relationships rather it comes through print and electronic media," (p. 97). It is through the savviness of African people that will assure them of success in the project of retrieving Africa from the mess it is in currently. Also see Rosenberg (2008); Calvalho (2007); and Green, *et al.,* (2004).

In Africa, under the cold war animosities, no priorities or attention were given to democracy, rule of law, human rights and the likes which Africans are supposed to struggle for and get. Instead, however, the premium was on carbuncular alliances either with the East or the West. There were only two choices for African countries to make; either to wilfully ally with the East or unwilfully the West and vice versa. Thereafter, some smart African thinkers such as Julius Nyerere envisaged the need of joining the Non-Aligned Movement (NAM) which however, did not counter the dichotomous banality of the cold war at the time. Due to the blanket and mistrust of the cold war, rulers would unleash any brutalities without being made accountable and responsible for their evil actions by the two powers that were at loggerhead almost in everything except exploiting Africa. Unfortunately though, despite the demise of one camp, the East, exploiting Africa still goes on unabated. You can currently see this almost everywhere in Africa. Formerly such double standard was evidenced in Ethiopia, Egypt, Equatorial Guinea, Gabon, Kenya, Libya, Malawi, the Republic of Congo, South Africa, Togo, Uganda the then Zaïre now the Democratic Republic of Congo (DRC), and many more countries in Africa to mention but a few. At the time, rulers, be they trustworthy or corrupt were above the law of their countries. Essentially, what mattered most, at the time, was nothing African rulers in the aforementioned to assure and safeguard the interests of superpowers, the US on the one hand and the then USSR.

Therefore, complicity was the only way for corrupt rulers as well as trustworthy leaders to bow in if they wanted to avoid any disturbances from superpowers of which the West accused those in its enemy's fold of human rights or rule of law while the East used accused the West of capitalism as the system that allows one person to exploit another instead of sharing equally and equitably. As argued above, there is nothing that assures corrupt African rulers safety in power except toeing the line. Hence, when they put themselves above the constitutions of their countries, nobody disturbed them provided his interests were intact. When it comes to being above the law, no African country was spared in this power game-cum-chicanery whereby a mortal being was above the law. By being above the law, the one is not duty bound or responsible or accountable to anybody except to himself and to those whose interests he protects. So, we can confidently say that Africans were not acquiescent to whatever miseries they found themselves in save that they were overpowered by the politics and *realpolitik* of the day based on their needs and aspiration.

Thirdly, there is nothing worthy we need to offer such as taking on rotten regimes by the way of exposing them through presenting the real situation as it has been. This will help those supposed to judge us to assess, evaluate and analyse themselves. Thereafter, they will be able to decide on what to do to avoid being blamed by the generations after them. Such approach balances the claims of the two sides. This is where academia becomes a very powerful and emancipatory weapon. This is where the importance of history becomes an asset-cum-weapon. For, by presenting, analysing and recording the epochs Africa went through, apart from preserving its history of sufferings, we will be able to give future generations a tool with which to use to avoid replicating the mistake we made. Importantly, to succeed, they need to judge us justly based on the real situation but not based on assumptions. By giving future generation such information, knowledge and tools, we are able to help them learn something from our past that they can use to forge ahead into the future, adeptly, confidently and safely. Such information will help them to avert repeating the same mistakes that pulled Africa back to where it is currently stuck.

We have shown a great deal of how Africa lost to insane and corrupt rulers that the West cloned, installed, and above all, used to rob it. Try to imagine how an individual spends her or his income. In a normal situation, a normal person, sometimes, and many times and cases, spends much more money than he or she saves due to the demands of daily life. We spend much money on food, clothing, housing, medication, education, transport and whatnot. Essentially, this is what life is all about for the majority of our people. For example, if you ask a professor or a medical doctor how much he or she has in the bank compared to how much one spent ever since one started working, you find that it is anecdotally a hell of money. If such a normal person wisely and frugally spent much more money than the one saved, what of our venal rulers whose expenditures were/ and are not subject to audit or any fiscal discipline, frugality or concern of others they used to rob? If thieves like Mobutu and Abacha were able to stash US$ 5 to 8bn apiece in banks abroad, how much did they squander? Here we do not mean the money that their wives, mistresses, children, friends, courtiers, relatives, armies and whatnot spent and squandered. We do not mean the money Western *godfathers-cum-masters* milked from their countries due to their myopia and greed. To gauge how much they robbed Africa, you can multiply such amount ten, even hundred times if you like. If you put such money together, you can understand how richer Africa would have been if it were managed by good managers. So, when we talk of Africa's worst managers or [mis-]managers, we mean exactly this. The other way you can evaluate how much money Africa lost, is by looking at how rich the West is, especially countries that do not have resources.

Arguably, it needs the courage of the mad or a high level of ignorance and indifference to wholesale condemn normal Africans who have nothing to do with politics or power for being coward and reticent for what happened to them after their countries were hijacked. They were not at all. The situation forced them to make do with such stinky and abhorring regimes. Again, the question can be raised as to why a few dictators are still in power committing the same sin-cum-robbery if the problem was the cold war? Yes, we admit. Africa still has many dictators doing the same monkey business despite the fall of the iron curtain. Moreover, we must underscore the fact that when the iron curtain fell, another type of curtain in neoliberalism based on globalism, capitalism, mercantilism, and many other isms was erected based on the archaic nature of the international system in which Africa has never been treated equally and fairly. Then one can ask: why didn't thing change? Mind you. Change takes time. It is a slow process that can be equated to slow ailments that may sometimes take a long time to kill a creature. Despite the fall of the iron curtain, some practices–especially clientele politics by the West, the sole power broker we currently have–are still ongoing unabatedly and unchallenged. The DRC provides an ideal example on how this rusty system works. Ever since colonial times, the DRC has always suffered a lot of miseries just because of its abundant resources that the West–and now China and India–needs the most. Stability in the DRC, Equatorial Guinea, Nigeria and other countries with abundant resources means a good bargaining chip for these countries which is a bad deal-cum-omen for countries that use unstable and unaccountable regimes to plunder the said countries. This is why you cannot hear the US preaching democracy to the DRC, Equatorial Guinea or Gabon. These countries have what a self-appointed *champion* and *guardian* of democracy needs and wants. So, rulers in these countries are not *bugged* with the democratisation of their countries or the protection of human rights. Arguably, human rights are not as precious as the interests of big countries are. Again, when the chips are down, the same exploiters blame their clones in order to get away with murder as it was in the cases of Bokassa and Mobutu. Mhango (2015) tackles this matter extensively. Those interested in exploring the reasons why Africa has always lagged behind as far as development is concerned should read this daring tome.

Verily, the history of Africa is littered with names of men who got drunk on power and received their comeuppance in due course, Leon (2008, p. 221). To the contrary, most of the best leaders of Africa had grand vision on how to deliver and develop it. This is why such decent and diligent persons did manage their countries well. Arguably, due to their grand visions, their countries were smaller than what they envisaged. There are managers of state business such as Julius Nyerere, Tanzania's founding father and Kwame Nkrumah, Ghana's founding father who were big fish in small ponds. Being a big fish in a small pond has its consequences. It makes it much easier for *fishermen* (the imperialists) to notice, and fish you or hunt you. If you are lucky you narrowly survive. If you are not, you end up being finished, fixed through coups. This is evident in two doyens of African politics mentioned above. Nyerere survived however, by facing a lot of hurdles that culminated in the felling of his vision in the early 80s while Nkrumah was fished (overthrown in 1966 which arguably became a very good lesson for Nyerere as far as survival tactics were concerned). Sadly though, some of the visionaries did not stay longer in power to fulfil their dreams-cum-vision of which one was the quest to unite Africa so that it could become a powerful player in the politics and economy of the world. There are two reasons why such amiable and capable leaders did not stay longer. On the one hand, some were toppled under the directions and orders of either the West as it happened in the DRC, Ghana, Togo, Uganda, Nigeria and elsewhere else. On the other hand, others were toppled under the directions of the East as it happened in Ethiopia however the regime in Ethiopia was not that competent and good to champion the interests of the country. This shows how both camps of the cold war had nothing to do with the betterment or interests of Africa except to exploit it and get what they needed and wanted. This speaks to the fact that colonialism is inhumane and brutal regardless of who is behind it.

Arguably, some of African best managers who survived; their governments were sabotaged, especially economically. International Financial Institutions (IFIs) such as the International Monetary Fund (IMF) and the World Bank (WB) were used to sabotage their economies not to mention using neighbours who frustrated or sabotaged their visions. We have seen this on Sankara whose sin–that warranted the West to topple and eliminate him–was nothing but his attempts to debunk the myth *vis-à-vis* Africa's dependence on handouts and aid. Despondently, some best managers of state affairs–especially those who showed their love of their continent and planned to suffocate imperialism such as Patrice Lumumba, Nkrumah and others–were overthrown and others killed after they proved to be a thorn in side to imperialists and their agents. Therefore, the simple solution that imperialists and their agents used–in making sure that is exploited; and thus held back–was toppling those stubborn leaders; thereby replacing them with their venal stooges; who would protect its interests at all costs; even if it meant to mercilessly slaughter and terrorise their own people. Notably, when it comes to hunting down and killing African stable leaders, the West did more harm than the East did. Again, what must be noted is the fact that all patriotic African leaders faced big challenges of which was the situation of not knowing who is a true friend or an enemy to them. As argued above, there are those who stayed put like Mwalimu Nyerere and those who succumbed before such challenges and machinations, especially the majority that ended up being toppled and other killed as we have indicated above in the cases of the DRC and Ghana. In fact, being a stable leader during the cold war, one had to see to it that either he or she puts the two big powers of the world on a collision course or becomes neutral or unspoken if not being compromised. The living example of those who were toppled simply because they didn't like to be stooges of any camp or subscribing to the lures of one camp against another were Nkrumah (Ghana), Lumumba (DRC), Sylvanus Olympio (Togo), Milton Obote (Uganda), Thomas Sankara (Burkina Faso) and Marien Ngouabi (Republic of Congo) to mention but a few. There are those who survived just because they offered everything the West wanted by receiving orders and protection. Such are, *inter alia*, Kenyatta (Kenya) Mobutu (DRC then Zaire), Banda (Malawi), and Houphouët-Boigny (Ivory Coast). Others stayed in between. They were neither birds nor animals. They were neither hot nor cold. Such are Kaunda (Zambia), Ahidjo (Cameroon) and Khama (Botswana). Others were totally weird before the eyes of the West. Those are Ahmed Sekou Toure (Guinea) Gamal Abdel Nasser (Egypt) and Nyerere (Tanzania).

In essence, after gaining independence, many African countries were not totally independent though. They were required to keep receiving orders from the former colonial monsters for the purpose of furthering exploitation and containment. Those who refused to take orders were toppled or their governments sabotaged as it happened in Tanzania for the whole period Nyerere was in power. The West shunned him completely. Such a situation, forced Nyerere to seek assistance from the East, thus, ushering *Ujamaa* and *Kujitegemea* or socialism and self-reliance that hanged on up until the

1990s when multiparty politics were introduced in Tanzania. Fortunately for Nyerere, he had already seen it coming. For, he relinquished power five years before.

While the best leaders of Africa strove to build and develop Africa, most of their worst counterparts had only one vision, rob Africa and its people pointlessly. Along with the Best African managers, we have discussed some of the worst managers who mismanaged and ruined their countries. Wiltshire (2011) argues that "when leaders display temperance through the effective management both of their own emotions as well as the emotional aspects of their relationships with others, they show themselves to be trustworthy," (p. 3). If you put this situation between African stable and reliable leaders and the gods of the West, you will be able to see how the situation was. Again, when they do vice versa, the result is to be hated, doubted and untrusted which force them to use terror as means of survival. If anything, this where the nexus of dictatorship in many African countries lies. Suffice it to use the conclusion that Ayittey (2002) makes that:

> The real tragedy of Africa is that most of its leaders don't use their heads. Even more tragic is the fact that the Western donors who, gushing with noble humanitarianism, set out to help the African people, don't theirs either. As long as the politics of exclusion is practiced in Africa, more states will collapse and the West would be obliged to go the rescue, (p. 17).

This conclusion is still logic. And it will always remain logic until Africa is truly and completely liberated from the grip of imperialists, dictators, thieves and *bêtes noirs*.

Special tributes
To all Africans inside, and outside of Africa who bore, and still go on bearing the sufferings and indignation resulting from the predicaments of Africa and shame on all those who–in one way or the other–arrested the development and prosperity of Africa. Among forces that have kept Africa abaft, poverty and underdevelopment resulting from perpetual exploitation play a very crucial role. As

Mandela nicely put it "poverty is not an accident. Like slavery and apartheid, it is man-made and can be removed by action of human being." All Africans of all works need to fight the desperation and awkward situation Africa is in thanks to being perpetually exploited by whoever using our own brothers and sisters. This is the story of Africa's best and worst president in managing and mismanaging Africa's resources and its people, future and wellbeing.

Figure 36: The way an African (Nkwazi N.Mhango) looks at Africa

God bless Africa
God reunite Africa
And so be it
Solemnise it
Make reunification a reality
Fill this dream in every heart
Let Africa like a bud sprout
Africa is ours to construct
It is ours to protect
Africans must build Africa
Africans must reunite Africa
They only have Africa
To them Africa is everything
Therefore, they must fear nothing
United we will overcome
So be it
Do it with exceptional tenor
Do it with committed vigour

Nkwazi Mhango
University of Manitoba
Winnipeg, Canada.

References

"'Africa can learn from Zambia's unity.", says Kenneth Kaunda, and he has no regrets." *Mail and Guardian*, 27 Oct, 2014.

"'Good old days' under Bokassa?" *BBC*, 2 January, 2009.

"'Greedy' West wants to re-colonise Africa–Museveni." *News 24*, 19 March, 2014.

"African dictator Bokassa's chateau sold at auction." *BBC* (12 January, 2011.

"An interview with Sir Dawda Jawara. *The Courier N° 119*, Jan,.- Feb., 1990

"Anatomy of an Autocracy: Mobutu's 32-Year Reign." *New York Times*, 17 May, 1997.

"BAE criticised by UK MPs over Tanzania corruption." *BBC*, 19 July, 2011.

"Burundi refugees flee attacks by ruling party's 'Watchmen'." *Daily Nation*, 12 May, 2015.

"Corruption and Despair Choke Zimbabwe." *New York Times*, October 19, 2003.

"Crabs, cannibals, diamonds and the echoes of Europe's sombre African empire." *Telegram*, 23 April, 2014.

"David Cameron calls Nigeria and Afghanistan 'fantastically corrupt'." *BBC*, 10 May, 2016.

"Death of the president." *New African*, December, 1986, No: 23.

"Despot planned 'Save Britain Fund'." *BBC*, 1 January, 2005.

"Dictator Idi Amin dies." *BBC*, 16 August, 2003.

"East Africa needs Dr Magufuli's forceful presence to move ahead." *Daily Nation*, 29 February, 2016.

"Former President Sir Dawda Jawara Leaves for Nigeria. *Foroyaa Newspaper Burning Issue, Issue No. 013/2007*, 2-4 February, 2007.

"Frontline States and African liberation." *Daily News*, 17 May, 2015.

"FW de Klerk's legacy in question on anniversary of Mandela's release." *Guardian*, 11 February, 2015.

"Gabon: Newspaper suspended over report on president's wealth." *New York Times*, 12 March, 2008.

"Gabon's President Offers Some of His Wealth 'to the People'." *New York Times*, 18 August, 2015.

"Graft Hobbles Iraq's Military in Fighting ISIS." *New York Times*, 23 November, 2014.

"Guptagate: The scandal South Africa's Zuma can't shake." *BBC*, 21 January, 2015

"Idi Amin Dada (History)." *CNN*, June 8, 2011.

"Idi Amin: 'Butcher of Uganda'" *CNN*, 16 January, 2003.

"Idi Amin's legacy of terror." *BBC*, 27 July, 1999.

"Is Magufuli the man Nyerere sought?" *Citizen*, 21 February, 2016.

"Kimathi widow cherishes encounter with ex-leader." *Daily Nation*, 8 December, 2013.

"Magufuli unveils cabinet, four ministries still vacant." *Citizen*, 10 December, 2015.

"Magufuli's shock therapy for Tanzania." *DW*, 12 February, 2016.

"Mandela visit helped bring back the swag in the ideals Kimathi died for." *Daily Nation*, 14 June, 2013.

"Mugabe and allies own 40% of land seized from white farmers– inquiry." *Guardian*, 30 November, 2010.

"Mugabe Has Recolonised His People." *Guardian*, 27 June, 2008.

"Mugabe vows to seize more farms." *BBC*, 28 February, 2009.

"Mugabe's anniversary speech." *BBC*, 18 April, 2000.

"Mugabe's Wife 'Gucci Grace' Said to Spark Party Split." *Bloomberg*, 27 October, 2014.

"Mwiraria faces arrest for failure to appear in court in Anglo Leasing case." *Daily Nation*, 23 November, 2015.

"Nelson Mandela: Barack Obama leads world tributes to man who 'bent history towards justice'." *Telegraph*, 6 December, 2003.

"Nigeria's Dasuki 'arrested over $2bn arms fraud'." *BBC* (1 December, 2015.

"OAU: African Leaders Speak out Against Military Coups." *IPS*, 2 June, 1997.

"Omar Bongo Ondimba, president of Gabon, died on June 8th, aged 73." *Economist*, 18 June, 2009.

"Omar Bongo." *New York Times*, 2004.

"Papa Bongo's 40 years in power." *Guardian,* 5 May, 2008.

"Political families own half of private wealth." *Daily Nation*, 20 February, 2014.

"Radar scandal: Few are fooled by the UK's public statements." *Guardian*, 12 August, 2012.

"Remarks with Kenyan President Daniel Arap Moi following their Meeting." *US Department of State* May 26, 2001.

"Samora Machel - flawed, feared and revered." *eNCA*, 13 June, 2013.

"Scores Killed in Burundi Violence." *Wall Street Journal*, 12 December, 2015.

"Tanzania President John Magufuli helps clean streets." *BBC*, 9 December, 2015.

"Tanzania president's reforms raise hope, awe in East Africa." *New Zimbabwe*, 10 January 2016.

"The father of the nation writes his autobiography." *Point Online*, April 9, 2010.

"The president, his church and the crocodiles." *New Statesman*, 23 October, 2008.

"Today in History: Archbishop Janan Luwum is shot dead." *Daily Monitor*, 16 February, 2015.

"TRA's Sh8 tn uncollected revenues due to snags." *Citizen*, 26 April, 2016.

"Uganda Poverty Strategy Paper." *IMF country Report no.05/307*, 2005.

"Watch Julius Malema praise Robert Mugabe." *Times Live*, 03 July, 2015.

"Where Concorde once flew: the story of President Mobutu's 'African Versailles'." *Guardian*, 10 February, 2015.

"Wife of Gambian president who committed £20,000 benefit fraud granted British asylum after SAS saved her from West Africa and brought her to UK." *Daily Mail*, 5 September, 2015.

"Will Mandela ever really retire?" *BBC*, 30 July, 2004.

Abwunza, Judith M. "Nyayo: Cultural contradictions in Kenya rural capitalism." *Anthropologica* (1990): 183-203.

Achankeng, Fonkem. "The Foumban" Constitutional" Talks and Prior Intentions of Negotiating: A Historico-Theoretical Analysis of a False Negotiation and the Ramifications for Political Developments in Cameroon." *Journal of Global Initiatives: Policy, Pedagogy, Perspective* 9.2 (2015): 11.

Acquaah-Gaisie, Gerald. "Combating third world corruption." *A paper presented at the International Conference on Corruption and Governance in Nigeria.* Vol. 6. 2008.

Adar, Korwa G. "The Internal and External Contexts of Human Rights Practice in Kenya: Daniel Arap Moi's Operational Code." *African Sociological Review* (2000): 74-96.

Adar, Korwa G., and Isaac M. Munyae. "Human Rights Abuse in Kenya Under Daniel Arap Moi, 1978." *African Studies Quarterly* (2001).

Adejumo, Ade. "Neo-Negritude Tempers in Okot p'Bitek's "Song of Lawino"." *International Journal of Humanities and Cultural Studies (IJHCS)ISSN 2356-5926 1.3* (2016): 360-367.

Africa, Black. "George BN Ayittey." *Cato journal* (1987).

Aghedo, Iro, and Oarhe Osumah. "Insurgency in Nigeria: A Comparative Study of Niger Delta and Boko Haram Uprisings." *Journal of Asian and African Studies* (2014): 0021909614520726.

Ajulu, Rok. "Politicised ethnicity, competitive politics and conflict in Kenya: A historical perspective." *African Studies* (2002): 251-268.

Akindès, Francis Augustin. The roots of the military-political crises in Côte d'Ivoire. No. 128. Nordic Africa Institute, 2004.

Akindès, Francis. "Côte d'Ivoire: Socio-political Crises, 'Ivoirité' and the Course of History." *African Sociological Review* (2004): 11-28.

Ambe, Hilarious N. "The Anglophone-Francophone Marriage and Anglophone Dramatic Compositions in the Cameroon Republic." *Davis and Marsden* (2004): 71-80.

Amundsen, Inge. "Political corruption: An introduction to the issues." *CMI Working Paper* (1999).

Anderson, David M. "Briefing: Kenya's Elections 2002: The Dawning of a New Era?." *African Affairs* (2003): 331-342.

Anderson, David M. "Vigilantes, violence and the politics of public order in Kenya." *African affairs* (2002): 531-555.

Arnold, Patricia, and Theresa Hammond. "The role of accounting in ideological conflict: lessons from the South African divestment movement." *Accounting, Organizations and Society 19.2* (1994): 111-126.

Asaala, Evelyne. "Exploring transitional justice as a vehicle for social and political transformation in Kenya." *African Human Rights Law Journal 10.2* (2010): 377-406.

Awasom, Nicodemus Fru. "Negotiating Federalism: How Ready Were Cameroonian Leaders before the February 1961 United

Nations Plebiscites?." *Canadian Journal of African Studies/La Revue canadienne des études africaines 36.3* (2002): 425-459.

Awasom, Nicodemus Fru. "The reunification question in Cameroon history: was the bride an enthusiastic or a reluctant one?." *Africa Today 47.2* (2000): 90-119.

Ayittey, George BN. "The Myth of Foreign Aid." *The Free Africa Foundation* (2002).

Ayittey, George BN. "Why Africa is poor." *Sustainable Development: Promoting progress or perpetuating poverty* (2002): 57-75.

Babo, Alfred. "The Crisis of Public Policies in Côte d'Ivoire: Land Law and the Nationality Trap in Tabou's Rural Communities." *Africa* (2013): 100-119.

Bachelard, Jérôme Y. "The Anglo-Leasing corruption scandal in Kenya: the politics of international and domestic pressures and counter-pressures." *Review of African Political Economy* (2010): 187-200.

Badmus, Isiaka Alani. "Even the Stones are Burning. Explaining the Ethnic Dimensions of the Civil War in Côte d'Ivoire." *J Soc Sci* (2009): 45-57.

Baker, Kathleen. "Images of West Africa, Past and Present." *The Changing Geography of Africa and the Middle East* (2002): 62.

Bartlett, Bruce R. "Capitalism in Africa: a survey." *The Journal of Developing Areas* (1990): 327-350.

Basedau, Matthias, and Andreas Mehler. Resource Politics in Sub-Saharan Africa. *Vol. 14. GIGA-Hamburg*, 2005.

Bechtolsheimer, Götz. Breakfast with Mobutu: Congo, the United States and the Cold War, 1964-1981. *Diss. The London School of Economics and Political Science*, 2012.

Beck, Linda J. "Reining in the marabouts? Democratization and local governance in Senegal." *African Affairs* (2001): 601-621.

Berry, LaVerie, *et al.* "Annotated Bibliography: Open Sources on Africa, April 1983." *Library of Congress Washington DC Federal Research Div*, 1983.

Besong, bate. "The Bernard Gonlon Tevolution: If Gold Should Rust, What Will Iron Do?." (2005).

Bierwirth, Chris. "The Lebanese Communities of Côte d'Ivoire." *African Affairs* (1999): 79-99.

Blay-Amihere, Kabral. "Côte D'Ivoire—an old man's party is nearly over." *Index on Censorship* (1990): 26-27.

Boschini, Anne D., Jan Peterson, and Jesper Roine. "Resource Curse or Not: A Question of Appropriability."*The Scandinavian Journal of Economics* (2007): 593-617.

Bridge, Lord. *"Opinion: Too high a price."* (1987): 2-40.

Brough, Wayne T., and Mwangi S. Kimenyi. "On the inefficient extraction of rents by dictators." *Public Choice* (1986): 37-48.

Brown-Peterside, Gally. "Why Balewa Died." *Africa Report 11.3* (1966): 15.

Bukurura, Sufian Hemed. "Between liberation struggle and constitutionalism." *Re-examining Liberation in Namibia* (2003): 34.

Burgess, Robin, *et al.* "Our turn to eat: The political economy of roads in Kenya." Manuscript, London, UK: London School of Economics and Political Science 2010.

Burrowes, Robert J. *The strategy of nonviolent defense: A Gandhian approach.* SUNY Press, 1996.

Bustin, Edouard. "Remembrance of sins past: unravelling the murder of Patrice Lumumba." *Review of African Political Economy* (2002): 537-560.

Byrne, Sean, and Cynthia L. Irvin. *"Reconcilable Differences. Turning Points in Ethnopolitical Conflict."* The Global Review of Ethnopolitics, Kumarian Press, 2000.

Campion, Edmund J. "Pierre Teilhard de Chardin's Importance in the Development of Léopold Sédar Senghor's Concept of the *"Civilisation de l'universel."* (2010).

Carvalho, Anabela. "Ideological cultures and media discourses on scientific knowledge: re-reading news on climate change." *Public understanding of science* (2007): 223-243.

Chege, Michael. "Kenya: back from the brink?." *Journal of Democracy* (2008): 125-139.

Chimuka, Tarisayi A. "Is 'Independence' for Africa: A Leap Forward Mirage?." *Idea* (2012): 42-57.

Chirere, Memory. "Armando Guebuza among the Poets." (2005).

Chiumbu, Sarah. "Redefining the national agenda—media and identity: challenges of building a new Zimbabwe." *Media, Public Discourse and Political Contestation in Zimbabwe, Elanders Infologistics Vast, Goteborg* (2004): 29-35.

Christopher, Anthony J. "'Divide and Rule': The Impress of British Separation Policies." *Area* (1988): 233-240.

Clague, Christopher, *et al.* "Contract-intensive money: contract enforcement, property rights, and economic performance." *Journal of Economic Growth* (1999): 185-211.

Clemens, Michael, and Todd Moss. "Costs and causes of Zimbabwe's crisis." *Center for Global Development 20* (2005).

CNN, December 6, 2013.

Cockcroft, Laurence. "Global corruption: An untamed hydra." *World Policy Journal 27.1* (2010): 21-28.

Cohen, Robin. "Class in Africa: analytical problems and perspectives." *Socialist Register* (1972).

Cohn, Stuart R. "Teaching in a Developing Country: Mistakes Made and Lessons Learned in Uganda." *Journal of Legal Education* (1998): 101-109.

Cole, Jonathan J. "The Congo question: Conflicting visions of independence." *Emporia State Research Studies* (2006): 26-37.

Cook, Amelia, and Jeremy Sarkin. Is Botswana the Miracle of Africa-Democracy, the Rule of Law, and Human Rights versus Economic Development. *Transnat'l L. & Contemp. Probs.* (2010): 453.

Cooksey, Brian, and Tim Kelsall. "The political economy of the investment climate in Tanzania." *Africa Power and Politics Programme Background Paper* 1 (2011).

Curtis, Tom. "The origin of AIDS." *Rolling Stone* (1992): 54-61.

Daddieh, Cyril K. "Elections and ethnic violence in Côte d'Ivoire: The unfinished business of succession and democratic transition." *African Issues* (2001): 14-19.

Daly, Sara, John Parachini, and William Rosenau. *Aum Shinrikyo, Al Qaeda, and the Kinshasa Reactor: Implications of Three Case Studies for Combating Nuclear Terrorism*. Rand Corp Santa Monica CA, 2005.

Darch, Colin, and David Hedges. "Samora Machel: the Beira speech." *African Yearbook of Rhetoric: Great speeches of Africa's liberation 2.3* (2011): 67-83.

Darch, Colin, and David Hedges. "Political rhetoric in the transition to Mozambican independence: Samora Machel in Beira, June 1975." *Kronos* (2013): 10-19.

335

De Gaay-Fortman, Bas. "Elections and civil strife: some implications for international election observation." Election Observation and Democratization in Africa. Palgrave Macmillan UK, 2000. 76-95.

De Klerk, F. W. "On leadership: words from leaders." *Verbum et Ecclesia* (2002): p-608.

De Rezende, Isabelle M. Visuality and Colonialism in the Congo: From the 'Arab War'to Patrice Lumumba, 1880s to 1961. *Diss. University of the Western Cape*, 2012.

De Witte, Ludo, and Ann Wright. *The assassination of Lumumba*. Verso, 2002.

Dearborn, Fitzroy. "Encyclopedia of African History." *Studies* (1986).

Deininger, Klaus, and Lyn Squire. "A new data set measuring income inequality." *The World Bank Economic Review* (1996): 565-591.

Deininger, Klaus, Hans Hoogeveen, and Bill H. Kinsey. "Economic Benefits and Costs of Land Redistribution in Zimbabwe in the early 1980s." *World Development* (2004): 1697-1709.

Dobris, Joel C. "Arguments in Favor of Fiduciary Divestment of South African Securities." *Neb. L. Rev. 65* (1986): 209.

Durrani, Shiraz. "Debating and documenting Africa: a conversation." *Information, society and justice Journal* (2008): 209-220.

Easterly, William. "Can Institutions Resolve Ethnic Conflict?*" *Economic Development and Cultural Change 49.4* (2001): 687-706.

Eckert, Andreas. "An African State and Society in the 1990s: Cameroon's political crossroads." *African Affairs* (1999): 289-290.

Eko, Lyombe. "It's a Political Jungle Out There How Four African Newspaper Cartoons Dehumanized and Deterritorialized' African Political Leaders in the Post-Cold War Era." *International Communication Gazette* (2007): 219-238.

Emizet, Kisangani NF. "Explaining the rise and fall of military regimes: Civil-military relations in the Congo." *Armed Forces & Society* (2000): 203-227.

Englert, Birgit. "Ambiguous relationships: youth, popular music and politics in contemporary Tanzania." *Wiener Zeitschrift fur kritische Afrikastudien 14.8* (2008): 71-96.

Erasmus, Gerhard. The Accord of Nkomati: Context and Content. *South African Institute of International Affairs*, 1984.

336

Etekpe, Ambily, and Philips O. Okolo. "Comparative Analysis of Post-Independence Social Formations in Ghana and Tanzania: Lessons for Africa in the 21st Century." Available at SSRN 1723204 (2010).

Fatton, Robert. "Clientelism and patronage in Senegal." *African Studies Review* (1986): 61-78.

Foeken, D., and T. Dietz. "Of Ethnicity, Manipulation and Observation: *the 1992 and 1997 Elections in Kenya.*" (2000).

Foucault, Michel. *The Foucault reader.* Pantheon, 1984.

Fouéré, Marie-Aude. "Julius Nyerere, ujamaa, and political morality in contemporary Tanzania." *African Studies Review 57.01* (2014): 1-24.

Fukuyama, Francis. "The imperative of state-building." *Journal of democracy* (2004): 17-31.

für Entwicklungsforschung, Zentrum. "*Volta basin water balance.*" (2000).

Gade, Christian BN. "The historical development of the written discourses on Ubuntu." *South African Journal of Philosophy* (2011): 303-329.

Gathii, James Thuo. "Corruption and donor reforms: expanding the promises and possibilities of the rule of law as an anti-corruption strategy in Kenya." *Connecticut Journal of International Law* (1999).

Gathogo, Julius. "*The History and Nature of Gitari's Leadership Prowess.*"

Gerard, Emmanuel, and Bruce Kuklick. *Death in the Congo: Murdering Patrice Lumumba.* Harvard University Press, 2015.

Gerard-Libois, Jules. "*The New Class and Rebellion in the Congo.*" Socialist Register (1966).

Ghura, Dhaneshwar, and Benoît Mercereau. Political Instability and Growth: *The Central African Republic. Vol. 4. International Monetary Fund*, 2004.

Gibson, James L. "Overcoming apartheid: can truth reconcile a divided nation?." *Politikon* (2004): 129-155.

Gillett, Simon. "The survival of chieftaincy in Botswana." *African Affairs 72.287* (1973): 179-185.

Girling, Fran. "Growing Young Gracefully: making development work for Tanzania's youth."

337

Glad, Betty, and Robert Blanton. "FW de Klerk and Nelson Mandela: A study in cooperative transformational leadership." *Presidential Studies Quarterly* (1997): 565-590.

Good, Kenneth. Diamonds, dispossession & democracy in Botswana. Jacana Media, 2008.

Gordon, Gregory S. "An African Marshall Plan: Changing US Policy to Promote the Rule of Law and Prevent Mass Atrocity in the Democratic Republic of the Congo." *Available at SSRN 1441541* (2009).

Grant, Michael, David Potter, and Chris Scarre. "Balewa, Abubakar Tafawa (1912–1966)." Famous Assassinations in World History: *An Encyclopedia* (2014): 30.

Gray, Clive, and Malcolm McPherson. "The Leadership Factor in African Policy Reform and Growth*." *Economic Development and Cultural Change* (2001): 707-740.

Graybill, Lyn S. "Pursuit of truth and reconciliation in South Africa." *Africa Today* (1998): 103-133.

Green, Melanie C., Timothy C. Brock, and Geoff F. Kaufman. "Understanding media enjoyment: The role of transportation into narrative worlds." *Communication Theory* (2004): 311-327.

Grice, Carter. *"Happy are those who sing and Dance:" Mobutu, Franco, and the struggle for Zairian Identity. Diss. Western Carolina University*, 2011.

Grossman, Blake R., and William F. Sharpe. "Financial implications of South African divestment." *Financial Analysts Journal 42.4* (1986): 15-29.

Guenther, Bruce. "The Asian drivers and the resource curse in Sub-Saharan Africa: the potential impacts of rising commodity prices for conflict and governance in the DRC." *The European Journal of Development Research* (2008): 347-363.

Hagberg, Sten, and Alexis B. Tengan. "Bonds and boundaries in northern Ghana and southern Burkina Faso." (2000).

Harsch, Ernest. *Thomas Sankara: An African Revolutionary*. Ohio University Press, 2014.

Hayward, Fred M., and Ahmed R. Dumbuya. "Political legitimacy, political symbols, and national leadership in West Africa." *The Journal of Modern African Studies* (1983): 645-671.

Hazlewood, Arthur. "The end of the East African Community: what are the lessons for regional integration schemes?." *JCMS: Journal of Common Market Studies* (1979): 40-58.

Henderson, Robert d'A. "Two aspects of land settlement policy in Mozambique, 1900-1961." Collected Seminar Papers. Institute of Commonwealth Studies. Vol. 20. *Institute of Commonwealth Studies*, 1976.

Henderson, Willie. "Independent Botswana: a reappraisal of foreign policy options." *African Affairs* (1974): 37-49.

Henderson, Willie. "Seretse Khama: A personal appreciation." *African Affairs* (1990): 27-56.

Hill, Garry Victor. "Akhenaten and Nefertiti: The Controversy and the Evidence."

Holmquist, Frank, and Michael Ford. "Kenyan politics: toward a second transition?." *Africa Today* (1998): 227-258.

Hooper, Edward. "Experimental oral polio vaccines and acquired immune deficiency syndrome." *Philosophical Transactions of the Royal Society B: Biological Sciences* (2001): 803-814.

http://mavulture.com/

http://www.ugandaforum.org/Africa/Idi%20Amin%20History/Idi%20Amin%204.html

http://ziomania.com/lumumba/The%20Last%20Letter%20of%20Patrice%20Lumumba.htm accessed on January 3, 2016.

https://wikileaks.org/wiki/The_looting_of_Kenya_under_President_Moi

Ibhawoh, Bonny, and J. I. Dibua. "Deconstructing Ujamaa: The legacy of Julius Nyerere in the quest for social and economic development in Africa." *African Journal of Political Science 8.1* (2003): 59-83.

Ikome, Francis Nguendi. "Personalisation of power." *Political economy of regionalisation in Central Africa* (2008): 15.

Isaksson, Ann-Sofie. "Neighbours and family first: donors should consider the effects of political favouritism in Africa." (2015).

Ishemo, Shubi L. "'A symbol that cannot be substituted': *The role of Mwalimu JK Nyerere in the liberation of Southern Africa, 1955–1990.*" (2000): 81-94.

Jaffré, Bruno. "*Assassination of Thomas Sankara: evidence of a documentary by RAI 3 involve France, CIA and Blaise Compaoré.*" (2009).

Jaffré, Bruno. "Features on Thomas Sankara's birthday." (2011).

Jaffré, Bruno. "Matyrdom of Thomas Sankara." (2010).

Jaffré, Bruno. "*The legacies of Thomas Sankara: a revolutionary experience in retrospect.*" (2014).

Jallow, Baba G., *et al.* "Leadership in Postcolonial Africa: *An Introduction.*" 2014.

Jawara, Dawda Kairaba. "The Commonwealth and human rights." *The Round Table* (1992): 37-42.

Johnson III, Boyd M. "Executive Order 12,333: The Permissibility of an American Assassination of a Foreign Leader." *Cornell Int'l LJ* (1992): 401.

Kagwanja, Peter Mwangi. "Clash of generations? Youth identity, violence and the politics of transition in Kenya, 997–2002." *Vanguards or vandals: Youth, politics and conflict in Africa* (2005): 83-108.

Kamusoko, C., and M. Aniya. "Land use/cover change and landscape fragmentation analysis in the Bindura District, Zimbabwe." *Land degradation & development* (2007): 221-233.

Kapp, Clare. "Operation "Restore Order" wreaks havoc in Zimbabwe." *The Lancet* (2005): 1151-1152.

Kaunda, Kenneth D. "The Struggle in South Africa."

Kegoro, George. "Money laundering patterns in Kenya." *Profiling Money Laundering in Eastern and Southern Africa, ISS Monograph* (2003): 135-165.

Kenyatta, Jomo, and Paul Halsall. "The Kenya Africa Union is Not the Mau Mau, 1952." (1998).

Kenyatta, Jomo. *Facing Mount Kenya: the traditional life of the Gikuyu. Vol. 219*. East African Educational Publishers, 2015.

Khama, Seretse. "African-American Relations in the 1970's: Prospects and Problems." *Africa Today* (1971): 25-34.

Khama, Seretse. "*Botswana-a developing democracy in southern Africa.*" (1970).

Kideghesho, Jafari R. "Elephant poaching crisis in Tanzania: A need to reverse the trend and the way forward." *Trop Conserv Science 9.1* (2016): 377-396.

Kirk-Greene, Anthony Hamilton Millard. "*The genesis of the Nigerian civil war and the theory of fear.*" (1975).

Kirwin, Matthew. "The Security Dilemma and Conflict in Côte d'Ivoire." *Nordic Journal of African Studies* (2006): 42-52.

Klein, Olivier, and Laurent Licata. "When group representations serve social change: The speeches of Patrice Lumumba during the Congolese decolonization." *British Journal of Social Psychology* (2003): 571-594.

Klerk, B. J. "Nelson Mandela and Desmond Tutu: Living Icons of Reconciliation." *The Ecumenical Review* (2003): 322-334.

Klopp, Jacqueline M. "Pilfering the public: the problem of land grabbing in contemporary Kenya." *Africa Today* (2000): 7-26.

Kofoed, Jacob Groes, and Martin Ingvarsson. "FW De Klerk."

Langer, Nicholas. "The American Empire in the Congo: The Assassination of Patrice Lumumba." *The Undergraduate Historical Journal at UC Merced* (2014).

Larcom, Shaun, Mare Sarr, and Tim Willems. "Dictators Walking the Mogadishu Line: How Men Become Monsters and Monsters Become Men." Available at SSRN 2434323 (2014).

Lawal, Gbenga. "Corruption and development in Africa: challenges for political and economic change." *Humanity and social sciences Journal* (2007): 1-7.

Lawson, Autumn Anne. Kwame Nkrumah's quest for Pan Africanism: from independence leader to deposed despot. *Diss. Wichita State University*, 2010.

Leão, Ana. "*A luta continua: children and youth in Mozambique's struggles.*" Angela McIntyre. (2005). Invisible Stakeholders: Children and War in Africa. *Institute for Security Studies. Pretoria. South Africa* (2005): 40-41.

Lebert, Tom. "An introduction to land and agrarian reform in Zimbabwe." Promised Land: *Competing visions for agrarian reform* (2003): 40-56.

Lederach, John Paul. *Preparing for peace: Conflict transformation across cultures.* Syracuse University Press, 1995.

Legault, Ghislain L. "Africa's newest friends." *China Rights Forum.* Vol. 1. 2008.

Leon, Tony. "On the contrary: leading the opposition in a democratic South Africa." *Jonathan Ball, Johannesburg* (2008).

Les, Leçons de Leadership pour, and Dirigeants Africains et du Monde. "*Hommages a Nelson Mandela.*"

Libya: First pictures of Gaddafi's bunker *BBC*, 25 August, 2011.

Lieberfeld, Daniel. "Nelson Mandela: Partisan and Peacemaker." *Negotiation Journal* (2003): 229-250.

Lonsdale, John. "Mau Maus of the Mind: Making Mau Mau and Remaking Kenya." *The Journal of African History* (1990): 393-421.

Lumumba, P. L. O. "The Leadership Kenyans Deserve." *Challenging the Rulers* (2011): 38.

Lumumba, Patrice Émery. "Patrice Émery Lumumba." *Pan-African History* (2003): 113.

Macartney, W. A. J. "Botswana goes to the Polls." *Africa Report* (1969): 28.

MacGinty, Roger, and Andrew Williams. *Conflict and development.* Routledge, 2009.

Machel, Mrs Graca, President FW De Klerk, and Mrs De Klerk. *"State of the Nation Address."* (2003).

Machel, Samora Moises. "Apartheid Must Be Eradicated." *The Black Scholar* (1987): 25-33.

Magaloni, Beatriz. "Elections under autocracy and the strategic game of fraud." Revised version of a paper presented at the 2005 Annual Meeting of the American Political Science Association, Washington, DC. 2007.

Makinda, Samuel M. "Kenya: out of the straitjacket, slowly." *The World Today* (1992): 188-192.

Mamdani, Mahmood. "Lessons of Zimbabwe: Mugabe in context." *London Review of Books* (2009).

Mandela, Nelson. *Notes to the future: Words of wisdom.* Simon and Schuster, 2012.

Mapuva, Jephias. "Governments of national unity (GNUs) and the preponderance of the incumbency: case of Kenya and Zimbabwe." *Int J Polit Sci Dev 1.3* (2013): 105-116.

Marchal, Roland. "France and Africa: the emergence of essential reforms?." *International Affairs* (1998): 355-372.

Mawere, Munyaradzi. "Coping with poverty in Rural Communities of Third World Africa: *The case of Mukonoweshuro Cooperative gardening in Gutu*, Zimbabwe." 2013.

Mazrui, Ali A. "Boxer Muhammad Ali and soldier Idi Amin as international political symbols: the bioeconomics of sport and war." *Comparative Studies in Society and History* (1977): 189-215.

Mazrui, Ali A. "The Sacred and the Secular in East African Politics (Sacré et profane dans la politique en Afrique orientale)." *Cahiers d'études africaines* (1973): 664-681.

Mazrui, Ali A. "Towards Re-Africanizing African Universities: Who Killed Intellectualism in the Post Colonial Era?." Alternatives: *Turkish Journal of International Relations* (2003): 135-163.

Mbaku, John Mukum. "Bureaucratic Corruption in Africa: The Futility of Cleanups." *Cato J.* (1996): 99.

Mbaku, John Mukum. "Decolonization, Reunification, and Federation in Cameroon." *The Leadership Challenge in Africa: Cameroon under Paul Biya* (2004): 30.

Mbigi, Lovemore, and Jenny Maree. *Ubuntu, the spirit of African transformation management. Knowledge Resources, 1995.*

Médard, Claire. "Indigenous' land claims in Kenya: A case-study of Chebyuk, Mount Elgon district." *Institut de recherche pour le développement (IRD), France. & Kenyatta University, Nairobi, Kenya* (2010).

Médard, Claire. "Indigenous' land claims in Kenya: A case-study of Chebyuk, Mount Elgon district." Institut de recherche pour le développement (IRD), France. & Kenyatta University, Nairobi, Kenya (2010).

Melady, Thomas, and Margaret Badum Melady. "*Idi Amin Dada: Hitler in Africa.*" (1977).

Meneses, Maria Paula. "S is for Samora: a lexical biography of Samora Machel and the Mozambican dream by Sarah Lefanu (review)." Africa: *The Journal of the International African Institute* (2013): 514-516.

Metz, Steven. "In lieu of orthodoxy: the socialist theories of Nkrumah and Nyerere." *The Journal of Modern African Studies* (1982): 377-392.

Meyns, Peter. "Liberation ideology and national development strategy in Mozambique." *Review of African Political Economy* (1981): 42-64.

Mhango, Nkwazi Nkuzi. *Africa Reunite or Perish.* Langaa, 2015.

Michel, Thierry. *Mobutu, roi du Zaïre.* Cinélibre, 1999.

Miguel, Edward. "Tribe or nation? Nation building and public goods in Kenya versus Tanzania." *World Politics* (2004): 328-362.

Mitchell, Thomas W. "The land crisis in Zimbabwe: Getting beyond the myopic focus upon black & white." (2014).

Mlambo, Alois S. "Becoming Zimbabwe or becoming Zimbabwean: Identity, nationalism and state-building." *Africa Spectrum 48.1* (2013): 49-70.

Mnthali, Felix. "Continuity and change in Conrad and Ngugi." *Kunapipi* (2014): 12.

Moore, David. *Raoul Peck's Lumumba: history or hagiography?*. na, 2007.

Muchie, Mammo, and Tutieri. "Africa's Elites Ways of Commodifying Politics to Valorise Economic Rent." *Transformacje* (2011).

Munslow, Barry. "Mozambique and the death of Machel." *Third World Quarterly* (1988): 23-36.

Murithi, Tim. "The African Union and the International Criminal Court: An Embattled Relationship?." *Institute for Justice and Reconciliation* (2013).

Mutonga, Sitwala. "Democratisation in the SADC Region: from one Party State to Multi-Party democracy in Zambia and Lessons for Swaziland." *Issues in the Economy and Politics of Swaziland Since 1968* (2003): 89.

Mutz, Diana C. "Facilitating communication across lines of political difference: The role of mass media." *American Political Science Association*. Vol. 95. No. 01. Cambridge University Press, 2001.

Mzumara, Macleans. *"Botswana a mono-diamond economy or not?."* (2012).

Mzumara, Macleans. "Mozambique from Marxist-Leninist to capitalism: has the country performed well economically?." (2011).

Ndikumana, Léonce, and James Boyce. "Congo's odious debt: external borrowing and capital flight in Zaire." *Development and Change* (1998): 195-217.

Ndikumana, Léonce, and Kisangani Emizet. "The economics of civil war: *The case of the Democratic Republic of Congo.*" (2003).

Ndikumana, Léonce, *et al.* "Enhancing Competitiveness in Four African Economies: The Case of Botswana, Mauritius, Namibia, and Tunisia." Forum économique mondial, Banque mondiale et Banque africaine de développement, Africa Competitiveness Report. 2009.

Nfi, Joseph Lon. "The Powerlessness of Cameroon's Reunification Monuments." (2013).

Nixon, Richard. "Non-Aligned Movement." *Cold War: The Essential Reference Guide* (2012): 153.

Njaya, T., and N. Mazuru. "Land Reform Process and Property Rights in Zimbabwe: Constraints and Future Prospects." *Journal of sustainable Development in Africa 12.4* (2010): 164-185.

Njie, Gibou, and Su layman Fie. "The Gambia." Ministries of Education in Small States: *Case Studies* (1989): 35.

Nkosi, Lethiwe. "Kenneth Kaunda: the dignity of labour." *African Yearbook of Rhetoric: Great speeches of Africa's liberation* (2011): 61-66.

Nkrumah, Kwame, Roberta Arrigoni, and Giorgio Napolitano. *Africa must unite*. London: Heinemann, 1963.

Nkrumah, Kwame. "*I Speak of Freedom1.*" (1961).

Nkrumah, Kwame. "Neo—colonialism: The Last Stage of Imperialism. 1965." *New York: International* (1966).

Norval, Aletta J. "Memory, identity and the (im) possibility of reconciliation: The work of the Truth and Reconciliation Commission in South Africa." *Constellations* (1998): 250-265.

Ntsebeza, Lungisile, and Ruth Hall. *The land question in South Africa: The challenge of transformation and redistribution*. HSRC press, 2007.

Nyamndi, George D. "Absented Presences in Recent Anglophone-Cameroon Poetry." *English Academy Review* (2009): 3-14.

Nyamnjoh, Francis B., and Jude Fokwang. "Entertaining repression: music and politics in postcolonial Cameroon." *African affairs 104.415* (2005): 251-274.

Nyanchama, Matunda. "Africa in the 21st Century: *The Future Economic Outlook.*" (2006).

Nyerere, Julius K. "Education for self-reliance." *The Ecumenical Review* (1967): 382-403.

Nyerere, Julius K. "Ujamma: the basis of African socialism." *The Journal of Pan-African Studies 1* (1987): 4-11.

Nyerere, Julius K. *The second scramble*. Tanganyika Standard, 1962.

Nyerere, Julius K. *Ujamaa*. Oxford University Press, 1968.

Nyerere, Julius. "Education in Tanzania." *Harvard Educational Review* (1985): 45-53.

Obwona, Marios B. "Determinants of FDI and their impact on economic growth in Uganda." *African Development Review* (2001): 46-81.

Oculi, Okello. "The Role of Economic Aspiration in Elections in Kenya." *Africa Development* (2011): 13-28.

Odari, Catherine J. A Blessing or Curse?: The Mboya-Kennedy Students' Airlift and its Implications. *Diss. Miami University*, 2011.

Odinkalu, Chidi Anslem. "Concerning Kenya: The current AU position on unconstitutional changes in government."*African Governance Monitoring and Advocacy Project* (2008): 1.

Ojuando, Margaret Achieng. "The Highridge Teachers' College experience with developing an institutional policy on HIV/AIDS." *Crafting institutional responses to HIV/AIDS: Guidelines and resources to tertiary institutions in Sub Saharan Africa* (2004): 63-73.

Oketch, Moses, and Caine Rolleston. "Policies on free primary and secondary education in East Africa: Retrospect and prospect." *Review of Research in Education* (2007): 131-158.

Olakunle, Akinwande Peter. "Cross-cultural Themes and the Challenges of Multilingualism and Translation, a Case Study of Leopold Sedar Senghor's *"Dialogue of Cultures."*

Oloka-Onyango, Joe. "Beyond the Rhetoric: Reinvigorating the Struggle for Economic and Social Rights in Africa." *Cal. W. Int'l LJ* (1995): 1.

Otenyo, Eric E. "New terrorism: Toward an explanation of cases in Kenya." *African Security Studies* (2004): 75-84.

Otley, David. "Performance management: a framework for management control systems research." *Management accounting research* (1999): 363-382.

Padelford, Norman J. "The Organization of African Unity." *International Organization 18.03* (1964): 521-542.

Parenti, Christian. "Chocolate's bittersweet economy Seven years after the industry agreed to abolish child labor, little progress has been made." *Fortune Magazine* 15 (2008).

Passas, Nikos. "Corruption in the procurement process/outsourcing government functions: Issues, case studies, implications." *Report to Institute for Fraud Prevention. Boston: Northeastern University* (2007).

Pereira, Luiz Carlos Bresser. "Administrative reform (through administrative reform!)."

Pondi, Jean-Emmanuel. "Cameroon and the Commonwealth of Nations." *The Round Table* (1997): 563-570.

Popkewitz, Thomas S. "The production of reason and power: Curriculum history and intellectual traditions." *Journal of Curriculum Studies* (1997): 131-164.

Post, Ken WJ. "Is there a case for Biafra?." *International Affairs (Royal Institute of International Affairs* 1944-) (1968): 26-39.

Quinn, Joanna R. "Constraints: the un-doing of the Ugandan Truth Commission." *Human Rights Quarterly* (2004): 401-427.

Qureshi, Sajda. "Lessons from the Age of Nelson Mandela: Information and Communication Technology in the Quest for Equality, Freedom and Justice." *Information Technology for Development* (2014): 1-5.

Raikes, Philip Lawrence. "Ujamaa and rural socialism." *Review of African Political Economy* (1975): 33-52.

Rajani, Rakesh. *"Is primary education heading in the right direction? Thinking with Nyerere." 6th UDSM Convocation Symposium.* University of Dar Es Salaam. 2003.

Ray, Ellen. "US Military and corporate recolonization of Congo." *Covert Action Quarterly* (2000): 4-15.

Ray, Ellen. "US Military and corporate recolonization of Congo." *Covert Action Quarterly* (2000): 4-15.

Reis, Guilherme Simões. *"The Political-Ideological Path of Frelimo in Mozambique, from 1962 to 2012."*

Reisman, W. Michael. "Humanitarian Intervention and Fledgling Democracies." *Fordham Int'l LJ* (1994): 794.

Reno, William SK. "Dark Age: The Political Odyssey of Emperor Bokassa." *Africa Today* (1998): 501.

Robinson, Tyler, and Jeffrey Boutwell. "South Africa's arms industry: A new era of democratic accountability?." *Armed Forces & Society* (1996): 599-618.

Romaldi, Christa. *"A Quiet Revolution? Youth Perception of State and Church Ideology in Zaire." (2010)*.

Rosenberg, Gerald N. *The hollow hope: Can courts bring about social change?*. University of Chicago Press, 2008.

Ross, Michael L. "What do we know about natural resources and civil war?." *Journal of peace research* (2004): 337-356.

Rotberg, Robert I. "Africa's mess, Mugabe's mayhem." *Foreign Affairs New York-* 79.5 (2000): 47-61.

Sadomba, Wilbert. "War veterans in Zimbabwe's land occupations: complexities of a liberation movement in an African post-colonial settler society." (2008).

Saine, Abdoulaye SM. "The 1996/1997 presidential and national assembly elections in The Gambia." *Electoral Studies* (1997): 554-559.

Santilli, Kathy. "Kikuyu Women in the Mau Mau Revolt: A Closer Look." *Ufahamu: A Journal of African Studies* (1977).

Saungweme, Sekai. "A Critical Look at the Charter on Democracy, Elections and Governance in Africa." *AfriMap paper*, May. http://www. afrimap.org/english/images/paper/ACDEG_Saungweme. Pdf (last accessed 16 December 2011).

Senghor, Léopold Sédar. "Negritude." *Indian Literature* (1974): 269-273.

Senghor, Léopold Sédar. "West Africa in Evolution." *Foreign Affairs* (1961): 240-246.

Shaw, William H. "'They Stole Our Land': debating the expropriation of white farms in Zimbabwe." *The Journal of Modern African Studies* (2003): 75-89.

Shepherd, Anne. "A wing and a prayer." *Africa Report* (1994): 40.

Shillington, Kevin. *History of Africa*. Palgrave Macmillan, 2012.

Skinner, Elliott P. "Sankara and the burkinabe revolution: Charisma and power, local and external dimensions." *The Journal of Modern African Studies* (1988): 437-455.

Skinner, Elliott P. "Sankara and the burkinabe revolution: Charisma and power, local and external dimensions." *The Journal of Modern African Studies* (1988): 437-455.

Sklar, Richard L. "Democracy in Africa." African Studies Review 26.3/4 (1983): 11-24.

Skurnik, Walter AE. "Leopold Sedar Senghor and African Socialism." *The Journal of Modern African Studies* (1965): 349-369.

Southall, Roger. "The Ndungu report: land & graft in Kenya." *Review of African Political Economy 32.103* (2005): 142-151.

Stark, Frank M. "Federalism in Cameroon: the shadow and the reality." *Canadian Journal of African Studies* (1976): 423-442.

Stone, J. H. "MK Gandhi: some experiments with truth." *Journal of Southern African Studies 16.4* (1990): 721-740.

Swanson, Dalene M. "Ubuntu: An African contribution to (re) search for/with a 'humble togetherness'." *Journal of Contemporary Issues in Education* (2008).

Taylor, Ian. *"The developmental state in Africa: the case of Botswana."* The Potentiality of Developmental States' in Africa. Dakar: *CODESRIA* (2005).

The Los Angeles Times, 3 November, 1991.

The New York Times, 2 November, 1991.

The New York Times, 21 December, 2001.

The New York Times, 5 October, 1987.

The *New York Times*, November 16, 1981,

Thompson, Paul. "Foundation and Empire: A critique of Hardt and Negri." *Capital & Class 29.2* (2005): 73-98.

Tiffen, Rodney. *"Domesticating Mandela."*

Tillmar, Malin. "Swedish tribalism and Tanzanian entrepreneurship: preconditions for trust formation." *Entrepreneurship and Regional Development* (2006): 91-107.

Tumfweko *Zambia News and Entertainment*, 27 December, 2013

Tutu, Desmond M. "Reflections on moral accountability." *International Journal of Transitional Justice* (2007): 6-7.

Van Acker, Frank. *Of clubs and conflict: the dissolvant power of social capital in Kivu (DR Congo).* UFSIA-University of Antwerp, 2000.

Van der Straeten, Jonas. "Legacies of a Past Modernism Discourses of Development and the Shaping of Centralized Electricity Infastructures in Late-and Postcolonial Tanzania." (2015): 273-278.

Vencovsk, Daniel. *"Presidential term limits in Africa."* (2007).

Venter, Albert, and Michele Olivier. "Human rights in Africa: Nyerere and Kaunda." *International Journal on World Peace* (1993): 21-33.

Villalón, Leonardo Alfonso. "Generational changes, political stagnation, and the evolving dynamics of religion and politics in Senegal." *Africa today* (1999): 129-147.

VO, NOT. *"David C. Preiss (Student Essay)"* (1973).

Wa Mutonya, Maina. "The Beat Goes On: Performing Postcolonial Disillusionment in Kenya." *Humania del Sur* (2010): 47-66.

Wanyeki, L. Muthoni. "Lessons from Kenya: Women and the post-election violence." *Standpoint, Feminist Africa* (2010).

Was Columbus, Nomzamo Winifred Zanyiwe Madikizela. *"See also African National Congress; Apartheid; Colonialism; Mandela, Winnie."*

Watia nia msimgeuze Nyerere sera." Dira ya Mtanzania, July 13th, 2015.

White, Bob W. "The Political Undead: Is It Possible to Mourn for Mobutu's Zaire?." *African Studies Review* (2005): 65-85.

White, Bob W. *Rumba Rules: the politics of dance music in Mobutu's Zaire.* Duke University Press, 2008.

Wilkins, Michael. "The death of Thomas Sankara and the rectification of the people's revolution in Burkina Faso." *African Affairs* (1989): 375-388.

Wiltshire, Eileen DesAutels. *"2011 Virtual Conference on Moral Leadership: The Classic Virtues in Organizational Leadership Temperance and Organizational Leadership: Control Yourself before Trying to Control Others."* (2011).

Wolf, Thomas P. "Immunity or accountability? Daniel Toroitich arap Moi: Kenya's first retired president." Legacies of Power. *Leadership Change and Former Presidents in African Politics* (2006): 197-232.

Woods, Dwayne. "State action and class interests in the Ivory Coast." *African Studies Review* (1988): 93-116.

Woronoff, Jon. *West African Wager: Houphouet Versus Nkrumah.* Metuchen, NJ: Scarecrow Press, 1972.

Wrong, Michela. *It's our turn to eat: the story of a Kenyan whistleblower.* London: Fourth Estate, 2009.

www.brainyquote.com/quotes/authors/i/idi_amin.html#fHRzctc4 BFlePXeO.99 accessed on 7 January, 2016.

Zürcher, Christoph, *et al. Costly democracy: peacebuilding and democratization after war.* Stanford University Press, 2013.

www.ingramcontent.com/pod-product-compliance
Lightning Source LLC
Chambersburg PA
CBHW072103040426
42334CB00042B/2141